ACCESS
PHILADELPHIA

W9-BHF-148

Sixth Edition © 2005 by **ACCESS**®PRESS. All rights reserved. No portion of this publication may be reproduced or transmitted in any form or manner by any means, including, but not limited to, graphic, electronic, and mechanical methods, photocopying, recording, taping, or any informational storage and retrieval systems without explicit permission from the publisher. **ACCESS**® is a registered trademark of HarperCollins Publishers Inc. Portions of this work were previously published in *Physicians Travel & Meeting Guide* magazine.

Permit Philadelphians a moment of expansiveness. After years of hearing their city distinguished mainly by the Liberty Bell and by its cheesesteaks, brick streets, and rabid sports fans, civic pride is on the upswing as a result of a massive dose of revitalization that began with the $500 million **Pennsylvania Convention Center** in July 1993. Meanwhile, **City Hall**, a stately granite and white-marble monolith finished at the turn of the 19th century, has seen its 584-foot-tall tower emerge from a face-lift that had kept it under scaffolding for years. And **30th Street Station**, a beautiful early 20th-century train station, has been restored to its Depression-era grandeur. Tour operators who once considered Philadelphia a day-trip destination—catch the Liberty Bell, **Betsy Ross House, Rodin Museum, Philadelphia Museum of Art**, and **Independence Hall** and get out before sundown—now urge visitors to spend a few leisurely days getting to know the city.

William Penn designed Philadelphia with the pedestrian in mind, and walking is still the best way to see this spirited metropolis. The town is laid out in quadrants, with City Hall at the center. Each of the four areas is arranged around a public square: **Franklin Square** near **Independence National Historical Park; Washington Square** near **Society Hill; Rittenhouse Square**, west of **Broad Street;** and **Logan Circle**, with the stunning **Swann Fountain**, at the **Benjamin Franklin Parkway.** Wander a few blocks from any of these tranquil greenswards to delve into Philadelphia's history. The past isn't confined to museums here, nor is it necessarily marked on your historic-sites map. You'll see it in the horse-and-buggy-size alleys; the **Old City** factories converted to restaurants and condos; the regal row houses flanking Rittenhouse Square, and at

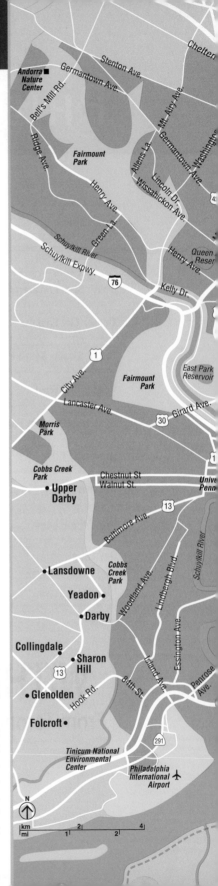

funky, down-home **Reading Terminal Market**, where you can stock up on **Lancaster County** produce, Amish baked goods, and Italian gourmet sauces.

Philadelphia also has a strong cultural scene, reflected in classic museums such as the Philadelphia Museum of Art, the **Museum of American Art of the Pennsylvania Academy of Fine Arts**, and the **University of Pennsylvania Museum of Archaeology and Anthropology**. For the past several years, the city has been developing an "Avenue of the Arts" corridor of buildings devoted to the performing arts near the **Academy of Music** on S. Broad Street, crowned in December 2001 with the dramatic $265 million **Kimmel Center for the Performing Arts**, the new home to the world-class **Philadelphia Orchestra**. The renaissance that began in the late 1970s continues to produce new coffee-houses, bookstores, and restaurants. Despite a spate of new steak houses, Philadelphia has shed its meat-and-potatoes tendencies, owing in part to the ethnic groups that have settled here. **Chinatown** boasts a number of authentic (and inexpensive) Vietnamese, Thai, and Malaysian restaurants as well as vegetarian diners and noodle shops. And if you search beyond the well-publicized trattorie of South Philadelphia, you'll find many menus that transcend the traditional spaghetti and meatballs.

Past the area that locals call **Center City** is **Fairmount Park**, a cool stretch of green popular for its bike and nature trails; the satellite neighborhoods of **University City**, trendy **Manayunk**, and ultraposh **Chestnut Hill**, home to the country's first cricket club; the **Main Line** community of **Merion**, which boasts the world-famous **Barnes Foundation** art gallery; and, even farther away in New Jersey, the gaming halls of **Atlantic City**. **Kelly Drive** snakes along the **Schuylkill River**, offering ringside seats for rowing competitions as well as urban skyline vistas, whereas a host of nightclubs along the **Delaware River** has inspired more than a few waterside pub crawls.

Many of these recent attractions, particularly waterfront bars and dance halls, wouldn't have had a prayer in what was a somewhat stodgy town in the mid-1970s. For decades, Philadelphia lived in the shadow of Manhattan, just 90 miles to the north, and omnipresent history—such as **Christ Church**, where brass plaques mark the pews once occupied by George Washington and Benjamin Franklin—represented the city's only draw. A reverse trend is in progress, however, with New Yorkers (among others) discovering a place that's quieter, cleaner, less frantic . . . and full of possibility. And though the City of Brotherly Love may still feel awkward in its urbane role, no one will fault Philadelphians for a little self-congratulation—the city has been modest for too long.

Area code 215 unless otherwise noted. You must dial all 10 digits (area code plus the number), even within 215.

Getting to Philadelphia

Philadelphia International Airport (PHL)

Located in southwest Philadelphia, 8 miles from Center City, **Philadelphia International Airport** (PHL; www.phl.org) handles direct flights to more than 100 national and international destinations. As part of an ongoing $1 billion renovation, the **Overseas Terminal** was replaced by **Terminal A**, and a new international terminal, which accommodates 12 wide-body gates. A 419-room newly renovated **Marriott** hotel (492.9000, 800/228.9290),

connected to the central terminal, opened in 1995. Another 17 airport hotels include **Extended Stay America** (492.6766, 800/398.7829; www.extendedstay.com) and **Microtel** (800/771.7171; www.microtelinn.com). Additional airport improvements, including moving sidewalks, have been installed. If getting around is still a problem, contact your airline for courtesy cart service. There are now more than 100 shops and eateries in the **Philadelphia Marketplace** adjacent to Terminal B.

Airport Services

Airport emergencies 937.3111
Customs 863.4271
Foreign-language assistance use white courtesy phones

How to Read This Guide

PHILADELPHIA ACCESS® is arranged by neighborhood so you can see at a glance where you are and what is around you. The numbers next to the entries in the following chapters correspond to the numbers on the maps. The text is color-coded according to the kind of place described:

Restaurants/Clubs: Red

Hotels: Purple | **Shops: Orange**

🐾 **Parks/Outdoors: Green** | **Sights/Culture: Blue**

♿ Wheelchair accessible

WHEELCHAIR ACCESSIBILITY

An establishment (except a restaurant) is considered wheelchair accessible when a person in a wheelchair can easily enter a building (i.e., no steps, a ramp, a wide-enough door) without assistance. Restaurants are deemed wheelchair accessible only if the above applies and if the rest rooms are on the same floor as the dining area and their entrances and stalls are wide enough to accommodate a wheelchair.

RATING THE RESTAURANTS AND HOTELS

The restaurant star ratings take into account the quality, service, atmosphere, and uniqueness of the restaurant. An expensive restaurant doesn't necessarily ensure an enjoyable evening; a small, relatively unknown spot could have good food, professional service, and a lovely atmosphere. Therefore, on a purely subjective basis, stars are used to judge the overall dining value (see the star ratings below). Keep in mind that chefs and owners often change, which sometimes drastically affects the quality of a restaurant. The ratings in this guidebook are based on information available at press time. The price ratings, as categorized below, apply to restaurants and hotels. These figures describe general price-range relationships among other restaurants and hotels in the area. The restaurant price ratings are based on the average cost of a dinner entrée for one person, excluding tax and tip. Hotel price ratings reflect the base price of a standard room for two people for 1 night during the peak season.

RESTAURANTS

★	Good
★★	Very Good
★★★	Excellent
★★★★	Extraordinary Experience
$	The Price Is Right (less than $15)
$$	Reasonable ($15–$25)
$$$	Expensive ($25-$40)
$$$$	Big Bucks ($40 and up)

HOTELS

$	The Price Is Right (less than $125)
$$	Reasonable ($125–$175)
$$$	Expensive ($175–$240)
$$$$	Big Bucks ($240 and up)

MAP KEY

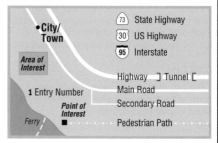

Ground transportation	937.9658
Immigration	594.4100
Information and paging	937.6755, 937.6937
Lost and found	937.6888
Parking	683.9825
Police	937.6918

AIRLINES

Air Canada............888/247.2262; www.aircanada.com

Air France ....800/237.2747; www.airfrance.com

Air Jamaica ....800/523.5585; www.airjamaica.com

AirTran ....800/825.8538; www.airtran.com

American..........................800/443.7300; www.aa.com

American Eagle ....800/443.7300; www.aa.com

American Trans Air..................................800/I-FLY-ATA;
www.americantransair.com

America West 800/235.9292;
www.americawest.com

British Airways 800/247.9797;
www.britishairways.com

Continental ....800/525.0280; www.continental.com

Continental Express 800/525.0280;
www.continental.com

Delta ....800/221.1212; www.delta.com

Delta Connection..........800/221.1212; www.delta.com

Lufthansa ....800/645.3880; www.lufthansa.com

Midwest Express 800/452.2022;
www.midwestairlines.com

National Airlines 888/757.5387

Northwest ....800/225.2525; www.nwa.com

Southwest ....800/435.9792; www.southwest.com

United Airlines............800/241.6522; www.united.com

United Express ....800/241.6522; www.united.com

US Airways............800/428.4322; www.usairways.com

US Airways Express................................800/428.4322;
www.usairways.com

Getting to and from Philadelphia International Airport (PHL)

BY BUS

Buses do not run directly between downtown and the airport, but from the airport you can take the *No. 37* to S. Broad Street and **Snyder Avenue** or the *No. 68* to S. Broad Street and **Oregon Avenue**, and then take the Broad Street subway line northbound to City Hall. Bus *No. 108* also leaves from the airport for the **69th Street Terminal** in **Upper Darby**. Look for **Southeastern Penn-sylvania Transportation Authority** (**SEPTA**) bus stops outside baggage-claim areas.

BY CAR

Center City is less than a 15-minute drive from the airport, but to be safe, allow half an hour. To get to Center City, take **Interstate 95** (**I-95**) north and get off at Exit 22 (Central Philadelphia). This puts you on the **Vine Street Expressway** (**I-676**), which has Center City exits for N. Broad Street, N 15th Street, and N 22nd Street.

To get to the airport from downtown, take the Vine Street Expressway (I-676) to I-95 south. From the western side of the city, take **I-76** east (the **Schuylkill Expressway**). Owing to the recent Federal Aviation Administration security requirements, ground-level parking in terminals has been discontinued. Short-term and long-term parking is available in the garages, and the economy lot is still available.

RENTAL CARS

The following rental-car companies have 24-hour counters at the airport (except for Dollar, which operates between 5:30AM and 12:30AM):

Alamo ....800/327.9633; www.alamo.com

Avis ....800/331.1212; www.avis.com

Budget ....800/527.0700; www.budget.com

Dollar ....800/800.4000; www.dollar.com

Hertz...............................800/654.3131; www.hertz.com

National ....800/227.7368; www.nationalcar.com

BY LIMOUSINE

The airport shuttle and limousine companies listed below offer a range of services, including drop-offs at the city's major hotels and door-to-door service to the suburbs. Call ahead to make reservations, or call 937.6958 for general ground transportation information.

Dave's Best Limousine Service........................288.1000

Lady Liberty Transportation 724.8888

USA Limousine Service/Car 1 ....800/872.6070

BY TAXI

Taxis line up outside baggage-claim areas. The fare from the airport to Center City is about $20.

BY TRAIN

SEPTA's high-speed rail line is the best means of public transportation to and from the airport. Trains pick up passengers at all five airport terminals for nonstop service to three Center City locations: 30th Street Station (N 30th Street, between Market and Arch Streets), **Suburban Station** (John F. Kennedy Boulevard, between N 16th and N 17th Streets), and **Market East Station** (N 11th and Market Streets). The trains (which are cleaner and faster than the subways) leave the airport every 30 minutes between 6:10AM and 12:10AM. (SEPTA claims the trains' on-time rate falls in the 90th percentile, which sure beats that of most of the airlines.) For more information, call 580.7800.

BUS STATION (LONG-DISTANCE)

Greyhound buses arrive at and depart from the **Greyhound Terminal** (N 11th and Filbert Streets; 931.4030); the ticket office is open daily between 6AM and 1AM. There's a taxi stand in front of the station.

TRAIN STATION (LONG-DISTANCE)

Philadelphia's major Amtrak rail station is 30th Street Station (N 30th Street, between Market and Arch Streets), the nation's second busiest, receiving trains from the major cities along the Boston–Washington, DC corridor, as well as from some points west. The ticket office is open daily between 5:10AM and 10:30PM. One Amtrak train per day also stops at the **North Philadelphia Station** (N Broad Street and Indiana Avenue). The ticket office is open Monday through Friday between 5:30AM and 2PM. Taxis are available at both stations. For general information, call Amtrak (824.1600, 800/872.7245; www.amtrak.com).

Getting Around Philadelphia

BICYCLES

Cycling in town is not for the faint of heart. The city's narrow streets, parked cars, and unsympathetic drivers create many difficulties for bicyclists, particularly in Center City. But just beyond the downtown core, you'll find lots of good places to ride your two-wheeler. **West River** and Kelly Drives, on either side of the Schuylkill River, offer more than 9 miles of biking and jogging paths; in addition, the two roads are closed to automobile traffic at designated times on summer weekends. In Center City, bikes may be rented from **Bike Line** (1028 Arch Street; 923.1310).

Both SEPTA (580.7800; www.septa.org) and the **Port Authority Transit Corporation** (**PATCO**; 922.4600; www.drpa.org/patco), New Jersey's high-speed interstate rail service, offer **Bike-On-Rail** permits that allow passengers to take their bicycles on board. A bike map of the **Delaware Valley**, showing several hundred miles of suggested routes in the three-state area, is available from the **Bicycle Coalition of the Delaware Valley** (P.O. Box 8194, Philadelphia, PA 19101; 242.9253; www.bicyclecoalition.org).

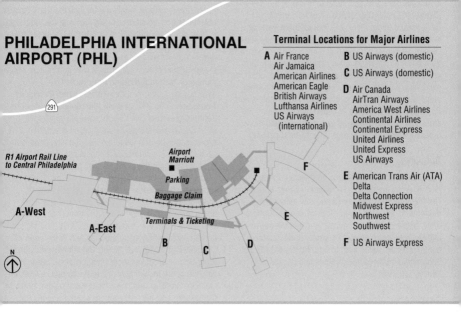

PHILADELPHIA INTERNATIONAL AIRPORT (PHL)

R1 Airport Rail Line to Central Philadelphia

Airport Marriott

Parking

Baggage Claim

A-West

A-East

Terminals & Ticketing

B   C   D   E   F

N

Terminal Locations for Major Airlines

A Air France
Air Jamaica
American Airlines
American Eagle
British Airways
Lufthansa Airlines
US Airways
(international)

B US Airways (domestic)

C US Airways (domestic)

D Air Canada
AirTran Airways
America West Airlines
Continental Airlines
Continental Express
United Airlines
United Express
US Airways

E American Trans Air (ATA)
Delta
Delta Connection
Midwest Express
Northwest
Southwest

F US Airways Express

BUSES

For the most part, bus service here is clean, reliable, and safe. SEPTA operates a large fleet of buses and trolleys that feed into the rail and subway systems, with several routes designed specifically with the tourist in mind. The *No. 38* will take you from Center City down the Benjamin Franklin Parkway all the way to the **Philadelphia Zoo**, and the *No. 42* connects Center City to the **Civic Center** and University City—home to the **University of Pennsylvania** and **Drexel University**. Base fare on most routes is $2; transfers are 60 cents. Senior citizens ride free during off-peak hours and holidays; children shorter than 42 inches tall pay 75 cents on weekends and ride free on weekdays. Exact change is needed for bus fares (paper money is accepted).

Discounted tokens and passes can be purchased at the SEPTA sales offices in 30th Street Station (N 30th Street, between Market and Arch Streets), **Suburban Station** (John F. Kennedy Boulevard, between N 16th and N 17th Streets), and **Market East Station** (N 11th and Market Streets); at the **Philadelphia Convention and Visitors Bureau** (17th and Sansom Streets; 636.3300) and at some Rite Aid drugstores. One of the best bargains going is SEPTA's Day Pass, which is good for a day's unlimited riding on all city public transit, plus a one-way trip on the **Airport High-Speed Line**. For more information, call 580.7800.

Also, a new bus service called **Phlash** (4-PHLASH; www. phillyphlash.com) operates on a downtown loop connecting historic sites, stores, hotels, restaurants, and bars. The Phlash buses stop at designated "Phlash points" about every 12 minutes daily between 10AM and 6PM. The all-day fare of $4, allowing unlimited rides, is a particularly good deal for travelers.

DRIVING

You no longer need to be an expert map reader to navigate Philadelphia. I-95 now has a number of Center City exits, complete with overhead signs directing motorists to the best routes. The main east–west highway through the city, the Schuylkill Expressway (I-76), has been completely reconstructed, though the shoulders still seem narrow in places. Also, some entrance ramps converge suddenly with speeding traffic, so be careful. The Vine Street Expressway (I-676) connects the Schuylkill Expressway with I-95 and provides a fast way to cut through Center City. The Schuylkill is infamous for traffic backups.

FERRIES

Before suspension bridges, commuters used to ferry across the Delaware River every day; now it's mostly used by tourists. When you're weary of pounding the city pavement, put your feet up aboard the **Riverbus Ferry** to **Camden, New Jersey**, for breathtaking views of Philadelphia, the **New Jersey State Aquarium** (www.njaquarium.org), and the **Tweeter Center** (www.tweetercenter.com/Philadelphia), Camden's 25,000-seat performing arts amphitheater. Departing on the hour from **Penn's Landing**, the 500-passenger ferry takes 12 minutes to cross and docks 100 yards from the aquarium. It departs every 40 minutes from 10AM to 5:20PM. The ferry terminal is located at Walnut Street and Columbus Boulevard, next to the **Independence Seaport Museum**. For more information, contact the **RiverLink Ferry** (925.LINK; www.riverlinkferry.org).

PARKING

At any given time, half the automobiles in the city seem to be cruising for a parking spot. Metered parking in Center City is hard to find, plus, for the most part, it's restricted to 2 hours unless you have a permit. (Warning:

Parking regulations are strictly enforced!) Your best bet is to leave the car at your hotel or in one of the many garages in Center City, then walk or take public transportation from there. The **Philadelphia Parking Authority** (**PPA**; 683.9600; www.philapark.org) operates several downtown garages that charge slightly lower rates than those at the commercial garages; the "early bird" rates (in by 9 or 10AM and out by 6PM) are as cheap as you'll find. If you insist on trying your luck with meters, come with a bankroll of quarters: downtown meters cost 25 cents per 15 minutes. Metered parking around the museums on the parkway is less expensive and more practical because most spots offer 12-hour parking.

SUBWAYS

The Broad Street subway runs north-south through the city, whereas the Market-Frankford line runs east–west. The Market East Station in Center City fairly gleams, but most others are pretty grim. Subway service is offered daily, between 5AM and midnight. Avoid the subway at night unless you're going to a game at the sports complex (when you're sure to be part of a crowd). For information on discounted tokens and passes, see "Buses" on page 7.

TAXIS

Cabs in Philly tend to be more expensive than in other cities in the Northeast. They are certainly plentiful, though—a fleet of about 1,400 cruises the city. Cabs line up in front of most hotels and taxi stands, and they also can be hailed on the street with a whistle or a "Yo!" Taxi companies include **Quaker City Cab** (728.8000), **Old City Taxi** (338.0838), and **Yellow Cab** (333.3333).

TOURS

Horse-drawn carriage excursions through the city's historic neighborhoods are offered by **'76 Carriage Co.** (stationed in front of Independence Hall at 6th and Chestnut Streets 10AM-6PM daily and at 2nd and South Streets 7PM-12PM nightly; 923.8516; www.phillytour.com). You also can take a walking tour of the historic area with guides from **Independence National Historic Park Tours** (597.8974; www.nps.gov/inde) and **Candlelight Stroll Centipede Tours, Inc.** (735.3123). **Walk Philadelphia**, run by the Center City District (440.5500, www.centercityphila.org), offers 50 different 90-minute tours, priced at a bargain $10, exploring neighborhoods and telling the city's stories as seen through 3 centuries of architectural change. Locals, passionate about the city and eager to share their enthusiasm, train for 12 weeks before they hit the streets. Tours are offered every weekend during the summer (440.5500; www.centercityphila.org). And you won't find a more enthusiastic tour guide than chef Joe Poon, who leads cultural and culinary tours daily from his self-named Asian fusion restaurant, located in the heart of Chinatown at 1002 Arch Street. The effervescent Hong Kong–born chef makes more than a dozen stops in the neighborhood, including a visit to Dr. Kieng Lim's herbal medicine store, an authentic Hong Kong bakery, a local fishmonger, and his own kitchen, where he winds up cooking dim sum or a dinner for the group. Tours, which last nearly 3 hours, are priced at $35 (**Joe Poon's Chinatown Tour**: 928.9333; www.josephpoon.com). Other sightseeing companies are listed below.

TOUR OPERATORS

American Trolley Tours/Choo Choo Trolley Company 333.2119

Liberty Belle Cruises ....757.0800; www.libertybelle.com

Philadelphia Trolley Works..............................925.TOUR; www.phillytour.com

Spirit of Philadelphia ....866/211.3808; www.spiritcruises.com

TRAINS

SEPTA's regional rail lines splay in every direction from three Center City locations: 30th Street Station (N 30th Street, between Market and Arch Streets), Suburban Station, (John F. Kennedy Boulevard, between N 16th and N 17th Streets), and Market East Station (N 11th and Market Streets). For some wonderful day trips, take a train ride to Merion (site of the wonderful Barnes Foundation art gallery), the college town of **Bryn Mawr**, and other stops on the famous Main Line. Another attractive option is to visit Chestnut Hill via the *R8 Chestnut Hill West*. For route information throughout the system, call SEPTA (580.7800).

PATCO (922.4600), New Jersey's regional transit company, operates the **Hi-Speedline**, which runs between four stops in Center City (S 16th and Locust Streets, S 12th and Locust Streets, S Ninth and Locust Streets, and S Eighth and Market Streets), then crosses the **Benjamin Franklin Bridge** to points in southern New Jersey. To reach the New Jersey Aquarium, take the Hi-Speedline to Broadway and then catch the Route 452 bus operated by **NJ Transit** (215/569.3752).

WALKING

To get a feel for both old and new Philadelphia, you're best off hitting the pavement, where one minute you'll find yourself dwarfed by the recent crop of skyscrapers, and the next, winding your way through narrow streets lined with brick row houses dating back to the American Revolution. Center City's hotels, historic sites, and museums are all conveniently close to one another, and parks and gardens offer good resting places for tired legs and feet. You can easily stroll from the Delaware River to the Schuylkill River in an hour; the most scenic route is along **Pine Street**, which starts in the residential neighborhood of Society Hill, turns into **Antique Row**, and ends near **Fitler Square** at the Schuylkill River. (*Warning*: Beware of motorists at intersections who have a habit of not yielding the right-of-way to pedestrians! Cars turning right on red pose a particular hazard to walkers.)

FYI

ACCOMMODATIONS

Hotel reservations aren't always necessary, but without a reservation you could be caught short if there's a big convention or other special event in town. Don't expect to find a room without a reservation the weekend of the Army–Navy football game in December. **Accommodations Express** (800/444.7666; www.design42.com/designs/ae) provides free hotel reservations service for all major Philadelphia hotels. The **Greater Philadelphia Hotel Association** (557.1900; www.philadelphiahotelassoc.org) makes referrals to area accommodations and provides

general information about hotels. If you're staying a month or longer, you may prefer to rent an apartment or condo. Places that offer long-term accommodations include **Henry on the Park Apartments** (7901 Henry Avenue, between Wise's Mill Road and Summit Avenue; 800/542.9909) at the edge of **Wissahickon Valley**, and **Oakwood Corporate Apartments** (16th and Sansom Streets; 800/832.8329) in Center City.

To find out about bed-and-breakfasts, contact the **Association of Bed & Breakfasts in Philadelphia** (P.O. Box 562, Valley Forge, PA 19481-0562; 800/448.3619; 610/687.3565; fax 610/995.9524; www.bnbphiladelphia.com)

CLIMATE

Although prolonged spells of extreme weather are rare in Philadelphia, the prime time to visit is April through October, when the weather is warmer. October is the driest month, and one of the prettiest times to visit. In April and May, the area runs rife with delicate new greenery and blossoms. On average, August brings the most sunny days, but it's also the most humid month of the year.

MONTHS	AVERAGE TEMPERATURE (°F)
December-February	33
March-May	53
June-August	75
September-November	57

DRINKING

The legal drinking age is 21. Liquor and wine are sold only at state-run stores and beer can be purchased only at beer distribution centers (but six-packs are sold in bars). Bars generally close at 2AM.

MONEY

Banks are generally open between 8:30 or 9AM and 3 or 4PM. Currency may be exchanged at several locations, including **Sovereign Bank** (1717 Arch Street, between N 17th and N 18th Streets; 854.3722) and **Thomas Cooke Currency Services** (1800 John F. Kennedy Boulevard).

PERSONAL SAFETY

The same rules apply here as they do to every other city—avoid down-and-out neighborhoods, guard pocketbooks and wallets, and, at night, stay in well-lit areas that have a lot of foot traffic. It's not a good idea at any time of day to venture into unfamiliar neighborhoods beyond the walking tours outlined in this book. Keep your car doors locked no matter where you're driving and whenever you park on the street.

PUBLICATIONS

The *Philadelphia Inquirer* (www.philly.com), the city's top all-around daily newspaper, has won 18 Pulitzers since the mid-1970s, largely for investigative series on topics as wide-ranging as police brutality, the energy crisis, and America's blood supply. The Friday edition includes a

Phun in Philly: Holidays and Special Events

January

Mummers Parade   Philadelphians line **Broad Street** on New Year's Day to watch the elaborately costumed Mummers strut their stuff in this unique annual daylong parade. For information, call 336.3050; www.mummers.org.

February

African-American History Month   The **African-American Museum in Philadelphia** sponsors a monthlong commemoration through exhibitions, lectures, and music. For information, call 574.0380; www.aampmuseum.org.

PECO Energy Jazz Festival   A weekend of jazz performances and musical events all over the city takes place annually in early or mid-February. For information, call 636.1666 or 800/537.7676; www.independence visitorcenter.com.

Junior Jazz Weekend   A celebration of jazz for little ones is held at midmonth at the **Please Touch Museum**. For information, call 963.0667; www.pleasetouchmuseum.org.

March

Philadelphia Flower Show   The largest and most prestigious indoor flower show in the world is held at the **Pennsylvania Convention Center** during the first 2 weeks of March. For information, call 988.8800; www.theflowershow.com.

St. Patrick's Day Parade   Irish and Irish-for-a-day Philadelphians transform downtown streets into a bit of old Ireland around 17 March. For information, call 945.0563.

April

Philadelphia Antiques Show   Museum-quality antiques are on exhibit at this mid-April show, which benefits the **Hospital of the University of Pennsylvania**. For information, call 662.3941; www.philaantiques.com.

Penn Relays   The world's oldest and largest track meet takes place the last week of the month at

Franklin Field on the **U Penn** campus. For information, call 898.6145.

World's Largest Garden Party   Simultaneous open houses celebrate spring at the 23 **Delaware Valley** gardens, historic homes, and arboreta of the **Gardens Collaborative** organization. For information, call 247.5777, ext 175; www.greaterphiladelphiagardens.org.

Philadelphia Festival of World Cinema   This 2-week festival in early April celebrates the best of international cinema, with premieres and film classics shown throughout the city. For information, call 733.0608.

PrideFest America   From the end of April into early May, PrideFest is the nation's premier celebration of gay, lesbian, bisexual, and transgender culture, including entertainment, education, and sporting events. For information, call 732.3378; www.equalityforum.com.

May

Italian Market Festival   The market's main street, **Ninth**, becomes a scene reminiscent of festivals in many small Italian towns, with plenty of food and lots of music, on the third Sunday in May. For information, call 922.5557.

Captain Morgan's Jam on the River   Philadelphia salutes the music and food of New Orleans in Memorial Day weekend festivities at **Penn's Landing**. For information, call 965.7676.

Devon Horse Show   This venerable outdoor horse show first took place in 1895 and still runs, between approximately late May and early June, at the **Show Grounds** in **Devon** on the **Main Line** between **Wayne** and **Paoli**. For information, call 610/964.0550; www.devonhorseshow.org.

June

Elfreth's Alley Fete Days   During the first week of the month, the oldest residential street in the US opens its homes to the public with a celebration that also includes colonial crafts and entertainment. For information, call 574.0560 or go to www.elfrethsalley.org.

"Weekend" section with comprehensive listings of events and entertainment. The *Philadelphia Daily News*; www.philly.com, a tabloid with no Sunday edition, emphasizes local news and sports. The *Philadelphia Tribune*; www.phila-tribune.com, serves the city's African-American population with editions on Tuesday, Thursday, and Friday. *City Paper*; www.citypaper.net, a freebie distributed in newspaper boxes throughout the city, has especially thorough coverage of cultural and entertainment events, as well as insightful political commentary on regional doings.

For a view of Center City from the people who live there, as well as entertainment and restaurant listings, pick up a copy of *Philadelphia Weekly*; www.philadelphiaweekly.com,

a free paper published on Wednesday. *Philadelphia Magazine*; www.phillymag.com, a full-color monthly glossy sold at newsstands, offers slick regional reporting, plus film, theater, and cultural listings. Featuring an extensive dining directory, the magazine gives the Best of Philly awards you'll see hanging in area restaurants. *Business Philadelphia* caters to the local business community. *PGN* (*Philadelphia Gay News*; www.epgn.com) serves the gay and lesbian population. Two free newspapers, *Metrokids*; www.metrokids.com, and *Parents Express*, offer listings of children's events and helpful kid-oriented ideas; both are available at bookstores, record stores, and some restaurants.

Wachovia US/Pro Cycling Championship The nation's only professional cycling race stretches over a 156-mile course that includes the grueling "Manayunk Wall." The race, in the first week in June, begins and ends on **Benjamin Franklin Parkway**. For information, call 610/676.0390 or go to www.procyclingtour.com.

July

Welcome America Philadelphia's Independence Day celebration starts in late June and climaxes on the Fourth of July with concerts, parades, ceremonies, and spectacular fireworks displays. The 12-day celebration also includes the presentation of the **Philadelphia Liberty Medal**—past recipients have included Jimmy Carter, Nelson Mandela and F.W. de Klerk, and Václav Havel. For information, call 965.7676 or go to www. americasbirthday.com.

August

Pennsylvania Dutch Festival Held at **Reading Terminal Market** on the first weekend of the month, this event highlights Amish culture, featuring crafts, music, and food. For information, call 922.2317; www.readingterminalmarket.org.

September

Yo! Philadelphia Sponsored by the *Daily News*, this Labor Day weekend festival at Penn's Landing celebrates the city's neighborhoods, foods, and musical talent. For information, call 636.1666 or 800/537.7676.

Philadelphia Harvest Show At midmonth, city and suburban gardeners compete for blue ribbons in the best flowers, baked goods, harvest baskets, and preserved products categories in the **Horticultural Center, West Fairmount Park**. For information, call 988.8800.

Von Steuben Day Gala & Parade A salute to the German general who trained patriots at **Valley Forge** takes place in Philadelphia in late September, traditionally 1 week after the big Steuben Day parade in New York City. For information, call 363.3300; www.independencevisitorcenter.com.

South Street Seven Arts Festival South Street is lined with crafts booths, performances, and artworks during this weekend event in late September or early October. For information, call 413.3713.

October

Columbus Day Parade Food and entertainment celebrate the great explorer at Penn's Landing. For information, call 363.3300.

Bach Festival of Philadelphia A series of eight concerts concentrating on the music of the Baroque period and featuring an international array of artists, at various Philadelphia churches and other venues, begins late in October, going on until April. For information, call 247.BACH or go to www.bach-fest.org.

November

Philadelphia Craft Show A major exhibition and sale of crafts by top artists from around the country is held yearly, either late October or early to mid-November. For information, call 684.7931.

Advanta Championships The former **Virginia Slims Tournament**, one of the 53 events on the premier women's international tennis tour, is held at **Villanova University** in the first half of the month. For information, call 591.0800. For tickets, call 866.TENNIS-5; www.advantachampionships.com.

Thanksgiving Day Parade Started in 1919, this is the oldest Thanksgiving Day parade in the country. The route goes from **20th** and **Market Streets** to the **Philadelphia Museum of Art**. For information, call 636.3300.

December

Army–Navy Football Game Midshipmen and cadets face off in their annual gridiron contest on the first Saturday in December. For information, call 636.3300; www.navysports.com.

Fairmount Park Historical Christmas Tours Colonial mansions are decorated for Christmas and open for candlelight tours during the first week of the month. For information, call 763.8100; www.philamuseum.org.

Radio Stations

Frequency	Call Letters	Format
AM:		
920	ESPN	Sports
1060	KYW	News
1540	WNWR	Ethnic/foreign
FM:		
88.5	WXPN	Eclectic folk, pop, and world music
90.1	WRTI	Jazz/classical
90.9	WHYY	National Public Radio
92.5	WXTU	Country
93.3	WMMR	Rock
94.1	WYSP	Classic rock
98.1	WOGL	Oldies
98.9	WUSL	Urban contemporary
101.1	WBEB	Adult contemporary
102.9	WMGK	Classic and light hits

Restaurants

As in most other cities these days, it's okay to dress casually in most restaurants. Usually, getting seated will

THE BEST

Deen Kogan

Managing Director, Society Hill Playhouse

Take a must-do "history walk," with stops at **Independence Hall**, the **Liberty Bell**, and **Ben Franklin's grave**. Toss a penny for good luck.

Two stops for art lovers: the **Philadelphia Art Museum**, one of the world's finest, and the **Barnes** in **Merion**, which boasts the finest collection ever assembled by one individual. Cézanne and Matisse hang next to Pennsylvania Dutch hex signs, and that's just right.

Have a picnic at **Bartram Gardens**, the oldest botanical garden in the country. Don't expect pretty flowers. For that, and spectacular displays, put **Longwood Gardens** on the schedule.

Browse and buy at the **Friends of the Free Library Book Store**, 20th and Vine. Among the reading copies, you might find the first edition you've been looking for. In any case, it's for a good cause.

Visit the residents at the **Zoological Gardens**, America's first zoo. It's particularly pleasant on a winter morning, when the animals seem to relish your company.

Enjoy baseball on a summer Sunday afternoon at **Lincoln Financial Field** watching the **Phillies**, football on a fall day with the **Eagles**, and any time at the **Spectrum** or **Center** when the **Flyers** and **Phantoms** play the special brand of Philadelphia-style hockey.

Drive "down the shore" winter or summer. Fifty minutes, and you are on the boardwalk in **Atlantic City** or walking on the beach in **Margate**. Add 45 minutes and experience **Cape May**'s gingerbread homes and bird sanctuaries.

Catch jazz at any one of a dozen spots from **Zanzibar Blue** to **Chris' Jazz Cafe**. Check the local paper for times and talent.

Declare a diet moratorium and have lunch at the **Palm** while you watch the power brokers interact over the daily specials; tea or any other meal at the **Four Seasons**; dinner at **Deux Chemines**, elegant French food in an incredible town house; an Italian egg cream at South Street's **Supreme Bean**; finish at 1AM standing on the pavement at Ninth and Passyunk eating a **Pat's** (or **Geno's**) steak "with" or "without."

depend more on your having a reservation than a jacket and tie.

SHOPPING

One of the trendy shopping areas in Philadelphia is the strip of South Street between **S 10th** and **Front Streets**, where nearly 150 shops and boutiques offer funky men's and women's clothing, cutting-edge CDs, and decorative New Age-style objects. The **Shops at Liberty Place** (S 17th Street, between Chestnut and Market Streets), with 60 shops and eateries under one roof, is another great place for both browsers and serious shoppers. Old City's shops and galleries on **Second** and **Third Streets**, between Arch and Market Streets, offers urban chic housewares, cutting-edge galleries, and vintage clothing shops. If you're looking for kitchenware and fresh foods, head over to the **Italian Market** (S Ninth Street, from Washington Avenue to Christian Street) or the **Reading Terminal Market** (N 12th Street, between Filbert and Arch Streets). Shopping with a small-town feel can be had in picturesque Chestnut Hill (on Germantown Avenue, between Willow Grove Avenue and Bethlehem Pike) and the gentrified neighborhood of Manayunk (on Main Street, between Pensdale Street and Green Lane). Most shops and department stores in Philadelphia stay open later on Wednesday evenings.

SMOKING

Pennsylvania state law requires restaurants seating 75 or more people to have a nonsmoking section. Smaller restaurants must either have a nonsmoking section or post a sign up front stating otherwise.

STREET PLAN

A neat little grid system developed in 1682 by Thomas Holme, surveyor for William Penn, makes it easy to figure out Center City. The grid's boundaries comprise the 2 square miles between the Delaware and Schuylkill Rivers and Vine and South Streets. Numbered streets run north-south, whereas those with names run east-west. Broad Street (an exception to the numbered rule) is the major north-south axis, and Market Street, the east-west axis. The two streets meet at City Hall. The Benjamin Franklin Parkway cuts diagonally across the grid from City Hall to the Philadelphia Museum of Art and Fairmount Park.

TAXES

Clothing and supermarket food can be purchased tax-free, but there is a 7% sales tax on almost everything else. The hotel tax is 13%, one of the highest in the country.

TELEPHONE

Two new overlay area codes have been added to the Philadelphia region: 267 alongside the traditional 215 for Philadelphia itself and its immediate suburbs, and 484 with 610 for the surrounding area to the north and west. *Note:* all calls within as well as between these area codes must be dialed with all 10 digits (area code plus seven-digit number; you need not dial 1 first, but you can, and your call will go through either way). To find out whether your call is local or long distance, which is becoming a pretty complicated issue, call the Bell Atlantic Hotline at 800/734.5910.

Phone Book

EMERGENCIES

Ambulance/fire/police 911
AAA Keystone Automobile Club 569.4321
Dental emergency 925.6050

HOSPITALS

Children's Hospital 590.1000
Graduate Hospital 893.2000
Hahnemann University Hospital 762.7000
Hospital of the University of Pennsylvania ..662.4000
Pennsylvania Hospital 829.3000
Thomas Jefferson Hospital 955.6000
Medical referrals 563.5343

PHARMACIES (24-HOUR)

CVS Pharmacy...465.2130
Rite Aid Pharmacy 467.2831
Poison Control Center 386.2100

VISITORS' INFORMATION

Better Business Bureau 985.9312
Disabled Visitors' Information.........................686.2798
Foreign language translation 893.8400
Greater Philadelphia Chamber
of Commerce 545.1234
Greyhound Bus 931.4075
Northeast Philadelphia
Chamber of Commerce 332.3400
Independence Visitors Center 800/537.7676
SEPTA 580.7800
Time 846.1212
Weather...936.1212
Western Union.......................................800/325.6000

TICKETS

Tickets for theater, ballet, concerts, and other performances are available at **Glassman's Ticket Office** (231 S 13th Street, at Locust Street; 735.9673), **John Wanamaker Ticket Office** (1500 Market Street; 568.2400), and **Upstages** (1412 Chestnut Street; 569.9700). Other ticket outlets include **Ticketron** (885.2515), **Ticketmaster** (465.2832), **Telecharge** (800/545.2559), and **William Penn Ticket Agency** (1218 Chestnut Street, between S 12th and S 13th Streets; 925.2511).

Tickets to baseball, basketball, football, and hockey games can be purchased either through Ticketron, Ticketmaster, or Telecharge (see above), or by contacting the individual teams: the **Phillies** (463.6000), **76ers** (339.7600), **Eagles** (463.5500), and **Flyers** (465.4500).

TIME ZONE

Philadelphia is on Eastern Standard Time, the same as New York City.

TIPPING

Restaurant servers and related service personnel should be tipped at least 15%, whereas the standard tip for cab drivers is 10%.

VISITORS' INFORMATION CENTERS

A new $38 million **Independence Visitor Center** (One North Independence Mall West, at 6th and Market Streets; 800/537.7676; www.independencevisitorcenter.com) is open 8:30 AM to 5PM daily.

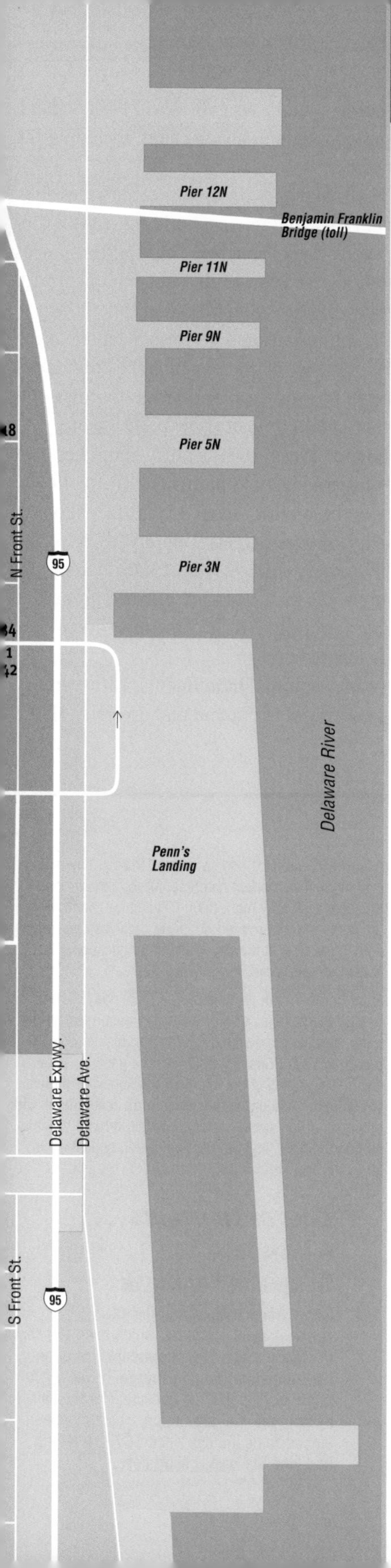

Pier 12N

Benjamin Franklin
Bridge (toll)

Pier 11N

Pier 9N

Pier 5N

N Front St.

95

Pier 3N

Delaware River

Penn's
Landing

Delaware Expwy.
Delaware Ave.

S Front St.

95

S Front St.

OLD PHILADELPHIA

As every schoolchild knows, colonial America came into being within the redbrick walls of **Independence Hall**. Here, a group of determined colonists, risking execution by order of King George III, signed the Declaration of Independence. And after the Revolutionary War, the US Constitution was written and made into law in this distinguished building. At first glance Independence Hall appears too modest for the momentous role it played in US history. But linger awhile and you'll begin to see how its very simplicity is the perfect backdrop for the major events that took place.

You could easily spend a day or two touring **Independence National Historical Park**, the district that encompasses Independence Hall; the famous **Liberty Bell**, which called citizens to **Independence Square** for the first public reading of the Declaration of Independence in 1776; the **Second Bank of the United States**, housing portraits of the government's founders; and many other historic buildings crucial to the country's early history. On the park's periphery are the **National Museum of American Jewish History**, with exhibits on early Jewish settlements; the **United States Mint**, the largest money factory in the world; and the **Arch Street Friends Meeting House**, a lovely Quaker building circa 1804.

Two neighborhoods intertwine with Independence Park—trendy **Old City**, a warehouse district reborn as a mecca for art galleries, bustling restaurants and cafés, and luxury condos, and **Society Hill**, a charming residential area that dates to colonial times. Old City, to the north and east of Independence Park (although technically the park is considered part of Old City), was the center of manufacturing and commerce and a crucial part of the bustling colonial seaport in the mid-1800s. Industry eventually moved west, and the area declined until the late 1960s, when Old City was rejuvenated.

Today it contains the largest concentration of contemporary art galleries in Philadelphia, along with popular restaurants, hipster bars and lounges, and historic sites, including the diminutive **Elfreth's Alley.**

Every September, the **Philadelphia Fringe Festival** makes the avant-garde accessible, filling the galleries, alleyways, sidewalks, vacant lots, and unused buildings of Old City with the performing arts. During this multiday event, there are nearly 1,000 performances by hundreds of performing arts groups. Productions are from a full spectrum of colorful work that falls within, between, and sometimes beyond the standard categories of theater, dance, music, poetry, and puppetry. National and international performers come to the Fringe to present new visions and thought-provoking work that expands the boundaries and directions of their art forms. For dates, more information, and program guide call the Live Arts Festival and the Philly Fringe at 413.9006 or visit www.pafringe.org.

In Society Hill, located south of Independence Park, 18th-century churches and modern town houses share the quirky brick-and-cobblestone pathways. In the **Powel House** and the **Physick House,** you can see how the wealthy lived 3 centuries ago; get a glimpse of how they live today on **Delancey** and **Spruce Streets.** Happily, there's little evidence of the squalor that characterized Society Hill in the 1960s, when the Philadelphia Redevelopment Authority took over the area, sold off historic properties one by one, and brought about the remarkable renewal. **Old St. Joseph's,** one of the oldest Catholic churches in the country, also is located here.

This is a district that has something for everyone—colonial monuments, 18th-century houses, and contemporary art galleries—and it continues to expand and diversify all the time.

OLD CITY

In colonial days, Old City and Society Hill constituted the city proper. But in the 1800s, as the city burgeoned, Old City benefited from its position alongside the Delaware River (now separated from the neighborhood by Interstate 95) and became a thriving mix of factories, banks, warehouses, and retail stores. This hectic district—bounded by **Chestnut** and **Vine Streets** and by **N Front** and **N Fifth Streets**—included a world-renowned sugar refinery, textile manufacturers, and a hoopskirt factory (probably responsible for the long-forgotten slogan "Philadelphia Dresses the World"). Many commercial buildings of that period—in brick, cast iron, and granite—survive alongside early colonial buildings, such as the magnificent **Christ Church**—where brass plaques mark the pews once occupied by George Washington and Benjamin Franklin, the Betsy Ross House, and the Arch Street Friends Meeting House, all giving Old City its character.

Eventually the city's manufacturing center moved west and Old City deteriorated. Then the construction of the highway along the river and the Benjamin Franklin Bridge cut the neighborhood off from the rest of the city. But with the gentrification of Society Hill in the late 1970s, many of Old City's former warehouses were converted into luxury apartments or condominiums and a number of small businesses opened their doors. The relatively cheap rent and spacious 19th-century buildings offered the perfect combination for contemporary art galleries. Today more than 40 galleries, performance theaters, and arts-related nonprofit organizations—many among the best in the city—call this unquestionably hip neighborhood home.

From October through June on the first Friday of each month, the galleries stay open late to host a big block party, attracting a generally young and fashionable crowd. At **First Friday,** people tour the galleries for a few hours, sampling the free hors d'oeuvres, and then eat dinner in one of the neighborhood's restaurants. Old City is an urban success story, a neighborhood that has rebounded from blight to become a trendy destination for locals and visitors alike.

1 *BOLT OF LIGHTNING . . . A MEMORIAL TO BENJAMIN FRANKLIN*

Isamu Noguchi designed this 60-ton stainless-steel sculpture, which rises 101 feet to mark the axis of **Independence Mall** and the **Benjamin Franklin Bridge**. It was a gift to the city's public art collection by the Fairmount Park Art Association, which has been embellishing the city since 1872. ◆ N Fifth and Vine Sts. www.philart.net

2 St. George's Church

This is the oldest Methodist church in the US, and Richard Allen, the country's first African-American preacher, was licensed here in 1785. Two years later, he left to found the African Methodist Episcopal Church. A historical center and museum adjoin the church. ♦ Free. Daily, 10AM-3PM. 235 N Fourth St (between Race and Vine Sts). 925.7788. www.gcah.org/Heritage_Landmarks/George

3 Painted Bride Art Center

Located in a former elevator factory just under the **Benjamin Franklin Bridge**, this multicultural art center hosts dance performances, poetry readings, plays, art exhibits, and concerts (mostly jazz and world music). This was the brainchild of a small group of artists who originally set up shop in 1970 in a former bridal store on South Street. It has since grown into a full-fledged nonprofit center—with funding from the National Endowment for the Arts—promoting multiculturalism in the arts. The **Bride** tends toward the avant-garde, offering spoken-word, dance, music, and vocal performances, along with photography exhibits and theater. ♦ Daily. 230 Vine St (at N Third St). 925.9914. www.paintedbride.org

4 DiNardo's Famous Seafood

★$$ The casual atmosphere at this popular Philadelphia branch of the notable Wilmington, Delaware, seafood house is ideal for families. Dark strip paneling, nautical doodads, large tables, and roomy booths set the scene for cracking into the blue-clawed hard-shell crabs, which come steamed and seasoned (Baltimore style) or in a bowl of garlic sauce. The fish is always fresh, and the salty, slightly spicy french fries taste great with beer. You may be in for a wait on weekends. ♦ Seafood ♦ M-Sa, lunch and dinner; Su, dinner. 312 Race St (between N Third and N Fourth Sts). 925.5115. ♿ www.dinardos.com

5 Mode Moderne

Designer furniture and decorative objects from the 1920s to the 1960s are displayed in this offbeat showroom. ♦ W-Sa, noon-6PM. 159 N Third St (between Quarry and Race Sts). 627.0299. www.modemoderne.com

6 Fireman's Hall

This turn-of-the-19th-century firehouse has been restored to showcase fire-related memorabilia spanning 2 centuries. Exhibits tell the story of firefighting, from its primitive beginnings in the American colonies to 21st-century technology. The museum's high-ceilinged main room contains examples of 19th- and 20th-century fire wagons, powered by hand, horse, or steam. Other highlights are a hand pump reputedly used by Benjamin Franklin, who founded the country's first fire company, and a radio dispatch system. Antique axes, helmets, badges, old posters, and ladders adorn the walls and fill the display cases. Don't miss the living quarters on the second floor. Children especially love this museum. ♦ Donation. Tu-Sa. 147 N Second St (between Elfreth's Alley and Race St). 923.1438. ♿ www.gophila.com /culturefiles/Museums/Firemanshall

7 The Clay Studio

Part gallery, part art school, and part group salon, this cooperative of more than 30 ceramic artists produces an eclectic array of pieces—from the wildly avant-garde to vases you could give your parents for Christmas. Two first-floor rooms feature juried exhibitions by local and national ceramic artists, and a small shop sells distinctive, reasonably priced designs. ♦ Tu-Su, noon-5PM. 139 N Second St (between Elfreth's Alley and Race St). 925.3453. www.claystudio.org

7 Nexus Foundation for Today's Art

This nonprofit organization displays the works of its 25 members and also hosts art exhibitions showcasing trends in experimental and innovative contemporary art. ♦ Tu-F, noon-6PM; Sa, Su, noon-5PM. 137 N Second St (at Elfreth's Alley). 629.1103. ♿ www.nexus philadelphia.org

8 United States Mint

Every day, 35 million coins come out of the manufacturing rooms of this money factory—the largest mint in the world—and each year, more than 100,000 working dies used in coin presses are produced here. Blanks are stamped out of strips of metal, and, eventually, the finished coins drop into large canvas bags, which are sewn shut and loaded onto pallets. Normally, visitors can watch the action through a plate-glass window on the second floor. As of summer 2002, however, the **Mint** was still closed to public tours, owing to post–September 11 security measures.

The monolithic, virtually windowless building, designed by **Vincent G. Kling and Associates** in 1969, is a descendant of the oldest mint in the country, which opened a few blocks away in 1792. David Rittenhouse, a famous mathematician and inventor, served as director of the first **Philadelphia Mint**, and the balance he invented in the 1700s is on display. Designs for all the commemorative coins made since 1892 are also here, plus numerous other samples of metallic art, including all the Congressional Gold Medals, and war medals such as the Purple Heart and the Bronze Star. A "hot off the press" display shows the latest mint medals authorized by Congress. In the lobby, two Tiffany glass mosaics dating from 1901 depict the history of coin making. Peter the Eagle, a real bird who adopted the mint as his home and was a mascot to mint workers in the early 19th century, has been stuffed and put on display (he may have been the model for the American eagle that appeared on silver dollars). Coins and medals can be purchased in the lobby store. ♦ Free. M-F. Bounded by Arch and Race Sts and by N Fourth and N Fifth Sts. 408.0114. ♿ www.usmint.gov

9 SNYDERMAN GALLERY

Richard and Ruth Snyderman, a husband-and-wife team, are the proprietors of this spacious gallery. Exhibits focus on contemporary art, furniture, paintings, and sculpture. ♦ Tu-Sa. 303 Cherry St (between N Third and N Fourth Sts). 238.9576. www.snyderman-works.com

9 F.A.N. GALLERY

This gallery's narrow room showcases contemporary art, including paintings, sculpture, and works on paper by local and national artists. ♦ Tu-Su. 311 Cherry St (between N Third and N Fourth Sts). 922.5155. www.fanartgallery.com

10 OLC

This lighting and furniture showroom specializes in artsy, contemporary light fixtures with European labels. There's also furniture from B & B Italia, Driade, Cassina, and others. Approximately 90% of the sales are to designers and architects, but walk-in traffic is welcome. ♦ Tu-Sa. 152-154 N Third St (between Cherry and Race Sts). 923.6085

11 INDIGO

This international bazaar of art and artifacts and its second-floor gallery, **Indigo Arts**, feature international folk art from Asia, Africa, and the Americas. Textiles, pottery, furniture, tribal masks, sculpture, antiques, and jewelry are the attractions at the shop. Upstairs, the gallery showcases Haitian paintings, Mexican prints and paintings, Nicaraguan "primitivista" paintings, West African barbershop signboards, and African and Oceanic sculpture. ♦ Tu-Su. 151 N Third St (between Cherry and Race Sts). 922.4041. Also at 4419 Main St, Manayunk. 482.1001. www.indigoarts.com

11 PENTIMENTI GALLERY

Exhibiting all manner of works—ranging from figurative to abstract—the gallery represents contemporary local, regional, and international artists. M-Tu, by appointment; W-Sa. 133 N Third St (at Cherry St). 625.9990. www.pentimenti.com

Old City Hall

12 ELFRETH'S ALLEY

Turn off Second Street into this postcard-perfect alley of 18th-century brick row houses, said to be the oldest continuously inhabited street in the US. The fact that most of the houses are still private homes makes the alley all the more enchanting. Named after Jeremiah Elfreth, a blacksmith and speculator who built and rented out some of the homes, the alley was right next to the Delaware River during the 18th century. Artisans, furniture makers, sea captains, school teachers, and a rabbi lived here.

Though at first glance the buildings look alike, take a closer look and you'll see signs of different periods. The oldest, **Nos. 120-122**, were built in the 1720s, and the newest, in the early 1800s. Small panes of glass (shipped all the way from England in early colonial days), pent eaves, and modest doorways distinguish the earlier homes. Later dwellings have stairs leading up to elaborate entrances and larger windows. Note the mirror contraptions that jut from the second floors of some of the houses. Called busybodies, they were used by residents as early as the 18th century to see who was knocking at their front doors below.

In 1997, two more houses—the **Windsor Chair Maker's House** (**No. 124**) and the **Mantua Maker's House** (**No. 126**)—were restored, furnished with 18th-century furniture, and opened to the public. No. 124 was occupied by two of Philadelphia's most famous Windsor chair makers, Gilbert Gaw and John Ackley. The two homes shared a rear garden, which is available to groups or individuals for special events.

The **Elfreth's Alley Museum** occupies the house in the middle of the south side of the block. Built in 1750, it's a classic Philadelphia "trinity"—a miniature three-story structure with one room on each floor and narrow, winding staircases. The museum is open daily; there's an admission charge. Halfway down the block is **Bladen's Court**, a tiny brick and cobblestone alley-within-an-alley that takes you to a small circular courtyard. ♦ Off N Second St (between Arch and Race Sts). 574.0560. www.elfrethsalley.org

13 RISTORANTE DE GHIOTTONE

★★$$ Devotees of Old City's art galleries pack the tiny but festive dining room in this brick-walled trattoria. Diners sitting elbow-to-elbow at tables with bright vinyl tablecloths indulge in such hearty fare as sausage with olives, fresh tomatoes, rosemary, and mozzarella. Be prepared to wait on weekend evenings. ♦ Italian ♦ M-F, lunch and dinner; Sa, Su, dinner. 130 N Third St (between Arch and Cherry Sts). 829.1465

14 RODGER LAPELLE GALLERY

A participant in First Friday, this highly regarded gallery exhibits contemporary paintings, sculpture, and graphics by local and national artists. ♦ W-Su, noon-6PM. 122 N Third St (between Arch and Cherry Sts). 592.0232

15 MODERNE GALLERY

Expensive European and American Art Deco furniture and decorative pieces, including paintings and sculpture, are on display at this gallery. The showroom has featured the ironwork of Edgar Brandt and furniture by Dominique, Leleu, and Adnet. ♦ Tu-Sa. 111 N Third St (between Arch and Quarry Sts). 923.8536. www.modernegallery.com

16 BETSY ROSS HOUSE

Upholsterer and seamstress Betsy Ross lived either in this house or in the one that stood in the courtyard next door. Though she was long believed to have designed the American flag, this claim has now been disproved (meager—not firm—evidence does indicate that she sewed a flag for the early federal government). Ross, who lived from 1752 to 1836 and was widowed twice and married three times, is buried in the courtyard. The 1740 house is typical of the period and contains the accoutrements of her trade. ♦ Donation requested. Tu-Su. 239 Arch St (between N Second and N Third Sts). 627.5343. www.ushistory.org/betsy

17 ROSENFELD GALLERY

Located in a former paint warehouse, this spacious first-floor gallery exhibits works by new artists from around the country. Popular shows have included clay monoprints by Mitch Lyons and handmade paper by Doug Zucco. ♦ W-Sa; Su, noon-5PM. 113 Arch St (between N Front and N Second Sts). 922.1376. ⅃. www.therosenfeldgallery.com

18 SMYTHE STORES

This 1857 Northern Italian Renaissance–style warehouse turned office building is one of the neighborhood's few remaining grand cast-iron structures. With its rows of arched windows and fluted columns, this edifice represents a significant departure from the area's original brick warehouses, which had small windows and little adornment. In 1900, plans to demolish the building so trolleys could turn around in the corner were averted. Instead, an ingenious idea evolved—remove only the middle section, thereby allowing trolleys to pass right through the center. The demolished portion was re-created with fiberglass in the

1970s, long after the trolley route had died. Can you tell where the old and new begin and end? ◆ N Front and Arch Sts

19 CHRIST CHURCH BURIAL GROUND

Some of the country's first leading citizens are buried in this cemetery three blocks from **Christ Church**, including Benjamin Franklin; numerous Revolutionary War heroes and patriots; and the Right Reverend William White, chaplain of the Continental Congress and first Episcopal Bishop of Pennsylvania. Franklin's grave is visible through the iron gate on the Arch Street side. Owing to acid rain and other environmental factors, the gravestones are in a state of advanced deterioration, and the burial ground is not open to the public, but it is possible to arrange a visit through the church offices. ◆ By appointment only. N Fifth and Arch Sts. 922.1695. www.oldchristchurch.org/burial

20 HOLIDAY INN HISTORIC DISTRICT

$$ A short walk from **Independence Park**, this 364-room hotel has a pleasant lobby and comfortable rooms (although those overlooking Arch Street don't have much of a view). You can relax in the shady courtyard of the **Arch Street Friends Meeting House** across the street or take a dip in the hotel's small outdoor pool. ◆ 400 Arch St (at N Fourth St). 923.8660, 800/843.2355; fax 923.4633. & www.sixcontinentshotels.com

Within the Holiday Inn Independence Mall:

BENTON'S GRILL

★$$ Decorated with old prints of Philadelphia and American colonial reproductions, this casual dining room serves breakfast, lunch, and dinner daily. ◆ American ◆ 923.8660. & www.hiphiladelphia-historicaldistrict.felcor.com/phlim/dining.html

21 ARCH STREET FRIENDS MEETING HOUSE

Owen Biddle's simple brick structure, the largest Quaker meeting house in the country, was built in 1804 on land donated by William Penn. It still hosts twice-weekly meetings, though today's congregants usually fill only a small portion of the pews in the main meeting room. The austere style—with white wooden shutters and none of the customary accoutrements of religious worship (statues, pulpits, stained-glass windows, and the like)— is common to all meeting houses. Believing that God resides in each person, the Quakers don't look to sermons or ministers for direction. Feel free to ask questions of the person at the front desk. ◆ Donation requested.

M-Sa. 320 Arch St (between N Third and N Fourth Sts). 627.2667. www.archstreetfriends.org

22 CHLÖE

★★$$ This intimate Old City café, owned by chef Mary Ann Ferrie and her husband Dan Grimes, is a friendly place to enjoy innovative New American cuisine. Ferrie's signature salad, panko-crusted goat cheese over mixed greens, is a good place to start, but the tuna, served rare with a soy-banana-ginger sauce, is equally satisfying. The chocolate *gâteau* is decadent, served with fresh whipped cream. The only downside is that no reservations are accepted, and there's no place to wait comfortably for a table. ◆ 232 Arch St. 629.2337. www.chloebyob.com

FLOTSAM + JETSAM

23 FLOTSAM & JETSAM

This interesting shop offers a way-cool blend of home and garden furnishings, many designed by local craftspeople and artisans. ◆ 149 N Third St (between Market and Arch Sts). 351.9914. www.flotjet.com

24 FOSTER'S URBAN HOMEWARE

This terrific store offers an eclectic array of contemporary housewares, both decorative and functional. Guaranteed, you'll find something you didn't know you couldn't live without. ◆ 124 N Third St (between Market and Arch Sts). 671.0588; fax 267/671.0587. www.fosterscookware.com

25 LARRY BECKER/ CONTEMPORARY ART

Located on the first floor of a narrow brick building, this gallery has built a solid reputation representing a select roster of about a dozen contemporary painters and sculptors. Some of the better-known local names have included Italo Scanga, Bill Walton, Darwin Nix, Stuart Netsky, and Rebecca Johnson. ◆ Tu-Th, by appointment only; F, Sa, 11AM-5PM. 43 N Second St (between Church and Arch Sts). 925.5389. & www.artnet.com/lbecker

26 NATIONAL MUSEUM OF AMERICAN JEWISH HISTORY

This museum devoted to the history of Jews in America is also home to one of the oldest continuously meeting congregations, **Kahal Kadosh Mikveh Israel**, which traces its roots to 1740. Jews came to the colonies in very small numbers and apparently did not encounter discrimination. After a procession celebrating the adoption of the Constitution, for instance, kosher food was served, and George Washington sent a letter to Jewish supporters publicly thanking them for their congratulations on his appointment as president. In 1800, when the US population was about 5.3 million, the Jewish population was a mere 2,000, most of it concentrated in seaport towns. Designed by **H2L2**, the museum opened and held the first service on 4 July 1976. Books and crafts are sold in the gift shop. ◆ Admission. M-Th, 10AM-5PM; F, 10AM-3PM; Su, noon-5PM. 55 N Fifth St (between Market and Arch Sts). 923.3811. &. www.nmajh.org

27 OLD CITY COFFEE

★$ Fresh-roasted coffee beans, brewed coffees, cookies, and muffins are sold in this fragrant storefront. Pass through the little hallway to the cozy dining room with marble-topped tables, and relax over a cappuccino, cold lemonade, or light lunch of Thai shrimp salad. ◆ Café ◆ Daily, breakfast and lunch. 221 Church St (off N Third St). 629.9292. www.oldcitycoffee.com

28 KEISER-NEWMAN

Aggressively stylish contemporary furniture made of wood, glass, marble, aluminum, and porcelain fills this showroom across Second Street from **Christ Church**. ◆ Tu-Sa; Su, noon-5PM. 21 N Second St (between Market and Arch Sts). 923.7438. www.keiser-newman.com

29 BLUE IN GREEN

★★$ This hip coffee shop serves some of the most consistently good breakfast and lunch fare in town, so expect a wait. Creative pancakes, omelettes, salads, and sandwiches generally run in the $8 range; the coffee keeps on coming; and the waitstaff is adorable. ◆ 7 N 3rd St (between Market and Church Sts). 928.5880. ◆ A second location, on jewelers' row, also serves up dinner. But the real deal there is the early-bird breakfast special: eggs, bacon, home fries, and toast or a short stack of pancakes for just $2.50. ◆ 719 Sansom St. 923.6883

30 CHRIST CHURCH

If you sailed into Philadelphia during the 1700s, the white steeple of this church would have welcomed you, just as the Statue of Liberty has long held out her hand to travelers from afar in New York. Completed in 1744, the design owes much to **Sir Christopher Wren**'s churches in London. **Dr. John Kearsley**, a physician, is believed to have laid out the plans for the elegant Georgian structure, and **James Porteus**, of the Carpenters' Company, was the builder. Master carpenter **Robert Smith** added the tower and 200-foot steeple in 1754. The exterior, dominated by a Palladian window on the east front, is in Flemish bond brick, common to residential structures of the period, and urns bearing flames crown the balustrade that runs along the roof.

This National Historic Landmark rings with the history of 18th-century Philadelphia. George Washington and Benjamin Franklin were among the key historical figures who belonged to the Anglican congregation; the baptismal font in the rear of the church, sent to Philadelphia in 1697 from All Hallow's Church Barking-by-the-Tower in London, is where William Penn was baptized; Bishop William White preached from the wineglass-shaped pulpit for almost 60 years; members of the Continental Congress attended services here while meeting in Philadelphia; and the signers of the Declaration of Independence came here on 5 July 1776 to pray. Not long after the colonies achieved independence, the church separated from the mother country as well, and the Protestant Episcopal Church in the United States was established in conventions here in 1785 and 1789. The American Book of Common Prayer also was approved here in 1789. Designated a national shrine in 1950, the church remains an active parish. There is a small gift shop on the premises, open during visiting hours. ◆ Donation suggested. M-Sa; Su, 1-5PM. Closed M and Tu Jan-Mar. Services Su, 9AM, 11 AM; W, noon. Second St (between Market and Church Sts). 922.1695. &. www.christchurchphila.org

31 LUCY'S HAT SHOP

★$$ This magnet for Old City hipsters features a central fireplace geared to casting a glow onto both diners and drinkers. Settle into the red-velvet banquette—**Lucy's** décor is early bordello—and sip a cocktail. Martinis are favored here. Expect smoke and noise as the evening wears on, which makes Lucy's a good choice for an early supper of gnocchi with broccoli rabe or artichoke-crusted monkfish along with salads, burgers, and the like. Best bet is to make Lucy's late-night haunt for libations and bar food. The garlic mussels and goat-cheese flat bread are stellar choices. ♦ 247 Market St. 413.1433. www.lucys.info.com

32 RED SKY LOUNGE

★★$$ Specialty cocktails, including the house special (aptly named) Red Sky, mulled fruit and vodka, set the stage for a chic eat-and-greet scene at this swank Old City lounge. Nibbles like tuna tartare, pan-seared foie gras, and lobster pot stickers mean you don't have to look good on an empty stomach. ♦ 224 Market St. 925.8080. www.redskylounge.com

33 THE CONTINENTAL RESTAURANT & MARTINI BAR

★★$$ Finding a spot at the crowded bar won't be easy, but it will be worth every "pardon me" and subtle nudge. Enjoy an icy martini, one of the best in town. Once seated in the newly expanded dining room, nibble your way around the globe with small plates (similar to tapas) of, say, lobster mashed potatoes, seared tuna with mushroom risotto, and Tandoori salmon. Taking the design honors in this redecorated 1960s diner is the bar itself—cast, polished concrete—and fanciful light fixtures shaped like olives, with skewers through them. A second location in Center City West opened in 2004 at 1801 Chestnut St. ♦ Eclectic ♦ Daily, dinner. 138 Market St (at S Second St). 923.6069. ㅎ. www.continentalmartinibar.com

34 PENN'S VIEW HOTEL

$$ Not far from the center of **Independence National Historical Park**, this small inn holds its own on a block of old warehouses that will probably be restored someday. The standard accommodations have windows with partial views of the **Delaware River**, whereas premium rooms feature Jacuzzis and full views of the river (and Interstate 95). All 27 guest rooms are furnished with colonial reproductions. Continental breakfast is included in the rate. ♦ 14 N Front St (at Market St). 922.7600, 800/331.7634. ㅎ. www.pennsviewhotel.com

Within Penn's View Hotel:

RISTORANTE PANORAMA

★★$$ A large wall mural of an Italian hill scene dominates the dining room of this less-expensive cousin of the fastidious **La**

Famiglia (see page 24). Specialties include lobster ravioli and more than 120 wines by the glass—the city's largest selection. ♦ Italian ♦ M-F, lunch and dinner; Sa, Su, dinner. 922.7800. ㅎ.

35 FORK

★★★$$ This stylish American bistro has earned national acclaim for its moderately priced menu and for helping transform Old City into one of Philadelphia's hippest areas for a night out. The 48-seat dining room features earth-toned banquettes with 7-foot-high backs. Works by top local artisans, including light fixtures with hand-painted shades; walls texturally painted in muted shades of green, blue, ochre, and gray; and velvet curtains with geometric patterns and symbols grace the interior. Sculpted walls slice through the space, creating semiprivate areas for dining. There's also a welcoming bar and 30-seat lounge area where guests may relax while sipping a glass of wine from the affordable wine list or a cocktail. A small, 10-seat sidewalk café is open as weather permits. Appetizers include warm beet, leek, and Gorgonzola bruschetta and poached salmon dumplings with lemon-grass broth. Try the bay scallops cooked lightly in a leek broth with sorrel and new potatoes, Mexican black-bean soup, Greek-style marinated lamb chops combined with lightly sautéed spinach, and for dessert, chocolate bourbon cake with butter-pecan gelato. ♦ American ♦ Daily, lunch and dinner. Reservations recommended. 306 Market St (between Third and Fourth Sts). 625.9425. ㅎ. www.forkrestaurant.com

35 FRANKLIN COURT

The ghost of Benjamin Franklin appears everywhere in Philadelphia, but perhaps most vividly here. It was in this brick courtyard that he built his 10-room, three-story house and printshop, nestled behind a row of tenements he rented out on Market Street. Now gone, the structures have been replaced by the underground **Franklin Museum**, with a towering postmodernist sculpture marking the spot once occupied by his house.

Before entering the courtyard, visit the restored rentals on Market Street, which contain exhibits about Franklin's life. At **322 Market Street** (a replica of the office of the *Aurora and General Advertiser*), you can see the newspaper published by Benjamin Franklin Bache, Franklin's grandson. Next door, at **320 Market Street**, are demonstrations of 18th-century printing and bookbinding equipment. The exposed foundation and original brick walls of **318 Market Street** explain how Franklin, influenced by the Great Fire of London, designed a fireproof structure. At **316 Market Street** is the **B. Free Franklin Post Office**, a working post office where both the furnishings and the clothing of the postal workers are colonial. (Unfortunately, however, the postage prices are strictly contemporary.) Alongside is the **United States Postal Service Museum**, which offers narrative displays of US postal history. Exhibits include pony express pouches and originals of Franklin's *Pennsylvania Gazette*. (Franklin was also the nation's first postmaster.)

To see the courtyard where the Franklin house once stood, pass through the archway in the center of the Market Street houses, where a sign reads: "Benjamin Franklin went to and from his house through this original passage." The painted steel sculptural outline of the buildings—known as **Ghost Structures**—was completed in 1976 according to designs by the noted Philadelphia architectural firm of **Venturi, Scott Brown and Associates** with **John Milner Associates** and rises 54 feet high. In the pavement beneath the metal frames are inscriptions by and about Franklin and concrete portals offering views into the foundation of his demolished home.

Next, visit the **Franklin Museum**, which celebrates Franklin's ingenuity. Displays showcase his many inventions: In addition to the Franklin stove, he designed the swim flipper; at age 80, he invented the wooden book clasp, a precursor of the shelf clasps now used in grocery stores; and he also developed an armchair with a seat that could be converted to steps for reaching books. The main room has a phone bank where you can dial numbers to hear comments made about Franklin by everybody from George Washington to D.H. Lawrence; and on a stage in the center of the room, a cast of moving dolls in period costumes act out scenes of Franklin's life. There's also the obligatory 20-minute biographical film. ♦ Museums free. Daily. 314-22 Market St (between S Third and S Fourth Sts). 597.8974. www.ushistory.org/franklin/court

36 BLUEZETTE

★★$$ This Old City restaurant may look grand, but it has humble beginnings—owner Delilah Winder is best known for her soul-food outlet in the **Reading Terminal Market** and her five other take-out eateries around town. With **Bluezette**, Winder has taken everything up a notch, working with designer Riccardo Gonzales to create two dining spaces, one nonsmoking and all white, the other a cool blue lagoon. Winder's menu is the real show stopper here, a collection of bold comfort cuisine drawing from Caribbean, Creole, and Southern influences. Try some of the best fried chicken you'll ever taste, cornmeal-encrusted catfish, salmon with mango and papaya salsa, and curried goat served with pigeon peas and rice. Whatever you do, leave room for the sweet-potato pie, a Winder family recipe. ♦ 246 Market St. 627.3866. www.bluezette.com

t a n • g e r • i n e

t a n • g e r • i n e

t a n • g e r • i n e

37 TANGERINE

★★★$$ This dreamy tribute to the Casbah offers French Moroccan cuisine served in an atmosphere of sexy candlelight and exotic dance music. Everything chef Chris Painter creates is worthy of an Arabian sheik, from the restaurant's signature lobster risotto to one of the traditional Moroccan tagines. Portions are generous, and dishes are served family style and meant to be shared. The arugula with honeyed almonds and Manchego cheese comes piled high with enough greens to satisfy a hungry trio, a bargain for just $8. ♦ 232 Market St. 215/627.5116. www.tangerine restaurant.com

38 CUBA LIBRE

★★$$ This restaurant–bar–movie set looks like a scene out of *The Godfather: Part II*, the part where Michael was being wined and dined in pre-Castro Havana. Chef Guillermo Veloso offers a deft *nuevo latino* touch in the kitchen, with the best deal being his all-you-can-eat feast for $33 every Monday night. There is also a respectable wine list. The menu changes weekly, but expect a menu of hot and cold tapas along with dishes like paella marinera, Peruvian chicken, and *vaca frita*. The paella is fragrant with saffron and spiced with chorizo, rock shrimp, baby clams, and monkfish; the chicken is simmered in coconut, mild with peanuts and cilantro; and the *vaca frita* is a wonder of crisped pulled beef laced with rosemary mojo and marinated onions. The bar gets very crowded on weekends. ♦ International/Cuban ♦ Reservations are suggested. 10 S Second St (between Chestnut and Market Sts). 627.0666. www.cubalibrerestaurant.com

---

Restaurants/Clubs: **Red** | Hotels: **Purple** | Shops: Orange | Outdoors/Parks: **Green** | Sights/Culture: Blue

39 CAFÉ SPICE

★★$$ This elegant Indian bistro, an outgrowth of the New York original, turns up the heat with traditional vegetarian curries, scrumptious Indian breads—the veggie *roomali* roll is a meal in itself—lentil, potato, and onion samosas, and vegetable kebabs. ◆ Indian ◆ 5 S 2nd St (between Chestnut and Market Sts). 627.6273. www.cafespice.com/philadelphia/welcome

40 METROPOLITAN BAKERY

★★$ This popular outpost of the locally owned and operated artisan bakeshop features a breakfast menu built on **Metropolitan**'s fine array of baked goods, such as French berry rolls, which you can top with French butter, cream cheese, jam, or English double cream. Lunch brings a changing array of sandwiches, including a hearty—and colorful—tuna with capers, black olives, red onions, Havarti cheese, tomato, and romaine on brioche. There are also pressed sandwiches (sort of panini), including ham and Gruyère, and small plates for the not-so-hungry, including a baguette with a wedge of cheddar and an apple or pear. ◆ M-F, 7:30AM-7PM; Sa, 8AM-6PM; Su, 9AM-5PM. 126 Market St. 928.9528. www.metropolitanbakery.com

41 SHANE CANDIES

Open since 1876, this charming storefront bills itself as the oldest candy store in the country. Whether or not this is true, the store has some of the best chocolates in Philadelphia. (Try the milk-chocolate almond bark.) At Eastertime, the store is packed full of chocolate crosses and coconut-cream eggs. ◆ M-Sa. 110 Market St (between S Front and S Second Sts). 922.1048. www.shanecandies.com

42 WARMDADDY'S

★★$$ The Bynum brothers, Robert and Benjamin, owners of **Zanzibar Blue**, the city's ultrasuccessful jazz club, have created Philadelphia's only venue with live, traditional Delta blues and authentic Southern cuisine. The food—including down-home smothered

The Liberty Bell received its name in the 19th century when antislavery groups, inspired by its inscription "Proclaim liberty thro' all the land to all the inhabitants thereof," coined the name.

St. Peter's Church, built to accommodate the overflow of people who wanted but couldn't get seats at Christ Church, was first called "the chapel of ease."

chicken and waffles, fried cornmeal catfish with Creole sauce, and Beale Street spicy sautéed shrimp—is prepared with dedication to original Southern recipes, and a mighty dose of Mississippi back-porch blues and Chicago blues is tossed in for good measure. The cover charge is waived if you're seated for dinner before 8:30PM. If you're coming for the music only, you'll be seated at the bar. ◆ Southern ◆ Cover, W-Su. Tu-Su, dinner. Reservations recommended. 4-6 S Front St (between Chestnut and Market Sts). 627.8400. www.warmdaddys.com

42 LA FAMIGLIA

★★★$$$$ Consistently first-class Italian cuisine is served in this formal and elegant drawing room appointed with fine moldings and sconces, ornate mirrors, and plush chairs. Start off with *crostini di porcini* (toasted bread topped with porcini mushrooms sautéed in olive oil with fresh basil) or hearts of artichokes sautéed in olive oil with fresh herbs. Then dig into the homemade pasta, including small ravioli in a cream sauce. Fresh fish is also a specialty here—try the whole fish grilled tableside. The wine list is long and wonderful. Stiff service is the only negative. ◆ Italian ◆ Tu-F, lunch and dinner; Sa, Su, dinner. Reservations required. 8 S Front St (between Chestnut and Market Sts). 922.2803. www.la-famiglia.com

43 SERRANO

★★$$ Exotic puppets dangle from the ceilings and gargoyles decorate the walls of this small international café. The menu features everything from Ceylon black curry chicken and Hungarian chicken paprikash to Malaysian pork chops, plus Indonesian satay, Texas chili, Asian-style fish, and Thai salads. ◆ International ◆ Daily, dinner. 20 S Second St (between Chestnut and Market Sts). 928.0770. www.tinangel.com/serrano.html

Above Serrano:

TIN ANGEL

Acoustic music is the draw at this cozy coffee-house where well-known artists, such as Livingston Taylor and Roger McGuinn (formerly of the Byrds), play. On Wednesday nights, anyone can get up and perform—just be sure to bring your own instrument. Candlelit tables are the setting for a wide array of coffee drinks, tea, alcoholic beverages, and desserts. A combination of dinner at **Serrano** and a show ticket is a good deal. ◆ Cover. Daily, 7PM-midnight. 928.0978; credit card orders, 928.0770. www.tinangel.com

44 THE BOURSE

In striking contrast to the colonial structures nearby is this massive, columned brownstone, a 19th-century office building reincarnated as a multilevel retail and office complex in 1982 according to designs by **H2L2**. The blocklong structure, originally designed by **George** and **William Hewitt**, architects of the **Bellevue Stratford Hotel**, features a red sandstone and Pompeian-brick exterior with flourishes of terra-cotta decoration. It opened in 1895 as home to the city's maritime, stock, and grain exchanges and ranks as the first commodities exchange in the US. After the financial center moved to the commercial district, the building fell into decline, until it was extensively renovated in the 1980s. The most dramatic space is the enormous great hall, illuminated by a huge skylight. The ground-floor food court has plenty of places to sit and offers hamburgers, salads, pizza, and sandwiches. Staircases with lacy railings ascend to the second floor, where tables can be reserved for large groups. The lower level houses **El Mariachi Restaurant** and, among other things, public rest rooms. ♦ Daily. 21 S Fifth St (between Ranstead and Ludlow Sts). 625.0300. ♿. www.bourse-pa.com

Within The Bourse:

Bain's Deli

$ Standard-issue corned beef brisket, tuna salad, and ham sandwiches are sold here. ♦ Deli ♦ Daily, lunch. Ground floor. 925.6646. Also at The Gallery I (N 10th and Market Sts). 928.9323; The Gallery II (N 11th and Market Sts). 592.1610; and One Liberty Pl (S 17th St, between Chestnut and Market Sts). 567.1685. ♿. www.bainsdeli.com

Liberty Chicken

$ Rotisserie chicken, chicken kebab, spicy noodle chicken salad, and plain old chicken salad are some of the options here. ♦ Chicken ♦ Daily, lunch. Ground floor. 629.0815. ♿. www.bourse-pa.com/7.html

45 Club 27

This sexy, New York–style dance club caters to the hipster 20- and 30-something crowd. Decked out in industrial décor—exposed air ducts, metal mesh fencing—**Club 27** includes an upstairs balcony–dance space that attracts a naughty fringe element. ♦ 27 Bank St (between Chestnut and Market Sts). 922.3020. www.club27philly.com

46 Ritz at the Bourse

This five-screen cinema shows foreign films and offbeat movies rarely played in more commercial theaters. Reduced parking rates are available. ♦ S Fourth and Ranstead Sts. 925.7900. www.ritzfilmbill.com

47 Hot Soup

Welcome to Philadelphia's only glassblowing studio and gallery, featuring live demonstrations, classes, and workshops. ♦ Daily. 26 S Strawberry St (between Chestnut and Market Sts). 922.2332. www.hotsoupstudio.com

48 Sassafras International Cafe

★$$ A carved wood bar, mosaic tiles, and a marble fireplace add charm to this small bistro that is best known for its burgers. Choices also include Mongolian dumplings and stir-fries. ♦ International ♦ Restaurant: M-Sa, lunch and dinner. 48 S Second St (between Chestnut and Market Sts). 925.2317

49 The Omni at Independence Park

$$$ Combining the efficiency of a large chain operation with the comforts of an elegant small hotel, this property is the most luxurious place to stay east of Broad Street. Most of the 150 rooms overlook Independence Park and are furnished with king-size beds and marbled bathrooms. Drinks and light fare, usually accompanied by piano music on weeknights, are served in the intimate lobby. Other highlights include a lap pool, a fitness center, voice mail, and a gourmet restaurant. Weekend rates are especially reasonable. ♦ 401 Chestnut St (at S Fourth St). 925.0000, 800/843.6664; fax 931.4217. ♿. www.omnihotels.com

Within The Omni at Independence Park:

Azalea

★★$$$ Plush and formal, this dining room is dressed in champagne tones with oversize cream-colored chandeliers, mirrored posts, banquettes, and white linen. The kitchen prides itself on using local produce, meats, and seafood. Dinner might include Maryland shore tuna baked in a black-olive crust, braised Vineland veal tenderloin, or roasted monkfish with oysters. ♦ Eclectic ♦ M-F, breakfast, lunch, and dinner; Sa, breakfast and dinner; Su, brunch and dinner. Reservations recommended. 931.4260 ♿

50 Cosí

★★$ This cheery combination coffeehouse, café, and lounge features brightly colored, comfy sofas and chairs and sidewalk seating in season. In addition to offering teas and coffee drinks (frozen and non-), delicious desserts and ice cream, and hearty-fare soups and salads, sandwiches, pizza, and wraps, **Cosí** has a full bar—hidden behind a

---

Restaurants/Clubs: Red | Hotels: Purple | Shops: Orange | Outdoors/Parks: Green | Sights/Culture: Blue

sliding mural; it opens ceremoniously at 4PM. ♦ Café/lounge ♦ Daily, lunch and snacks until 2AM. 325 Chestnut St (between S Third and S Fourth Sts). 399.0215. ᚔ. Also at numerous locations throughout the city. www.getcosi.com

BUDDAKAN

50 BUDDAKAN

★★★$$$ Named for a Japanese concert hall of the same name, Stephen Starr's Old City restaurant features modern Asian cuisine, including Japanese, Chinese, Vietnamese, Thai, and Indian fare, interpreted with a French technique. The room's white décor, designed by Starr himself, pays homage to renowned restaurant and hotel designer Philippe Starck, using his signature pieces, such as curved, high-backed banquettes and surreal chairs decorated with the hand-painted, photographic image of a face on the back, throughout the 100-seat main dining room. (Many of the faces are those of Philadelphians.) The 20-foot-high walls are swathed in white fabric and illuminated with soft lights from behind. Cherrywood floors add warmth. A 10-foot-high, gold-leafed Buddha dominates the setting. The social center of the 170-seat restaurant is the onyx-topped community table for 22 that provides an area where guests may mingle. Inventive appetizers might include Thai lobster crepe with shiitake mushrooms and cognac curry sauce; tuna carpaccio; and duck-and-foie gras dumplings with vanilla jus. Entrées such as dry, aged beef with Szechuan fries and watercress salad, and *pad thai* with jumbo shrimp are popular dishes. *Be forewarned*: Saturday nights are booked months in advance. ♦ Asian ♦ Daily, dinner. 325 Chestnut St (between S Third and S Fourth Sts). 574.9440. ᚔ. www.buddakan.com

51 THE NATIONAL LIBERTY MUSEUM

This unique museum honors more than 350 men, women, and young people for their contribution to American liberty and fight against injustice, violence, and bigotry. A highlight is an extraordinary collection of glass art by sculptors including Dale Chihuly and an exhibit paying tribute to the heroes of 9/11. The exhibit illustrates that liberty must be protected—or it can easily shatter. ♦ Admission. Tu-Su, 10AM-6PM. 321 Chestnut St. 925.2800. www.libertymuseum.org

52 UNITED AMERICAN INDIANS OF THE DELAWARE VALLEY

Philadelphia's only true source of Native American culture—it's wholly owned and operated by 42 different tribes of Native Americans—offers a museum displaying contemporary and ancestral art, ancient tools, and over 20 audio and video presentations. The **Trading Post** gift shop is stocked with silver jewelry, dance shawls, music, pottery, paintings, collectible dolls, and handmade clothing. The facility also hosts book signings and artists' receptions, offers a speakers' bureau, and provides instruction in Native American social ways, including dancing. ♦ Daily. 225 Chestnut St (between Strawberry and S Third Sts). 574.9020. www.communicator.com/indianpa.html

53 PHILADELPHIA FISH & Co.

★$$ Walk through the extremely popular and noisy bar to reach this casual dining room where a wide selection of fresh seafood is served. The restaurant imports about 100 pounds of mesquite from Texas every day to feed its grill and give the seafood a nice nutty flavor. Besides the grilled red snapper with tarragon vinaigrette, there are seared Asian-Cajun tuna, fire-roasted jumbo shrimp, and Chesapeake Bay crab cakes, a specialty of the house. This is the go-to place for locals in search of friendly service and the freshest fish in town. ♦ Seafood ♦ M-Sa, lunch and dinner; Su, dinner. 207 Chestnut St (at S Second St). 625.8605. www.philadelphiafish.com

54 ROCOCO

★★★$$$ The century-old **Corn Exchange Bank** has been transformed into an elegant and, true to its name, ornate cobalt blue-and-butterscotch-colored restaurant, complete with a grand staircase, towering ceilings, and a 40-foot-long serpentine bar of poured amber resin embedded with futuristic fiber optics. The menu features panko-crusted salmon, fire-grilled swordfish, shrimp and steak, and jumbo lump crabmeat served in a mild Java curry. A private cigar lounge is located on the second floor. ♦ American ♦ Daily, dinner. Reservations recommended. 123 Chestnut St (between S Front and S Second Sts). 629.1100

54 THE PLOUGH & THE STARS

★★$$ This friendly Irish pub offers better-than-average pub fare, including baked river trout stuffed with Irish smoked-salmon mousse, roast loin of pork wrapped in a rasher of Irish bacon, and traditional shepherd's pie and Irish stew. Other draws are afternoon tea, 12 premium beers on tap, and Irish music on Sunday afternoons and evenings. Dine on the mezzanine for a good look at activity on Second Street. ♦ Irish ♦ M-F, lunch and dinner; Sa, Su, brunch, lunch, and dinner. Music: Su, 3-10PM. 123 Chestnut St (between S Front and S Second Sts). 733.0300. www.ploughstars.com

55 POSH

★$ Located on the first floor of **Brasil's Restaurant**, this new dance lounge has a retro theme—think Rat Pack meets the Girl from Ipanema. ♦ Music and dancing W-Su. 112 Chestnut St. 413.1701

56 THOMAS BOND HOUSE

$$ This bed-and-breakfast offers a country inn atmosphere in the middle of the city. Built in 1769 by Thomas Bond, an eminent colonial physician who helped found **Pennsylvania Hospital**, the elegant Georgian brick structure was a residence until 1810, when it became a commercial building. It was restored as an inn in 1988 and offers a wide range of rates. A marble fireplace warms the parlor, where wine and cheese are served nightly. Guests enjoy continental breakfast during the week and a full breakfast on weekends. All 12 guest rooms feature TVs and hair dryers. ♦ 129 S Second St (between Walnut and Chestnut Sts). 923.8523, 800/845.2663; fax 923.8504. www.winston-salem-inn.com/philadelphia

57 INDEPENDENCE VISITOR CENTER

Located on **Independence Mall**, the $38 million center serves as the gateway to **Independence National Historical Park** and the surrounding historic district, and, on a broader scale, the city and entire region. At the center, park rangers and exhibits and displays will help visitors gain a contextual understanding of the park and its surroundings. Here also will be the place to purchase tickets to tours, attractions, and events in the area; make reservations for accommodations, restaurants, and transportation; purchase gifts, books, and souvenirs; see films documenting the creation of the nation and ones about the attractions of Philadelphia and the region; and have a light meal. Public rest rooms are also available. This is also the place to get free tickets for timed admission to **Independence Hall**.

Independence Park Institute, contiguous to the **Independence Visitor Center**, is another component in the expansion project, the foundation for the park's educational programs, accommodating the more than 400,000 schoolchildren, 15,000 teachers, and 20,000 chaperons who visit the park each year. In addition to serving as the central orientation point for school groups, the Institute will offer fee-based programs on a reservation basis, and pre-visit, on-site, and post-visit curriculum materials, as well as teacher training and family and youth programs. A sculpture on the building's south wall depicts a most unusual view of the Declaration of Independence—words pertaining to slavery that were drafted but cut from the document will be shown once again, but filled in with crushed glass. ♦ One N Independence Mall W, at 6th and Market Sts. 965.7676. www.independencevisitorcenter.com

58 DECLARATION HOUSE

"Neither aiming at originality of principle or sentiment, nor yet copied from any particular document and previous writing, it was intended to be an expression of the American mind." So Thomas Jefferson said of the Declaration of Independence, which he drafted in rented rooms on this site. The 18th-century brick row house where he labored was demolished in 1883, then reconstructed the year before the US bicentennial celebration. An 8-minute film featuring a rather unconvincing Jefferson plays regularly, and memorabilia from his life are displayed in large glass cases. The two upstairs rooms Jefferson rented from Jacob Graff have also been re-created. ♦ Free. Daily. S Seventh St (at Market St). 597.8974. www.nps.gov/inde/declaration-house.html

59 LIBERTY BELL CENTER

Every year, some 1.6 million people (up to 10,000 on busy days) visit the **Liberty Bell**. Originally commissioned for the 1750 bell tower of the **State House** (later known as **Independence Hall**) in commemoration of the 50th anniversary of the Pennsylvania colony's Charter of Liberties, the famous bronze bell was made by Whitechapel Foundry in London. Its prophetic inscription (from Leviticus) reads: "Proclaim liberty thro' all the land, to all the inhabitants thereof." In 1753, it was placed in the belfry and tolled on important occasions, including 8 July 1776, when it rang out to call citizens to the first public reading of the Declaration of Independence in **Independence Square**. In 1777, when the British occupied Philadelphia, patriots moved the bell to Allentown for safekeeping. The 2,000-pound bell—which could not be repaired—cracked several times during the 1800s, then was silenced for good when it rang out for George Washington's birthday in 1846. During the Civil War, abolitionists adopted it and its biblical inscription as a symbol of liberty.

As more visitors began making the pilgrimage to Philadelphia to pay tribute to the cracked symbol of freedom, officials deemed Independence Hall too small to accommodate them and lobbied for the construction of the bell's home from 1976 to 2003, a contemporary structure designed by **Mitchell/Giurgola** and completed in time for the country's bicentennial, where it can be visited 24 hours a day.

The famed symbol of our nation's freedom moved to a new $12.6 **Liberty Bell Center** in 2003. Located in the same block as its old structure, between 5th and 6th on Market, the new complex enhances visitors' experience and understanding of what the bell stands for by adding a new exhibit hall and a bright, spacious chamber to house the bell. The entire area accommodates 400 visitors at a time. At night, the bell is illuminated, and a 5-minute audio account of its history is activated by pushing a button outside the pavilion. During the day, park rangers do the talking.

The new Liberty Bell Center is part of a master plan for the renewal of the three blocks north of Independence Hall as **Independence Mall**. The project, completed in 2003, includes facilities for tourism, educational programs, and scholarly research. The underground parking garage was enlarged and renovated; an open-air café, gardens, seating areas, and spaces for special events have been added.

In the second block, the new $38 million **Independence Visitor Center**, located on Independence Mall, serves as the gateway to **Independence National Historical Park** and the surrounding historic district, and, on a broader scale, the city and entire region (see page 27). ♦ One N Independence Mall W, at Sixth and Market Sts. 965.7676. www.constitutioncenter.org

To circumvent Pennsylvania's conservative provincial assembly, Benjamin Franklin and other liberal leaders began meeting at City Tavern to discuss revolutionary measures combining mass involvement and economic tactics. Such discussions laid the groundwork for a revolution in Pennsylvania, and soon radical committees were operating in every county in the state—with the de facto popular government's headquarters in City Tavern.

Elfreth's Alley was created in 1703 when two property owners on Front Street extended a cartway to the rear of their lots to subdivide their land.

The **National Constitution Center**, a $185 million homage to our nation's most important document, opened on 4 July 2003. A stirring interactive museum, the Center is the first dedicated to honoring and perpetuating the ideas embodied in the US Constitution. The engaging 132,000-square-foot monument presents the history of the document, as well as its contemporary relevance examined through discussion and display. The Center is also a hub for study and debate, the site for special lectures, film screenings, and other thought-provoking events. About 1,000,000 people visit annually. A cheery upstairs café offers substantial fare and terrace dining. ♦ 111 S Independence Mall E at Market St (between S Fifth and S Sixth Sts). 923.0004. www.constitutioncenter.org

60 PECO ENERGY LIGHTS OF LIBERTY CENTER

A high-tech addition to **Independence National Historical Park**. Billed as the world's first ambulatory sound and light show, this $12 million production unfolds at five different points in the park, where visitors can see and hear images and sounds that depict events that led up to the colonists' fight for independence from the British. The voices of celebrities Walter Cronkite, Ossie Davis, Charlton Heston, Claire Bloom, Frank Langella, and others bring the story to life. Produced by Miziker and Co. of L.A.—the same outfit that puts together Super Bowl halftime shows and Olympic ceremonies—**Lights of Liberty** also boasts sound editing by George Lucas's Skywalker sound engineers for *Star Wars* and *Titanic*, among other movies. The 60-minute experience begins and ends at **PECO Energy Liberty Center**, 6th and Chestnut, where tickets are sold and guests pick up the three-dimensional headsets that they'll wear throughout the show. Visitors in groups of 50 then follow a route where full-color, five-story images will be projected, including **Independence Hall**, **Carpenters' Hall**, **Second Bank of the United States**, and **Franklin Court**. The audio track is available in seven languages, and there is a special "children's channel." Open 7 days a week, just after dark, with groups leaving every 10 minutes. ♦ Admission. 601 Chestnut St. 512.3789, 877/GO.2.1776. www.lightsofliberty.org

61 CONGRESS HALL

Completed in 1789 as a county seat, the Federal-style west wing of **Independence Hall** housed the **US Congress** between 1790 and 1800, when Philadelphia was the nation's capital. During that period, Congress officially added the first 10 amendments—the Bill of Rights—to the Constitution; established the United States Mint; and admitted Vermont,

Kentucky, and Tennessee to the union. Now a National Historic Site, the building has been authentically restored to its 1793 condition with a mixture of original and period furnishings. George Washington took the oath of office for his second term in the Senate chamber, an elegant room decorated with red silk curtains, an ornate plaster ceiling, a huge carpet (a reproduction) bearing floral patterns, the seal of the US, and 13 state shields. Four years later, John Adams, the nation's second president, was inaugurated in the House of Representatives' meeting room. ◆ Free. Daily. S Sixth and Chestnut Sts. 597.8974. www.nps.gov/inde/congress-hall.html

61 RIDE THE DUCKS

Amphibious sightseeing is all its quacked up to be for this one-if-by-land, two-if-by-sea sightseeing experience. The 80-minute adventure takes off at 6th and Chestnut daily, squiring tourists by sights including Independence Hall, the Liberty Bell, and Betsy Ross House before taking to the Delaware for a cruise around Penn's Landing. Your ticket includes a plastic duck call (aka "wacky quacker"), which means you can hear the Duckmobile coming before you see it. Kids just love it. Buy tickets at a kiosk at Sixth and Chestnut, or at the Independence Visitor Center. ◆ Departures daily. Sixth and Chestnut Sts. 215/227.3825. www.phillyducks.com

62 INDEPENDENCE HALL

So often has this brick building been called the birthplace of American government that doing so seems a cliché. But the events that took place here were indeed momentous, and anyone with the slightest interest in American history will find this beautifully preserved structure filled with all the integrity the history books suggest. Best of all, the building speaks for itself, with no hype or extraneous exhibits.

The hall actually originated as headquarters of the Pennsylvania colony at a time when this plot of land stood on the outskirts of Philadelphia. In 1729, Pennsylvania leaders saw the need for a central government building, and Andrew Hamilton, a prominent lawyer and amateur architect who was Speaker of the Assembly, began planning the **State House** (as **Independence Hall** was then known) with master carpenter **Edmund Wooley**. (In colonial times, master carpenters often served as architects.) They completed construction in 1748, at a time when no one foresaw just how useful such a building might be as a meeting place for a fledgling federal government. Less than 30 years later, delegates

from 13 colonies, including Benjamin Franklin, Thomas Jefferson, and John Hancock, congregated here and hotly debated the Declaration of Independence, which they finally approved on 4 July 1776 and signed a month later. The State House then went on to further fame: The Second Continental Congress, which drafted the Articles of Confederation, met here, and the first-floor Assembly Room served as the venue for the Constitutional Convention, which in 1787 produced the document that became the US Constitution. Much later, on 22 April 1865, 85,000 people came here to view the body of slain president Abraham Lincoln.

This is one of the country's most outstanding examples of Georgian architecture, noted for its symmetry and for reflecting the city's early taste for Quaker plainness. The building is restrained and unpretentious, with a white bell tower that seems a quaint souvenir in contrast to the monumental temples of government in Washington, DC. The brick-and-wood tower, also believed to be the work of Edmund Wooley, was added in 1750 to mark the 50th anniversary of William Penn's Charter of Liberties, which listed the founding principles of the Pennsylvania colony. The centerpiece is the great clock with its ornate dial plate, a replica of the original clock, installed in 1752. William Strickland designed the steeple, which was added in 1828.

The first floor's two rooms and large central hallway—all with handsome carved moldings—are decorated in mostly period furnishings that are not authentic to the rooms. (British troops used the building's earliest furniture as firewood when they occupied the city in 1777 and 1778.) The **Supreme Court Chamber**, on the right when you enter, is where Pennsylvania's highest court met. Note the large rendition of the Pennsylvania coat of arms, dating to 1785, over the judge's chair. King George III's coat of arms originally occupied the wall but was burned in **Independence Square** after the first public reading of the Declaration of Independence.

Across the hall is the **Assembly Room**, where the most significant events took place. The room's original fixtures include an inkstand made by silversmith Philip Syng in 1752 and used for the signing of both the Declaration of Independence and the US Constitution, along with the chair used by George Washington during the Constitutional Convention. The back of the chair has a carving of the top half of the sun. After the Constitution was adopted, Franklin reportedly said, ". . . now at length I have the happiness to know that it is a rising and not a setting sun." Two fireplaces and tables covered with green baize cloth, pewter

---

Restaurants/Clubs: Red | Hotels: Purple | Shops: Orange | Outdoors/Parks: Green | Sights/Culture: Blue

inkstands, and brass candlesticks dominate the room. The beautiful cut-glass chandelier, added in 1976, resembles a fixture that hung here in 1776.

On the second floor are the **Governor's Council Chamber**; the **Long Gallery**, used by British troops as a prison for American patriots during the Revolution; and the **Committee of the Assembly's Chamber**, which has a collection of weapons used during the war.

You need a ticket for the free tour of Independence Hall, offered every 15 minutes by the National Park Service. Tours average 25 minutes. Tickets are available at the **Independence Visitor Center** the day of the tour or can be reserved as early as a year in advance by calling 800/967.2283 between 10 AM and 10PM daily or by going to http://reservations. nps.gov. Unless you're satisfied with a quick zip through the building, it's best not to come for a tour between 10AM and 2PM during the busiest times—May through June, the last 2 weeks of September, and October—when the rangers have less time to talk. ♦ Free. Daily. Chestnut St (between S Fifth and S Sixth Sts). 597.8974. www.nps.gov/inde/indep-hall.html

63 OLD CITY HALL

The "newest" part of the original **State House** complex is the east wing of **City Hall**, a Federal-style twin of **Congress Hall**, designed by master carpenter **David Evans** and completed in 1791. Plans for the building, now a National Historic Site, were first discussed in the 1730s, but actual work didn't begin until after the Revolutionary War. Although it was built to house the city government, the structure was used as the US Supreme Court from 1791 to 1800, when Philadelphia was the nation's capital. When the capital moved to Washington, DC, the building served as city hall; then, in 1901, the local government relocated to Center Square. ♦ Free. Daily. S Fifth and Chestnut Sts. www.nps.gov/inde /old-city-hall.html

When the Declaration of Independence was first read outside Independence Hall on 8 July 1776, the British royal coat of arms was torn down and burned, and not one but two Liberty Bells were rung.

Just how many cheesesteaks can Philadelphians consume? More than a million hoagie rolls are baked each week in the ovens at Amoroso's Bakery, and South Philly's Pat's King of Steaks, where the cheesesteak is said to have been invented, uses about 5,000 pounds of beef in an average week.

64 SECOND BANK OF THE UNITED STATES

Architecture students often come to admire **William Strickland**'s 1824 marble-faced edifice, a National Historic Site, which established the trend in Greek Revival public buildings. (Strickland, who modeled the bank after the Parthenon, also designed the **Independence Hall** steeple and other noteworthy buildings of the period.) Classical architecture became the preferred style for government buildings in the 19th century as the country sought a more sophisticated image and a link between its democratic principles and those of ancient Greece.

The bank was one of the world's most powerful financial institutions until President Andrew Jackson vetoed the renewal of its charter in 1832 after disagreeing with the bank's conservative policies. Between 1844 and 1935, the building served as the US Customs House, then was restored in 1974 to house the **Portrait Gallery** (see below) as part of the **Independence National Park** complex. The main banking room is beautiful, with a barrel-vaulted ceiling in salmon and green tones, black-and-white marble floors, arched windows, and Doric columns. ♦ Free. Daily. 420 Chestnut St (between S Fourth and S Fifth Sts). www.nps.gov/inde/second-bank.html

Within the Second Bank of the United States:

PORTRAIT GALLERY

Charles Willson Peale, the nation's most prominent early portraitist, opened the forerunner to this gallery on the second floor of **Independence Hall**. His museum, an idiosyncratic collection of portraits and mounted animal specimens (natural history fascinated him), closed in 1828. Today this gallery houses many of Peale's paintings of the nation's founders, including Alexander Hamilton and Declaration of Independence signers Thomas Mifflin and Robert Morris. Also on display are a Henry Inman portrait of William Penn; William Rush's lifesize likeness of George Washington, carved in pine; an extremely rare authentic print of the first edition of the Declaration of Independence, in broadside form, from 8 July 1776; a draft of the first official version of the preamble of the Constitution; and early prints of Philadelphia. ♦ Free. Daily. 597.8974. www.ushistory.org/tour/tour_2bank.htm

65 CARPENTERS' HALL

Patterned after England's trade guilds, the **Carpenters' Company** has been active since its founding in 1724, making it the oldest trade organization in the country. The group greatly influenced the creation of the city, spreading information about building techniques and setting prices. Its master carpenters, most notably **Robert Smith** (who also designed **St. Peter's Church** in Society Hill), often served as architects as well. Smith designed this handsome Georgian building as a meeting place for members of the Carpenters' Company, but it served as the site of the First Continental Congress in 1774, the year it was completed. Exhibits include Windsor chairs used by the delegates, a scale model of the building under construction, and early carpentry tools. ♦ Free. W-Su, Jan-Feb; Tu-Su, Mar-Dec. 320 Chestnut St (between S Third and S Fourth Sts). 925.0167. www.ushistory.org/carpentershall

66 PHILOSOPHICAL HALL

Directly behind **Old City Hall** stands the Federal-style headquarters of the **American Philosophical Society**, the nation's oldest learned society. Founded in 1743 by Benjamin Franklin—who else?—the organization has included as members Thomas Jefferson, John Audubon, Marie Curie, Thomas Edison, Charles Darwin, and Albert Einstein. In the 18th century, the society promoted astronomical research, silk cultivation, and canal development. Today it continues to encourage research in diverse fields, including quantum physics, neurobiology, computers, literary studies, and medical science. The building, a National Historic Landmark, was designed by **Samuel Vaughan** and completed in 1789. ♦ By appointment only. 104 S Fifth St (between Walnut and Chestnut Sts). 440.3400. www.nps.gov/inde/philhall.html

INDEPENDENCE NATIONAL HISTORICAL PARK

Consider this L-shaped swath of land—bounded roughly by Second and Sixth Streets and by Walnut and Arch Streets—one large American history museum, with more than 20 buildings and monuments central to the early founding of the country. The 46-acre park is home to **Independence Hall**, **Old City Hall**, **Congress Hall**, **Philosophical Hall**, and the new **Liberty Bell Pavilion**, and covers 17 city blocks, blending into the neighborhoods of Old City and Society Hill. Operated by the National Park Service, it was created by an act of Congress in 1948. Rangers at the new **Independence Visitor Center** can answer general questions about the park. Pick up a map at Independence Hall, the best starting place for your tour. Some sites—including Independence Hall, the **Todd House**, and the **Bishop William White House**—can be seen only as part of an organized tour. Disability accessibility maps are available at any of the sites within the park, and wheelchairs can be rented at the Independence Visitor Center. There's a parking garage on Second Street between Chestnut and Walnut Streets as well as 2-hour on-street meter parking for shorter visits. Be sure to have quarters on hand—the meter maids are vigilant.

67 INDEPENDENCE SQUARE

The inviting plot of green behind **Independence Hall** is filled with benches, arching trees, and a rustic peace. It's a lovely place to sit or stroll, particularly when the trees take on the first leaves of spring or the foliage turns lush and generous with shade in summer. At the rear of the colonial buildings, pathways radiate south to Walnut Street, west to Sixth Street, and east to Fifth Street. The first public reading of the Declaration of Independence took place here. ♦ Bounded by S Fifth and S Sixth Sts and by Walnut and Chestnut Sts. www.gophila.com/index-independencehall.htm

68 LIBRARY HALL

The **Library Company of Philadelphia**, founded in 1731 as the first subscription library in the colonies and a forerunner of the Library of Congress, moved its headquarters to this site in 1789 and stayed until the building was demolished some 99 years later.

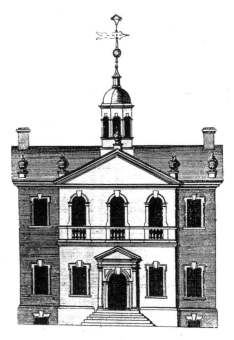

COURTESY OF THE CARPENTERS' COMPANY OF THE CITY AND COUNTY OF PHILADELPHIA

Restaurants/Clubs: Red | Hotels: Purple | Shops: Orange | Outdoors/Parks: Green | Sights/Culture: Blue

NORTHERN LIBERTIES

These days, there's tasty doings in **Northern Liberties**, a warehouse-filled industrial neighborhood north of Old City now being discovered by some of the city's newest eateries. Whether you're in the mood for above-average pub fare or *pommes frites*, you'll find it here. www.northernliberties.org

N. Third (Third and Brown Streets; 413.3666; www.northird.com) is comfort food all the way, with hearty Southern-style American fare prepared by chef Terry Cherry, previously in the kitchen at **Ortlieb's Jazzhaus** (www.ortliebsjazzhaus.com) the venerable neighborhood jazz joint and restaurant just up the street. His menu, reasonably priced at $14 or less for entrées, includes buttermilk pan-fried chicken, ribs, and grilled salmon.

You won't find a friendlier neighborhood pub than **Standard Tap** (901 N 2nd Street; 238.0630), a former plumbing-supply shop turned bar and restaurant. Terrific duck salad, a hearty chicken pot pie, and perfectly grilled burgers are among the anything-but-standard charms of this local watering hole. www.standardtap.com

Las Cazuelas (426 W Girard Avenue; 351.9144), located on the edge of Northern Liberties, is home to truly authentic Oaxacan cuisine, from brooding *moles* to freshly stuffed tamales and salsa verde. The appetizer sampler, which offers tortillas stuffed with refried beans and cheese, and *tacos dorados* (chicken wrapped in tortillas, then deep-fried), is a great way to start the south-of-the-border experience. Family owned and run, Las Cazuelas is a bright spot on an otherwise barren stretch of Girard Avenue. www.lascazuelas.net

Built in its place in 1954 (with a reproduction of the original façade designed by **William Thornton**, architect of the Capitol building in Washington, DC), this structure by **Martin, Stewart & Noble** houses the library and offices of the **American Philosophical Society**, whose headquarters are across the street at **Philosophical Hall** (see page 31; the Library Company is now located in Center City East—see page 63.) The 200,000-plus volumes and manuscripts in the library include historical treasures, such as first editions of Newton's *Principia* and Darwin's *Origin of Species*, Lewis and Clark's field notes, and a copy of the Declaration of Independence handwritten by Thomas Jefferson. The Philosophical Society rotates small exhibits from its collection in the lobby. ♦ Free. Lobby, M-F. 105 S Fifth St (between Walnut and Chestnut Sts). 440.3400. www.ushistory.org/tour/tour_library.htm

69 FIRST BANK OF THE UNITED STATES

This is one of the oldest bank buildings in the country, designed and completed with a classical façade by architect **Samuel Blodgett Jr.** in 1797. The structure still conveys a sense of indomitable power, with its marble facing and two-story Corinthian portico. Note the carved American eagle in the mahogany pediment over the entranceway. (The eagle was gaining in stature as a national symbol at the time the bank formed.) The bank lost its federal charter in 1811 but served as a working bank until 1926. Now a National Historic Site, much of this building is vacant, with only a few floors used for park offices. It is not open to the public. ♦ S Third St (between Walnut and Chestnut Sts). www.ushistory.org/tour/tour_1bank.htm

70 CURTIS CENTER

For more than a half-century, the Curtis Publishing Company was the country's leading publisher of popular magazines, including the phenomenally successful *Ladies Home Journal*, begun in 1883. Curtis also bought the *Saturday Evening Post* in 1897 and increased circulation to 500,000 by 1903. *Dream Garden*, a 15-foot-high Maxfield Parrish glass mosaic mural made by Louis C. Tiffany Studios in 1916, dominates the lobby of this building, designed by Edgar Seeler. ♦ 601 Walnut St (at S Sixth St). 238.6450. www.ushistory.org/tour/tour_curtis.htm

71 DILWORTH-TODD-MOYLAN HOUSE

Lawyer John Todd lived here until 1793, when he died of yellow fever (an epidemic that claimed the lives of many Philadelphians). His widow, Dolley Payne Todd, later married James Madison, the nation's fourth president. The Georgian brick house, a typical late 18th-century middle-class dwelling constructed by carpenter Jonathan Dilworth, is open to the public only as part of the daily tours led by park rangers from **Independence Visitor Center**. ♦ Free. Tours daily. S Fourth and Walnut Sts. 597.8974. www.independencevisitorcenter.com

72 BISHOP WILLIAM WHITE HOUSE

Originally built in 1787 as the home of the first bishop of the Episcopal Diocese of Pennsylvania, this restored upper-class residence is now open to the public. The Right Reverend William White was an esteemed civic leader, chaplain to the Continental Congress, and rector of **Christ Church** and **St. Peter's Church**. Furnished with 18th-century period pieces, the house has eight levels, including a root cellar, wine cellar, and ice pit, plus a feature that was a novelty at the time: a clothes closet. You can only see the house on one of the daily tours, which depart from the Visitor Center. (It's best to reserve a spot on these tours in the morning; sign up at **Independence Visitor Center**.) ♦ Free. Tours daily. 309 Walnut St (between S Third and S Fourth Sts). 597.8974. www.ushistory.org/tour/tour_bishop.htm

73 MERCHANTS' EXCHANGE

This masterpiece of Greek Revival architecture, with a sweeping semicircular Corinthian portico and a lantern tower, is a dramatic departure from the Federal and Georgian brick buildings in the area. Designed in the early 1830s by **William Strickland**, it is also notable for its adaptation to a very irregular site. The Philadelphia Exchange Company, the oldest stock exchange in the country, opened here in 1834. Business transactions took place in the luxurious exchange room—with its marble columns and a mosaic floor—until the Civil War. A National Historic Site, it's now used by the National Park Service as an office and is closed to the public. ♦ S Third and Walnut Sts. www.ushistory.org/tour/tour_merchan.htm

74 CITY TAVERN

★★$$$ Proprietor Walter Staib has reestablished dining excellence at this historic tavern, which John Adams called "the most genteel in America." Paul Revere arrived here on horseback in 1774 with news that Boston Harbor had been closed by the English Parliament, and George Washington enjoyed a lavish dinner here on his way to New York City for his 1789 inauguration. The present building is a reconstruction of the 1773 structure that was a famous watering hole for both delegates to Continental Congresses and the city's elite. Join these celebrated patrons (in spirit, if not in person) with a mug of beer made according to recipes perfected by George Washington and Thomas Jefferson and served by waitstaff dressed in colonial garb. Any of the tavern's 10 dining rooms are good places to try early American dishes, such as medallions of venison, turkey stew, West Indies pepper pot soup, slow-roasted prime rib, and lobster pie.♦ American ♦ Daily, lunch and dinner. 138 S Second St at Walnut St. 413.1443. www.citytavern.com

SOCIETY HILL

One of the most pleasant city neighborhoods in the country, this district—bounded by Lombard and Walnut Streets and by Second and Seventh Streets—boasts a delightful mix of 18th- to 20th-century residences, handsome colonial churches, and charming walkways with benches and greenery. **St. Joseph's** and **St. Peter's Ways** are brick walkways that wend from **Old St. Joseph's Church** below Walnut Street to **St. Peter's Church** on Pine Street. **Lawrence Court**, off the 400 block of Pine Street, is a similar walkway. Both have been enlivened with sculptures, and St. Peter's Way also has a small playground.

The absence of tall buildings puts the area on an intimate scale, reminiscent of the city that stood here more than 200 years ago. Named after the Free Society of Traders, a stock company that invested in William Penn's new colony, this was one of the principal residential areas of colonial Philadelphia. When the city served as the capital of the nation between 1790 and 1800, many of the federal government's leaders lived here. But the neighborhood was not always so posh: In the 1940s, it ranked as one of the worst slums in Philadelphia. Its rebirth is a story of ingenious urban renewal. Today the area contains more 18th-century architecture than anywhere else in America.

Fifty short years ago, Society Hill was dominated by a food distribution center on Dock Street, commercial buildings, and run-down boardinghouses. Spurred in part by the renewal of **Independence Park**, the city relocated the food center to South Philadelphia in the 1950s, tore down the dilapidated commercial buildings, and surveyed the neighborhood's historical treasures. The Philadelphia Redevelopment Authority acquired many of these deteriorated colonial structures and sold them to private individuals for what would be considered a pittance today, but with a binding agreement that required restoration of the buildings. During the next 2 decades, more than 600 of the area's historic houses were renovated. And fortunately, the architecture of the contemporary town houses constructed on empty lots doesn't attempt to replicate colonial structures, à la Williamsburg, Virginia, but complements the older buildings instead. Though a few historic houses are open to the public, notably the **Physick House** and **Powel House,** the vast majority are private residences.

75 PENN MUTUAL LIFE INSURANCE

Completed in 1970 and designed by **Mitchell/Giurgola**, this 18-story office building overlooking **Independence Square** is actually an addition to the buildings next door, designed

---

by **Edgar Seeler** in 1913 and **Ernest Matthewson** in 1931. Note how the dark glass and concrete façade of the old building blends in with the newer ground-level entrance. ♦ 510 Walnut St (between S Fifth and S Sixth Sts). www.ushistory.org/tour/tour_washsq.htm

76 LAMBERTI'S CUCINA

★$$ Indulge a craving for garlic, tomatoes, and olive oil in this second-story, glass-enclosed restaurant across the cobblestone street from the **Ritz Five** movie theater. The menu is heavy on pasta, as well as Italian preparations of chicken, veal, and seafood. Try the penne with garlic and broccoli in olive oil, or the jumbo lump crabmeat tossed with plum tomatoes, garlic, and basil. A breezy outdoor terrace is open in warm weather. ♦ Italian ♦ Daily, lunch and dinner. 212 Walnut St (between S Second and S Third Sts). 238.0499. ♿ www.lambertis.com

76 RITZ FIVE

This five-screen movie theater is popular with locals in search of something besides the latest Hollywood blockbuster. You can count on finding at least one good movie here, and it's clean and comfortable—with cushy chairs that lean back. Arrive early for weekend shows. ♦ 214 Walnut St (between S Second and S Third Sts). 925.7900. www.ritzfilmbill.com

77 PHILADELPHIA CONTRIBUTIONSHIP FOR INSURING HOUSES FROM LOSS BY FIRE

One of the city's earliest insurance firms, formed by Benjamin Franklin in 1752, the **Contributionship** actually kept its own brigades to help in fighting fires. The Greek Revival–style headquarters was designed by **Thomas Ustick Walter** and completed in 1836. The building is closed to the public. ♦ 212 S Fourth St (between Locust and Walnut Sts). www.ushistory.org/tour/tour_contrib.htm

Philadelphia often touts itself as America's most historic city—which has led some to think of it as America's most illustriously haunted city! Frequently cited are: the ghost of Benjamin Franklin on a jolly jaunt around the streets of Rittenhouse Square, our forefathers busy at work in the dead of night in Independence Hall, and Benedict Arnold taking care of unfinished business at Powel House.

78 SHERATON SOCIETY HILL

$$$$ A block from **Penn's Landing** and only steps from Old City and **Independence Park**, this luxurious hotel has 365 rooms, an indoor pool, and atrium lobby. The brick exterior fits in nicely with the neighborhood. ♦ 1 Dock St (at S Second St). 238.6000, 800/325.3535; fax 238.6652. ♿ www.sheraton.com

Within the Sheraton Society Hill:

HADLEY'S

★$$$ This formal dining room offers grilled Atlantic salmon and Sterling beef with string potatoes, and its own seasonal cobbler with cinnamon ice cream for dessert. ♦ American ♦ Daily, breakfast, lunch, and dinner. 238.6000 ♿

THE COURTYARD

★$ Sink into a comfortable chair by the fountain in the sunny lobby for a drink, cup of coffee, or lunch of chicken salad or seafood chowder. ♦ American ♦ Daily, breakfast and lunch. 238.6000 ♿

WOODEN NICKEL STEAKHOUSE

★$$ A casual chop house serving steak and seafood in a sports-bar atmosphere. ♦ American/steak house ♦ Daily, from 2 PM to midnight. 238.6000 ♿

79 WASHINGTON SQUARE

Among the original five parks laid out by William Penn, this square is one of the most inviting and underused outdoor spaces in Philadelphia. It has a checkered past: During the city's first decades, it was a ragged plot of green used as a cemetery for transients and paupers, and later for victims of the yellow fever epidemic. The **Tomb of the Unknown Soldier** in the center of the square commemorates the American patriots who were buried here during the British occupation of the city in 1778. When the neighborhood improved during the 19th century, the square became a gracious common, as the Federal town houses on the southwest end attest. Christopher Morley, the famous Philadelphia writer, lived as a young man in the third house from the corner of Seventh Street. In the 1800s, offices were built around the square, and it became the headquarters of the city's publishing industry. Today the plaza has a mix of residences, office buildings, and small businesses. On its streets are the oldest publishing house in the country, a contemporary art gallery, and one of the city's oldest and most unusual private clubs. Dominated by shade trees and furnished with benches, it's a good place to take a break and feed the pigeons. ♦ Bounded by S Sixth St and Washington Sq W and by Washington Sq S and Walnut St. www.ushistory.org/tour/tour_washsq.htm

80 THE ATHENAEUM OF PHILADELPHIA

Two gaslit lampposts stand outside the front door of this private library, which opened as a subscription library for well-to-do bibliophiles in 1814. The elegant Italian Renaissance Revival building was one of the first brownstones in the city, designed by **John Notman**, the Scottish-born architect who brought Gothic and Renaissance designs to 19th-century America. Inside, the elegant rooms seem made for sipping sherry and poring over texts by Aristotle or Virgil. The library is known for its architectural and design collection, which includes early architectural drawings of the US Capitol and **Independence Hall**, as well as decorative arts from the Victorian period. The building also serves as headquarters of the **Victorian Society of America** and houses a wide range of Victorian interior design samples that are often used by people researching house restorations. Exhibits on the first floor are open to the public. ♦ Free. M-F. Tours by appointment only. 219 S Sixth St (between Spruce and Walnut Sts). 925.2688. www.athenaonline.org

81 OLD ST. JOSEPH'S CHURCH

Hidden from view by an alley and courtyard, this structure built in 1733 (and reconstructed in 1838) was the first Roman Catholic church in the city. Though state founder William Penn tolerated all religious practices, England forbade Catholic services, so this parish sought to be discreet (its pastor is said to have gone about town in Quaker dress). The original parishioners, less aristocratic than those at nearby **Old St. Mary's**, were mostly Irish and German craftspeople and domestics. Stop at the rectory to tour the church when services aren't taking place. ♦ M-F, by appointment. 321 Willing's Alley (between S Third and S Fourth Sts). 923.1733. www.oldstjoseph.org

82 WASHINGTON SQUARE

★★★$$$ Another Stephen Starr production, this restaurant on the park boasts inspired global cuisine by executive chef Marcus Samuelsson, the 33-year-old wunderkind behind New York's celebrated Aquavit and Riingo restaurants. Samuelsson has created a terrific global sharing menu of specialties like scallop-and-lobster-hotdog with spicy sauerkraut and tomato jam, grilled lamb chops

with peanut-chili sauce, and minced lamb pie. Strikingly designed by the Rockwell Group (Striped Bass, Nectar, Buddakan), Washington Square has a way-cool outdoor living room for lounging when weather permits, complete with cloth sails overhead, intimate couch-and-chair groupings, teak and rattan finishes, and a hipster tile mural by Todd Oldham. Fans circulate cool or warm air, depending on the season, gaslit torches cast a warming glow, and the kicky drink menu includes exotic daiquiris and muddled fruit martinis. Inside, the 1929 vintage Ayers Advertising Agency building is equally inviting, all flowing curtains, pony-hair banquettes, and baroque woodwork. ♦ Seventh and Locust Sts. 592.7787. www.washingtonsquare-restaurant.com

83 LOCKS GALLERY

The former headquarters of the Lea & Febiger publishing firm has been converted into this prestigious commercial gallery for contemporary art. Behind the wrought-iron door and columned façade are three floors of exhibition space. Artists displayed here include Louise Bourgeois, whose exquisite but disturbing sculptures address gender and identity; Elizabeth Murray, whose comic-shaped autobiographic canvases straddle high and low culture; and Anthony-Petr Gorny, whose dense multimedia works comment on vision, representation, and power. ♦ Tu-Sa. 600 Washington Sq S (at S Sixth St). 629.1000. www.locksgallery.com

84 POWEL HOUSE

Samuel Powel and his wife, Elizabeth Willing Powel, were legendary hosts who entertained George Washington, General Lafayette, and other prominent figures at this elegant Georgian town house. Powel, a wealthy patron of the American Revolution, was evidently able to accommodate both sides of the dispute; he was the first mayor of Philadelphia after the war and the last mayor under the crown.

Built in 1765, the house contains its original fixtures and furnishings, including a staircase made of Santo Domingo mahogany. Powel hired furniture carvers to create the intricate doorways, moldings, and paneling. (The woodwork from two of the original rooms is displayed in New York City's Metropolitan Museum of Art and the **Philadelphia Museum of Art**.) One amenity in short supply, however, is closet space. It was local custom at the time to levy taxes on all rooms that could be walked into—including closets. One way to decrease taxes was to use a massive wooden armoire like the piece on the second floor. Don't miss the elegant ballroom or the formal

It's a Grand Old Flag

It wasn't until 14 June 1777—a date now commemorated as Flag Day—that the US adopted the Stars and Stripes. The Continental Congress resolved "that the flag of the thirteen United States be thirteen stripes, alternate red and white; that the union be thirteen stars, white, in a blue field, representing a new constellation."

It was a modification of the so-called Great Union Flag, in use since 2 January 1776, when it was unfurled by General George Washington himself over the camp of the Continental Army at Cambridge, Massachusetts.

Back in Philadelphia, the Continental Congress appointed a committee consisting of Washington, Robert Morris, and Colonel George Ross to prepare a new flag of popular design. The committee decided the 13 white stars on the blue background should be placed in a circle, emblematic of continuity and even

eternity. Then, or so the story goes, they called on Betsy Ross at her home at 239 Arch Street in Philadelphia and asked her to sew the flag they had envisioned. Ross was already a seamstress in government employ—during the war, she sewed the small packets that American rebels used to hold gunpowder. In fact, there is a government receipt for a flag she made, but there is no indication that it was the nation's first flag.

But whatever the case, the first display of the new flag, the Stars and Stripes, as it soon came to be called, was over Fort Stanwix, now Rome, New York. It flew over a battlefield for the first time at the Battle of Brandywine on 11 September 1777. The flag was first raised on foreign soil 22 January 1778, when American forces captured Fort Nassau, in the Bahamas, from the British.

garden adjacent to the house, which contains trees and shrubs common to 18th-century gardens.

The house is one of seven residences known collectively as **Mansion Row**, which starts at 232 S Third Street. Some of the city's leading citizens had homes here in the 18th and 19th centuries, including John Penn, grandson of William and the last colonial governor of Pennsylvania, who lived in the house that stood at **No. 242** between 1776 and 1810. **No. 236** was built in 1824 by master bricklayer Amos Atkinson. Only the Powel House is open to the public. ♦ Admission. Th-Sa. 244 S Third St (between Spruce St and Willing's Alley). 627.0364. www.ushistory.org/tour/tour_powel.htm

85 Old St. Mary's Church

Built in 1763 by carpenter Charles Johnson, this was Philadelphia's central Roman Catholic church during the American Revolution. It became the city's first cathedral in 1810 after the creation of the Philadelphia Diocese. The Continental Congress attended services here four times; George Washington and John Adams both visited; and on 4 July 1779, the first public religious commemoration of the Declaration of Independence was held at this church. The earliest version of the building was plain brick; the Gothic façade was added during the late 1800s when the church was expanded. The cemetery to the west has been a Catholic burial ground since 1759. ♦ M-Sa; Su, 8AM-1PM. Services Sa, 5PM; Su, 9AM, 10:30AM. 252 S Fourth St (between Spruce and Locust Sts). 923.7930. www.stmaryholytrinity.org/mary.html

86 Society Hill Towers

These high-rises, the only ones in Society Hill, are the result of a design competition held in the late 1950s to select a new building for the site of a demolished food distribution center. Architect **I.M. Pei** won with these concrete towers, completed in 1964. The apartments inside are spectacular, with floor-to-ceiling windows and views of the river. At the base of **West Tower** is Old Man, Young Man, The Future by Leonard Baskin, a work commissioned (as required) by Philadelphia's One Percent for Art program and completed in 1966. In the center of the adjacent square of town houses, also by Pei, is a second casting of Gaston Lachaise's Floating Figure, originally completed in 1927. ♦ S Second and Locust Sts. www.societyhilltowers.com/history

87 Society Hill Synagogue

Designed by **Thomas Ustick Walter**, architect of the Capitol dome in Washington, DC, this Greek Revival building was erected in 1829 as a Baptist church. It was purchased by a Romanian Jewish congregation in the early 1900s, and the attics and cupolas that originally stood atop the squat corner towers were removed. ♦ 418 Spruce St (between S Fourth and S Fifth Sts). 922.6590. www.societyhillsynagogue.org

88 Physick House

The only freestanding Federal mansion left in Society Hill is an excellent place to get a sense of how the wealthy lived in the early part of the 19th century. The 32-room house was built in 1786 by Henry Hill, an importer of

Madeira wine, and later occupied by Dr. Philip Syng Physick, known as the father of American surgery. Physick lived here between 1815 and 1837, courageously remaining during the yellow fever epidemic. After his death, the house was remodeled by family members and then neglected until the 1960s, when the property was donated—along with its original furnishings—to the Philadelphia Society for the Preservation of Landmarks and restored. Next to the house is a Federal-style garden with a serpentine path and antique cannons. ♦ Admission. Tours: Th-Sa, 11AM, noon, 1PM, and 2PM; group tours by appointment. 321 S Fourth St (between Delancey and Cypress Sts). 925.7866. www.ushistory.org/tour_physick.htm

89 DELANCEY STREET

This charming side street has an eclectic array of colonial structures and contemporary houses. It's one of a number of intimate narrow streets in Society Hill—others include **American**, **Cypress**, and **Philip**—that are ideal for a stroll. Most of the houses were built individually or in pairs instead of in speculative rows. On the south side of the 200 block of **Delancey Street** is a typical colonial courtyard with tiny houses that were rented out by the merchant who owned the main house in front. ♦ From S Front to S Sixth Sts

90 OLD PINE STREET CHURCH

Established in 1768 as the third Presbyterian church in the city, and the only colonial parish still in existence, this structure dominates the block with its wrought-iron fence, yellow exterior, and classic columns. It was originally constructed as a simple Georgian church from plans by master carpenter **Robert Smith**. In 1837, as the Greek Revival style came into fashion, Corinthian columns were added, giving it the appearance of a classical temple. During the British occupation of Philadelphia, royal troops used the church as a hospital and stable. Later, several of the parish's 19th-century pastors were in the forefront of the region's antislavery movement. As does **St. Peter's**, this church has a peaceful courtyard with tombstones standing in crooked rows. Mathematician, astronomer, and inventor David Rittenhouse is buried here, as are a number of Revolutionary War heroes. Eugene Ormandy, the famed conductor of the **Philadelphia Orchestra**, was also laid to rest here. ♦ M-F, 9AM-3PM. Services: Su, 10:30AM. 412 Pine St (between S Fourth and S Fifth Sts). 925.8051. ♿. www.oldpine.org; www.ushistory.org/tour/tour_oldpine.htm

91 ST. PETER'S CHURCH

Perhaps more than any other place in the city, this lovely 18th-century church and its serene, otherworldly graveyard will transport you to the colonial era. Miraculously, the building has changed very little in its more than 2 centuries. The William Penn family donated the land for an Anglican church when the pews at **Christ Church** north filled to overflowing. Designed by master carpenter **Robert Smith**, the church opened for worship in 1761. In the first sermon given here, Reverend Dr. William Smith noted that the church was "decently neat and elegantly plain." In keeping with the Georgian style of the time, the earliest version of the church had no exterior ornament aside from the large Palladian window on the chancel wall and arched windows on the side walls. The intimate interior is unusual because the pulpit and altar are at opposite ends of the main aisles. The high-backed box pews, once occupied by George Washington and other leading citizens, were raised off the floor to prevent drafts. Two wooden angels by local sculptor William Rush, brought here from **Old St. Paul's Church** in 1831, flank the organ case. The tower and spire, designed by Philadelphia architect **William Strickland**, were added in 1842 and contain eight bells made at the Whitechapel Foundry in London, birthplace of the **Liberty Bell**. Several Revolutionary War figures are buried in the churchyard, including Dr. John Morgan, chief physician of the Continental Army and founder of the **University of Pennsylvania School of Medicine**, and John Nixon, a lieutenant colonel who read the Declaration of Independence for the first time in public on 8 July 1776. Portrait painter Charles Willson Peale is buried here as well, as are the chiefs of seven Native American tribes who died during the yellow fever epidemic of the 1790s. The churchyard, surrounded by a brick wall built in 1784, is shaded by beautiful trees, including robust hollies that spill over to the street side and Osage oranges, said to have been grown from seeds brought from the West by Lewis and Clark. The parish still houses an active congregation. ♦ Tu-Sa, 9AM-noon (knock on the parish house across the street if the church is locked). Services: Su, 9AM, 11AM. S Third St (between Lombard and Pine Sts). 925.5968. ♿. www.stpetersphila.org

---

Restaurants/Clubs: Red | Hotels: Purple | Shops: Orange | Outdoors/Parks: Green | Sights/Culture: Blue

SOUTH STREET/WATERFRONT

South Street is the closest thing Philadelphia has to New York's Greenwich Village. Its hip reputation was immortalized in the 1960s, when a popular song intoned, "Where do all the hippies meet? South Street, South Street," and again in the 1980s, when a song by the Dead Milkmen mentioned **Zipperhead**, a South Street hangout. Though national chain stores started taking up residence in the 1980s, South Street has managed to maintain its counterculture character with an eclectic mix of boutiques, restaurants, pubs, music clubs, and people (keep an eye out for the Kazoo Lady and other wacky street performers). The crowds tend to be on the young and tattooed side, less sophisticated than the see-and-be-seen crowd that frequents Old City bars and lounges.

As in other trendy urban neighborhoods, many of South Street's establishments come and go with the seasons. The water-ice shop that attracted hordes last summer may well vanish in the fall. Vacant storefronts suddenly become costume shops for Halloween, then hastily transform into last-minute gift centers in time for the winter holidays. Even the secondhand stores, which keep all the slackers looking frowsy-chic, change frequently. On weekends during warm-weather months, South Street closes to vehicular traffic from **Eighth** to **Front Streets**, creating a wide walkway that grows more Dionysian by the hour. During any season, first-time visitors should start either at the river and work west or around **10th Street** and walk toward the water.

Although the bohemian pleasures of South Street are easy to explore on foot, restaurants and nightclubs on the piers along the nearby Waterfront are spread too far afield for walking. Despite water-taxi services, it's difficult to bounce between nightclubs on the different piers, as some are miles apart. But waterfront establishments have taken care of the proximity problem with one-stop restaurant-nightclubs, dinner cruises on the **Delaware,** and theme "entertainment complexes," where you can dine and dance the night away under one roof.

1 CAVANAUGH'S RIVER DECK

★$ Formerly **Maui**, this waterfront pub went from a tropical theme to an Irish one, now boasting the city's largest outdoor Irish grill and bar. The grub is decent, the mood casual, with live music and dancing under the stars featured from May to September. ◆ Pier 53, N Columbus Ave (a half-mile north of Spring Garden St). 629.7400. www.cavanaughsriverdeck.com

2 EGYPT

A split-level dance floor, impressive sound and light systems, pyramids, and other thematic decorations make this one of Philadelphia's top clubs in which to dance the night away. ◆ Cover. W-Su, 9PM-2AM. 520 N Columbus Blvd (between Callowhill and Spring Garden Sts). 922.6500, 800/622.3497. www.egypt-nightclub.com

3 SHAMPOO

Inspired by the frolicking 1975 hit movie of the same name, this dance club lures the crowd with two floors of varied entertainment, including eight bars and three dance floors. Crafted by New York City–based couple Colleen and Arthur Weinstein (she's the interior designer and he's the lighting designer), the tone is set by 1970s retro furniture, vibrant colors, and pop art. Each dance floor has its own kind of music—from classic alternative to hip-hop and house—played by resident and visiting disc jockeys. Friday is gay dance night, complete with drag shows and great DJs. In the summer, visit the tent-covered outdoor area called the **Groove Garden**. The **Very Brady Backyard** offers patio furniture, an extra DJ, a Jacuzzi, and a bit of fresh air. ◆ Cover. W-Sa, 5PM-2AM. 417 N Eighth St (at Willow St). 922.7500

4 KATMANDU

★$$ Built to resemble Rick's in Jamaica—complete with imported palm trees—this American bistro shines with a Caribbean flair. The ambitious menu runs the gamut from nachos and hummus to sesame-crusted ahi

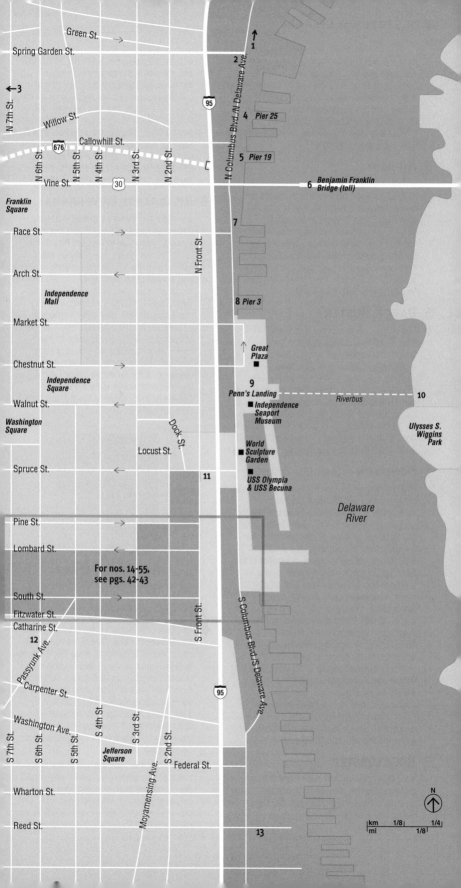

Green St.

Spring Garden St.

1

2

3

Willow St.

N 7th St.

95

4 *Pier 25*

Callowhill St.

676

N 6th St.

N 5th St.

N 4th St.

N 3rd St.

N 2nd St.

5 *Pier 19*

Vine St.

30

6 **Benjamin Franklin Bridge (toll)**

Franklin Square

7

Race St.

N Front St.

Arch St.

Independence Mall

8 *Pier 3*

Market St.

↑ **Great Plaza**

Chestnut St.

9

Independence Square

Penn's Landing *Riverbus* 10

Walnut St.

■ **Independence Seaport Museum**

Washington Square

Dock St.

Ulysses S. Wiggins Park

■ **World Sculpture Garden**

Locust St.

Spruce St.

■ **USS Olympia & USS Becuna**

11

Delaware River

Pine St.

Lombard St.

For nos. 14-55, see pgs. 42-43

South St.

Fitzwater St.

S Front St.

Catharine St.

12

Passyunk Ave.

Carpenter St.

95

Washington Ave.

S 7th St.

S 6th St.

S 5th St.

S 4th St.

S 3rd St.

S 2nd St.

Jefferson Square

Moyamensing Ave.

Federal St.

Wharton St.

S Columbus Blvd./S Delaware Ave.

Reed St.

N

13

| km | 1/8 | 1/4 |
| mi | 1/8 | |

tuna and surf-and-turf Maryland style, with a crabcake and filet. Reggae and world music carry you farther along on your island escape. ◆ Caribbean/American/Asian ◆ Daily, lunch, dinner, and late-night snacks, mid-Apr–Sept. Pier 25, N Columbus Blvd (between Callowhill and Spring Garden Sts). 629.7400. www.katmanduphilly.com

5 HIBACHI

★★$$ This waterfront Japanese steakhouse is all about eat-ertainment, with communal dining around sizzling grills manned by showman chefs, who chop veggies, flip shrimp, and generally entertain the crowd. You can also eat at the sushi bar, or order à la carte at traditional tables, many with good river views. But the group scene is lots of fun. ◆ Pier 19, N Columbus Blvd (between Race and Callowhill Sts). 592.7100

5 DAVE & BUSTER'S

This mega-club features a restaurant and five bars. The fifth and biggest link in the Texas-based chain entertains with billiards, shuffleboard, and a carnival midway with casino games and 120 virtual-reality video games. Refuel with choices from an extensive menu, including pizzas, burgers, steak, pasta, and chicken. ◆ Su-Tu, 11:30AM-midnight; W, Th, 11:30-1AM; F, Sa, 11:30-2AM. Pier 19, N Columbus Blvd (between Race and Callowhill Sts). 413.1951. ⑯. www.daveandbusters.com

6 BENJAMIN FRANKLIN BRIDGE

This defining piece of public architecture was designed by **Paul Philippe Cret** and completed in 1926, when it was the largest suspension bridge in the world. Rising from the buildings of Old City and towering over the waterfront piers, the bridge's massive blue hulk is visible for miles. A symbol of the city's solid traditionalism, it has served as the backdrop for movie sets and album-cover photographs and is much more than just a conduit for cars, bikes, and commuter trains. To fully appreciate the bridge, you must see it at night, when it becomes a veri-table light sculpture. A computer-driven lighting system, designed by Philadelphia architect **Steven Izenour** of **Venturi, Scott Brown and Associates**, was added during the US bicentennial. Each cable is illuminated, and as the trains pass, the lights blink in a sweeping, domino-like succession that reminds one of the bridge's utility while celebrating its beauty.

7 ROCK LOBSTER

★$$ One of the deck 'n' tent brigade that disappears when the winter winds blow, this restaurant has an upscale Cape Cod–style beach house atmosphere, and prices to match. The seafood—particularly the lobster

and shrimp salads—is worth the investment, and the rest of the menu has improved dramatically. There is now a heated tent and a larger redecorated bar area. Come for happy hour and listen to live rock (usually light) or jazz. On Wednesday through Saturday nights, top-40 dance bands perform after 9:30PM. ◆ Seafood ◆ Cover after 8:30PM. Daily, lunch and dinner (open seasonally); happy hour M-F, 5:30-8PM. 221 N Columbus Blvd (between Race and Callowhill Sts). 627.7625

8 RISTORANTE LA VERANDA

★★$$$$ This **Penn's Landing** institution, under new ownership as of 2002, offers romantic waterside views from **Pier 3**. The rustic Roman interior is equally pleasant. An extensive menu featuring the cuisine of Rome and Abruzzi offers fresh fish imported from the Mediterranean and prime cuts of beef. All meats are cut to order and prepared on a wood-burning grill, then carved tableside. Fish entrées are filleted tableside too. A visit to the antipasto table before the main course is highly recommended. All breads, pastas, pastries, and desserts are freshly made on the premises. ◆ Italian ◆ Daily, lunch and dinner. Reservations recommended. Pier 3, N Columbus Blvd (between Market and Arch Sts). 351.1898

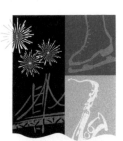

Festival Pier
PENN'S LANDING

9 PENN'S LANDING

This tract of waterfront land, extending from **South Street** to **Vine Street**, was once the city's primary commercial area. This is where William Penn's surveyor, Thomas Holmes, started parceling out land grants. Early settlers dug caves into the steep slope rising from the water until housing could be built, and by 1700, most Philadelphians lived within three or four blocks of the river on tiny congested lots—a far cry from Penn's dream of a green country town.

Through the 18th and 19th centuries and well into the 20th century, the docks were central to city commerce. Sailors, pilots, riggers, and shipwrights worked and lived nearby. In 1967, with most of the shipping concentrated in the south end of Philadelphia, the rotting piers were replaced with the current system of walkways and the tiered river-view amphitheater known as the **Great Plaza**. In the summer, the plaza and festival pier are the site of outdoor concerts—including a Memorial Day weekend New Orleans festival and a Yo Philadelphia celebration of the city in September—as well as other themed celebrations. Pedestrian walkways at **Market**, **Chestnut**, **Walnut**, and **South Streets** cross **Interstate 95** to connect the city with the waterfront. Penn's Landing is perpetually under development and has yet to reach its full potential. Although big names like Disney and Comcast have been close to anchoring the Delaware River entertainment scene with an Inner Harbor–type complex, the deals always seem to fall through. The latest disappointment was the 2004 announcement that the Please Touch Museum was in fact not going to relocate to Penn's Landing. Proposals are under consideration for future development, but locals don't hold their breath. ♦ From I-95, take Exit 16 (Columbus Blvd–Delaware Ave); from I-76, follow I-676 to I-95 South; from Ben Franklin Bridge, take I-95 South. For parking information, call 923.8181. SEPTA bus routes 21 and 42 stop nearby. For information on events at the Great Plaza, call 923.4992. www.pennslandingcorp.com

Within Penn's Landing:

CHART HOUSE

★$$$ A salad bar loaded with fresh veggies and seasonal fruits, excellent treatments of surf and turf, and spectacular views of the Delaware make this the waterfront's most notable expense-account restaurant. Tops among the seafood choices are steak-size cuts of grilled swordfish and tuna, served with various sauces, some of them light enough to satisfy those who tally their fat grams. ♦ Continental/seafood ♦ M-Sa, lunch and dinner; Su, brunch and dinner. Reservations recommended. 555 S Columbus Blvd (between Catharine and Spruce Sts). 625.8383

SPIRIT OF PHILADELPHIA

★$$$ Where there's a waterfront, there's a dinner cruise operation. The *Spirit of Philadelphia*, which has both open and enclosed decks, takes to the water year-round from its moorings beside the **Chart House** and offers lunch, dinner, and moonlight cruises up and down the **Delaware**. Live dance music follows the dinner show. Theme cruises have included a 1950s sock hop and Jamaican and Caribbean meals. There's a cash bar. ♦ Continental ♦ Daily, lunch and dinner. Reservations required. S Columbus Blvd (between Catharine and Spruce Sts). 923.1419

LIBERTY BELLE II

★$$$ Another smaller dinner-cruise operation, the *Liberty Belle II* covers the basics, with at least two entrée options at lunch and dinner. There's a cash bar. ♦ Continental ♦ Daily, lunch and dinner. Call for schedule and reservations. S Columbus Blvd (at Lombard Cir). 629.1131

USS OLYMPIA

One of America's first steel ships, the *USS Olympia* was Admiral Dewey's flagship at the battle of Manila Bay in 1898 and one of the few survivors of the Spanish-American War. Its final assignment came in 1921, when it brought the body of the Unknown Soldier from France to Arlington National Cemetery. The ship has been transformed into a museum, where you can climb around and view the restored cabins, top deck, and boiler room. It's now part of the **Independence Seaport Museum** (see page 42), located to its north. ♦ Admission included in ticket to Independence Seaport Museum. Daily, Apr-Dec. S Columbus Blvd and Spruce St. 922.1898

USS BECUNA

Berthed a few feet from the **Olympia** (and also part of the **Independence Seaport Museum**), the submarine *USS Becuna* is a 1,526-ton vessel commissioned in 1944. The *Becuna* saw action in the South Pacific during World War II and served in the Atlantic during the Korean and Vietnam Wars before being decommissioned in 1969. Veterans of World War II volunteer time to answer questions on board. *Warning:* A submarine is no place for the claustrophobic. ♦ Admission included in ticket to Independence Seaport Museum. Daily, Apr-Dec. S Columbus Blvd and Spruce St. 922.1898

HYATT REGENCY PENN'S LANDING

$$$ The deluxe hotel across the road from the **World Sculpture Garden** has 350 rooms and suites; a health club with indoor swimming pool; **Keating's Grille**; an indoor-outdoor restaurant, bar, and take-out café; and a six-level, 500-car parking garage. Modern rooms offer spectacular views of the city skyline and the **Delaware River**. ♦ N Columbus Blvd (between Spruce and Walnut Sts). 800/233.1234. www.hyatt.com

WORLD SCULPTURE GARDEN

This grassy 2-acre sculpture garden is a welcome respite in the midst of Philadelphia's frenzied waterfront development. Attractions at this favorite picnic spot stretching along the

---

Restaurants/Clubs: Red | Hotels: Purple | Shops: Orange | Outdoors/Parks: Green | Sights/Culture: Blue

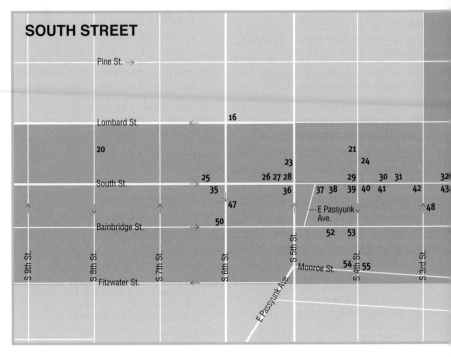

SOUTH STREET

Pine St. →

Lombard St. ←   16

20   21

23   24

25   26 27 28   29   30 31   32

35   36   37 38   39 40 41   42   43

47   E Passyunk   48
Ave.

50   52 53

S 9th St.   S 8th St.   S 7th St.   S 6th St.   S 5th St.   Monroe St.   54   55   S 3rd St.

Bainbridge St. →

Fitzwater St. ←

E Passyunk Ave.

S 4th St.

waterfront include a bronze statue of William Penn at the age of 38 in 1682, an obelisk erected in 1992 commemorating Christopher Columbus, and a 20-foot totem pole from Canada. The garden in currently being refurbished. ♦ S Columbus Blvd (between Spruce and Chestnut Sts)

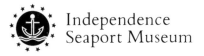

Independence Seaport Museum

INDEPENDENCE SEAPORT MUSEUM

This museum offers an interactive look at Philadelphia's heritage as a port city. Although life in Philadelphia no longer revolves around its port, water had everything to do with the city's initial development. The **Delaware River**, with its links to the Atlantic Ocean and its tributary the **Schuylkill**, provided the prime means of transportation and trade in colonial times. Eighteenth-century Philadelphia was also the country's key entry point for immigrants. This fascinating museum showcases more than 10,000 maritime artifacts, including uniforms, flags, navigational instruments, and models of small crafts and ships. The library counts more than 12,000 volumes in its collection, as well as 750 maps and 9,000 ship plans, and is one

of the nation's premier regional maritime research centers. In *Home Port: Philadelphia*—an exhibit that explores the port's role in immigration, commerce, defense, and recreation—you can unload a giant container ship, experience a drill aboard a naval destroyer, and try your hand at ship-welding. The *Workshop on the Water* offers hands-on opportunities to learn traditional boat-building techniques in a working boat shop. ♦ Admission. Daily. 211 S Columbus Blvd (between Spruce and Chestnut Sts). 925.5439. ♿. http://phillyseaport.org

RIVERLINK FERRY

Known locally as the "Delawhale," this 100-foot vessel offers quick passage between Philadelphia and Camden's **New Jersey State Aquarium** on the hour and half hour. The ship takes 400 passengers on a 12-minute trip that retraces the route of the 19th-century ferries Walt Whitman rode, providing a scenic view of both waterfronts: Camden, once the biggest naval shipyard in the country, and Philadelphia, the largest freshwater port in the world. ♦ Admission. Mar 23–Nov 30, 9AM-6:30 PM; departures every 40 minutes. Express service is also available up to 2 hours before Tweeter Center concerts and Riversharks baseball games on the Camden Waterfront. Call for winter and holiday schedules. S Columbus Blvd (between Spruce and Chestnut Sts). 925.5465. ♿. www.pennslandingcorp.com

BLUE CROSS RIVERRINK AT PENN'S LANDING

Practice your figure-eights at this new outdoor public skating rink along the **Delaware River**. The hockey-size (200 by 85 feet) rink offers public skating, instructional programs, and special events. If you don't have your own skates, rent them here. On weekends, get to the rink up to an hour ahead of time to beat the crowds. Refreshments are available inside a heated tent. Public sled skating for physically challenged children and adults is also available. ◆ Admission. Nov-Mar: M, W, noon-2PM, 3:30-5PM, 6-9PM; Tu, Th, noon-2PM, 3:30-5PM; F, noon-2PM, 3:30-5PM, 6-10PM; Sa, 8-10AM, noon-2PM, 3-5PM, 6-8:30PM; Su, noon-2PM, 3-5PM. S Columbus Blvd (between Chestnut and Market Sts). 925.RINK. ♿. www.riverrink.com

GAZELA

The **Philadelphia Ship Preservation Guild** maintains and operates this 177-foot square-rigged sailing ship built in 1883. The *Gazela* was the oldest of the tall ships to participate in the 1976 OpSail tall ship celebration in New York and was on hand for the Statue of Liberty centennial in 1986. The ship, which functions as a training vessel and is a permanent working exhibit, has a busy sailing schedule during the summer. ◆ Admission. Open to visitors May–mid-Oct (when in port). Call for schedule and reservations. S Columbus Blvd (between Market and Race Sts). 923.9030. www.gazela.org

10 CAMDEN CHILDREN'S GARDEN

This innovative attraction along the Camden Waterfront is a 4-acre interactive horticultural park. Located alongside the aquarium, it features themed exhibits, including *Dinosaur, Storybook and Picnic Lunch Gardens, Giant Chimes,* the *Violet Fountain Plaza,* and the *Underground Maze.* A kids' carousel and train ride are also featured activities. The **Children's Garden** is easily accessible by car, bus, **RiverLink Ferry** from **Penn's Landing,** or the **PATCO Hi-Speedline.** Visitors can save by buying a combination ticket at the **New Jersey State Aquarium.** 3 Riverside Drive, Camden, NJ. 856/365.TREE(8733). www.camdenchildrensgarden.org

10 USS *NEW JERSEY* BATTLESHIP MUSEUM

One of the most decorated battleships in US Navy history, the **Battleship *New Jersey*** is permanently berthed at the southern end of the Camden Waterfront. The USS *New Jersey* is a signature waterfront attraction to veterans, patriots, and families from around the world. Her keel was laid at the **Philadelphia Navy Yard** in 1940, and the hull was launched on 7 December 1942. Involved in a long list of operations in the Pacific during World War II, the USS *New Jersey* also served during the Korean and Vietnam wars and in the Middle East. Visitors can view the *Berthing and Life at Sea* and *History of the USS New Jersey* exhibits, as well as the interactive **Combat Engagement Center.** The tour route also features a look inside the ship's legendary 16-inch gun turrets, the bridge, captain's and admiral's cabins, officers' wardroom, and two mess areas. A flight simulator is an added attraction with separate admission. ◆ 9AM-5PM, Apr-Sept; 9AM-3PM, Oct-Mar. Admission; free to military in uniform. Becket St at the Delaware River, next to the New Jersey State Aquarium. 856/966.1652. www.battleshipnewjersey.org

11 VIETNAM VETERANS MEMORIAL

This outdoor plaza, dedicated in 1987, was built with volunteer contributions to honor the 80,000 Vietnam veterans from the Philadelphia area. A semicircle of wide brick steps faces a high black-granite wall painted with a mural depicting military scenes—aircraft carriers, fighter jets, and the like. Another wall

---

Restaurants/Clubs: Red | Hotels: Purple | Shops: Orange | Outdoors/Parks: Green | Sights/Culture: Blue

is inscribed with the names of Philadelphians killed in the conflict. Both the American flag and black MIA flag fly overhead. ◆ Daily, 24 hours. Spruce and S Front Sts

12 DESSERT

For the perfect way to sweeten any Wednesday through Sunday evening, stop by Dessert, the Queen Village dessert and coffeehouse featuring brewed-to-order coffees and teas and scrumptious goodies like cherry pie, banana Napoleon crème brûlée, and chocolate brioche bread pudding. ◆ 806 S Sixth St (between Passyunk and Catharine Sts). 923.9733

13 ENGINE 46 STEAKHOUSE

★$$ Large portions (doggie bags are practically de rigueur) make this bustling steak house a good bet for a meal with a group or the family. Kids like the ambiance—it's a restored 1894 firehouse, complete with firefighters' memorabilia. ◆ American ◆ Daily, lunch and dinner. United Artists Riverview Plaza, 10 Reed St (at S Columbus Blvd). 462.4646

14 ARTFUL DODGER

★★$ While the **Dark Horse** (see below) represents the high end of pub dining, this is a neighborhood watering hole—with above-average pub food. One room is a bar; the other has large wooden booths and a fireplace. In addition to sandwiches, the kitchen makes excellent stews and chili that's spicy enough to warm you up in the middle of winter. The specials—including grilled swordfish in a warm Oriental salsa and grilled tuna in lemon butter—are worth considering, as are the preparations of fried fish and the grilled chicken Caesar salad. ◆ British/American ◆ Daily, lunch and dinner. 400-402 S Second St (at Pine St). 922.1790

15 HEADHOUSE SQUARE

In 1745 sheds were erected on this square between South and Pine Streets to facilitate commerce; in the early 1800s firehouses, called headhouses, were built at either end of the square. Each headhouse had a cupola, an alarm bell, and a firemen's social club. The station at Second and South was torn down before 1860, but its market shed remained until 1950, when it was razed to make room for a parking lot. The shed between Lombard and Pine, called the **Shambles**, was restored in the 1960s; in the summer, it serves as an open-air crafts market on weekends. The remaining Georgian-style headhouse, at Second and Pine, was built in 1805. ◆ S Second St (between South and Pine Sts).

16 MOTHER BETHEL AFRICAN METHODIST CHURCH

Considered the birthplace of the African-American church, the massive stone **Mother Bethel** is the most important historic building in the South Street area. Richard Allen and Absalom Jones, two prominent freedmen of colonial Philadelphia, founded this sanctum in 1787. It later served as a stop on the Underground Railroad. Four churches have been built on the site; the current one, known for its gospel choir and fiery preaching, opened in 1890 and was restored in 1987. ◆ Museum: by appointment only, Tu-Sa, 10AM-3PM. Services: Su, 8AM, 10:45AM. S Sixth and Lombard Sts. 925.0616

17 THE DARK HORSE

★★$$ Formerly **Dicken's Inn**, this pub was retooled by the winning team responsible for the **Black Sheep**, located in the heart of Rittenhouse Square. The Dark Horse serves dinner 7 nights a week, lunch every day but Monday, and Sunday brunch. The chalkboard menus include authentic pub grub, specialties like chipotle wings and crisp roast duck, in addition to sandwiches and salads. Nothing is over $20. ◆ 421 S 2nd St (between Lombard and Pine Sts). 928.9307

18 THE MOSHULU

★★★$$$ This regal sailing ship turned fine restaurant offers one of the best dining experiences in town, either on land or sea. A century old in 2004, the shipboard restaurant, all done up in South Seas rattan and polished wood, features the inspired cuisine of executive chef Ralph Fernandez and the festive Bongo Bar and Deck, topside, for cocktails and snacks with a view when the weather is fine. ◆ 401 S Columbus Blvd (between Lombard and Pine Sts). 923.2500. www.moshulu.com

19 LE CHAMPIGNON OF TOKIO

★★$$$ This cozy bistro with live jazz on the weekends has a globe-trotting menu of inventive Japanese food (including artfully prepared sushi), Thai standbys, and French cooking. Just reading the regular menu can take an evening. If the range of dishes is too much of a good thing, choose one of the house specialties—lobster hara or bouillabaisse. The weekend lunch menu also offers Japanese-style dim sum. ◆ Japanese/French/Thai ◆ W-F, dinner; Sa, Su, lunch and dinner. 124 Lombard St (between S Front and S Second Sts). 922.2515

20 SOCIETY HILL PLAYHOUSE

Over the last few years, this neighborhood theater has become one of the most consistent venues for drama in Philadelphia. Its two stages are small and rather ordinary, but the productions—popular shows and family fare—have received critical acclaim. The season runs year-round, and there are cabaret shows on weekends. ♦ Call for schedules and ticket prices. 507 S Eighth St (between South and Lombard Sts). 923.0210. www.societyhillplayhouse.com

21 DJANGO

★★★$$ The word is out about Django, a quirky BYOB owned by husband-and-wife team Bryan Sikora and Aimee Olexy. Substance rules over style at this neighborhood restaurant, featuring European dishes, regional ingredients, informed and careful service, and moderate prices. ♦ 526 S 4th St (between South and Lombard Sts). 922.7151

22 PIZZERIA UNO

★$ The chain's trademark deep-dish pie is served with a view of one of Philadelphia's oldest commercial areas from the second-floor windows. On most weekend nights there's live musical entertainment upstairs. ♦ Pizza ♦ Daily, lunch and dinner. 509-511 S Second St (between South and Lombard Sts). 592.0400. ♦. www.pizzeriauno.com

23 TIRA MISU

★★$$$ Playing fast and loose with Southern Italian cuisine, this is the closest thing South Street has to a cozy white-tablecloth trattoria. Chef-owner Alberto Del Bello is from Rome's Jewish neighborhood, and he mixes elements of both traditions to create his imaginative dishes. The wood oven produces exceptional bread, but be sure to save room for the filling entrées: *Ravioli con aragosta* (lobster ravioli and lump crabmeat in a cognac sauce) is a crowd pleaser. A piano bar on the premises offers live music Wednesdays, Fridays, and Saturdays. ♦ Italian ♦. M-F, lunch and dinner; Sa, Su, dinner. Proper attire requested. Reservations recommended. 528 S Fifth St (between South and Lombard Sts). 925.3335

24 611 RECORDS

This shop is the last word in wax, with knowledgeable sales help and an outstanding selection of house, drum and bass, and straight-up techno. You won't find pop and top 40, but you will find the latest DJ mixes, trance, and techno music. For used vinyl and CDs, try **611**'s offshoot, **612**, right across the street. ♦ M-Th, noon-9PM; F, Sa, noon-11PM;

Su, noon-7PM. 611 S Fourth St (between South and Bainbridge Sts). 413.9100. www.611records.com

25 BEAN CAFÉ

A peaceful island amid South Street's sea of seemingly ceaseless activity, this cozy coffeehouse is outfitted with a working fireplace, books for browsing, original art (all for sale) on the walls, and the occasional piano player. Enjoy coffee, flavored cappuccino, tea, and homemade pastries while taking in the street scene. In warm weather, try to snag one of the outdoor tables. ♦ Daily, 7AM-midnight. 615 South St (between S Sixth and S Seventh Sts). 629.2250

26 GARLAND OF LETTERS

When your inner child calls, this New Age bookstore with a welcoming, low-key environment offers music, crystals, and objets d'art, along with the expected instructional guidebooks. Come here to hook into Philadelphia's growing healing-arts scene. Sign up for yoga or meditation classes and learn about lectures and community events. ♦ Daily, 10AM-10PM. 527 South St (between S Fifth and S Sixth Sts). 923.5946. ♦. www.garland ofletters.com

27 SOUTH STREET SOUVLAKI

★★$ This popular Greek taverna has an open-flame grill and kitchen facing the street, so you can see—and smell—the options before ordering. Just about everything that comes off the grill is delectable. Best bets include such staples as gyro sandwiches and souvlaki, grilled fresh fish specialties, and roasted chicken. The swordfish kebabs—prime chunks of fish and veggies served on a stick over yellow rice, with a lemon cream sauce—are excellent. ♦ Greek ♦ Tu-Su, lunch and dinner. 509 South St (between S Fifth and S Sixth Sts). 925.3026

28 THE BOOK TRADER

A daunting, floor-to-ceiling repository of more than 100,000 used books, this bookworm's paradise may very well have those long out-of-print volumes you've been stalking. The fiction titles are crammed on the first floor, whereas the more spacious second level has enough room for a miniature art gallery. An adjacent center for used records, tapes, and CDs, though not as comprehensive, has been known to contain a few gems. ♦ Daily, 10AM-midnight. 501 South St (at S Fifth St). 925.0219. www.abebooks.com/home/discountrarities

29 PEARL ART & CRAFT

You don't have to be an art enthusiast to appreciate the vast selection of art and craft

---

supplies spread over three floors at this branch of the national discount store. Everything from pens, clay, paints, canvases, and frames to drafting supplies, games, and one-of-a-kind greeting cards awaits. ♦ Daily. 417 South St (between S Fourth and S Fifth Sts). 238.1900. www.pearlpaint.com

29 ZIPPERHEAD

On the cutting edge when it comes to the latest fashion fads gripping American youth, this store has seen trends swing from safety-pin punk to biker leather and back again. Even if you're the khakis type, it's fun to examine the odd accessories, pre-ripped flannel shirts, and all types of gear in basic black. A skateboard shop caters to the skate-punk community. Both floors offer rock and rap T-shirts and other music-related items. ♦ M-W, Su, noon-10PM; Th, noon-11PM; F, Sa, noon-midnight. 407 South St (between S Fourth and S Fifth Sts). 928.1123. www.simplyfiendish.com

30 ISHKABIBBLE'S EATERY

★$ This short-order eatery offers window service to the sidewalk and a small counter inside. The tiny kitchen whips up an impressive array of foods. Try the joint's signature chickensteak, mushroom cheesesteak, or the famous Fourth Street cookies (baked on the premises). Vegetarian chili and a veggie hoagie are two of the alternatives for those who pass on meat and dairy products. ♦ American ♦ Daily, breakfast, lunch, and dinner. 337 South St (between S Third and S Fourth Sts). 923.4337

30 AMERICAN PIE CONTEMPORARY CRAFTS

Kitschy cow-shaped wall clocks and other goofy items share the shelves with decorative contemporary crafts and an interesting selection of jewelry. Prices are fair. ♦ M-Th, 11AM-9PM; F, Sa, 11AM-10PM; Su, noon-6PM. 327 South St (between S Third and S Fourth Sts). 922.2226. Also at 4303 Main St (at Roxborough Ave), Manayunk. 487.0226. ₺. www.americanpiecrafts.com

31 MINERALISTIC

The front door painstakingly marbled with white paint over black (or is it black over white?) should be a sign that this eclectic gift shop offers an engaging selection of fine objects. Much of the stock has either a medieval or a Victorian theme. Find silver jewelry, minerals and crystals, fierce and fanciful gargoyles for your walls or shelves, and glass and pewter items. ♦ M-Th, noon-9 PM; F, Sa, 11AM-10PM; Su, noon-8PM. 319 South St (between S Third and S Fourth Sts). 922.7199. www.mineralistic.com

32 CHEF'S MARKET

Put together a picnic or last-minute brunch at this upscale market. In addition to the fresh fish and meat counters, there are innumerable prepared entrées, cheeses and gourmet sauces, and the best selection of bread on South Street—crispy French baguettes, sourdough rolls, round Italian loaves. When you order one of the specialty coffees (by the cup or pound), it's hard to resist the cookies and other enticing baked goods, placed to encourage impulse purchases. ♦ Daily, 8AM-9PM. 231 South St (between S Second and S Third Sts). 925.8360. www.chefsmkt.com

33 MALLORCA RESTAURANT

★★$$ This elegant Spanish restaurant located in the heart of South Street offers authentic tapas, a good Spanish and Portuguese wine list, and delicious dishes like *mariscada* (mixed seafood) in green sauce, a huge portion of fresh shrimp, scallops, mussels, clams, and a half lobster bathed in a sauce made from creamed asparagus, garlic, white wine, onions, and parsley. Homemade sangria is a Mallorca trademark. ♦ 119 South St. 351.6652. www.mallorcaphilly.com

34 DOWNEY'S

★$$ Happy hour brings a happy crush to this Irish bar with turn-of-the-19th-century décor, and many stay on for dinner. The bartenders are skillful and generous, and the waiters cheerfully steer indecisive diners toward the best items on the basic menu of steaks and seafood. A second-floor balcony—open for dining in nice weather—overlooks the **Delaware River**, and there's a rooftop deck too. ♦ American ♦ Daily, dinner. 526 S Front St (at South St). 625.9500. www.downeysrestaurant.com

35 TOWER RECORDS

South Street's premier music store requires three floors to house all of its compact discs and cassettes. How does this one differ from others in the chain? Its extraordinarily deep jazz section caters to the area's discriminating listeners, and its rap bins contain a full line of local and international hip-hop. Staff members are knowledgeable and friendly. There's a **Ticketmaster** outlet on-site. ♦ Daily. 610 South St (between S Sixth and S Seventh Sts). 574.9888. Also at Broad and Chestnut Sts. 568.8001. ₺. www.towerrecords.com

36 PHILADELPHIA RECORD EXCHANGE

Well before chain stores brought the yuppies to South Street, young slackers swarmed the neighborhood, their only ambition to find the latest punk records on the cheap. This store is still a haven for alternative-rock culture, and though it does a brisk used-CD business, it hasn't lost faith in vinyl, which ensures the business of the downwardly mobile. The store—packed to capacity, hot, and always loud—also carries local and national fanzines. ◆ M-Th, Su, noon-7:30PM; F, Sa, noon-9PM. 608 S Fifth St (between Bainbridge and South Sts). 925.7892. www.philarecx.com

37 CHEERS TO YOU

★$ In this well-liked corner pub, television sets, tuned to different channels, radiate from various angles. It's a great place to drink, and especially busy on weekends. But come to socialize, not to eat—the food is unremarkable. ◆ Italian ◆ Daily, lunch and dinner. 430 South St (at E Passyunk Ave). 923.8780

37 GUACAMOLE COMPANY

Avocado-colored doors and peach-and-bright blue walls dominate this trendy fashion boutique. The clothes are funky (red rubber jumpers and black vinyl pants, for example) and fine for the 15-to-25-year-old club-going female. A soundtrack of club music completes the appeal. ◆ Daily. 422 South St (between S Fourth St and E Passyunk Ave). 923.6174

38 ATOMIC CITY COMICS

Fanatics and dabblers can select from collector comics, trading cards, buttons, T-shirts, and other superhero-related merchandise in this invariably busy store. Some epic game is usually in progress at the huge game table, where players talk strategy and mull over options with enough candor to help an alert beginner learn the basics. ◆ M-Th, noon-9PM; F, Sa, 11AM-10PM; Su, noon-8PM. 640 South St (between S Fourth St and E Passyunk Ave). 625.9613. & www.atomiccitycomics.com

39 PHILADELI

★$ This informal diner is filled with local color. Breakfast, available all day, is a highlight; start with fresh-squeezed orange or grapefruit juice, and sample one of the various bagel treatments. The creamy cheesecakes and other gooey desserts are to die for, just as the waitstaff claim. If you're on the move, they'll also package cold drinks, snacks, and sandwiches to go. ◆ Deli ◆ Daily, breakfast, lunch, and dinner. 410 South St (between S Fourth St and E Passyunk Ave). 923.1986

39 EYES GALLERY

One of the first gift shops to locate on South Street in the 1970s, this place helped spark the South Street renaissance and spawned a number of neighboring imitators. The boutique features high-quality exotic jewelry, clothing, and handicrafts from various developing and Latin American countries, all artfully displayed. ◆ M-Th, 11AM-7PM; F, Sa, 11AM-8PM; Su, noon-6PM. 402 South St (between S Fourth St and E Passyunk Ave). 925.0193. www.eyesgallery.com

39 JIM'S STEAKS

$ The scent of fried onions wafting through the intersection of Fourth and South Streets is the only advertising this black-and-white-tiled joint needs. A brawny bruiser behind the counter slaps together a classic Philadelphia cheesesteak: thin strips of steak cooked on an open grill, cheese, and usually onions, served in a hoagie roll. Although some locals maintain that both **Pat's** and **Geno's** in South Philly have superior steaks, **Jim's** has earned devoted followers with its special sauces, fresh toppings, and excellent fries. Pick up your meal at the ground-level cafeteria, then sit upstairs for an excellent view of the street action. ◆ American ◆ Daily, lunch, dinner, and late-night snacks. 400 South St (at S Fourth St). 928.1911. www.jimssteaks.com

40 ALYAN'S

★$ Though short on décor, this Middle Eastern restaurant comes out a winner with tasty food and low prices. Such standbys as hummus and falafel are skillfully rendered, and the homemade home fries—seasoned with onions and peppers—are a meal in themselves. ◆ Middle Eastern ◆ Daily, lunch and dinner. 603 S Fourth St (between Bainbridge and South Sts). 922.3553

41 THEATER OF LIVING ARTS (TLA)

Once a cinema, then a venue for counterculture drama, followed by a repertory film theater, and then a theater dedicated to live music, the TLA is now a rock 'n' roll hall with no permanent seats, though folding chairs are brought in for the quieter shows. The generous stage, unobstructed sight lines, and good acoustics make this a terrific place for live music, and somebody interesting plays at least twice a week. The Pretenders and Squeeze have rocked the house; local rap

The Continental Congress, meeting in Philadelphia, passed a resolution on 2 July 1776 that "these United Colonies are, and of right ought to be, Free and Independent States" and that "they are absolved from all allegiance to the British Crown." This resolution, of course, was the official Declaration of Independence.

In an average week, Philadelphia Soft Pretzel Bakery makes 325,000 pretzels.

Restaurants/Clubs: Red | Hotels: Purple | Shops: Orange | Outdoors/Parks: Green | Sights/Culture: Blue

and rock groups also perform here. Just inside the door, **That Little Bar** (open only during shows) serves drinks and snacks. ◆ Call for schedules and prices. 334 South St (between S Third and S Fourth Sts). 922.1011. www.theateroflivingarts.net

42 Jon's Bar & Grille

★★$ Large umbrella-covered tables, comfy chairs, and trees strung with Christmas lights create the most pleasant outdoor-dining experience on South Street. The basic menu offers everything from nachos to grilled chicken sandwiches. A plaque in the bar area marks this site as the birthplace of Larry Fine, one of the Three Stooges. ◆ American ◆ M-F, lunch, dinner, and late-night snacks; Sa, Su, brunch, dinner, and late-night snacks. 606 S Third St (at South St). 592.1390. www.jonsbarandgrille.com

43 Next BYOB

★★$$ Opened by a talented team of twentysomethings—co-owners Jason Taylor (Avenue B, Striped Bass, Bluezette) and Rich Podulka (Rouge, Striped Bass, Five Spot) and chef Terry Owens (Rouge, Four Seasons), Next is another reason besides Django to head to South Street for dinner. The simple yet soothing and intimate décor sets the stage for a really terrific meal. Standout menu items include what may be the best tuna carpaccio in town, served with crunchy daikon, pea shoots, and a wasabi drizzle, and an awesome bucco of bacon-wrapped monkfish, served with risotto carbonera and black-eyed peas. Beets adorn a perfect toss of greens, goat cheese, haricots verts, and hazelnuts— chef Owens manages to get a pleasing crunch into almost every dish. Don't forget to bring your own wine. ◆ New American. 223 South St. 629.8688

44 Ristorante San Carlo

★★$$ This small, elegant, and unpretentious *ristorante* has earned the devotion of many discerning pasta lovers, who rave over the sauces. Fresh tomatoes and garlic are the primary ingredients in the full-bodied but never heavy tomato sauce. ◆ Italian ◆ Daily, dinner. Reservations recommended. 214 South St (between S Second and S Third Sts). 592.9777

45 Bridget Foy's South Street Grill

★$$ This eatery has outgrown its beer-and-burger roots and has taken on a more elaborate (and expensive) menu. Fare billed as "turbo-charged American" includes grilled items, pastas, salads, and a still dependable burger. Bridget's also offers a front-row seat to the three-ringed South Street circus. Venture inside to find one of the friendliest bars in town. Patrons can quench their thirst with German EKU lager or a hearty house microbrew. ◆ American ◆ Daily, lunch and dinner. 200 South St (at S Second St). 922.1813. www.bridgetfoys.com

46 Monte Carlo Living Room

★★★$$$ Ambitious Northern Italian creations, an understated yet elegant atmosphere, and attentive service make this the most outstanding restaurant in the South Street area. The pasta is homemade, and the beef and veal dishes are among the best available anywhere. Dessert options include an incredibly smooth gelato. The dance floor in the upstairs lounge attracts the over-40 set. ◆ Italian ◆ Daily, dinner. Upstairs club open until 2AM. Proper attire required. Reservations required. 150 South St (at S Second St). 925.2220. www.montecarlolivingroom.com

47 South Street Antiques Market

Many of the old houses a few blocks from the commercial area have been passed from generation to generation in the same family, proving a gold mine for the 25 or so dealers in this market. Vintage castoffs include clothing, postcards, jewelry, Depression-era glassware, and Art Deco furniture. The dealers are ready with information about their merchandise, but they're also aware that most people who wander in are just browsing. The lower level can be counted on for a few black-velvet paintings too. ◆ W-Th, Su, noon-7PM; F, Sa, noon-8PM. 615 S Sixth St (between Bainbridge and South Sts). 592.0256 &

48 Azafran

★★$$ Caracas-born owner Susanna Goihman brings a New World sensibility to dishes like grilled salmon papillote, brightened with a flavorsome orange-and-beet sauce, or chicken "steak" with arugula and tomatoes. Expect to wait on the weekends, and don't forget to bring your own wine. ◆ 617 S Third St (between Bainbridge and South Sts). 928.4019

48 Hostaria Da Elio

★★$$ This newcomer is creating quite a buzz, thanks to chef-owner Elio Sgambati's inspired take on authentic regional Italian cuisine. The 42-seat restaurant offers delectable homemade pasta—don't miss the ricotta gnocchi with Gorgonzola sauce—along with traditional veal, fish, and meat dishes, with entrée prices from $10 to $24. Sgambati, a native of Rome, previously worked at Il Gallo Nero, Cafe Calamari, and La Collina in Belmont Hills. ◆ 615 S Third St (between Bainbridge and South Sts). 925.0930

ALL THAT JAZZ (AND BLUES)

In recent years, Philadelphia's jazz and blues scene has exploded, exposing listeners to music that was once the domain of a few select clubs. In addition to the well-known and big-name venues, such as **Zanzibar Blue** (www.zanzibarblue.com) for jazz and **Warmdaddy's** for blues, there are now a number of other nightspots where the jazz ranges from very cool to white hot, and the blues from down-home to big city. Call ahead to find out who's playing and what the cover charge is and, in most cases, to make reservations. An up-to-date view of the whole scene is available at www.phillyjazz.org.

As noted, Zanzibar Blue, now comfortably ensconced in new digs at the **Park Hyatt Hotel at the Bellevue,** presents local and national big-name acts, including the likes of the Ernie Hopkins Quartet, Keisa Brown, FVC Connection, and Renaissance, 7 days a week, including a very popular jazz brunch on Sunday (200 S Broad Street, at Walnut Street; 732.5200).

Among Philly's hipster spots for live band, hip-hop, and house, the Five Spot also holds events that are a bit more contemporary, like hip-hop poetry slams and musical trips back to modern rock. The music starts at 10PM and continues until 1AM (5 S Bank Street, between Chestnut and Market Streets; 574.0070).

In nearby Mt. Airy, about 15 minutes outside of Center City, **North by Northwest** is a new venue worth checking out. This Woolworth-turned-restaurant and jazz-blues club is a cavernous space filled with tables from shop windows to stage. Most evenings, a band appears around 10PM. Southern fare is served (7165 Germantown Avenue; 248.1000; www.NXNWphl.com).

Ortlieb's Jazzhaus, a quintessential Philadelphia jazz club housed in a former bowling alley-cafeteria for the old Ortlieb's brewery, swings every night but Monday, and there's no cover charge. This neighborhood favorite hosts hometown heroes like Bootsie Barnes and His Organ Trio (847 N Third Street, at Poplar Street; 922.1035.

The **Philadelphia Clef Club of the Performing Arts**, a recent addition to the much-touted **Avenue of the Arts**, is a concert space and educational facility rather than a club. There are a 220-seat auditorium, classrooms, rehearsal studios, and jazz archives. The list of performers has been as distinguished as it gets, including Lionel Hampton, Clark Terry, Grover Washington Jr., and other jazz giants. Call for a concert schedule (736-738 S Broad Street, at Fitzwater Street; 893.9912).

Other good places to hear jazz include the **Swann Lounge** at the **Four Seasons Hotel** on Friday and Saturday nights (1 Logan Square, between Benjamin Franklin Parkway and N 19th Street; 963.1500), **Chris' Jazz Cafe** (1421 Sansom Street, between S Broad and S 15th Streets; 568.3131), **Rembrandt's Restaurant & Bar** in Fairmount every Thursday night (741 N 23rd Street; 763.2228), and the **Prime Rib**, where a pianist accompanied by a bass player is featured nightly between 6 and 11PM (1701 Locust Street, at the Warwick Hotel; 772.1701). For a real change of pace, check out **Bob and Barbara's Lounge**, a boho shot-and-beer bar that features suave house band Nate Wiley and the Crowd Pleasers Friday and Saturday nights beginning around 10. Drag shows are another of this bar's calling cards, so expect a diverse crowd (1509 South Street, between S 15th and S 16th Sts. 545.4511).

Enjoy Sunday brunch to a jazz accompaniment at Zanzibar Blue (see above), the **White Dog Cafe** (3420 Sansom Street, between S 34th and S 36th Streets, University City; 386.9224), the **Marker** in the **Adam's Mark Hotel** (City Line Avenue and Monument Road; 581.5000), the **Courtyard** (in the Sheraton Society Hill Hotel, 1 Dock Street, at S Second Street; 238.6000), and **Allie's American Grill** (in the Philadelphia Marriott Hotel, 1201 Market Street, at N 12th Street; 625.2900).

To hear the blues in Philadelphia, try **Warmdaddy's** (4 S Front Street, between Chestnut and Market Streets; 627.2500); the **Tin Angel** (20 S Second Street, between Market and Chestnut Streets; 928.0978); **South Street Blues** (21st and South Streets; 546.9009); **Ulana's**, especially for blues jam sessions, which happen every Tuesday night (S Second and Bainbridge Streets; 922.4152); and **Dawson Street Pub** (100 Dawson Street at Cresson Street, Manayunk; 482.5677).

49 CEDARS

★★$ The Lebanese fare in this family-owned storefront is impressive—from the grape-leaves appetizer and the tabbouleh salad to the combination platter (tabbouleh and hummus with tahini sauce). ◆ Lebanese ◆ Daily, lunch and dinner. 616 S Second St (between Bainbridge and South Sts). 925.4950. www.cedarsrestaurant.com

50 BEAU MONDE

★★$$ This handsome Breton-style creperie boasts a working ceramic fireplace and wall panelings with hand-painted flowers, fruits, and herbs. Dark wood furniture contrasts with light wood floors. Two types of crepes native to Northwest France and Brittany—blé noire (savory crepes), made from buckwheat flour, and froment (sweet crepes), made from

---

Restaurants/Clubs: Red | Hotels: Purple | Shops: Orange | Outdoors/Parks: Green | Sights/Culture: Blue

PHILADELPHIA BY THE BOOK

Before you visit Philadelphia, you may want to explore the city through the many books that have been written about it. Here are just a few recommended titles to begin your literary tour:

Andrew Wyeth: A Secret Life, by Richard Meryman (HarperCollins, 1996): In this account of America's most popular artist, biographer Meryman, a member of the Wyeth family's inner circle for some 30 years, paints Wyeth as a dark, complex man and offers a closer look into Wyeth's very private life.

Fool's Gold, by Albert DiBartomoleo (St. Martin's Press, 1993): Here is a fast-moving, well-written tale about the mob set partly in South Philadelphia.

The Frog/Commissary Cookbook, by Steven Poses et al. (Doubleday, 1985): Although the Frog and Commissary restaurants are no more, their culinary memory lives on in this book of recipes compiled by their owner. Among the highlights are the butterflied shrimp with soy, garlic, ginger, and lemon and the killer chocolate-chip fudge cake.

From Home and Abroad, American and British Writers in Philadelphia, 1800–1910, by John J. Burke (University Press of America, 1996): Burke has assembled a telling compendium of what famous writers, such as Samuel Clemens, Charles Dickens, and Oscar Wilde, thought and wrote of Philadelphia.

Gardens of Philadelphia and the Delaware Valley, by William M. Klein Jr. (Temple University Press, 1995): Essays by the former director of Philadelphia's **Morris Arboretum** on the history of 44 of the region's gardens, arboretums, and public parks. The more than 200 photographs were taken by Derek Fell.

God's Pocket, by Pete Dexter (Random House, 1983): Dexter, once a popular local news reporter, tells the story of the chain of events set in motion when a Philadelphia construction worker is killed while taunting a colleague.

Hostile Witness, by William Lashner (HarperCollins, 1995): This is the first novel by Philadelphia's answer to John Grisham. Lawyer-turned-novelist Lashner inserts a lot of local color in his story of a small-time attorney's foray into the dangerous world of shady politics and unscrupulous law practices.

I'd Rather Be in Philadelphia, by Gillian Roberts (Ballantine, 1993): One of the popular series of mystery stories featuring Amanda Pepper, a high-school teacher turned amateur sleuth.

Imagining Philadelphia, by Philip Stevick (University of Pennsylvania Press, 1996): Stevick's collection of visitors' observations in travel narratives, correspondence, diaries, and fiction captures what the author calls "a parallel city to the place on the map and the street under foot, a city of the mind, an imagined Philadelphia."

Main Line Wasp, by W. Thacher Longstreth (Norton, 1990): This book contains the humorous memoirs of Philadelphia's longtime city councilman-at-large, a descendant of one of the city's first families.

Miracle at Philadelphia: The Story of the Constitutional Convention, May to September 1787, by Catherine Drinker Bowen (Little, Brown, 1986): This is a readable, entertaining account of the dramatic sessions that produced the Constitution.

The Philadelphia Experiment: Project Invisibility, by William L. Moore (Fawcett Crest, 1979): This documented report tells the story of a World War II experiment to make matter invisible, particularly the strange disappearance of the *U.S.S. Eldridge*, a fully manned destroyer escort, from Philadelphia, and its reappearances in Norfolk, Virginia, and again Philadelphia, all in some kind of molecule-meshing green fog.

Philadelphia: Portrait of an American City, by Edwin Wolf II (Camino Books, 1990): Originally written for the occasion of America's bicentennial, this lavishly illustrated history of Philadelphia life has been updated and re-released.

Principato, by Tom McHale (Viking, 1970): An Italian-American from South Philly marries into an arch-conservative Irish-Catholic family in this merciless satire of the Catholic Church.

Public Art in Philadelphia, by Penny Balkin Bach (Temple University Press, 1992): Written by the executive director of the Fairmount Park Art Association, this work is considered to be the definitive book on the sculptures, fountains, and statuary adorning the city's parks and public spaces.

Rabbit, Run, by John Updike (Knopf, 1960): Set in the fictional town of Brewer, Pennsylvania, on the outskirts of Philadelphia, this is the first of Updike's novels about Harry "Rabbit" Angstrom and his attempts to cope with the ups and downs of life. Also check out the other books in the series: *Rabbit Redux*, *Rabbit Is Rich*, and *Rabbit at Rest*.

South Philadelphia: Mummers, Memories, and the Melrose Diner, by Murray Dubin (Temple University Press, 1996): South Philadelphia resident Dubin takes readers on an insider's tour, exploring hundreds of years of history, including ethnic strife and community solidarity.

Third and Indiana, by Steve Lopez (Viking, 1995): The mean streets of Philadelphia's drug-ridden Badlands are the focus of this well-received first novel by a *Philadelphia Inquirer* columnist.

wheat flour—are offered here. Lunch and dinner crepe choices include shrimp, spinach, and roasted leeks with seafood sauce; andouille sausage, ratatouille, and herb butter; and grilled vegetables with salsa verde. Be sure to try one of the mouth-watering sweet crepes—such as banana, Nutella, and vanilla ice cream—for dessert. A full bar offers your choice of accompanying drinks. On Saturday and Sunday between 10AM and 3PM, a brunch menu is available in addition to the standard menu. L'Etage Cabaret and Bar offers music entertainment Tu-Su. ♦ Creperie ♦ Tu-F, lunch and dinner; Sa, Su, brunch and dinner. 624 S Sixth St (at Bainbridge St). 592.0656. www.creperie-beaumonde.com

51 New Jersey State Aquarium

In 1995, the area's largest aquarium—which had previously focused on native mid-Atlantic sea life—launched a $16 million repopulation, importing over 1,200 tropical fish and other aquatic creatures for a total of 5,000 specimens in all. In addition to the popular touch tanks—where you can gently pick up (and return) starfish and sea anemones—interactive exhibits include a mini-television studio where kids can record their thoughts about the environment. Strollers are allowed, and backpacks are provided for parents who want to carry small children through the exhibits. ♦ Admission. Open daily; closed Thanksgiving, Christmas Day, and New Year's Day. 1 Riverside Dr, Camden, New Jersey. 856/365.3300. ♿. www.njaquarium.org

51 Judy's

★★$$ Stuffed meat loaf, superlative buttery mashed potatoes, and other unpretentious eats have kept this restaurant going for nearly 2 decades. The menu changes daily, and the specials are truly special. Several varieties of fresh fish are always available. ♦ American ♦ Daily, dinner. 627 S Third St (at Bainbridge St). 928.1968

52 Shippen Way Inn

$$ The South Street area's only bed-and-breakfast inn has nine rooms—most with double beds and each with a private bath and reproductions of furnishings from the colonial era. Common areas include a living room, breakfast room, and courtyard. Locals coping with spillover houseguests favor this inn, which has discount rates for stays longer than 3 nights. A continental breakfast (included in the rate) is served daily, as is wine and cheese at happy hour. ♦ 418 Bainbridge St (between S Fourth and S Fifth Sts). 627.7266, 800/245.4873. www.shippenwayinn.members.easyspace.com

53 The Pink Rose Pastry Shop

★★★$ The pastry chefs at this bakery pour the finest ingredients and lots of TLC into the batter of their cookies, muffins, and cakes. The carrot cake deserves a special mention. If you choose to have a bite here, settle down at a table and enjoy the unhurried atmosphere and relaxing music. The coffee is great too. ♦ Bakery ♦ Tu-Th, 8AM-10:30PM; F, 8AM-11:30PM; Sa, 9AM-11:30PM; Su, 9AM-8:30PM. 630 S Fourth St (at Bainbridge St). 592.0565. www.pinkrosepastry.com

53 Famous 4th Street Deli

★$ Family owned and operated for three generations, this deli is one of the few remaining signs that South Street was once a Jewish enclave. The oversize sandwiches are legendary—try the pastrami or the Reuben—as are the bagels and homemade cookies. Don't judge this place by the décor or the paper plates. It's cluttered and a little chaotic when the line gets long, but the food is terrific, and the dining room is extraordinarily clean. ♦ Deli ♦ Daily, breakfast and lunch. 700 S Fourth St (at Bainbridge St). 922.3274. www.famouscookies.com

54 House of Tea

This store may just be North America's most comprehensive purveyor of high-quality loose tea from the world's best suppliers. Blends hail from every imaginable exotic port, but you can also find traditional brews like Earl Grey, Darjeeling, English Breakfast, and the like. Prices start at around $7 for a 4-ounce sampling and go as high as $28 per pound. Tea accessories are also on hand. Brewing advice is free for the asking. ♦ Tu-Sa. 720 S Fourth St (between Monroe and Bainbridge Sts). 923.8327

55 Essene

★$ With all the high-cholesterol food on South Street, it's comforting to know about this shrine to the fresh and wholesome just a few blocks away. In addition to an abundance of organically grown produce, this spotless health-food emporium has a restaurant in back that turns out vegetable juices, spicy sesame noodles, tofu hot dogs, and more. ♦ Health food ♦ M, W-Su, lunch and dinner. 719 S Fourth St (at Monroe St). 922.1146. www.essenemarket.com

Old bricks are making way for a neighborhood of multiple personalities extending from **Washington Square** to **Broad Street**. Robbed of its commercial heart by a slump in retail business when suburban malls siphoned away customers, the area is currently in the midst of urban renewal. Adding considerably to its revitalization was the construction of the massive brick **Pennsylvania Convention Center**, strategically positioned in the downtown core between **Independence National Historical Park** and the **Benjamin Franklin Parkway**'s museums to encourage visitors to take advantage of the city's history and commerce.

Reminders of Philadelphia's development from colonial seaport to confident metropolis are visible in this varied neighborhood. Foxglove, queen of the prairie, and saffron crocus growing in the brick walls of the 18th-century garden at **Pennsylvania Hospital** are reminiscent of a time when the city's doctors relied on medicinal plants as remedies. A few blocks to the north, gaslights flicker outside the **Walnut Street Theater**, as they did in the days when Sarah Bernhardt contracted a fatal cold while performing here. And just west of the theater, one of the world's first modernist skyscrapers, the **PSFS Building**, now the luxury hotel **Loews Philadelphia**, rises with clean, elegant lines above the busy street.

Market, Chestnut, Walnut, Spruce, and **Pine Streets**—long, walkable thoroughfares that traverse Center City from the **Delaware** to the **Schuylkill Rivers**—characterize Philadelphia as much as redbrick and cobblestones. Strolling down these streets, you can find farmers selling produce at the **Reading Terminal Market**, as they have since 1893; step into the Pennsylvania Convention Center; then take a stroll through the lofty **Grand Court** of **Lord & Taylor** (formerly the Philadelphia institution known as **Wanamaker's**). If you have time, indulge in some cheese fries at the **Gallery at Market East**, a contemporary shopping mall, and while away an afternoon browsing in **Chinatown** for oyster sauce or bok choy, perhaps, or along Pine Street's **Antique Row**, with its eclectic shops, shade trees, secondhand bookstores, coffee shops, and small park dedicated to renowned Philadelphia architect **Louis I. Kahn**.

Pine and Spruce Streets, with larger, more-stately row houses than those in Society Hill, have none of the hard edges found in the commercial districts just a short distance away.

1 HAWTHORN SUITES

$$ This 16-story tower includes spacious studio and one-bedroom suites located one block from the **Pennsylvania Convention Center**. The renovation of this former clothing factory has retained the distinctive Art Deco flair, whereas guest rooms feature data ports, voice mail, cable TV, and free local phone calls. Meeting space is available for up to 200. There's also a fitness center.♦ 1100 Vine St. 829.8300; fax 829.8104. www.hawthornsuites.com

2 SPAGHETTI WAREHOUSE

★$ This massive, barnlike family restaurant has a train dining car in the middle of it. The approach is simple and effective: Meals consist of a fresh-baked loaf of bread, huge drinks, a garden salad, and a good-size plate of pasta with a choice of sauces. The 15-layer lasagna is popular. ♦ Italian ♦ Daily, lunch and dinner. 1026 Spring Garden St (between N 10th and N 11th Sts). 787.0784. www.meatballs.com

3 HAMPTON INN PHILADELPHIA CONVENTION CENTER

$$ This new hotel is steps away from the convention center, with 250 rooms, including king/queen suites, an indoor pool, spa and fitness facility, and 3,500 square feet of meeting space. A complimentary breakfast is a plus, although you may be tempted to eat all your meals in the neighborhood—between **Reading Terminal Market** and **Chinatown**,

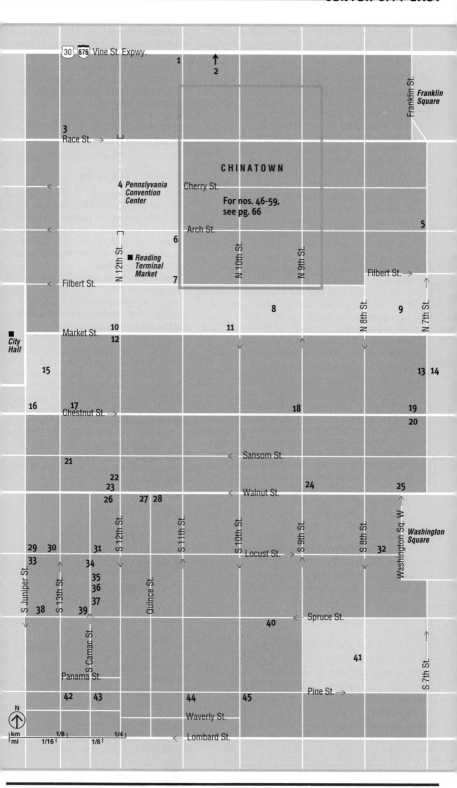

30 676 Vine St. Expwy.

1

2

3
Race St. →

Franklin St.

Franklin Square

CHINATOWN

4 *Pennslyvania Convention Center*

Cherry St.

For nos. 46-59, see pg. 66

Arch St.

5

6

N 12th St.

N 10th St.

N 9th St.

■ *Reading Terminal Market*

7

Filbert St. →

← Filbert St.

8

N 8th St.

9

N 7th St.

■ *City Hall*

Market St.

10

12

11

15

13 14

16

17
Chestnut St. →

18

19

20

21

← Sansom St.

22
23

← Walnut St.

24

25

26

27 28

S 12th St.

S 11th St.

S 10th St.

S 9th St.

S 8th St.

Washington Sq. W

Washington Square

29 30

31

34

← Locust St. →

32

33

S Juniper St.

S 13th St.

35
36
37

Quince St.

38

39

S Camac St.

40

← Spruce St.

41

S 7th St.

Panama St.

42

43

44

45

Pine St. →

N
↑

km
mi   1/16   1/8   1/8   1/4

Waverly St.

← Lombard St.

Restaurants/Clubs: Red | Hotels: Purple | Shops: Orange | Outdoors/Parks: Green | Sights/Culture: Blue

your taste buds won't get bored. ♦ 1301 Race St. 665.9100; fax 665.9200. www. hamptoninn.com

4 PENNSYLVANIA CONVENTION CENTER

Philadelphia is a consistent player in the competitive "meet market" with this 1.3-million-square-foot complex, which is set for expansion in the next few years. With a final bill of more than $500 million, the center, which opened in 1993, was the costliest construction project in Philadelphia history. Architects **Thompson, Ventulett, Stainback & Associates** of Atlanta, Georgia, designed the handsome brick and limestone mammoth, with a main hall that covers four square blocks. The convention center boasts two unusual structures that set it apart from blander public buildings: the old **Reading Railroad**'s historically certified **Train Shed**, which has been renovated and is now the grand hall and ballroom, and the ornate terra-cotta **Headhouse**, which has become the complex's showcase entrance. There is already talk of expanding the facility, although no definite plans are on the drawing board.

From the moment officials proposed it, the convention center was one of the city's hottest controversies. Many adamantly opposed such an addition to this already extremely dense neighborhood with narrow streets. Despite the crowds, however, the location is very convenient. It's within easy walking distance of **Chinatown**, **The Gallery**, **Liberty Place**, and the commercial core of Center City; **Independence National Historical Park** is a mere six blocks away; and the **Reading Terminal Market** has been renovated and made part of the convention complex. In addition to the usual conventions and meetings, the center hosts several annual city events, including March's spectacular **Philadelphia Flower Show**, the largest and most prestigious show of its type.

Driving and parking in the area remain a problem, but the center can be reached by mass transit. Commuter rail lines, including the **Airport Express**, stop at the **Market East Station**; there are subway stops at 11th and Market Streets and 13th and Market Streets; and the purple **Phlash** buses run along Market Street and stop right outside the door of the adjacent **Philadelphia Marriott**, which is connected to the convention center by a skyway. ♦ Bounded by N 11th and N 13th Sts and by Market and Race Sts. 418.4700. ♿ www.paconvention.com

Within the Pennsylvania Convention Center:

READING TERMINAL

Once a hurry-scurry commuter rail station built by the **Philadelphia and Reading Railroad** in 1892, this terminal has embarked on a new career as a welcoming point for visitors. It's the site of two of Philadelphia's most distinctive landmarks, the **Reading Headhouse** and the **Reading Train Shed**, designed by the **Wilson Brothers** and completed in 1893. The Train Shed—the nation's only surviving single-span arched train shed—has become the grand hall of the **Pennsylvania Convention Center**. The Headhouse has become the convention center's entrance hall. Waiting rooms and offices once occupied the Headhouse, distinguished by its ornate Italian Renaissance exterior, wrought- and cast-iron columns, terra-cotta details, brick floors, and copper cornice. The region's transit system was reconfigured in the late 1970s, when **Market East Station** became the major transportation hub. The **Philadelphia Marriott** has built 210 oversize guest rooms at the Headhouse, as an extension of the existing hotel (see page 59). ♦ Market St (between N 11th and N 12th Sts)

READING TERMINAL MARKET

When the **Philadelphia and Reading Railroad** decided to build its terminal on Market Street in 1892, the company faced the prospect of having to displace two 30-year-old farmers' markets. The railroad company, in a stroke of genius, built a new market underneath its train shed as a compromise. Today people treasure this chaotic bazaar. Cooks depend on the market as a source of high-quality groceries, and locals say it's the best lunch spot in the city.

In its prime, in the decades before World War I, the Baldwin Locomotive Works was Philadelphia's largest employer and produced an average of 3,000 locomotives a year. Workers earned about $15 per week for a 55-hour work week on the day shift or 65 hours on the night shift.

There are 985 licensed food vendors in Philadelphia.

The Tasty Baking Company turns out 3.5 million Peanut Butter Kandy Kakes a week.

In its early years, the market was a marvel of turn-of-the-19th-century technology, with sawdust-covered floors, 78,000 square feet of aisles and stalls, a 400-line telephone system, and 250,000 cubic feet of cold storage in the basement. It instantly flourished, appealing to all classes and tastes. Ordinary folks came for the New Jersey seafood and corn, Lancaster County poultry and vegetables, cranberries from the Pine Barrens, and huckleberries from the Poconos. Chefs from the city's fanciest hotels, the **Bellevue Stratford** and the **Barclay**, bought fresh produce and herbs.

The market survived the Depression, when Philadelphians waited in line for rationed meat, but met its enemy with the advent of the modern supermarket and the exodus of the middle class to the suburbs. Thus began a serious decline. As the *Trenton Times* put it, "it became easier to find a secondhand paperback [there] than a fresh fish for dinner." In the 1970s, there was talk of tearing the market down to make way for new development along Market Street, but sympathetic management took over in 1980. Farmers and purveyors signed new leases, and merchants who had been there for years decided to stay. Happily, the demand surged for local produce, quality meats, fresh fish, and superior lunch fare. Once again, the market is jammed during lunch hours and on weekends, and renovations have created an even more cheerful atmosphere.

The northwestern corner of the market is still almost exclusively for Amish merchants from Lancaster County, known for their superior poultry and produce. Grab a bite to eat at one of the tempting food stalls (barbecued ribs at **Delilah's**, grilled chicken sandwiches at **Fireworks!**, and fried seafood at **Pearl's Oyster Bar** are among the choices). At lunchtime, long lines form at the Amish pretzel stall, origin of the very best soft pretzels on earth. (Note: Most of the food stalls close by 3PM, and the Amish businesses are open from Wednesday to Saturday only.) Dinner can be had at the **Down Home Diner**. Maps of the market hang from the walls and are available at the office near the Arch Street entrances. Discount parking is available at the lot at 12th and Filbert Streets. ♦ M-Sa. N 12th St (between Filbert and Arch Sts). 922.2317. ♿. www.readingterminalmarket.org

Within Reading Terminal Market:

12TH STREET CANTINA

★★$ This started out as a tiny stand, but it's grown into a full-fledged eat-in and take-out Mexican restaurant. You can get the standard fast food—tacos, burritos, and enchiladas—as well as excellent homemade dishes: Oaxacan beef stew, turkey in classic red *mole* sauce, Yucatán-style chicken tamales, or spicy vegetable casseroles. Salsas, tortillas, and fresh peppers can be purchased here too. ♦ Mexican ♦ 625.0321. ♿. Also at Shops at the Bellevue, 200 S Broad St (at Walnut St). 790.1578; Manayunk Farmer's Market, 4120 Main St (near Lock St), Manayunk. 930.0272

SPATARO'S

★$ Cold buttermilk and old-fashioned sandwiches have been standouts at this deli since 1947, where such choices as ham, liverwurst, turkey, tuna salad, and cream-cheese-and-olive spread are the same as when Truman was president. Just one of these substantial sandwiches can satisfy two restrained appetites. ♦ Deli ♦ 925.6833 ♿

FISHER'S SOFT PRETZELS AND ICE CREAM

If the only kind of soft pretzel you've ever tasted came from a street vendor, you're in for a treat. Here, Amish women roll out the dough just before it's placed in the oven, and waitresses brush the baked pretzels with butter. The result is as memorable as a warm slice of homemade bread. If you want a scoop, however, you're better off going to **Bassetts Ice Cream**. ♦ 592.8510 ♿

BASSETTS ICE CREAM

Even when the market was desolate in the 1960s and 1970s, you could always find people lining up here. Louis DuBois Bassett started an ice cream business out of his backyard in Salem, New Jersey, in 1861, which makes **Bassetts** the oldest commercial ice cream operation in the country. The family moved the business from the Garden State to the **Reading Terminal** in the 1890s, where it's been ever since. It's no wonder the customers sitting at the counter have glazed looks of contentment. Heavy, smooth, and intensely flavored, this ice cream has a treacherously high butterfat content. Double chocolate chip, Irish coffee, French vanilla, butter almond, and rum raisin are the most highly recommended flavors. The Bassett family has also introduced its own frozen yogurt, and they expanded nationally in the 1980s. ♦ 925.4315 ♿

KAMAL'S MIDDLE EASTERN SPECIALTIES

★★$ Falafels, made fresh daily, are stuffed into pita with the requisite salad greens and tahini sauce. There's also shish kebab, hummus, *baba ghanouj*, rice pilaf, and Greek pizza. ♦ Middle Eastern ♦ 925.1511 ♿

Restaurants/Clubs: Red | Hotels: Purple | Shops: Orange | Outdoors/Parks: Green | Sights/Culture: Blue

THE BEST

Meryl Levitz

President and CEO, Greater Philadelphia Tourism Marketing Corporation

EAT!

People are eating their way through Philadelphia! BYOBs, sidewalk cafés, and coffee shops have popped up all over.

And we still have diners, diners, diners—a few favorites are the **Melrose** in South Philly, the **Mayfair** in the Northeast, and **Little Pete's** on 17th Street, so you can eat steak and eggs, open-face turkey sandwiches, meat loaf and mashed potatoes, creamed chipped beef on toast, and deep-dish pies 24 hours a day (cheap!). Don't forget **Famous 4th Street Deli**, too, for everything from lox and bagels to killer cookies.

Fresh, hot, soft pretzels, sticky buns, prosciutto hoagies, spit-roasted chicken, crabs and beer, homemade water ice, and much more can be found at the **Reading Terminal Market**, located smack in the middle of town. And you can even shop for jewelry, cookbooks, fresh flowers, spices, cheeses, and Bassett's ice cream on your way out.

Have tea and cakes at the **Pink Rose** in the afternoon (just off South Street) or late Sunday brunch at the **Standard Tap** in Northern Liberties.

High tea comes complete with sandwiches, scones, tarts, and a harp in the **Swann Lounge** at the **Four Seasons**.

Moving upscale, try the lobster dumplings at **Susanna Foo**, Champagne by the glass and a dessert sampler at Georges Perrier's **Le Bar Lyonnais**; the prix-fixe lunch at Perrier's **Le Bec-Fin**; the guacamole at **El Vez** and the gelato across the street at **Capogiro**; Sunday brunch at the **Fountain** in the **Four Seasons**; cozy yet chic dining at the **White Dog Café** followed by

shopping at the adjoining **Black Cat**; the live jazz accompanying the etoufée at **Zanzibar Blue**; mojitos and ceviche at **Alma de Cuba**; chocolate to eat and to go from **Lacroix** at the **Rittenhouse**, and everything at **Buddakan**.

SHOP!

And shop some more! There is no sales tax on clothing here! Hurray!

Museum gift shops are terrific: the **Philadelphia Museum of Art**, the **Franklin Institute** (science), the **Penn Museum** (archeology and anthropology), the **Kimmel Center** (performing arts), **PAFA** (American art), and the **Independence Visitor Center** and **Lights of Liberty** at the **PECO Energy Center** for all things Philadelphia.

The grid system of Center City makes it very organized: we have **Jewelers' Row**, **Antique Row**, **Fabric Row**, **Rittenhouse Row**, etc.; the **Center City District** (department stores, **Liberty Place**, and wonderful small shops); **South Street**, famous and funky; **Old City**, retro chic and galleries galore; **Manayunk**, trendy with plenty of great restaurants; and **Pine Street**, with new one-of-a-kind galleries, gifts, housewares, and clothes.

Go to **Fante's** in the **Italian Market** for every gadget, odd-size baking pans, unique cookie cutters, and any other kitchen paraphernalia you could ever need.

Within 30 minutes of downtown Philadelphia are the huge **Franklin Mills Outlet Mall**; **Suburban Square**, for a slice of the Main Line in Ardmore; the vast **King of Prussia Mall**, with over 400 stores, including Neiman-Marcus, Nordstrom's, Bloomingdale's, Crate & Barrel, etc.

CELEBRATE!

Sunoco Welcome America! celebrates America's birthday in America's birthplace—what could be better? Ten days and dozens of free events, over the Fourth of July.

FAMOUS 4TH STREET COOKIE CO.

Few of the usual shopping-mall cookie stands match the quality found here. The selection typically includes oatmeal raisin, several varieties of chocolate chip, white chocolate, and peanut. ♦ 629.5990 ♿

DIENNER'S BAR-B-Q-CHICKEN

★★$ If you see people at a market table bent over pieces of aluminum foil and rising piles of bones, you know they've been here. Hot roasted chicken is sold whole or in parts, and, in addition to spicy barbecued chicken, you can also get simple roasted chicken with salt and mild seasonings. Dive into it here or take it out. ♦ Barbecue ♦ 925.8755 ♿

LE BUS BAKERY

The breads, almond croissants, muffins, cakes, and cookies are oven-fresh. ♦ 592.0422 ♿

5 AFRO-AMERICAN HISTORICAL AND CULTURAL MUSEUM

Built in 1976 on land that was once part of a historic black community, this contemporary building houses exhibits of African-American art and historical photographs and artifacts. The rotating displays might illustrate the migration of blacks from the southern states, the civil rights movement, or the rise of the black church. Other popular shows have included the abstract collages of the late Romare Bearden and narrative silk screens by Jacob Lawrence. Don't miss the museum's gift shop,

Philadelphia Flower Show is a drop-dead gorgeous horticultural wonderland at the Pennsylvania Convention Center every March—the oldest flower show in America.

The **Wachovia US Pro Cycling Championships** is one of the country's most celebrated races.

First Friday—on the first Friday of every month, Old City's art galleries invite you to stroll, browse, have wine and cheese, and see what's new.

Take **candlelight tours** at Independence Park, Fairmount Park, and Bucks County.

There are also the **Craft Show**, **The Antiques Show**, **The Book and The Cook**, and **Manayunk Arts Festival**—the events never stop.

And, of course, the feathered, sequined, musical **Mummers Parade** on January 1 (and huge fireworks on New Year's Eve). Oh, dem golden slippers!

GREAT STREETS!

Elfreth's Alley is the oldest continually occupied (teeny-tiny) street in America.

Walnut Street, between Fifth and Seventh, behind Independence Park (site of the Liberty Bell, Independence Hall, and more) features leafy green spaces and gardens backed by the genuine beginning of America.

The Avenue of the Arts (Broad Street) is a performing arts mecca, with the new **Kimmel Center for the Performing Arts**, **Academy of Music**, **Philadelphia Orchestra**, **Pennsylvania Ballet**, **Opera Company**, **Wilma Theater**, **Merriam Theater**, **Prince Music Theater**, **Clef Club** (jazz), and the **Arts Bank**—all within a few blocks of each other. And don't forget the new **Freedom Theater** on North Broad Street.

Jog, bike, blade, stroll, or drive your way from the Philadelphia Museum of Art onto Kelly Drive, then **Lincoln Drive**, the most beautiful urban roadway in America. The **Schuylkill River** ("hidden river" in Dutch) and **Fairmount Park** with its trees, sculpture, bridges, and curves and hills flank the Drive—a must-see, must-do experience.

Latches Lane, 20 minutes from Center City, is the street where the **Barnes Foundation** lives. There are 181 Renoir portraits and other works, plus a mind-boggling, heart-stirring private collection of Impressionist, post-Impressionist, and early Modern works of art.

There are great "Main Street" places to explore in the region, including charming central avenues in **Chestnut Hill, Manayunk, Doylestown, New Hope**, and **Kennett Square**.

BEST RESOURCES

Closest to my heart is www.gophila.com, a great resource for choosing and booking hotels; finding restaurants, itineraries, nightlife, and attractions, and seeing it all in virtual brochures. It's one-stop shopping for planning a unique Philadelphia itinerary.

The **Philly Fun Guide** is a great place for ideas to plan weekend activities with a weekly listing of special discounts. Visit phillyfunguide.com.

CultureFiles™ is an online "what's what" site showcasing 300 of Philadelphia's greatest cultural institutions, including such lesser known treasures such as **The Wharton Esherick House** (home and working studio of the late craftsman); **The Mercer Museum**, an immense and startling collection of American implements; the **Brandywine River Museum**, a countryside museum devoted to the art of three generations of Wyeths; the **Eastern State Penitentiary**; the **Insectarium**, and more. Visit www.gophila.com.

which has an excellent collection of literature on black history and culture. ♦ Admission. Tu-Sa; Su, noon-6PM. N Seventh and Arch Sts. 574.0380. www.aampmuseum.org

6 HILTON GARDEN INN

$$$ One of a handful of new hotels opened near the **Pennsylvania Convention Center** in the past few years, the **Hilton Garden Inn** includes 259 spacious rooms, each outfitted with a work space, data ports, a fridge and microwave, and either one king or two double beds. There is a restaurant on premises and dozens within steps of the front door. The location is close to just about everything. ♦ 1100 Arch St. 923.0100; fax 925.0800. www.hiltongardeninn.com

MAGGIANO'S
LITTLE ITALY®

7 MAGGIANO'S LITTLE ITALY

★$$ This popular chain, known for its mega-portions of red-sauce Italian and faux–Little Italy décor, is now open across from the **Pennsylvania Convention Center**. Hopefully the first sign of restaurant activity in the neighborhood dominated by **Chinatown** and the **Reading Terminal**, **Maggiano's** is the quintessential Italian restaurant—you know, the red-and-white-checkered tablecloths, Frank Sinatra and

Restaurants/Clubs: Red | Hotels: Purple | Shops: Orange | Outdoors/Parks: Green | Sights/Culture: Blue

CHILD'S PLAY

With its abundance of museums, parks, and historic sites, Philadelphia provides the ideal combination of fun and education for kids as well as for adults. Here is a list of activities that will keep even restless tykes entertained:

1. Dig for dinosaur bones in a simulated fossil pit at the **Academy of Natural Sciences**.

2. Strut like a mummer at the **Mummer's Museum**.

3. Roar at the rare white lions in the **Philadelphia Zoo**, the nation's oldest zoo.

4. Pick up a starfish and stroke a shark at the **New Jersey State Aquarium** in Camden.

5. Walk through a larger-than-life model of a human heart at the **Franklin Institute**.

6. Watch coins stamped out of strips of metal at the **US Mint**, the largest mint in the world.

7. Clamber through a World War II submarine at the *USS Becuna*.

8. Get lost in a maze at the children's garden at **Longwood Gardens**.

9. Marvel at the medieval armor and weaponry at the **Philadelphia Museum of Art**.

10. Laugh and play with Big Bird, Bert and Ernie, and friends at **Sesame Place**.

Dino tunes, and gigantic portions. Like Mama used to make—if you grew up in South Philly. The extensive menu of southern Italian faves is served family style. There's a $1 bar menu during happy hour. ◆ 12th & Filbert Sts. 567.2020. www.maggianos.com

8 THE GALLERY AT MARKET EAST

If you like the variety and convenience of a suburban shopping mall but want to do your buying in the city, this is the place for you. When the initial phase of this complex was completed in 1977, it was the first major retail building in Philadelphia in more than 40 years. At the time, the idea of putting a retail center in the middle of the city was new and exciting. Now you can find shopping malls like this (with skylit atriums, escalators, glass-enclosed elevator, and fountains) in other urban centers across the country.

Designed by **Bower and Fradley/Bower Lewis Thrower** and **Cope Linder Associates**, the building covers a three-block area, with the main entrance at Ninth and Market Streets. **Strawbridge's** and **Kmart** are the anchor department stores. The other stores (170 of them on four levels) are mostly chain outlets, such as **Radio Shack**, **The Gap**, and **Kay-Bee Toys**, and themed restaurants, such as the **Hard Rock Cafe**. There are three busy food courts. ◆ Daily; open until 8PM W, F. Market St (between N Eighth and N 11th Sts). 625.4962. www.galleryatmarketeast.com

Within The Gallery at Market East:

STRAWBRIDGE'S

If you see lots of people on Market Street clutching bright green shopping bags, you'll know it's Clover Day, one of the monthly sales events at this local retail giant. In 1861, Justus

Strawbridge opened a dry-goods store on what was then known as High Street. He later formed a partnership with Isaac Clothier and launched one of the most successful businesses in Philadelphia. **Strawbridge's** eight-story building dates from 1896 and has been expanded several times, with the last addition in the 1930s. The local chain was sold by the Strawbridge family to the St. Louis–based May Company in 1996. First-rate service and good sales remain hallmarks of the store. ◆ M-Tu, 10AM-7PM; W, F, 9AM-9PM; Th, 10AM-8PM; Sa, 9AM-7PM; Su, noon-6PM. 629.6000. &. www.strawbridges.com

Within Strawbridge's:

THE FOOD HALL

$ Chocolate-chip cookies, smoked-turkey sandwiches, pasta salad, fresh-roasted coffee, chocolates, and excellent breads are all sold in a marketlike setting on the first floor. There are a few tables and chairs where weary shoppers can rest and refuel. ◆ Deli ◆ 629.6000 &

MARKET EAST STATION

You can access the commuter rail lines and subway through **The Gallery** shopping complex. The station entrance is on the mall level. Notice the colorful tile wall mural designed by David Beck. ◆ N 11th and Market Sts. 580.7800. www.septa.org

9 MARKET PLACE EAST

Without this delightful block of five Victorian buildings, also known as the **Mellon Independence Center**, miraculously spared from demolition in the 1970s and later restored, the city would be diminished. Their gay and ornate façades designed and built between 1859 and 1907 by **Collins and Autenreith** create a creamy white wedding cake that profoundly enhances the character of Market Street east of Broad Street. One of the structures is cast iron, and the others are brick with marble or granite sheathings and galvanized iron trim, but their arched windows and common color give the appearance of a single exterior with octagonal towers at either end. Notice the sign, evocative of another era, that reads "Hats Trimmed Free of Charge."

Lit Brothers Department Store occupied the Victorians from 1893 until it went out of business in 1977. In 1987, the buildings were converted into an office and shopping complex, a triumph for preservationists. The first-floor and basement retail sections are situated around an attractive six-story atrium. Be sure to see the splendid paneling by **John Haviland**, designed originally for **Independence Hall**, installed near the elevator lobby. ♦ M-Sa, 10AM-6PM; Su, noon-5PM. 701 Market St (at N Seventh St). 592.8905 &

Within Market Place East:

China Pagoda

$ This is a good place to pick up basic Chinese fare—egg rolls, pepper steak, roast pork with vegetables, lo mein, fried rice, egg foo yong, chop suey, and chow mein—to enjoy in the food court area. ♦ Chinese ♦ Daily, lunch and dinner. 592.1035

Au Bon Pain

★$ Tarragon chicken salad, smoked turkey, and ham are stuffed into croissants—assembly-line style—at this popular chain operation. ♦ French café ♦ M-F, breakfast and lunch. 922.8942. Also at Liberty Place, S 17th St (between Chestnut and Market Sts). 567.9005; S 15th and Ranstead Sts. 567.8539; S 18th and Market Sts. 854.9980. & www.aubonpain.com

10 Philadelphia Marriott Downtown

$$$ Located just across the street from the **Pennsylvania Convention Center**, this mammoth hotel earns high marks for service and amenities, including 24-hour room service. Prices rise when convention business comes to town (room rates typically rise above the $200 mark). For top-drawer noshing, choose **J.W. Steakhouse**; otherwise, there's casual dining at **Allie's American Grill**, a lively scene at **Champions Sports Bar**, and gourmet coffee at a **Starbucks** outlet. Hotel amenities include a 64,000-square-foot conference space, 27 meeting rooms, a fully equipped business center, fitness center, indoor lap pool, whirlpool, massage service, and health club. ♦ 1201 Market St (at N 12th St). 625.2900, 800/320.5744; fax 625.6000. & www.marriott.com

Within the Philadelphia Marriott Downtown:

J.W. Steakhouse

★★$$ Situated on the second floor under an atrium ceiling, this upscale restaurant serves steaks, chops, and seafood at reasonable prices. ♦ Steak ♦ Daily, dinner. Reservations recommended. 625.2900. &

Allie's American Grill

★$ All-American favorites are served family style in this lobby-level eatery, including such Philadelphia specialties as cheesesteaks and "Chinatown flautas" (deep-fried wontons stuffed with chicken, mozzarella, and spices). Breakfast and lunch buffets, and a Sunday brunch, are also offered. ♦ American ♦ M-Sa, breakfast, lunch, and dinner; Su, brunch and dinner. 625.2900. & www.marriott.com

11 Hard Rock Cafe

★$ The rock 'n' roll memorabilia is the calling card at this popular chain—but the food won't let you down either. Order sandwiches, salads, burgers, barbecue—something for everybody. And you'll have fun looking at Madonna's bustier, Bob Dylan's guitar, and Prince's see-through black shirt. ♦ 1113-31 Market St. 235.1000. www.hardrock.com

12 Loews Philadelphia Hotel

$$$$ The former **Philadelphia Saving Fund Society Building** (**PSFS Building**), the first modernist skyscraper in the world and a building revered by architecture lovers for its combination of rich materials—marble, stainless steel, and polished granite—and sleek lines, has been transformed into a 585-room luxury hotel. When Philadelphia architect **George Howe**, also known for the **Bird House** at the **Philadelphia Zoo**, and **Walter Lescaze**, a Swiss architect, finished their building in 1932, it embodied the very latest in European design, referred to as the International style. (It was also the second skyscraper in the world to be air-conditioned.) The design takes full advantage of the building's historical features, including the sculptural curve of the gray granite base and the three-story former banking room, which has been preserved as a dramatic banquet space. The room on the rooftop, formerly used for the board of directors, has been renovated as a spectacular setting for catered events. In addition to a 15,000-square-foot fitness center, spa, and indoor swimming pool, the hotel contains a 360-seat restaurant featuring fine regional American cuisine. ♦ 12 S 12th St (at Market St). 627.1200, 800/23.LOEWS. www.loewshotels.com

---

Restaurants/Clubs: Red | Hotels: Purple | Shops: Orange | Outdoors/Parks: Green | Sights/Culture: Blue

13 THE BALCH INSTITUTE FOR ETHNIC STUDIES

Well-conceived exhibits of photographs and artifacts in the small museum here celebrate the city's ethnic diversity. Learn about the successive waves of immigration to the Philadelphia area, including that of German Jews who arrived in the 18th century and Italians who worked as stonemasons and laborers on the first skyscrapers in the 1920s. Photographs capture the **Headhouse Square** marketplace around 1916 and stooped laborers in early sweatshops. A research library housing 60,000 volumes and 12,000 photographs is in the process of being moved to the **Historical Society of Pennsylvania** at 1300 Locust Street, where it was scheduled to be open to the public for research projects by the fall of 2002. The institute also hosts workshops, film screenings, and lectures. ♦ Admission. Free Sa, 10AM-noon. Museum: M-Sa, 10AM-4PM. Library: Tu, Th, Sa, 10AM-4PM. 18 S Seventh St (between Chestnut and Market Sts). 925.8090. &. www.balchinstitute.org

14 ATWATER KENT MUSEUM, THE HISTORY MUSEUM OF PHILADELPHIA

Objects of everyday life in Philadelphia over 3 centuries are showcased in this museum. The collection includes Native American stone tools, an 18th-century cockroach trap, a wooden pipe that carried water from the **Schuylkill River**, and photographs of some of the city's seedy types in an 1890 rogues' gallery from the **Philadelphia Police Department**. The **Atwater** is now home to the world's largest and most complete collection of Norman Rockwell's illustrations, including the entire collection of *Saturday Evening Post* covers, formerly housed at the **Curtis Center**. **John Haviland** designed the Greek Revival structure (the original home of the **Franklin Institute**), which was completed in 1827. ♦ Admission. Tu-Sa. 15 S Seventh St (between Chestnut and Market Sts). 922.3031. &. www.philadelphiahistory.org

15 LORD & TAYLOR

What had been the **John Wanamaker Store**, a local landmark since 1911, was sold by the Wanamaker family in 1996 and is now **Lord & Taylor**. The store's selling space has been somewhat reduced, but treasured Wanamaker's traditions have been devoutly retained, such as the Christmas light and music show, which delighted generations of Philadelphians, and the bronze statue of an eagle, a meeting place for countless multitudes over the years. Purchased at the 1904 Louisiana Purchase Exposition in St. Louis, the eagle soon became such a Philadelphia icon that the expression "Meet me at the eagle" became part of the city's vernacular. The store's 30,000-pipe organ, which dominated the Grand Court, a lofty work of marble and arches, has also been kept, and is featured in daily concerts, Monday through Saturday, at 11:15AM and 5:15PM.

The building, designed in the Italian Renaissance style by famed Chicago architect **Daniel Burnham**, is a magnificent survivor from a bygone era when department stores looked like palaces. John Wanamaker began his career as a clerk in a trading house on Market Street, eventually becoming a multimillionaire. He built this granite and limestone monolith between 1902 and 1911, with construction proceeding even as he ran his original store on the site. At the time, the concept of selling everything from stationery to lingerie in a single building was still novel. The 1.9 million–square-foot store dazzled the public with a post office, children's playrooms, a books and periodicals department large enough to publish its own newsletter, and pneumatic tubes that carried money from every part of the building to the cashier's office on the second floor. ♦ M-Tu, Th-Sa, 10AM-7PM; W, 10AM-8PM; Su, noon-6PM. S 13th and Market Sts. 241.9000. &. www.lordandtaylor.com

16 COURTYARD BY MARRIOTT

$$$ The historic **City Hall Annex** was built in 1926 and transformed into the unique 17-story, 498-room **Courtyard Hotel** in 1999. Rooms feature extra-large desks, data ports, and two-line phones. The hotel is in a prime location for both business and leisure travelers. ♦ 21 North Juniper St at City Hall. 496.3200; fax 496.3696. www.courtyard.com

17 CHESTNUT STREET

In the early 1970s, city officials closed this street (then one of Philadelphia's premier shopping streets) to car traffic between Eighth and 18th Streets, widened and bricked the sidewalks, and added modern light fixtures and benches. The street was reincarnated as a "transitway" for the exclusive use of buses and pedestrians—which unfortunately coincided with downtown losing business to suburban shopping malls and their ample free parking. **Chestnut Street** is once again open to traffic, and business is on the upswing. West of Broad Street, the street's appearance improves noticeably. Two of the outstanding buildings found there are **Liberty Place** and the old **Jacob Reed's Store**, now a bookstore with a café. Longtime independent retailers include **Boyd's for Men**. ♦ Open to car traffic daily, 7PM-6AM

LET FREEDOM RING: THE STORY OF THE LIBERTY BELL

The story of America's Liberty Bell begins in 1749, when the **State House**'s belfry was built and an order was placed for a bell. In a letter written to the London foundry, where it was cast, State House superintendents Isaac Norris, Thomas Leech, and Edward Warner were quite specific about the bell: "Let the bell be cast by the best workmen, and examine it carefully before it is shipped with the following words, well shaped, in long letters around it, viz.: 'By order of the Assembly of the Province of Pennsylvania, for the State House in the city of Philadelphia, 1752.' And underneath—'Proclaim Liberty through all the land unto all the inhabitants thereof.'—Levit. XXV.10."

The bell arrived in Philadelphia in August 1752, was hung in place, and, when tested, immediately cracked. Two Philadelphians, by the names of Pass and Stow, were hired to repair the bell. The two artisans successfully recast it, and, in the process, determined that the crack was a result of too much copper in the mix.

Pass and Stow completed their work in the spring of 1753, and the recast bell was placed in the State House belfry on 17 April. In celebration, workmen

feasted on beef, cheese, potatoes, bread, and rum that day. But despite the feelings of good cheer, people didn't care for the sound of the recast bell, so Pass and Stow were hired to recast it a second time. To improve the sound, they supposedly added silver to the mix. The 2,080-pound bell was raised again in the first week of June. Today, their bell, the one world knows as the Liberty Bell, may be seen at the new $12.6 million **Liberty Bell Center** on the east side of Sixth Street between Market and Chestnut Streets.

A number of commemorative bells, perhaps as many as 48, have been cast around the country, including one made for Philadelphia in 1876 to honor the 100th anniversary of American independence. That bell was cast in Troy, New York, and it and a new steeple clock were presented to the city by a wealthy citizen named Henry Seybert. The bell was in place to be rung on Independence Day, but again, city fathers didn't like its tone, so it too had to be recast. Philadelphians, it seems, are very picky about their bells. Nevertheless, it is the Seybert bell that booms forth from Independence Hall each hour.

18 NATIONAL ARCHIVES AND RECORDS ADMINISTRATION

A total of 42,000 cubic feet of paper records is housed here, including the papers of the Continental Congress, passenger lists for the ports of Philadelphia and Baltimore between 1800 and 1950, and the federal census records for the entire country between 1790 and 1910. The **Archives** hosts two major exhibits from its collections each year. ♦ Free. M-F; second Sa of every month, 8AM-4PM. US Court House and Post Office Building, 900 Market St (at 9th St). Entrance to National Archives is on Chestnut St (at 9th St). 597.3000. ♿. www.nara.gov

19 MORIMOTO

★★★$$$$ Masaharu Morimoto's collaboration with Philly restaurant scene-stealer Stephen Starr offers East-meets-West cutting-edge Asian cuisine in an eye-popping, high-tech atmosphere that includes pulsating lighting and a wave of exotic bamboo wood overhead. The chef's tasting menu is priced at $80, $100, and $120. Morimoto was the executive chef at Nobu in New York for 6 years before becoming the star of the Japanese-produced *Iron Chef* on the TV Food Network. ♦ 723 Chestnut St. 413.9070. www.morimoto restaurant.com

20 ANGELINA

★★★$$$ Out with the Angel, in with the Angelina. Formerly **Blue Angel**, this modern Italian restaurant features a rosy-hued, sexy bar—decorated wall-to-ceiling with paintings of fleshy, Italian beauties—and an authentic Italian menu by chef Christopher Painter, with the emphasis on simple preparation and fresh ingredients. The restaurant's standout items include the ricotta Caesar, a delicious twist on the traditional fave; homemade pastas like oxtail ravioli with white beans and diced root vegetables; and a Sicilian-style black bass fillet with toasted pine nuts and sun-dried tomatoes. ♦ 706 Chestnut St (between S Seventh and S Eighth Sts). 925.6889

21 EL VEZ

★★★$$ El Vez does a trendy take on regional Mexican food. Tableside guacamole-making, a huge margarita menu, and delicious rare tuna tostadas owe it all to the deft talents of chef José Garces in the kitchen. The bar scene is happening, the margaritas are shaken, never stirred, and seating is first come, first served. ♦ 121 S 13th St (at Sansom St). 928.9800

22 MACCABEAM

★★$ If you tried to get an idea of Philadelphia's demographics from its ethnic restaurants, you would think the Chinese

---

Restaurants/Clubs: Red | Hotels: Purple | Shops: Orange | Outdoors/Parks: Green | Sights/Culture: Blue

population was huge and the Jewish relatively small. In fact, the reverse is true, though this is one of the few *glatt* kosher restaurants in Center City. The tidy storefront with a galley kitchen, framed posters, and black lacquer chairs offers homey Israeli cooking, including turkey *kubba*, a mixture of turkey and cracked wheat formed into a ball and stuffed with pine nuts, and outstanding homemade falafels. ◆ Israeli/American ◆ M-Th, Su, lunch and dinner; F, lunch. 128 S 12th St (between Walnut and Sansom Sts). 922.5922

23 PORTOFINO

★★$$ Rediscovering a classic restaurant is like remembering what it's like to fall in love all over again. For more than 30 years, Portofino has brought northern and central Italian cuisine to Philadelphia diners, with owner Ralph Berarducci ever present in the front of the house and chefs Raymond Moscardelli and Bob Cholminski keeping the kitchen in tip-top shape. Newly renovated, the restaurant features traditional and updated Italian specialties. The veal is outstanding, the pasta al dente and perfectly sauced, and the service wonderfully attentive. ◆ 1227 Walnut St. 731.2000

24 WALNUT STREET THEATER

Built in 1809, the oldest theater in continuous operation in the country is located here in a restored Greek Revival building designed by **John Haviland**. The theater filled a void in a city slow to embrace the stage, and soon, it became a nationally recognized center for the dramatic arts. Many famous actors graced its stages, including Sarah Bernhardt, the Barrymores, Lunt and Fontanne, the Marx Brothers, Katharine Hepburn, and Helen Hayes.

In 1983, the theater opened its own nonprofit production company, drawing actors from around the country. Its main theater seats more than 1,000 and hosts a five-show season, usually with a big Christmastime production and a new musical at the end of the season. A mix of comedy and drama round out the rest of the year. Small, intimate productions are staged in an 80-seat studio theater between January and May. ◆ Box office: M-Sa, 10AM-6PM; Su, noon-4PM. 829-833 Walnut St (at S Ninth St). 574.3550. www.wstonline.org

25 PILEGGI BOUTIQUE

Good-looking womenswear with an emphasis on younger New York and European fashion designers is sold in this store that adjoins a trendy beauty salon. The owners keep the selection unusual and fresh, favoring designers such as Vivienne Tam, Dolce & Gabbana, and Teenflo. There's also a large selection of costume jewelry. Prices range from moderate to expensive. ◆ M-Sa. 715 Walnut St (between S Seventh and S Eighth Sts). 922.3526

26 AOI

★$ For a sampling of the food here, order the 20-piece sushi-sashimi combination entrée. There are also buckwheat noodle dishes, chicken teriyaki, beef tempura, and for dessert, fried ice cream and fruit tempura. ◆ Japanese ◆ M-F, lunch and dinner; Sa, Su, dinner. 1210 Walnut St (between S 12th and S 13th Sts). 985.1838

26 RODEWAY INN

$$ This delightful family-run 19th-century establishment includes 25 guest rooms, outfitted for the business traveler. The location is ideal, just a stone's throw from the **Pennsylvania Convention Center** and historic sights. Ask for a room at the back to avoid traffic noise. ◆ 1208 Walnut St. 546.7000; fax 546.7573. www.rodeway.com

27 CARIBOU

★$ This homey Parisian-style café with a large storefront window, marble tables, and an amiable French-speaking owner offers croissants and muffins for breakfast, and *croque monsieur*, salmon mousse, and croissant sandwiches for lunch. Try the satisfying version of the standard French onion soup, vegetarian lasagna, chicken cordon bleu, or baked escargot for dinner. ◆ French ◆ Daily, lunch and dinner. 1126 Walnut St (between S 11th and S 12th Sts). 625.9535. www.cariboucafe.com

28 FORREST THEATER

Phantom of the Opera, *Les Misérables*, and most of the other big hits eventually make their way to this stage, which has been hosting major Broadway shows for more than 60 years. The 1,800-seat theater opened in 1927 as an offshoot of the original **Forrest** at Broad and Sansom Streets. ◆ Box office: Tu-Sa, 10AM-8PM, and Su, noon-6PM, when a show is playing; M-Sa, 10AM-6PM, for pre-opening sales. 1114 Walnut St (at Quince St). 923.1515 ♿

29 CLARENCE MOORE HOUSE

Built as the home of businessman Clarence Moore in 1890, this delightfully complex mansion was designed by **Wilson Eyre**, an Italian-born architect known for his playful, imaginative residential structures. The exterior is an appealing mixture of rough-cut and smooth limestone, brick, and slate, and features a Venetian loggia, French tower, arched windows, sculptures, and gargoyles. The building now houses offices. ◆ 1321 Locust St (at S Juniper St)

30 GIRASOLE

★★★$$ This newly remodeled trattoria, its name the Italian word for "sunflower," will seem especially appealing on a gray winter night, with golden walls and summery lighting. Chef Rene Vergara and owner Franco Lovino maintain consistently high standards. Pastas—orecchiette with broccoli rabe and sun-dried tomatoes, and farfal with smoked salmon, to name a couple—are made by hand, not by food processor; carpaccio, prepared warm or cold, is served with arugula and Parmesan or smoked mozzarella and endive; and chicken paillard, veal with mozzarella and arugula, and daily fish entrées are made at the grill. Most popular of all are the pizzas, baked in a wood-burning oven lined with volcanic lava. Choose from a variety of toppings, including arugula and prosciutto or four cheeses. ♦ Italian ♦ M-F, lunch and dinner; Sa, Su, dinner. Reservations recommended. 1305 Locust St (at S 13th St). 985.4659

31 DEUX CHEMINÉES

★★★★$$$$ This first-class French restaurant was named for the original building and its two huge fireplaces. Fire destroyed the old location on Camac Street in the late 1980s, and today the restaurant occupies a former town house designed by **Frank Furness**, with five fireplaces and four elegant dining rooms furnished with silks, Oriental rugs, and fine old portraits. Chef-owner Fritz Blank produces a changing fixed-price menu that includes soup, salad, entrée, vegetable, dessert, and coffee. Crab velouté soup laced with Scotch whiskey, poached asparagus with orange-onion vinaigrette and curried whipped cream, rack of lamb *à la périgourdine*, and steamed Norwegian salmon in beurre blanc sauce were on the menu during a recent visit. ♦ French ♦ Tu-Sa, dinner. Jacket and tie requested. Reservations recommended. 1221 Locust St (at S Camac St). 790.0200. www.deuxchem.com

32 RISTORANTE LA BUCA

★★★$$$ Descend an indoor staircase a few steps from **Washington Square** and you'll find yourself inside a grottolike basement with brick and stucco walls, wine racks, elegant brocades, pottery, and baskets. This restaurant draws businesspeople at lunch and a well-heeled older clientele in the evening. The items on the somewhat staid Italian menu are executed with high-quality ingredients, and the kitchen's strengths are manifested in grilled foods: Sweet, smoky-tasting langostine; veal loin with radicchio; and grilled chicken are among the highlights. ♦ Italian ♦ M-F, lunch and dinner; Sa, dinner. Jacket and tie requested. Reservations recommended. 711 Locust St (between Washington Sq W and S Eighth St). 928.0556. www.ristlabuca.com

33 LIBRARY COMPANY OF PHILADELPHIA

Founded by Benjamin Franklin and his associates in 1731, this organization maintains the largest collection of rare books in the area, including the libraries of James Logan and Benjamin Rush. When the Continental Congress, Constitutional Convention, and US Congress were meeting in Philadelphia between 1774 and 1800, the **Library Company** served as the Library of Congress. Stop in to see the changing exhibits on Philadelphia's history. ♦ M-F. 1314 Locust St (between S 13th and S Juniper Sts). 546.3181. & www.librarycompany.org

34 CAMAC STREET

Though William Penn hoped that each house in his "Greene Country Town" would be surrounded by open space, the lots he sold to various individuals were soon divided and subdivided. The city's well-to-do built large dwellings on the main streets, whereas workers erected modest row houses on the smaller streets and back alleys. (**Panama, Iseminger, Jessup,** and **Quince Streets,** which lie just west of Washington Square, are only a few of the narrow, almost hidden, pockets of tiny houses and trees within steps of the city's skyscrapers.) **Camac** (pronounced "Cuh-*mack*") **Street** offers a mix of early-19th-century row houses. Between **Spruce** and **Locust Streets,** Camac becomes the "Street of Clubs," so nicknamed because it's a haven for the city's oldest artists' organizations. Some of the clubs remain, buoyed by the large numbers of artists drawn to the neighborhood since World War II. (The **Franklin Inn Club,** between Locust and **Walnut** Streets, is a literary club founded in 1902—Christopher Morley and Howard Pyle were dues-paying members.) ♦ Between S 12th and S 13th Sts

35 PHILADELPHIA SKETCH CLUB

Thomas Eakins, N.C. Wyeth, and Thomas Anshutz all belonged to this 137-year-old artists' club. Regular exhibits are open to the public. ♦ During exhibits: F-Su, 1PM-4PM. 235 S Camac St (between Spruce and Locust Sts). 545.9298. www.sketchclub.org

35 THE CHARLOTTE CUSHMAN CLUB

Started in 1907 (at another location) as a boardinghouse for actresses, this private theater club continues as a gathering place for people in the theater business and their avid followers. The club's collection of memorabilia includes Sarah Bernhardt's crown from *Medea,*

Restaurants/Clubs: Red | Hotels: Purple | Shops: Orange | Outdoors/Parks: Green | Sights/Culture: Blue

antique theater bills, and a grand piano donated by Fanny Brice. "Your responsibility is to speak with clarity, wit, and eloquence, and you never know what might happen," the voice on the club's answering machine used to advise. Past recipients of the annual Charlotte Cushman Award (in honor of the famous 19th-century actress) include Katharine Hepburn, Richard Burton, Helen Hayes, and Julie Harris. Though there are no regular hours for the public, it's worth calling in advance to arrange a visit. ♦ Visits by appointment. 239 S Camac St (between Spruce and Locust Sts). 735.4676

36 PLASTIC CLUB

A small sign on the door points out that this is the location of the country's oldest art club for women, opened in 1897. (At that time, the word *plastic* was commonly used to refer to an artist's molding of various materials and to the idea that a piece of art is never completely finished.) The club hosts one or two exhibits a year that are open to the public. ♦ 247 S Camac St (between Spruce and Locust Sts). 545.9324. www.libertynet.org/plasticc

37 THE INN PHILADELPHIA

★★$$ Fine dining is offered in style at this quiet, elegantly appointed Center City restaurant, housed in two former private homes built in 1824 and 1825, respectively. The first-floor lobby and bar, lit by candlelight and two fireplaces, leads to three second-floor dining rooms—**Franklin**, and smoke-free **Green** and **Gallery**—where entrées include Australian rack of lamb, pork roulade, and chilled poached salmon. In spring and summer, open-air dining in the **Secret Garden**, which dates to 1822, is available. Ask about the house ghost, a form seen by several guests and staff. ♦ American ♦ Tu-Sa, dinner; Su, brunch and dinner. Reser-

Benjamin Franklin, destined to become Philadelphia's most famous citizen, arrived in the city as a 17-year-old apprentice printer in 1723.

Philadelphia's first corrupt politician was Colonel William Markham, William Penn's cousin. While serving as Penn's deputy governor, between 1693 and 1699, Markham offered safe haven to pirates, including the notorious Captain Kidd, for a price of 100 British pounds for every crew member.

The first European to set foot in what is now Philadelphia was probably Cornelius Hendricksen of the Netherlands in 1615. While exploring the Delaware River, or the South River, as Henry Hudson had called it, Hendricksen discovered and named Philadelphia's other river, the Schuylkill, a word meaning "hidden stream."

vations recommended. 251-253 S Camac St (between Spruce and Locust Sts). 732.2339. www.innphiladelphia.com

38 VETRI

★★★★$$$$ Chef/owner Marc Vetri creates truly innovative regional Italian cuisine—very much like what Mario Batali is doing at Babbo in New York's Greenwich Village. Interesting ingredients, beautifully presented and lovingly served—an expensive night out, but worth every penny. Your best bet is the chef's tasting menu, $65, $90 with wine. There are only 35 highly coveted seats, so be sure to reserve in advance. ♦ 1312 Spruce St. 732.3478

39 VALANNI

★★$$ Pull up a seat at the bar or settle into one of the cozy banquettes at this comfortable Center City restaurant, and you're in for a treat. Chef R. Evan Turney has crafted a menu he's calling Medi-Latin—specialties drawn from South and Latin America as well as from the Mediterranean coast. Try the maple-walnut-crusted duck breast, the paella, and the pan-seared bay scallops. There are also small plates to share, tapas-style. The mezze plate is excellent. And don't miss sampling the Latin cocktails that are a house specialty, classics like mojitos and caipirinhas. ♦ 1229 Spruce St. 215/790.9494. www.valanni.com

40 PORTICO ROW

In the 1830s a speculator hired architect **Thomas Ustick Walter**, famed for his design of the Capitol dome in Washington, DC, to draw up plans for a block of elegant row houses in what was then a very posh area. Compared with earlier homes built closer to the **Delaware River**, the residences here were extremely large, with protruding porticos (each is actually an entrance to separate houses) and marble columns distinguishing their brick exteriors. The interiors of these private residences, which were restored in the 1980s, are richly detailed with walnut, mahogany, and marble. ♦ 900-930 Spruce St (between S Ninth and S 10th Sts)

41 PENNSYLVANIA HOSPITAL

From its **Spruce Street** entrance, there's no hint of the central role this hospital played in colonial times. But approach the complex from **Pine Street** and you'll get a sense of its significance. The lovely brick building with a rotunda was the country's first full-fledged hospital, and its domestic scale, at once modest and majestic, proves a dramatic contrast to more modern hospitals. Designed by **Samuel Rhoads** (a friend of Benjamin Franklin, who helped raise funds for the building), the hospital was built in three parts: The **East Wing** was completed in 1756; the **West Wing**, 2 years later; and the center building, an outstanding example of Federal architecture, opened in 1804.

Thomas Bond, an eminent colonial physician, founded the hospital, initiating the first clinical studies of medicine in the country when he took his students on hospital rounds. Early modern surgical techniques were performed in the domed amphitheater at the top of the center building, which now houses the **History of Nursing Museum** and the **Historic Library of Pennsylvania Hospital**, said to be the country's oldest medical library. Benjamin West's painting *Christ Healing the Sick in the Temple* hangs in the gallery pavilion in the **Cathcart Building**, and there's a lovely 18th-century herb garden on the hospital's original grounds on Pine Street.

For information on 30-minute self-guided tours, stop by the marketing office on the second floor of the **Pine Building** (enter on Spruce Street). ♦ Self-guided tours M-F; group tours available by special arrangement. S Eighth St (between Pine and Spruce Sts). 829.3971. www.pahosp.com

42 SAHBABA

★$ Brick walls and café tables create a casual atmosphere for a quick bite to eat. Order chicken kebab, falafel, or hummus at the counter, and they'll bring it to your table. ♦ Middle Eastern ♦ M-Sa, lunch and dinner. 1240 Pine St (at S 13th St). 735.8111 ♿

43 ANTIQUE ROW

In the early 1800s, cabinetmakers who set up shop on Pine Street crafted some of the finest furniture of the century. But when factories started churning out furniture, the street turned to the antiques trade and before long, earned a reputation for dusty, intriguing shops and idiosyncratic dealers. Some of the finest antiques in the country have been bought and sold on these blocks, along with (so the story goes) a few rather ingenious fakes. In recent years, antiques shopping at auction houses and traveling shows has increased, but Pine Street is still a prime haunt for veteran shoppers who thrive on ferreting out obscure treasures. You'll find more than a dozen stores stocked with furniture, lamps, and accessories, as well as boutiques offering an eclectic selection of 1950s kitsch, estate jewelry, contemporary painted furniture, and South American crafts. ♦ Pine St (between S Ninth and S 13th Sts)

44 JEFFREY L. BIBER ANTIQUES

This shop offers an appealing selection of bronze statuettes, paintings, lamps, vases, and lots of silver (letter openers, vases, toilet articles, and tea sets). European antiques are also sold—perhaps a Louis XVI walnut settee,

a Chippendale looking glass, or an 18th-century Scottish grandfather clock. ♦ M-Sa, 11AM-5PM. 1030 Pine St (between S 10th and S 11th Sts). 574.3633

45 M. FINKEL AND DAUGHTER

A striking quilt typically hangs in the window of this refined shop, which has turned to catalogs to market much of its stock of samplers, needlework, and, of course, antique quilts. The store also carries expensive, high-quality American antique furniture and decorative objects. ♦ M-F; Sa, Su, by appointment. 936 Pine St (at S 10th St). 627.7797. www.finkel antiques.com

CHINATOWN

The area's Chinese roots date back to the mid-19th century, when the first Chinese came to Philadelphia from Guangdong Province. In the 1860s, Lee Fong opened a laundry at 913 Race Street, the first business in what is now known as Chinatown. Today the six-block area is home to dozens of Chinese restaurants, grocery stores, shops, churches, a cultural center, a hotel, fortune-cookie bakeries, an Asian bank, and about 3,000 people, a fraction of Philadelphia's Asian community.

Chinatown is a dense little neighborhood that has had to fight for its survival. After years of vying for space with the city's red-light district, it was later threatened by the expansion of the Vine Street Expressway and the construction of the **Pennsylvania Convention Center** right next door. But, so far, so good—it seems that conventioneers often crave a quick order of shrimp fried rice. Though Chinatown has much more to offer than restaurants, most visitors come here to eat, whether it be Chinese, Vietnamese, Malaysian, Taiwanese, Burmese, or Thai fare. There are a number of good places, and prices are always reasonable. Finding street parking can be difficult, so resign yourself to paying for a space in one of the nearby lots if you don't find anything after a couple of swings around the area.

46 VIETNAM

★★★$$ More delicate than Chinese cuisine, Vietnamese food doesn't get better than at this friendly restaurant, owned by Benny Lai and his family. A Chinatown favorite with a polished ambiance a cut above most local joints, **Vietnam** showcases *pho* noodles in veggie broth, an outstanding barbecue platter, vegetarian spring rolls, noodle dishes spiked with lemongrass and cilantro, steamed fish, and more. ♦ 221 N 11th St (between Race and Vine Sts) 592.1163. www.eatatvietnam.com

46 LEE HOW FOOK

★★$$ Refreshing lemon chicken, steamed sea bass, and hacked fried chicken with seasoned salt are among the nice and light dishes served

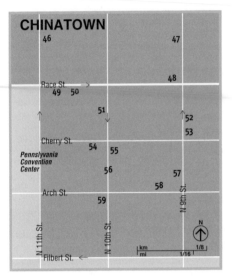

CHINATOWN

49 JOY TSIN LAU

★$$ The gaudy red décor, featuring columns festooned with dragons, tanks of live fish, and lots of mirrors, is quite a backdrop for a traditional Chinese restaurant. Moo shu pork, roast duck, *wu-nan*–style lamb, and lemon shrimp are among the dozens of listings. Whole lobster is also available, and dim sum, offered daily, includes stuffed crab claws and shrimp dumplings. ♦ Chinese ♦ Daily, lunch and dinner. 1026 Race St (between N 10th and N 11th Sts). 592.7227. www.phillychinatown.com/joytsinlau.htm

50 CLARION SUITES

$$ The only place to stay in the heart of Chinatown is this 96-suite hotel on the National Register of Historic Places, a restored Victorian building that was originally home of the Heywood Brothers Furniture Company, producers of the first American bentwood rocker more than a century ago. Rooms have exposed-brick walls and oversize windows. A complimentary continental breakfast buffet is served every morning. ♦ 1010 Race St (between N 10th and N 11th Sts). 922.1730, 800/628.8932; fax 922.6258. www.clarioninn.com

51 IMPERIAL INN

★$$ If you've never had dim sum (Chinese finger foods in a variety of wrappings, sauces, and dumplings), you can get a good introduction here. Choices on the dim sum carts rolled around by servers at lunchtime range from spareribs, steamed dumplings, and a chewy Chinese version of lasagna to the more exotic chicken feet in brown sauce. The massive restaurant has one of those booklike menus packed with all the Cantonese, Szechuan, and Mandarin standards, but it's better to wait until the cart rolls by and you can just point at what looks good to you. ♦ Chinese ♦ Daily, lunch and dinner. 142 N 10th St (between Cherry and Race Sts). 627.5588

at this spartan Chinese restaurant. Bring your own beer or wine. Dim sum on Sunday is the best. ♦ Chinese ♦ Tu-Su, lunch and dinner. No credit cards. 219 N 11th St (between Race and Vine Sts). 925.7266. www.leehowfook.com

46 BAR SAIGON

Benny Lai opened this third-floor lounge upstairs from his family-owned Vietnam Restaurant in the fall of 2004, and the scene is cooler than cool—more Old City than Chinatown. Not only do hungry diners have a place to wait for their tables instead of spilling out onto the street, but the vibe is sophisticated, the sound system—including plasma TVs—is state of the art, and the drinks are top shelf. There's even a locker to store your own bottle, if you really want to feel at home. ♦ 221 N 11th St (between Race and Vine Sts). 592.1163

47 SANG KEE PEKING DUCK HOUSE

★★$ The dishes here are a cut above those served at neighboring restaurants, though the dining room can get noisy and crowded. Try the shrimp with black pepper sauce, spicy beef and eggplant, or chicken in black-bean sauce. Regulars recommend the noodles with ginger and scallions, and the huge servings of wonton noodle or vegetable soup are a meal in their own right. ♦ Chinese ♦ Daily, lunch and dinner. 238 N Ninth St (between Race and Vine Sts). 925.7532. Also at Reading Terminal Market, 51 N 12th St. 922.3930. www.phillychinatown.com/sangkee.htm

48 JOE'S PEKING DUCK HOUSE

★★$ A select Chinese menu is available in this proverbial hole in the wall. Best bets are crispy duck in its natural juices; mussels, in a variety of Asian sauces; and dumplings. ♦ Chinese ♦ Daily, lunch and dinner. 925 Race St (between N Ninth and N 10th Sts). 922.3277

51 TING WONG RESTAURANT

★★$ Nothing fancy about this spare Chinese restaurant, but you'll be concentrating on the food, not the atmosphere. **Ting Wong** offers such Hong Kong specialties as barbecued pork ribs, pan-fried noodles, and traditional favorites like steamed sea bass and sesame chicken. What's different about Ting Wong is that the restaurant is open for breakfast. You can have congee—the Chinese answer to cream of wheat—flavored with extras like roast pork, shrimp, preserved egg, and squid, for an average of $3.50. Beats having Wheaties any day. ♦ 138 N 10th St (between Cherry and Race Sts). 928.1883. www.phillychinatown.com/tingwong.htm

52 RAY'S CAFE & TEA HOUSE

★★$ Never will you see coffee served with more finesse than in this compact, contemporary café, which serves specialty coffees and Taiwanese cuisine. The coffee beans are roasted daily, and water is heated in an elaborate glass siphon over a tiny flame—all very mysterious and elegant. Your small, expensive cup of coffee comes in a china cup or exotic mug on a delicate wooden tray, with a gold spoon and a butter cookie that's topped with sugar sprinkles. Daily coffee specials range from Jamaican blue mountain to Brazilian Bourbon Santos, Sumatra Mandheling, Yemen Mocha, and plain Colombian. The "amazing iced coffee" takes 12 hours to prepare, as spring water drips, drop by drop, through a basketball-size crystal ball. No hot water is used in the process, so the resulting beverage lacks bitterness. The Taiwanese menu features excellent dumplings stuffed with vegetables or pork and cabbage; and the house noodle soup is a meal in itself, thick with shrimp, pork, chicken, egg, and vegetables. Rice noodles come with stir-fried pork and vegetables. The place is bright and clean, compared with many of the restaurants in this neighborhood. Bring your own wine or beer. ♦ Coffeehouse/Taiwanese ♦ Daily, lunch and dinner. 141 N Ninth St (between Cherry and Race Sts). 922.5122

53 HARMONY CHINESE VEGETARIAN

★★$$ All the "meat" and "seafood" dishes here are imitations fashioned from wheat gluten and soy protein, using no real meat or fish. The "shrimp" may not taste like it was just pulled from the Atlantic, but it's tasty. Bring your own libations and enjoy the cozy, small dining rooms. ♦ Chinese vegetarian ♦ M-F, lunch and dinner; Sa, Su, dinner. 135 N Ninth St (between Cherry and Race Sts). 627.4520

54 CHERRY STREET CHINESE VEGETARIAN

★$$ It doesn't look Jewish—and, indeed, it's thoroughly Chinese—but this pleasant pastel room is deemed kosher (except on Saturday) by the city's rabbis. You'll see pork, beef, and poultry on the menu, but it's all made from wheat gluten. Yet another place to bring your own beer and wine. ♦ Chinese vegetarian ♦ M-F, lunch and dinner; Sa, Su, dinner. 1010 Cherry St (between N 10th and N 11th Sts). 923.3663

55 PENANG MALAYSIAN CUISINE

★★★$$ This is the place in town for spicy Malaysian cuisine, a meld of bold Thai and Asian flavors that employ fiery chilies, a powerful blend of curry, and lots of garlic to get the job done. Order the house special crab with spicy chile and dried shrimp sauce, and you know it's fresh—the chef pulls it live out of the tank up front. Appetizers such as Indian pancake, baby oyster omelette, and spicy crispy squid and entrées that include spicy Thai chicken, Malaysian-style spareribs, and salted fish with Chinese broccoli seem to satisfy all. ♦ Malaysian ♦ Daily, lunch and dinner. 117 N 10th St (between Arch and Cherry Sts). 413.2531. www.phillychinatown.com/penang.htm

56 GATE

This decorative arch is hard to miss as you stroll down 10th Street. It's one of the most attractive landmarks in Chinatown, a neighborhood with lots of commercial signs but almost no outdoor artwork. The arch was a joint project between Philadelphia and its Chinese sister city, Tianjin. Chinese artisans completed it in 1984 with materials brought from Tianjin. ♦ N 10th St (between Arch and Cherry Sts). www.phillychinatown.com

57 RANGOON BURMESE RESTAURANT

★$ The city's only Burmese restaurant offers a tempting menu. Try crispy taro roots or Burmese-style wonton or one of several salads, including string bean and peanut salad, followed by beef mint kebab or curried fish cake. ♦ Burmese ♦ Daily, lunch and dinner. 112 N Ninth St (between Arch and Cherry Sts). 829.8939. www.phillychinatown.com/rangoon.htm

58 SIAM CUISINE

★★$$ Cold grilled beef salad, jumbo shrimp and rice noodles, Thai herbal cake, and grilled chicken have kept this restaurant busy for more than 10 years. Linen tablecloths—still a rarity in Chinatown—and pastel walls distinguish the large dining room. ♦ Thai ♦ M-Sa, lunch and dinner; Su, dinner. 925 Arch St (between N Ninth and N 10th Sts). 922.7135. www.phillychinatown.com/siamcuisine.htm

59 JOSEPH POON

★★$$ The ever excitable Joe Poon, whose **Joseph Poon Asian Fusion** restaurant is known for its healthful and delicious Chinese cuisine, also happens to be the culinary spokesperson for the National Watermelon Board. Which is why he was on the *Tonight Show* a few summers ago, carving a watermelon in the shape of Jay Leno's head. Now that's talent. ♦ 1002 Arch St. 928.9333. www.josephpoon.com

BROAD STREET/SOUTH PHILADELPHIA

Philadelphia wears Broad Street like a fine old tuxedo. Twelve miles long and 69 feet wide, this grand avenue lined with some of the city's best architecture seems ready-made for parades and presidential motorcades. Most of the buildings date from the late 19th and early 20th centuries, recalling a time when the area was the city's nerve center of banking, business, and local government. Though many businesses have relocated to the modern glass and steel skyscrapers to the west, Broad Street remains a prestigious address as well as a hub of activity.

A walk south along this street can stir memories of Philadelphia as it was before the 1940s, with all its self-confidence, hopes, and pretensions. Highlights include the **Museum of American Art of the Pennsylvania Academy of the Fine Arts**, in a spectacular Victorian designed by Philadelphia architect **Frank Furness**; City Hall, a Second Empire colossus and the largest municipal building in the world; the **Union League**, an elegant club for the city's conservative elite since the Civil War; the **Land Title Building**, an early skyscraper of classic proportions; and the famed **Academy of Music**, the oldest concert hall in the country and home to the **Philadelphia Orchestra**. Also on this stretch of Broad are the opulent exterior of the former **Bellevue Stratford Hotel**, now a hotel, shopping, and office complex, which dresses up its surroundings like a fancy bow tie; and the **Girard Trust Company** building, a classical temple in marble transformed into a hospitality focal point by the tony **Ritz-Carlton** hotel.

Broad Street, from **Susquehanna Avenue** in the north to **Washington Avenue** in the south, is now called the **Avenue of the Arts**. More than 16 venues for the performing arts are either open for business or on the drawing board, a project with a price tag of more than $350 million. The Philadelphia Orchestra, **Pennsylvania Ballet, Opera Company of Philadelphia, Wilma Theater, University of the Arts**, and **Philadelphia Clef Club of the Performing Arts** already call the avenue home. The latest addition is the stunning $265 million **Kimmel Center for the Performing Arts**, but face-lifts for existing buildings are ongoing. The avenue features patterned granite sidewalk slabs, old-fashioned street lamps, landscaping, and granite curbs.

Just south of South Street, Broad enters—what else?—South Philadelphia, a neighborhood with a distinct working-class personality. In the early years of the 20th century, many immigrant groups settled here, with Italians and a colorful array of Asian cultures dominating the neighborhood today. South Philly Italian style is characterized by neat rows of brick houses with metal awnings, spaghetti and meatballs, Mario Lanza, Mummers, the **Italian Market**, and more than its share of funeral homes. Increasing numbers of *pho* noodle houses, Asian supermarkets, and Vietnamese signage mark the neighborhood's changing population. The best walking routes are in the vicinity of the Italian Market at Ninth and Christian Streets. Drive or take the subway even farther into South Philadelphia to reach the city's sports centers, **Wachovia Spectrum**, the brand-new **Citizen's Bank Park**, and **Lincoln Financial Field**, homes of the **Phillies, Eagles, Flyers**, and **76ers**.

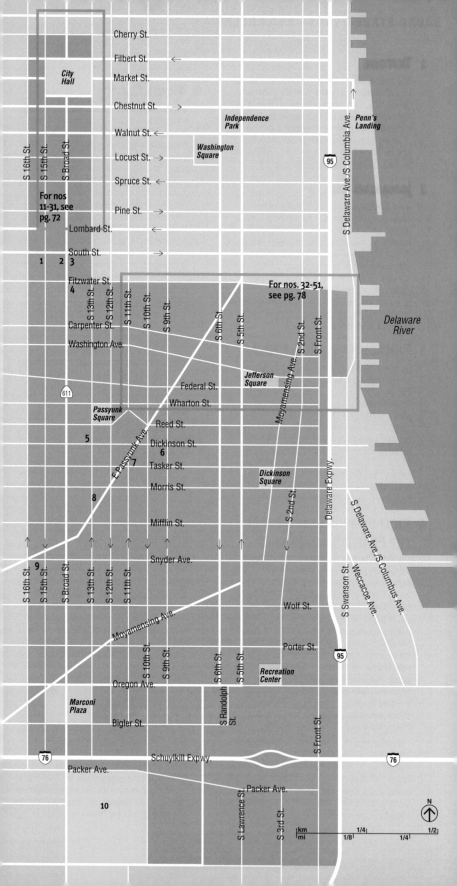

1 TRITONE

This casual watering hole offers a small stage for live music that draws a rotating lineup of bands, DJs, and other performing types most nights Wednesday through Saturday. The bar is friendly and casual, attracting a diverse mix of locals from the neighborhood. Standard pub fare is served until 1 AM. ♦ 1508 South St. 545.0475. www.tritonebar.com

2 JAMAICAN JERK HUT

★★$ Chef-owner Nicola Shirley has been cooking up spicy jerked chicken and fish, curried goat, and meat pies from her native Jamaica at this modest South Street restaurant for close to 7 years. When the weather is fine, a steel band entertains out back. Shirley is in the process of writing a combination cookbook and travel guide to Jamaica. Until your next visit to her homeland, the Jamaican Jerk Hut will have to hold you over. ♦ 1436 South St. 545.8644

3 PHILADELPHIA ARTS BANK

Formerly the **South Philadelphia National Bank**, renovated by **Mitchel Kurtz Architect PC**, this theater hosts an eclectic mix of the performing arts, from dance concerts and wind ensembles to film festivals and classical plays. In case you have trouble finding the building, look up 10 stories for a huge red Art Deco sign lighting the Philadelphia sky. Discounted evening parking is available nearby. ♦ Box office: M-F, 10AM-6PM; Su, noon-4PM. 601 S Broad St (at South St). 545.0590. www.uarts.edu/newhub.html

4 PHILADELPHIA CLEF CLUB OF THE PERFORMING ARTS

The Clef Club was founded in 1966 as the social unit of Musicians' Protective Local 274 of the American Federation of Unions, a black local started at a time when African-American musicians were denied access and representation in the white-dominated local here, as in many other American cities. The club quickly became a haven for jazz lovers as well as some of the greatest exponents of the art, boasting as members John Coltrane, Shirley Scott, Philly Joe Jones, and the Heath brothers; Philly native Dizzy Gillespie always stopped in when he was in town, as did out-of-towners Duke Ellington, Sarah Vaughan, Dinah Washington, and Max Roach.

The club's new 16,000-square-foot, $3.5 million building in the Avenue of the Arts development features a 220-seat performance hall, members' lounge, gift shop, educational wing with class-rooms and practice rooms, library, and catering facilities and is fast becoming one of the most significant jazz performance venues in this jazz-loving town. ♦ 736-38 S Broad St (at Fitzwater St). 893.9912. www.clefclubofjazz.8m.com

5 VICTOR CAFE

★★$$$ Waiters regularly break into song in this special restaurant, founded in 1925 by the late John DiStefano and named after the recording company. (A replica of the RCA Victor mascot, Nipper, stands guard above the door.) Starched linens cover the tables, pictures of opera greats decorate the walls, and a back room houses a collection of 20,000 records. This is how it works: Recorded opera music plays until a waiter rings a little bell; then a record starts—perhaps an old show tune, more likely an aria—and the waiter begins to sing. The scene is repeated every 20 minutes or so. Most of the performing waiters are opera students or professionals between contracts.

The kitchen's ambitions aren't always fulfilled, but you can't go wrong with the pasta dishes, including specialties like goat-cheese ravioli and spinach fettuccine in a champagne cream sauce. The vocalizing is memorable and perfect for special occasions—the waitstaff sing a mean "Happy Birthday." ♦ Italian ♦ Daily, dinner. Reservations recommended; jacket and tie requested. 1303 Dickinson St (between S 13th and S Broad Sts). 468.3040. www.victorcafe.com

6 IO E TU

★★$$ "You And I" is the name of this comfortable little restaurant close to South Philadelphia's famous **Italian Market**. Its two cozy dining rooms are invitingly romantic. Tables are granite-topped and etched glass dividers separate the two rooms. It also has a full-service bar (no seats at the bar). Naples-born Giovanni and Concetta Varallo offer a fine selection of authentic Italian cuisine: whole-wheat spaghetti with crabmeat and anchovies in onion sauce; homemade fusilli with Bolognese sauce; veal topped with prosciutto and sauced with wine; and a seafood dish of lobster, scallops, shrimp, clams, and mussels—in a light marinara sauce. Chef Varallo insists on preparing every dish to order, so there is usually a bit of a wait; but it's worth every second. ♦ Italian ♦ Tu-Su, dinner. 1514 S Ninth St (between Tasker and Dickinson Sts). 271.3906

7 TRE SCALINI

★★$$ Despite its underwhelming surroundings, the cuisine at this South Philly BYOB trattoria is not your typical red-gravy fare. A tasty bouillabaisse, grilled polenta and broccoli rabe, squid-ink pappardelle, and shrimp in a tomato crabmeat sauce are a few specialties of the house. All desserts are imported from Italy. ♦ 1533 11th St (at Tasker St). 551.3870

8 MARRA'S

★$ Philadelphia's first pizzeria now serves veal, chicken, and pasta in every Southern Italian variation—but stick with the pizza. Ease into one of the old red upholstered booths, ask for the Marra Special, and sit back and anticipate the classic, thin South Philly pie with mushrooms, pepperoni, and roasted peppers. Take a look at the oven in the foyer, made with bricks brought from Naples more than 70 years ago. South Philly lore has it that the bricks get hotter than their American counterparts. ◆ Italian ◆ Tu-Su, lunch and dinner. No credit cards. 1734 E Passyunk Ave (between Morris and S 12th Sts). 339.9042

9 MELROSE DINER

★★$ People from all walks of life frequent this South Philadelphia institution known for its comfort food, 24-hour breakfast, shared booths, and friendly waitresses—they'll all call you "hon." The diner food is predictable but tasty—try the meat loaf, homemade mashed potatoes, and warm apple pie next time you're in need of a culinary hug. The Melrose buys steaks from the same purveyor as many of the fancy steak houses—and serves them up at half the price. Try the cheesecake—it's among the best in the city. ◆ Diner ◆ Daily, 24 hours. No credit cards accepted. 1501 Snyder Ave (at S 15th St). 467.6644. www.melrose-diner.com

10 SPORTS COMPLEX

At the far end of South Philadelphia, the residential streets empty into sports-fan heaven, the site of two brand-new stadiums: the 43,500-seat **Citizen's Bank Park**, home to the Phillies, and the $512 million **Lincoln Financial Field**, home to as many as 68,532 Eagles fans. Both parks are state of the art, offering improved seats and sight lines, dramatically improved entertainment systems, exterior plazas, and lots more luxury seating. Citizen's Bank Park is open on the outfield side, offering a terrific view of the city skyline. Check out the wall of fame in the ground-level pavilion, a historic look at the team's highlights over the years. Kids 8 and under love the Phanatics' Fun Zone, where activities like face painting and rock climbing are featured before the games. At the Linc', where 66 percent of the seating is on the sidelines, there is room for three times as many luxury seats as at the old Vet, some 3,040 in 172 suites. Behind-the-scenes group tours are offered most days, Monday through Saturday, for $7 (267/570.4510). www.lincolnfinancialfield.com; http://philadelphiaphillies.mlb.com; www.philadelphiaeagles.com

Philadelphia's sports teams are enormously popular: The Phillies draw more than 2 million fans a season, and the Eagles sell out almost every game. Because most Eagles seats are held by season-ticket holders, the best you can hope for on game days are seats near the end zones or in the upper reaches of the stadium. Though the Phillies pull in a great crowd, they rarely sell out, so it's usually possible to buy tickets at the gate. ◆ Phillies box office: M-F, 9AM-8PM. Eagles box office: M-F. 3501 S Broad St. Phillies, 463.1000; Eagles, 463.5500

WACHOVIA COMPLEX

Together, the **Wachovia Spectrum**, built in 1967, and **Wachovia Center**, opened in 1996 and constructed on the site of the demolished **JFK Stadium**, form the Wachovia Complex. The complex hosts more than 330 major sporting events, family shows, concerts, and competitions that attract nearly 3 million people annually.

The new Wachovia Center is home to the **Philadelphia Flyers** of the National Hockey League, the **Philadelphia 76ers** of the National Basketball Association, and the **Philadelphia Wings** of the Major Indoor Lacrosse League. This state-of-the-art facility boasts 21,000 seats (19,500 for Flyers games), compared to 18,000 at the Spectrum. The arena's oval design assures that virtually every seat affords a clear sight line to the floor.

The Wachovia Spectrum, where the Flyers and Sixers used to play, is now home to the Philadelphia Phantoms of the American Hockey League and the Philadelphia KiXX of the National Professional Soccer League and the site of men's and women's college basketball, including LaSalle and Villanova Universities. Although the Spectrum doesn't host the 300 or so events a year it once did, it's still a popular venue for rock concerts and other forms of entertainment. ◆ Box office: M-F, 9AM-6PM; Sa, Su, 10AM-4:30PM. General information, 389.9560; Complex box office, 336.3600; Flyers, 755.9700; 76ers, 339.7676; Wings, 389.9464; Phantoms, 465.4522; KiXX, 888/888.5499 (toll free)

11 MUSEUM OF AMERICAN ART OF THE PENNSYLVANIA ACADEMY OF THE FINE ARTS

Frank Furness designed this High Victorian building for the oldest art school and museum in the country (founded in 1805 at another location). The compact foyer leads to a stairhall bursting with color. Bronze

---

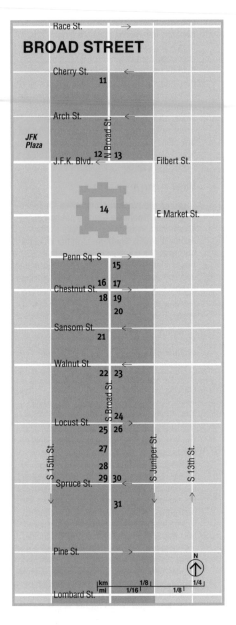

BROAD STREET

Race St. →

Cherry St. ←
11

Arch St. ←

N. Broad St.

JFK Plaza

J.F.K. Blvd. ← 12 13   Filbert St.

14   E Market St.

Penn Sq. S →
15

Chestnut St. 16 17
18 19
20

Sansom St. ←
21

Walnut St. ←
22 23

S. Broad St.

Locust St. 24
25 26
27
S Juniper St.
S 13th St.
S 15th St.
28
29 30 ←
Spruce St.
31

Pine St. →

N

Lombard St.

| km | 1/8 | 1/4 |
| mi | 1/16 | 1/8 |

centennial. Furness chose brick, sandstone, terra-cotta, and Conshohocken rough-cut stone for the exterior and further embellished them with a mansard roof and an eclectic mix of decorative details.

Founded by portraitist Charles Willson Peale and artist William Rush, the Academy's distinguished art school has had a number of famous teachers: Thomas Eakins, Gilbert Stuart, Cecilia Beaux, and Alexander Stirling Calder, to name a few. (Eakins taught at the academy between 1876 and 1886 and introduced the study of human anatomy to American artists. Although Eakins is a point of pride to the school today, he was dismissed from the staff after he allowed nude male models to pose in front of his female students.)

The academy likewise boasts a superb museum with a permanent collection of more than 1,700 paintings, 300 sculptures, and 14,000 works on paper, a portion of which is always on display. The inventory includes Benjamin West's *Death on a Pale Horse*, spared from destruction when a firefighter cut the canvas from its frame during a blaze; portraits of George Washington; *The Cello Player*, by Thomas Eakins; and sculptures by Howard Roberts, Nancy Graves, and Louise Nevelson.

Renovations in 1994 added a first-floor café, which offers light fare during museum hours and a jazz brunch on Sunday. The museum now also features an orientation theater—where a video on the history of the academy plays every 10 minutes—and an electronic self-guided tour. The **Museum Shop** sells art books and gifts. Check the schedule for lectures, films, concerts, and workshops. Classes meet in a separate building (at 1301 Cherry Street), where the school gallery exhibits works primarily by students and faculty. ◆ Admission; free W, 5-7:30PM. M-Sa; Su, 11AM-5PM. Guided tours Sa, Su, 12:30PM, 2PM. 118 N Broad St (at Cherry St). 972.7600. ይ. www.pafa.org

12 FRANK RIZZO STATUE

Directly across John F. Kennedy Boulevard, on the north side of City Hall, as if he were descending the street-level steps of the **Municipal Services Building** on his way out to the sidewalk, stands a statue of the late Frank Rizzo, a former mayor of Philadelphia. The 10-foot-high bronze of the "Big Bambino," as Rizzo was affectionately known to supporters, looks away from another sculpture on the Municipal Services Building steps, Jacques Lipchitz's *Government of the People*, a towering jumble that the controversial Rizzo did not like but learned to tolerate. ◆ N Broad St and John F. Kennedy Blvd and Filbert St. www.philart.com

ornamental railings, carved marble posts, ceramic tile mosaics, a star-studded cerulean blue ceiling, and a multitude of floral patterns (some cut in stone and gilded) combine for an exhilarating effect. The gilded walls were painted over and the floors covered with carpeting at one point (when some critics deemed the academy excessively ornate), but happily, opinions changed and the interior was restored according to designs by **Day and Zimmerman** for the 1976 bicentennial.

This is the third home of the academy, built just in time to celebrate the country's 1876

13 MASONIC TEMPLE

The first American Freemasons (now the largest fraternity in the world) met in Philadelphia in 1732, and this 1873 building was their sixth temple in the city. **James Windrim,** a 27-year-old Freemason, designed the opulent structure, which resembles a medieval Norman church with its imposing carved doorway and stone façade. George Herzog, one of a number of distinguished German craftsmen who came to this country in the second half of the 19th century, designed the halls. These main rooms vary dramatically in style, with the **Oriental Hall** modeled after the Palace of the Alhambra in Spain, and the **Egyptian Hall** after the temples of Luxor. **Renaissance Hall**, **Gothic Hall**, **Ionic Hall**, and **Norman Hall** are among the others. The **Masonic Museum** houses such memorabilia as George Washington's Masonic apron (a ceremonial garment designed after the working clothes of stonemasons). ◆ Tours M-F, 10AM, 11AM, 1PM, 2PM, 3PM; Sa, 10AM, 11AM. Closed Sa in July and Aug. 1 N Broad St (at Filbert St). 988.1917. &. www.pagrandlodge.org

14 CITY HALL

Few buildings are as fascinating, controversial, grandiose, expensive, misunderstood, and, some would say, beautiful as this one. With more than 600 rooms, 14 entrances, and 14.5 acres of floor space, it is the largest municipal building in the world. It took $25 million and 30 years to build and has been undergoing renovation and restoration virtually from the moment it was completed in 1901. When Thomas Holme, the colonial surveyor-general, laid out his plans for five public squares in Philadelphia, he designated the 10 acres in the center of the city for civic buildings. Years later, architect **John McArthur Jr.** said of his own plan to put an enormous and spectacularly ornate city hall at Center Square, "It cannot fail to make that portion of our city one of the choicest architectural spots in America." Still later, in 1953, City Councilman Victor Moore expressed a commonly held opinion at the time when he called McArthur's final product "an ugly monstrosity which sooner or later must come down."

The granite and white marble exterior is adorned with an eclectic mix of columns, pilasters, pediments, dormers, and sculptures. Note how the tall marble columns at the entranceway and each corner make the building appear as if it has three stories instead of eight. Crowning it all is a 548-foot tower and Alexander Milne Calder's famous bronze statue of William Penn (at 37 feet in length, it's the largest single piece of sculpture on any building in the world—the nose alone is 18 inches long). Calder also designed the other 250 sculptures on the building, most of them allegorical figures representing seasons, elements, virtues and vices, heroes, and trades. A sculpture's face sits above each of the four archways leading to Broad and Market Streets, representing Penn, Benjamin Franklin, Moses, and Sympathy.

Attempts to accommodate the workings of city government have led to the destruction or obscuring of many of the original interior details—the polished marble, coved ceilings, and carved woodwork, to name a few. But some rooms still point to what the building once was—and may someday be again. **Philadelphia Hospitality Style** offers tours of the impressive public spaces, including the **Mayor's Reception Room**, which features Honduran mahogany paneling, a 3-ton chandelier, and portraits of the city's mayors. Be sure to see the marble balconies in the **City Council Room**; the rotunda ceiling and pedimented niches in the **Council Caucus Room**; and the marbled walls, hand-set mosaic floors, and ceiling ornamented with gold leaf in the beautifully restored **Conversation Hall**. All of City Hall was restored in time for the building's centennial in 2001.

A noteworthy modern-day addition to City Hall is the giant **Philadelphia Compass Rose**, hand-painted on the brickwork in the center of the courtyard. The painting—which serves as a full-scale model for an eventual marble, granite, and bronze plaza—locates the exact center of the city where Market and Broad Streets intersect. Fifty-eight feet in diameter, it depicts a zodiac dial; a compass indicating true north, south, east, and west poles; and two axes, one coinciding with Broad Street and the other with Market Street. Etched in the center is William Penn's 1682 city plan, which echoes the surrounding layout. Suspended above the painting is a mirrored ball that allows visitors a fish-eye view of the compass, statue of Penn, shafts of light radiating from the four archways, and themselves as their position relates to the whole. Honoring Penn's 350th birthday in 1994, the artwork was a gift to the city from former city planner Edmund Bacon.

For a breathtaking view of Philadelphia, visit the **Observation Deck** at the base of the Penn statue. (To reach it, take the elevator to the 7th floor, an escalator up two more flights, and then a five-passenger elevator to a platform 30 stories up.) A volunteer tour guide is always standing by to answer questions. In addition to the guided tours of the public rooms, the **Foundation for Architecture**

Restaurants/Clubs: Red | Hotels: Purple | Shops: Orange | Outdoors/Parks: Green | Sights/Culture: Blue

(569.3187) offers occasional tours of the exterior. It's a good idea to call ahead even if you're just interested in the Observation Deck trip—sometimes morning hours are canceled to accommodate school groups. ◆ Guided tours of interior: M-F, 12:30PM. Tours of exterior: schedule varies. Observation Deck: M-F. Broad and Market Sts. 686.9074. www.phila.gov

15 BORDERS

Can a single store change a city? It must be possible, because no one can recall what Philadelphia was like before this chain of bookstores opened its original doors in 1990. A move to Broad Street still makes locals pine for its original Rittenhouse Square location. In addition to selling new publications on all subjects, this is a place to meet other readers, sip coffee (at the espresso bar upstairs), and fantasize about the novels you'd read if you only had the time. The espresso bar offers a full range of coffees, teas, exotic soft drinks, scones, dipping biscuits, and other sophisticated desserts. In the basement, a comfy children's department invites young readers (and their parents) to sprawl in the aisles. This is a main stop on the book-tour circuit, with author readings nearly every weeknight, and a children's hour every Saturday at 11:30AM. Most adult readings of adult books start at 7:30PM on the second floor; come early if you want a seat. ◆ M-F, 8AM-10PM; Sa, 9AM-10PM; Su, 10AM-7PM. 1727 Walnut St (between S 17th and S 18th Sts). 568.7400. www.borders.com. Also at numerous locations throughout the area.

16 THE RITZ-CARLTON, PHILADELPHIA

$$$$ A few years ago, this opulent hotel chain took over the **Girard Trust Company/ Mellon Bank**, which was originally built as a reproduction of the Roman Pantheon. With a solid Georgia marble rotunda, a bas relief of Girard Trust Company founder Stephen Girard carved into the tympanum, and a $1.5 million price tag at the time of its construction, the building is one of Philadelphia's most striking examples of neoclassical architecture. The hotel's 331 rooms, including a 2,100-square-foot penthouse, all have high-speed Internet access, cordless phones, and an exhaustive list of amenities. There's even a "technology butler" on call 24 hours a day, in case your computer acts up. Afternoon tea and cocktails are served in the dramatic **Rotunda** lobby, and restaurants include the **Paris Bar & Grill** and the Italian-flavored **Pantheon**. There's also **The Vault**, a posh cigar bar and cocktail lounge located in—what else?—the bank's former walk-in vault. 10 Ave of the Arts (Broad and Chestnut Sts). 735.7700; fax 735.7710. www.ritzcarlton.com

17 J.E. CALDWELL & CO.

When Horace Trumbauer designed this elegant Beaux Arts structure in 1916, he adorned it with black and gold Belgian marble floors, terra-cotta tile ceilings, and Baccarat chandeliers. Philadelphia's premier jeweler—a family-owned business since it opened in 1839—**Caldwell** used to operate a fleet of Rolls Royces to dispense diamonds, engraved calling cards, and European china to the homes of the city's elite. But the seven-store chain fell on hard times in 1992 and is now in the hands of a corporation that also markets less exclusive merchandise. ◆ M-Sa. 1339 Chestnut St (between S Juniper and S Broad Sts). 864.7800

18 LAND TITLE BUILDING

Chicago architect **Daniel Burnham** designed this 16-story "skyscraper." The Ionic arcade running along the two-story base of the buff brick and granite façade seems to lift the distinguished building upward, and the arches, projecting and flat windows, and decorative cornice set it apart from its neighbors. This was Burnham's first East Coast commission, completed in 1897. ◆ S Broad and Chestnut Sts. www.philadelphiabuildings.com

19 McCORMICK & SCHMICK'S SEAFOOD RESTAURANT

★★$$$ This upscale chain, based in Portland, Oregon, is known for its emphasis on Pacific Coast seafood—flown in daily. Although the regular menu is pricey, its $1.95 bar menu, offered between 3:30 and 6PM and between 10:30PM and midnight M-F, is a steal. ◆ One South Broad St (on the Avenue of the Arts at Chestnut St). 568.6888. www.mccormickandschmick.com

19 CAPITAL GRILLE

★★$$$ This restaurant, the 14th location for the upmarket chain, is known for oversize portions of perfectly prepared dry, aged steaks, fresh seafood, and outstanding customer service. **Capital**, which is also known for its award-winning wine list, is not a budget experience—the average check per person is $85, a bit higher than at its original incarnation. It is located in what used to be **Horn & Hardart**, one of the original automats in downtown Philly. ◆ 1338 Chestnut St. 545.9588. www.thecapitalgrille.com

20 POMPEII CUCINA D'ITALIA

★★$$ This Avenue of the Arts restaurant, popular both for concert- and theater-going diners and for lunchers from the business community, is thoroughly Italian. Chef Frank Chiavaroli offers regional Italian-inspired flavors and a creative selection of artistically presented chicken, fish, beef, veal, and homemade pasta dishes. Exquisite salad and appetizer choices abound, as well as a constantly evolving menu of top-notch desserts. The décor, in line with the restaurant's name, with a hand-painted mural, is Italianate, with tons of drapery, cherry wood chairs, hardwood floor, and marbleized walls. The 24-foot granite-topped bar is a hot spot after work. ♦ Italian ♦ M-F, lunch and dinner; Sa, Su, dinner; Su, brunch. Reservations recommended. 121 S Broad St (between Sansom and Chestnut Sts). 735.8400. ぐ. www.pompeiirestaurant.com

21 UNION LEAGUE CLUB

Known widely for two things—its conservatism and its magnificent building—this club is a descendant of an organization that raised money for the Union cause during the Civil War. Today it offers the city's lawyers and businesspeople a place to meet and lunch. In the 1980s, after much fuss, the club allowed women to join for the first time. The dark brick and sandstone building—designed by **John Fraser** and built in 1865, despite the Civil War—is a fine example of the Second Empire style, with a mansard roof, dormer windows, and a sweeping semicircular staircase. Horace Trumbauer's 1909 Renaissance Revival addition on the western side is a sharp contrast to the earlier structure. ♦ 140 S Broad St (at Sansom St). 587.5576. www.unionleague.org

22 THE BELLEVUE

Prussian immigrant George Boldt opened the **Bellevue Stratford Hotel** in 1904 at a cost of $8 million. It was one of the fanciest hotels in the world, featuring in-house orchestras, three ballrooms, a rooftop rose garden, and rooms ranging from Colonial to Greek in style. Designed by **George** and **William Hewitt**, the elaborate behemoth has a slate-covered mansard roof with dormers and chimneys and an exterior of terra-cotta, slate, and rusticated stone. It began losing its luster in the 1950s, and then, in 1976, as Philadelphia celebrated the country's bicentennial, tragedy struck. At an American Legion convention, Legionnaires' disease, as the media dubbed it, killed 29 Legionnaires and forced the hotel to shut down. (A bacterium transmitted in the hotel's air ducts apparently caused the disease.) The Bellevue Stratford changed hands, reopened in 1979 as the **Fairmont Hotel**, and then closed again 7 years later. In 1989, after a reported $100 million in renovations, the building was reopened once again, this time as the **Park Hyatt Philadelphia at The Bellevue** hotel, office, and shopping complex. Many of the building's outstanding features were beautifully restored or spared from further

deterioration, including the hotel's legendary 14,000-square-foot ballroom, where Philadelphia's socialites continue to hold balls and lavish fund-raisers, just as they have for more than 90 years. ♦ 200 S Broad St (at Walnut St). www.bellevuephiladelphia.com

Within the Park Hyatt at The Bellevue:

SHOPS AT THE BELLEVUE

The former hotel lobby is now a grand entranceway to this elegant retail complex. Among the upscale shops here are **Tiffany & Co.**, **Polo/Ralph Lauren**, **Williams-Sonoma**, **Nicole Miller**, and **Pierre & Carlo European Spa and Salon**. Downstairs at The Bellevue is a food court offering food to eat in or take out. ♦ M-Sa. 875.8350

THE PALM

★★$$$$ Saddle-size steaks and chops, grilled fish, and fancy hash-brown potatoes make this branch of the coast-to-coast chain as popular as it is in other cities. Well-turned caricatures of local celebrities grace the walls; the ceilings are painted to look like old-fashioned pressed tin. ♦ American ♦ M-F, lunch and dinner; Sa, Su, dinner. Reservations required. 546.7256 ぐ

PARK HYATT PHILADELPHIA AT THE BELLEVUE

$$$ Only the top eight floors of the old **Bellevue Stratford** remain devoted to luxury hotel accommodations. With its richly paneled library bar, hushed elegance, palatial **Grand Ballroom**, and intriguing nooks and crannies, it would make the perfect setting for a murder mystery. All 172 rooms come with a host of amenities like two-line telephones, minibars, VCRs and stereo systems, and use of the adjacent **Sporting Club**. Some rooms overlook a wonderful skylit conservatory. From the hallway known as **The Promenade**, you can look past the city's row houses east to the **Delaware River**. The dining rooms and lounges have been beautifully restored. ♦ 1415 Chancellor Ct (off S Broad St). 893.1234, 800/221.0833; fax 732.8518. ぐ

The statue of William Penn atop City Hall weighs 27 tons and stands 37 feet tall. It is the largest sculpture at the top of any building in the world.

The longest strike in the 100-year history of the Philadelphia Orchestra ended on 18 November 1996. The unprecedented work stoppage lasted 64 days.

Within Park Hyatt at The Bellevue:

Founders

★★★$$$$ Decorated with prints of old Philadelphia, statues of Benjamin Franklin and David Rittenhouse, and handsome upholstered chairs, this is a luxurious institution with wonderful views of the city's skyline. Chef Robert Capella's menu is a mix of classic and modern dishes, like rich lobster bisque spiked with Armagnac and smoky caramelized sea scallops studded with truffles, seared tuna and clam served over a rich tomato sauce, and chateaubriand for two, carved tableside. The restaurant won a Wine Spectator Award for Excellence in 2001. ♦ American/French ♦ Daily, lunch and dinner. Jacket and tie recommended. Reservations required. 790.2814 &

The Ethel Barrymore Room

★$$ Enjoy afternoon tea, light snacks, and evening cocktails in what looks like a boudoir. Floral murals and ornate plasterwork enhance the sky-blue domed ceiling. ♦ Tearoom ♦ Daily, 5PM-midnight; tea W-Sa, 3-5PM; dancing and live music F, Sa, 10PM-1AM. 893.1776 &

Philadelphia Library Lounge

The type of aristocratic wood-paneled library you see in movies is re-created here, complete with Oriental rugs, rows of old books on the shelves, and a fire blazing in the hearth. Stop in for drinks, hors d'oeuvres, or pastries. ♦ Daily, from 11:30AM. 893.1776 &

Zanzibar Blue

★★★$$$ This legendary jazz club's relocation to the **Park Hyatt**, from its longtime home on S 11th Street, gave a big boost to the developing Avenue of the Arts. Brothers Robert and Benjamin Bynum have brought some of the world's best jazz, and equally fabulous food, thanks to chef Al Paris, to their new venue. The room, with low ceilings, black walls trimmed with dark wood, and black-and-white portraits of jazz greats, is bathed in warm lighting. The menu includes classic Southern cooking, soul food, Latin and French dishes, with highlights like warm spinach salad, Portobello mushroom Napoleon, crab cakes, and rack of lamb with a red-wine and mustard sauce. As for music, expect to see contemporary giants like the Ernie Hopkins Quartet and vocalists Regina Carter, Juanita Holiday, or Brenda Smith. There are two or three sets each night, and there's no cover charge during the week. ♦ American ♦ M-Sa, dinner; Su, brunch and dinner. 732.5200. &. www.zanzibarblue.com

23 Italian Bistro

★$$ A trendy Italian menu, eclectic interior studded with neon and kitschy statues, and glass-enclosed café area jutting onto the Broad Street sidewalk all bring in a steady crowd. Pizzas pulled from the wood-burning oven are offered with tasty toppings such as eggplant, goat cheese, arugula, and prosciutto. Other dishes include shrimp scampi with rosemary, garlic, and bacon, and chicken cooked on a rotisserie. ♦ Italian ♦ Daily, lunch and dinner. 211 S Broad St (between Locust and Walnut Sts). 731.0700. &. www.italianbistro.com

24 Upstares at Varalli

★★$$ Diners near the upstairs windows here always seem to be having such a great time, perhaps because they're looking down on the envious "upstares" of others still searching for parking spaces. They also have great views of the **Academy of Music** and the lighted trees on the Avenue of the Arts. Pasta, pizza, and risotto are the kitchen's specialties. If you aren't famished, have a half order of risotto with duck and artichokes, pasta with sun-dried tomatoes and cheese, or agnolotti (round ravioli) with sweet sausage, peas, cream, and Parmesan. The pizza with duck and fontina cheese and the arugula salad with pine nuts, berries, red onion, Gorgonzola, and orange poppy-seed dressing are superb. Below, **Sotto Varalli** presents an alternative menu in about the same price range but focusing on seafood. ♦ Northern Italian ♦ M-Sa, lunch and dinner; Su, dinner. 1345 Locust St (at S Broad St). 546.4200. &. www.varalliusa.com

25 Academy of Music

The late Philadelphia writer John Francis Marion once described the sense of pride Philadelphians feel when they sit in the plush red seats of this beautiful concert hall: "They are secure, enfolded, enveloped in one of their favorite monuments to a rich and colorful past." For many, the Academy of Music is a more important cultural symbol than the **Liberty Bell**, particularly because it is home to the premier **Philadelphia Orchestra**. Plans for the building, completed in 1857, initially called for a more elaborate exterior, but funds ran short and architects **Napoleon LeBrun** and **Gustave Runge** settled on a dark brick façade with Italian Renaissance arches. No expense was spared on the Baroque interior, however, a gilded setting for performances and social events modeled after La Scala in Milan. German artist Karl Heinrich Schmolze, who died in his thirties from lead poisoning, painted the fresco on the domed ceiling. Medallions, urns, and sculptured figures ornament the barrel-shaped interior, and Corinthian columns flank the proscenium.

LUCRETIA MOTT: FRIEND OF THE FRIENDLESS

Quaker preacher and abolitionist Lucretia Mott was not born in Philadelphia. But like so many others, she fulfilled her destiny in the City of Brotherly Love. For her, the city's well-known motto became the sentiment that resonated through her life's work, as one who labored for the good of her fellow human beings, particularly for those who suffered in bondage of any kind.

Born in Nantucket on 3 January 1793, she and her husband James came to Philadelphia to stay in October 1814, after several visits. In 1818, Mott became a preacher of the Quakers, or Society of Friends. Over the next 15 years, she continually focused and fine-tuned her antislavery convictions, and in 1833, she helped found the American Anti-Slavery Society.

After hearing her speak at a national antislavery convention in Philadelphia that same year, a gentleman in attendance remarked, "I had never heard a woman speak at a public meeting. She said only a few words, but these were spoken so modestly, in such sweet tones and yet so decisively, that no one could fail to be pleased."

In 1840 Mott was a delegate to the World's Anti-Slavery Convention in London but was barred from the meeting when she arrived. That incident led to the second great mission of her life: the fight for women's rights. In 1848, she and Elizabeth Cady Stanton organized the first Women's Rights Convention in Seneca Falls, a meeting that began the long campaign for women's suffrage. On 21 November 1881, Lucretia Mott died in Philadelphia at nearly 90 years of age. Thousands attended the funeral. When someone sought to break the silence of the solemn service with the question "Will no one speak?" the answer came, "Who can speak now? The preacher is dead."

Many famous musicians and speakers, ranging from Tchaikovsky to Garrison Keillor, have appeared on this stage. The Philadelphia Orchestra, once described by the *New York Herald-Tribune* as the city's "chief contribution to civilization," first performed here in 1900 and was in residence until moving to the new **Kimmel Center for the Performing Arts** in December 2001. Three legendary conductors presided over the world-class orchestra: Leopold Stokowski, Eugene Ormandy, and Riccardo Muti. Current music director Wolfgang Sawallisch celebrated a decade at the helm with the 2003 season. Stokowski, who led the orchestra between 1912 and 1936 and insisted on adding modern composers to the Philadelphia diet of Beethoven and Brahms, received a lukewarm response when he conducted Stravinsky's *Le Sacre du Printemps* and supposedly resigned in frustration.

Though once celebrated for its acoustics as an opera house (LeBrun and Runge placed a dry well under the floor near the orchestra pit to enhance the music), the Academy is considered inadequate for orchestral music according to today's standards. The $265 million Kimmel Center solved that problem, providing a near-perfect acoustic backdrop to the orchestra, as well as to the **Chamber Orchestra of Philadelphia**, **Peter Nero and the Philly Pops**, **PHILADANCO**, and other arts organizations. The first new performing arts center for a top orchestra since New York's Avery Fisher Hall in the 1960s, the facility includes the 2,500-seat **Verizon Hall**; the 650-seat **Perelman Theater**; studio and rehearsal space; an education center; and a café, restaurant, and gift shop. The building's soaring 150-foot glass-vaulted roof, designed by architect **Rafael Vinoly**, is a dramatic addition to the changing face of the Avenue of the Arts. ♦ Academy of Music: Broad and Locust Sts; box office open M-Sa, 10AM-9 PM; 893.1930; tickets by phone: 893.1999; fax 545.4588. Kimmel Center for the Performing Arts: Broad and Spruce Sts; open daily, 10AM-6PM, later on performance evening; 790.5800. ⅃. www.academyofmusic.org

26 DOUBLETREE HOTEL

$$$ If you want to be in the center of Center City and the arts district, with a bird's-eye view of the new **Kimmel Center**, this 26-story hotel with 434 rooms and tall windows is a good choice. Amenities include the **Academy Café**, which serves breakfast, lunch, and dinner; a health club; indoor pool; racquetball courts; and rooftop track. Ask for a room facing Broad Street. ♦ S Broad St (at Locust St). 893.1600, 800/222.8733; fax 893.1664. ⅃. www.doubletree.com

Within the Doubletree Hotel:

JACK'S CENTER CITY TAVERN

★$$ The mural on the ceiling, with its heavenly equestrian scenes, is worth pondering while enjoying your favorite libations and such treats as artichoke and green-chili dip, dim sum, or spiced chicken pizza. Relax with friends on soft leather

---

Restaurants/Clubs: Red | Hotels: Purple | Shops: Orange | Outdoors/Parks: Green | Sights/Culture: Blue

couches or fan-backed chairs in one of two raised sitting areas overlooking the tables in this forest-green and sand-colored marble dining area. ◆ American ◆ Daily, lunch and dinner. 893.1600. www.doubletree.com

27 BLISS

★★$$ Chef Francesco Martorella, whose stylish new restaurant puts diners in touch with their inner gourmand, has created a menu of Mediterranean and Asian cuisine that includes terrific balsamic-glazed baby-back ribs, tiger shrimp spring rolls, scallops with a miso glaze served with soy-spiked cucumbers, and an outstanding five-spice lobster and shrimp risotto with a ginger black bean sauce. The restaurant's cool blue backdrop and hipster soundtrack is a natural mood elevator. ◆ 220 Broad St (between Spruce and Locust Sts). 731.1100

28 MERRIAM THEATER AT THE UNIVERSITY OF THE ARTS

Since the old **Shubert Theater** opened here in 1918, dozens of big-name Broadway stars have appeared on its stage, including Laurence Olivier, Ethel Merman, and Gertrude Lawrence. The **University of the Arts** purchased the 1,668-seat theater in 1971 and, in the 1980s, restored the inside, renovated the lobby, and refurbished some of the theater's original murals and bas-reliefs. Now managed by the **Philadelphia Theater League**, the Merriam presents Broadway hits, gospel shows, and some stand-up comedy, as well as student productions and performances by the **Pennsylvania Ballet** and the **Pennsylvania Opera Theater**. ◆ Box office: M-Sa. 250 S Broad St (between Spruce and Locust Sts). 732.5446. ♿ www.avenueofthearts.org/merriam.htm

29 RUTH'S CHRIS STEAK HOUSE

★★★$$$ Marble and wood contribute to the clubby feel of this gregarious and comfortable link in the upscale steak-house chain on the ground floor of the **Atlantic Building**. Obscenely large crustaceans stock the lobster tanks, and the marbled steaks, seared in the broiler and served on burning-hot plates, are huge. *Beware:* The sizzle you hear under your porterhouse or filet mignon is the sound of butter (you can ask the waiter to omit it). For extras, order the simple broccoli or fried shoestring potatoes, or share a baked potato with a hungry friend—each one weighs at least 1 pound. ◆ American ◆ M-Th, Sa, Su, dinner; F, lunch and dinner. Jacket and tie requested. Reservations recommended. 260 S Broad St (between Spruce and Locust Sts). 790.1515 ♿ www.ruthschris.com

30 WILMA THEATER

A curving neon-and-steel sign, spelling out a stylized *Wilma* above the door, greets theatergoers at this dynamic presence along Philadelphia's Avenue of the Arts. The first new theater constructed in Center City since the **Forrest** opened in 1928, this 295-seat

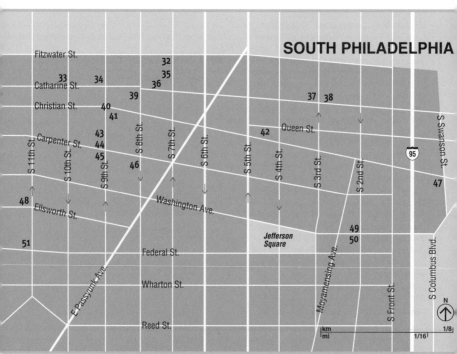

SOUTH PHILADELPHIA

theater, designed by **Hugh Hardy** of **Hardy Holzman Pfeiffer Associates** of New York, was built at a cost of $8 million. Its novel setting is the three lower floors of a six-story parking garage (the top three floors are still a garage). Color and glitz are restricted to the lobby: The décor of the small auditorium—the back row is only 38 feet from the stage—is intentionally neutral, its walls painted in warm tones so as not to compete with the productions. Artistic Directors Jiri and Blanka Zizka, who opened the original **Wilma** at 2030 Sansom Street in the 1980s, present material praised for originality and courage. ♦ Box office: daily, noon-5PM; until 7PM on show nights. 265 S Broad St (at Spruce St). 546.7824. &. www.wilmatheater.org

31 UNIVERSITY OF THE ARTS

Two art schools, the **Philadelphia College of Art and Design** and the **Philadelphia College of Performing Arts**, joined in 1987 to create this university. Housed in a Greek Revival-style building designed by **John Haviland** in 1825 as the **Asylum for the Deaf and Dumb**, the university offers degree programs in fine arts, graphic arts, dance, theater, and music. (It also operates the **Merriam Theater**—see above—where student dance and theater performances are held.) In 1875, **Frank Furness** designed the additions in the back. The university's first-floor **Rosenwald-Wolf Gallery** hosts rotating exhibits of acclaimed artists such as conceptual sculptor Donald Lipski and figurative painter Gregory Botts. ♦ Free. Gallery: M-F; Sa, Su, noon-5PM. Closed in August. 333 S Broad St (at Pine St). 875.1117. &. www.uarts.edu

32 SALOON

★★★$$$ Dress your best if you want to mesh with the fur coats and finely tailored suits in this chic Italian restaurant. Super-cushy chairs, reddish walls, and oversize paintings set the mood for an innovative menu that might feature such items as veal cordon bleu stuffed with prosciutto and cheese; shrimp with wild rice in a cognac cream sauce; and clams filled with shrimp, crabmeat, and cheese. ♦ Italian ♦ M, W-Th, Sa, dinner; Tu, F, lunch and dinner. American Express only. Jacket and tie recommended. Reservations required. 750 S Seventh St (between Catharine and Fitzwater Sts). 627.1811. &. www.saloonrestaurant.net

33 DANTE'S AND LUIGI'S

★$$ Stucco walls and white linoleum set the scene in this South Philly classic. Start with roasted peppers and proceed to one of the standbys: osso buco, pork chops cacciatore, sautéed broccoli rabe, or good old spaghetti and meatballs. Order a side of spaghetti with any of the dishes for a taste of the neighborhood's typically rich tomato "gravy." (Only outsiders call it sauce in South Philly.) ♦ Italian ♦ Tu-Su, lunch and dinner. 762 S 10th St (at Catharine St). 922.9501

34 L. SARCONE & SON BAKERS

Three times a day, hot Italian bread—seeded, plain, round, or oblong—comes out of the brick oven in this no-frills storefront, which opened more than 75 years ago. There might be a line, but the bread (dense and spongy with a thick crust) is worth the wait. There are also rolls, rings, twists, bread sticks, and pepperoni breads. Count on empty shelves if you arrive close to closing time; the bakery is known to close its doors early if the bread sells out. ♦ Tu-Sa, 7:30AM-3PM; Su, 7:30AM-1PM. 758 S Ninth St (between Catharine and Fitzwater Sts). 922.0445

34 RALPH'S

★$ The room downstairs is sedate and plain, so ask to be seated upstairs in the huge hall with old-fashioned Italian murals. Try the mussels in white-wine sauce, breaded veal cutlet, or spaghetti with meatballs. ♦ Italian ♦ Daily, lunch and dinner. Reservations recommended. 760 S Ninth St (between Catharine and Fitzwater Sts). 627.6011. www.ralphsrestaurant.com

35 CENT'ANNI

★★$$ Both traditional and contemporary Italian fare are offered, with an emphasis on fresh vegetables, Portobello mushrooms, sun-dried tomatoes, and lots of garlic. The cozy 24-table restaurant has exposed-brick walls and big murals capturing the lively personality of the **Italian Market**. Choose from osso buco; chicken and Portobello mushrooms in light cream sauce with penne; or veal and lobster tails in lemon butter, white wine, and garlic. If you're counting calories, the chef will prepare your meal, on request, with soy milk instead of cream. ♦ Italian ♦ Daily, Tu-Su. Reservations recommended. 770 S Seventh St (between Catharine and Fitzwater Sts). 925.5558

36 SAMUEL S. FLEISHER ART MEMORIAL

In 1898, Samuel S. Fleisher, a wealthy woolens manufacturer, founded a free art school called the **Graphic Sketch Club**, which he eventually moved to this unusual series of buildings (an Episcopal church, a church

---

Restaurants/Clubs: **Red** | Hotels: **Purple** | Shops: Orange | Outdoors/Parks: **Green** | Sights/Culture: Blue

school, and four residential abodes). The former house of worship, designed by the architectural firm of **Frank Furness** and completed in 1886, far outshines its immediate neighbors. Modeled after a medieval Italian church, the narrow brick structure is profoundly beautiful. Fleisher purchased the church (along with the adjoining houses) in 1922, renamed it "the sanctuary," and filled it with treasures of medieval and Renaissance ecclesiastical art. The **Philadelphia Museum of Art**, which now administers the galleries and school, enhanced the collection by adding 15th- and 16th-century European paintings and sculpture. Among the treasures are two large paintings by Pablo Vergos, 13th- and 14th-century statues of saints, Russian icons, a 15th-century French abbot's chair, stained-glass windows by John LaFarge and Nicola D'Ascenzo, wrought-iron gates by Samuel Yellin, and an altarpiece by Violet Oakley.

The school is still in operation, and students and faculty frequently exhibit their works here. Louis I. Kahn studied at **Fleisher**, and today a sparse lecture room by artist Siah Armajiani pays tribute to his ideas. Each year the museum hosts four art shows; more than 400 artists vie for the chance to exhibit their work at one of these prestigious, high-visibility events. ♦ Free. M-F, 11AM-5PM; M-Th, 6:30-9:30PM; Sa, 10AM-3PM. Closed July and Aug. No evening hours when school is closed. 709-721 Catharine St (between S Seventh and S Eighth Sts). ♿. 922.3456. ♿. www.fleisher.org

37 New Wave Café

★★$$ When you walk in, you think you're in a sports bar. And you are—satellite beams sports to every TV, baseball memorabilia adorns the walls, and the crowd is eager to discuss the Eagles' chances for the Super Bowl. Come for darts or Quizzo, and stay for dinner. ♦ 784 S Third St (at Catharine St). 922.8484. www.newwavecafe.com/

38 Dmitri's

★★★$$ On any given night, a hundred or more people may descend on this tiny two-room restaurant, which seats only 32 (reservations aren't accepted). If you're up to the wait, pass the time on a bar stool at the marble counter with a view of the open kitchen or hop across the street to **New Wave Cafe**, where the hostess will roust you when a table is ready. Owner-chef Dmitri Chimes prepares some of the best grilled fish in town, including whole baby salmon, swordfish steaks, and mackerel. The *baba ghannouj* and hummus are excellent. The restaurant doesn't have a liquor license, so bring your own wine and beer. ♦ Seafood/Middle Eastern ♦ Daily, dinner. 795 S Third St (at Catharine St). 625.0556

39 Michael's Ristorante

★★$$ Hearty, reasonably priced Italian food, served in an elegantly rustic setting with fireplace, candlelit tables, and a long oak bar, distinguishes this restaurant. Try the stuffed veal chops with mozzarella, spinach, and wild-mushroom–port sauce. The homemade cannelloni makes a perfect finish. There's even valet parking. ♦ Italian ♦ Tu-Su, dinner. 824 S 8th St (between Christian and Catharine Sts). 922.3986

40 Italian Market

This lively five-block stretch of 120 open-air stalls and specialty stores is the focal point of South Philadelphia's Italian neighborhood, where locals gather to shop, gossip, and people-watch. Plucked geese and whole pigs hang in the butcher windows; fish lie wide-eyed on packs of ice; and a huge variety of olive oils, vinegars, capers, pasta, and Italian cheeses line the store shelves. The low prices and selection of products draw crowds from all over Philadelphia. On Friday and Saturday, the sidewalks become nearly impassable as buyers try to squeeze past the outdoor vegetable, fish, and dry-goods vendors. The atmosphere is particularly electric around Christmas and Easter. In winter, merchants burn their packaging materials in metal barrels to keep warm, which produces a thick, acrid odor; in the sweltering summer heat, the street emits a pungent odor of a different sort. Even though driving up Ninth Street is legal, don't attempt it during market hours. Local parking lots don't charge much, and you can often find spaces on the streets nearby. ♦ Daily. Hours vary for different vendors. S Ninth St (from Washington Ave to Christian St). www.phillyitalianmarket.com

41 D'Angelo Brothers

Forty kinds of sausage and eight types of pâté can be found in this third-generation family-run shop. The sausages include Cajun boudin; seafood; turkey Santa Fe (turkey, cilantro, and jalapeño); and pork with spinach, pine nuts, and ricotta cheese. Run by Sonny D'Angelo, the store also claims to be the country's largest retail distributor of game meats, selling alligator, llama, ostrich, and 57 other kinds of exotic animals. If you must take home some turtle stew or buffalo chili, **D'Angelo**'s will happily pack it up in one of the shop's coolers. ♦ Tu-Sa; Su, 10:30AM-3:30PM. 909 S Ninth St (between Carpenter and Christian Sts). 923.5637. www.dangelobros.com

42 Mario Lanza Institute and Museum

Born Freddie Cocozza on Christian Street near Sixth Street, Mario Lanza is South

MUMMER'S THE WORD

Every New Year's Day, some 25,000 sequined, feathered, face-painted, banjo-playing men (plus a handful of women and children) dance and strut along a 2-mile stretch of S Broad Street. These colorful characters (known as Mummers) make their way up the urban boulevard to the hoots and hollers of dense, boisterous crowds.

The **Mummers Parade**, an official city function since 1901, has been called the oldest continuous folk festival in the United States. *Mumme* is a German word for "mask"; thus, a Mummer is one who disguises or masquerades. Whether the Mummers' tradition originated from English mummery plays (an early form of burlesque featuring harlequins dressed in silk and satin) or from a Swedish and Finnish custom of roaming bands of merrymakers who observed Second Christmas remains unclear. In the 1700s, Philadelphia's first Mummers wandered the city on New Year's Eve and at midnight shot pistols; they were nicknamed Shooters at the time. The bands became larger (and cut out the gunshot salute) in the 1850s, parading around the lower part of the city as far as Market Street by 1876. Eventually Broad Street from South Philadelphia to City Hall became the official site of the Mummers Parade.

Unless you've seen it firsthand, the Mummers' strut is hard to visualize (try to imagine a kind of high-stepping, one-arm-flapping walk). It probably evolved from the Cakewalk, a popular late 19th-century dance. The Mummers march to music produced by bands made up of (and limited to) accordions, saxophones, drums, violins, banjos, bass fiddles, glockenspiels, and clarinets—a tinny sound that some people find grating and others rousing.

The Mummers (who come from clubs representing different neighborhoods) devote a full 12 months to practicing the music, devising the routines, and, most important, designing and creating the costumes (elaborate productions of sequins, dyed feathers, lamé, and mirrors). One of the remarkable feats of the Mummers is that they manage to move at all in these getups, let alone march for hours. A typical costume worn by a string-band member weighs 150 pounds and consists of a steel-rod frame covered with cardboard, fabric, and gaudy ornaments. Each costume includes hundreds of ostrich feathers.

Four divisions of Mummers, called Comic, Fancy, String, and Fancy Brigade, trek down Broad Street. The Comic Division (aka the Clowns), which steps off first, specializes in first-class, unadorned strutting. They precede the more disciplined Fancies, who in turn are followed by the String Division, the true stars of the parade. Every year, each string band picks a different theme for its 5-minute routine. It could be a Broadway show like *The Sound of Music*, a fairy tale, or a concept like pirates or savages. The bands perform their routines at various intervals along Broad Street and again before the judging stand at City Hall, where they compete for modest prizes. Like the Fancy Brigade, a division with elaborate choreographed routines, the string bands have 55 members each.

The parade starts around 8:45AM and has been known to last well over 12 hours, a bit much unless you're a true Mummerphile. If you're averse to the cold, you can always watch the antics on television. Better yet, catch a live performance as the Mummers practice for the big day at the **Pennsylvania Convention Center** in preparation for New Year's Day. For more information, contact the **Independence Visitor Center** at 800/537.7676.

Philadelphia's favorite expatriate. The singer, who died in 1959 at the age of 38, achieved fame in seven Hollywood movies, including his most famous film, *The Great Caruso*, in 1951. Lanza never gained widespread respect as a serious opera singer, but this small, homey museum in the **Settlement Music School** is a touching memorial to his aspirations. Vintage films are often on the schedule. ◆ Free. M-Sa, 10AM-3:30PM. Closed Sa, July and Aug. 416 Queen St (between S Fourth and S Fifth Sts), third floor. 468.3623. ⅊. www.mario-lanza-institute.org

43 CLAUDIO KING OF CHEESE

Fat wheels of Parmigiano-Reggiano, oily jars of sun-dried tomatoes, slabs of prosciutto, and vats of olives fill this redolent shop. ◆ M-Sa; Su, 9AM-2PM. 926 S Ninth St (between Carpenter and Christian Sts). 627.1873

43 VILLA DI ROMA

★$ Everybody's "hon" to the waitresses dressed in the neighborhood's trademark black outfits in this traditional pasta joint with three plain-as-can-be dining rooms. Lasagna, cannelloni, and manicotti are mainstays, and the chicken and veal dishes come with tomato gravies, mozzarella, peppers, and sausages—in a variety of familiar combinations. Mussels are served in a choice of atypically thin red gravy or white garlic sauce. The cannolis are made at a local bakery. ◆ Italian ◆ No credit cards. Tu-Sa, lunch and dinner; M, Su, dinner. 934 S Ninth St (between Carpenter and Christian Sts). 592.1295. www.phillyitalianmarket.com/market/villa_di_roma

---

Restaurants/Clubs: Red | Hotels: Purple | Shops: Orange | Outdoors/Parks: Green | Sights/Culture: Blue

44 TALLUTO'S AUTHENTIC ITALIAN FOOD

This all-around Italian deli sells olive oils, fresh and frozen pastas, olives, pizza, meats, and antipasti. The smoked mozzarella and the fresh cannolis—crisp shells filled with sweetened ricotta cheese and chocolate chips—are both excellent. ♦ Tu-Sa; Su, 8:30AM-1PM. 944 S Ninth St (at Carpenter St). 627.4967. www.phillyitalianmarket.com/market/tallutos_pasta

45 FANTE'S COOKWARE

Cooking enthusiasts may have to muster some willpower here. There's always one thing more you could use, whether it be a $250 copper pot or $3 worth of plastic cake decorations. The prices aren't discount, but the selection of kitchen gadgets, knives, pot racks, cookbooks, earthenware, and high-quality pots and pans is unbeatable. A small shop adjoining the main store peddles gourmet oils, chocolates, coffees, and spices. ♦ Tu-Sa; Su, 9:30AM-12:30PM. 1006 S Ninth St (between Washington Ave and Carpenter St). 922.5557. www.fantes.com

46 PIF

★★$$ Located in a former pho shop, Pif is the first and only authentic French bistro in the **Italian Market** neighborhood. A welcome addition it is, thanks to chef David Ansill in the back of the tiny house, and the management skills of his charming French wife Catherine up front. The country French menu

changes daily, depending on what Ansill finds at the market. Don't miss the signature appetizer, escargot in a Pernod sauce and stuffed into a head of garlic. The fish is always good, as is the luscious dark Valrhona *chocolat pot de crème*. BYOB. ♦ Tu-Sa, 5:30-10PM. 1009 S 8th St (between Carpenter and Kimball Sts). 625.2923

47 GLORIA DEI (OLD SWEDES' CHURCH)

Swedish Lutherans first settled what is now Philadelphia nearly 40 years before the arrival of the English Quakers under William Penn. They built a simple log church on this site in the early 1640s and replaced it with the current brick structure in 1700. With its white steeple, classical gables, and steep roof, it resembles colonial churches built by British settlers more than the typical early log architecture of the Swedes. Today the church and its quiet graveyard—where Johan Printz, governor of the New Sweden colony, is buried—seem out of place along this industrialized section of the **Delaware River**. **Old Swedes'** became an Episcopal church after the American Revolution, when Sweden cut off aid to its churches in the former colonies. ♦ M-F, by appointment only; Sa, Su. Services: Su, 9AM, 11AM. 916 S Swanson St (between S Columbus Blvd and Christian St). 389.1513. ♿ www.nps.gov/glde

48 FELICIA'S

★★$$ Pictures of the old country brighten the main dining room of this row-house Italian restaurant, where the versatile kitchen turns out calamari sautéed with olives, capers, and fresh tomato; strip steak with brandy, Marsala, cream, and black peppercorn; grilled veal chop; and a fresh fish of the day. ♦ Italian ♦ Tu-F, lunch and dinner; Sa, Su, dinner. Reservations recommended. 1148 S 11th St (at Ellsworth St). 755.9656

49 SNOCKEY'S

$$ You'll know the instant you walk in that this oyster bar—around, in various locations, since 1912—is no-frills South Philly. Maybe it's the linoleum brickwork on the walls and the little red lobster prints on the white curtains. Ask to be seated in the front room, where you can watch the shucking at the raw bar, rather than in the main dining room in back. Start out with an appetizer from the raw bar before digging into the popular seafood combo platter—a deviled clam, fried scallops, fried oysters, a fried flounder fillet, cole slaw, and french fries. ♦ Seafood ♦ M-Sa, lunch and dinner; Su, dinner. 1020 S Second St (at Washington Ave). 339.9578. www.snockey.com

50 MUMMERS MUSEUM

The annual **Mummers Parade**, held on New Year's Day, is Philadelphia's Mardi Gras, when thousands of working-class citizens draped in elaborate costumes made of feathers and sequins strut down Broad Street to the sound of tinny string music. Crowds stationed on the sidewalks shout and heckle—and drink a fair amount of beer. Discussing the pagan roots of mummery, Temple University Professor Morris J. Vogel writes: "We can imagine the despair of primitive European peoples as autumn and winter brought ever less daylight, ever colder temperatures, fewer nuts and berries to gather, and fewer animals to hunt." At today's glitzy, televised Mummers Parade, however, thoughts of nuts and berries inevitably get lost in the revelry.

This museum, designed by **Veland and Junker** and completed in 1976, has two floors filled with items related to Mummers. In one particularly eerie room, mannequins model prize-winning costumes made over the years. A large digital clock ticks away the time remaining until New Year's Day, and plaques and photographs memorialize some of South Philadelphia's champions, such as the late Mayor Frank Rizzo. Between May and September, string band concerts are held on Tuesday nights between 8PM and 10PM (weather permitting) in the parking lot. ♦ Admission. Tu-Sa; Su, noon-5PM. 1100 S Second St (at Washington Ave). 336.3050. www.mummers.org

50 KRISTIAN'S

★★$$ Chef Kristian Leuzzi brings an uptown culinary sense to this downtown South Philly Italian, with specialties like pasta fagioli and osso buco, homemade pastas, and creative sauces distinguishing Kristian's as something special. The staff is friendly, and the atmosphere warm and casual. ♦ M, W-Sa, 5-10PM; Su, 3:30-8PM. 400 S 11th St (at Federal St). 468.0104. www.kristiansrestaurant.com

---

Restaurants/Clubs: Red | Hotels: Purple | Shops: Orange | Outdoors/Parks: Green | Sights/Culture: Blue

Center City West

Arch St.

Arch St. ←

30th Street
Station
(Amtrak)

John F. Kennedy Blvd.

8

9

Market St.

14

16

Chestnut St. →

18

Sansom St. ←

26   2

S 30th St.

76

Walnut St. ←

3

55

S 22nd St.

S 21st St.

Locust St. →

70

Rittenhou

78

Schuylkill River

82

83

Spruce St. ←

84
Schuylkill
River Park

Delancey Pl.

S 26th St.

S 25th St.

Panama
St.

S 24th St.

90
Fitler
Square

S 23rd St.

Pine St. →

Lombard St. ←

S 27th St.

94   South St. →

Grays Ferry Ave.

Bainbridge St. →

Arch St. ←

Kennedy
Plaza

Suburban
Station
2

3

N 19th St.

City
Hall

5   6
        7
Market St. →

10   11   12   13

15

17   Chestnut St. →

19   20   21   22   23

Sansom St. ← 24   25
29   30   31   32   33 34

38   39
Walnut St. ← 40 4142 43   44 45   46   47
        49 50   51   52   53   54

48   57 58
56   Chancellor St.   60

59
Rittenhouse   61
Square
                        62   63 64
        66   Locust St. →   67   68
                                    69

71   Latimer St. ←
        72   73   74   75   76   77
Rittenhouse Sq.
        79   80
Manning St.

81   Spruce St. ←
                                    85
                            86

88   Delancey St.
        89

S 20th St.   S 19th St.   S 18th St.   S 17th St.   S Smedley St.   S 16th St.   S 15th St.   S Broad St.

91   Pine St. →

Lombard St. ←
93

The Graduate
■ Hospital

South St. →

Bainbridge St. →

N
↑

km   1/8   1/4
mi   1/16   1/8

CENTER CITY WEST

The engines of investment and commerce roar from on high in the sleek glass towers of Center City West, the city's principal downtown core and site of the **Philadelphia Stock Exchange**. A fashionable residential area in the 19th century and a stronghold of investment houses and banks in the early 20th century, Center City West's skyline was transformed with the 1987 construction of the $225 million, 60-story **Liberty Place** skyscraper (home to **The Shops at Liberty Place** and the **Westin-Philadelphia** hotel). Several new skyscrapers are in the planning stages for the coming decade, as the city's skyline continues to expand.

On weekdays, **Chestnut Street** and the main thoroughfares of **Market Street** and **John F. Kennedy Boulevard** teem with businesspeople scurrying to and from their high-rise offices. Retail outlets stand shoulder to shoulder with little boutiques, hobby shops, great restaurants, and smart cafés in the stylish area south of Chestnut Street. **Rittenhouse Square,** a well-landscaped island of civility, is the most inviting public space in Philadelphia and the site of art exhibitions and flower shows. Some of the city's finest shops are located along **Walnut Street** between Rittenhouse Square and **Broad Street**, drawing an older, well-heeled clientele, whereas chic urbanites frequent the specialty shops that are found on the numbered cross streets and on narrow **Sansom Street.**

Farther down, tree-lined **South Street** is dominated by distinctive town houses, hardly changed since the 1890s. World-renowned Philadelphia architects **Frank Furness** and **John Notman** built many of the neighborhood's fine homes. Even subdivided into apartments, these brownstone or brick structures retain their character and originality. Also on these tree-lined streets are art galleries and several of the city's most unusual museums, including the **Mütter Museum,** which has a wealth of medical exotica, and the **Rosenbach Museum and Library**, with its priceless collection of literary manuscripts and first editions.

Except for restaurants, theaters, and a few outposts of commerce, Center City West above Walnut Street essentially shuts down at night. However, the Rittenhouse Square area and nearby **Pine** and **Spruce Streets** remain lively and safe, particularly in the warmer months. The faded first-run movie theaters on Chestnut Street are mostly a thing of the past; the neighborhood's innovative playhouse, the **InterAct Theater Company,** satisfies a more sophisticated audience with its multicultural approach to professional theater.

1 PENNSYLVANIA HORTICULTURAL SOCIETY

This organization was founded in 1827 for the purpose of promoting the science of horticulture. From its glass-curtained headquarters in Center City, the society runs the **Philadelphia Flower Show**—the world's largest indoor show of its kind, held every March at the **Pennsylvania Convention Center** and synonymous with spring in Philadelphia. It also holds more than 90 workshops, lectures, symposia, and clinics each year and maintains a library of some 15,000 books, periodicals, videos, and catalogs. ♦ Free. M-F. N 20th St (at Arch St). 988.8800. www.pennsylvaniahorticulturalsociety.com

2 SUBURBAN STATION

Downstairs in this refurbished 1930 Art Deco marble and brass building by **Graham, Anderson, Probst, and White** (the Chicago firm that also designed **30th Street Station**) are a shopping concourse and commuter rail station for trains to and from the Philadelphia suburbs. (You can also catch a fast train here to the airport.) Entrances to the concourse run from **City Hall** to **18th Street** along **John F. Kennedy Boulevard** and **Market Street**. ◆ John F. Kennedy Blvd (between N 16th and N 17th Sts). 580.7800. www.septa.org

3 JOHN F. KENNEDY BOULEVARD

The elevated **Pennsylvania Railroad** tracks, which ran from **30th Street Station** to **City Hall**, stymied development of Center City West for decades. Nicknamed the Chinese Wall, the tracks were finally torn down in 1953, making room for this thoroughfare and for the 14-acre **Penn Center** complex, which is connected by an underground concourse to **Suburban Station**.

4 COMMERCE SQUARE

I.M. Pei, architect of prominent buildings throughout the country, and **Henry Cobb**, who designed the John Hancock Tower in Boston, teamed up to create these 40-story twin corporate towers of textured gray granite (completed in 1987 and 1992). The diamond-shaped cutouts that adorn the top floors make the buildings easy to spot from blocks away. A wonderful midblock park designed by landscape architect **Hannah Olin** separates the towers. ◆ Market St (between N 20th and N 21st Sts)

Within Commerce Square:

TWENTY21

★★$$ This popular after-work spot boasts an expansive bar, along with a handsome dining room and outdoor seating when the weather is fine. Chef Rainer Floeter, formerly private chef to Main Line high society, has created a bold menu of new American favorites, including wild mushroom risotto ravioli, glazed salmon rolled in roasted tomato tapenade, and filet with roasted garlic Chianti sauce. Or let him surprise you with a tasting menu, five courses for $75. ◆ 2005 Market St (at N 20th St). 851.6262. www.twenty-21.com

5 THE FAMILY

This outdoor sculpture of a man, woman, and child was completed by Timothy Duffield in 1981. ◆ N 18th and Market Sts. www.philart.net/

6 MELLON BANK CENTER

The pyramid that covers the cooling system of the Mellon Bank Center has become a distinc-

tive element of the city's skyline, and its gray granite and white marble base dominates the block at street level. The building's tapering corners, which evoke an Egyptian obelisk, culminate in a latticework pyramid that's dramatically illuminated at night. Construction of the 54-story building, completed in 1990, followed the designs of **Kohn Pederson Fox Associates**, though the terrazzo floors and other stylish furnishings suggest an edifice of much greater age. Be sure to see the silvery vaulted ceilings inside. The underground concourse connects to **Suburban Station**. ◆ 1735 Market St (between N 17th and N 18th Sts). www.emporis.info/en/wm/bu?id=117939

7 THE TURF CLUB

This wood-paneled and brass-railed betting parlor broadcasts live from **Philadelphia Park** and other local horsetracks. It attracts a diverse mix of bettors: retirees, brokers from neighboring investment firms on their lunch hour, and regular players. There's also a restaurant and a bar. ◆ Daily, 11AM-11:15PM. 7 Penn Center (at N 17th and Market Sts). 246.1556. Also at 700 Packer Ave (at S Seventh St). 551.8270; 69th and Walnut Sts, Upper Darby. 352.5666. www.philadelphiapark.com/turfclubs/

8 MARKET STREET BRIDGE

The great granite eagles at each end of the bridge may look familiar to New Yorkers. Designed by **Adolph Alexander Weinman**, the 5,500-pound birds were installed on the roof of New York's Pennsylvania Station in 1903. When the station was demolished in the 1960s, the eagles were moved to diverse places, including this otherwise undistinctive bridge. None of the Schuylkill bridges are recommended for a casual walk; the traffic and wind can make them unpleasant for pedestrians.

9 BISTRO ST. TROPEZ

★★★$$ This restaurant is hard to find—it's on the fourth floor of an office building—but well worth the search. Enlivened with sunny Mediterranean Provençale colors, and with a superb view of the **Schuylkill River** and **Philadelphia Art Museum**, it serves excellent, reasonably priced French cuisine. Offerings include shrimp-and-lump-crab cake; filet mignon with Boursin cheese demiglacé; and pan-seared rainbow trout with arugula, sun-dried tomatoes, and goat cheese in a vegetable broth. The three-course prix-fixe dinner is a steal. ◆ French ◆ M-Tu, lunch; W-F, lunch and dinner; Sa, Su, dinner. Free parking after 8PM. 2400 Market St (between S 23rd St and the Market Street Bridge). 569.9269. ఈ. www.bistrosttropez.com

---

Restaurants/Clubs: Red **|** Hotels: Purple **|** Shops: Orange **|** Outdoors/Parks: Green **|** Sights/Culture: Blue

10 PHILADELPHIA STOCK EXCHANGE

Dating to 1790, the exchange was a key institution to the early American economy; now, however, it is overshadowed by the Big Board in the Big Apple. In 1981, it moved into its current comfortable quarters, designed by **Cope Linder Associates**, with an eight-story atrium under a greenhouse skylight as its centerpiece. Three selling floors, littered with call slips, offer stock equity, stock options, and foreign currency options. The traders stare at computer monitors like NASA flight controllers, furiously auctioning stocks and currency, signaling their bids across the floor, then shouting the puts and calls at each other, all making for good theater. ◆ 1900 Market St (at S 19th St). 496.5200. www.phlx.com

11 CROWNE PLAZA PHILADELPHIA

$$$ This 455-room hotel caters to business travelers, with each room outfitted with a coffeemaker, hair dryer, phones with computer jacks, an iron and ironing board, and other amenities. The convenient location is close to the stock exchange and a 10-minute walk to the convention center. ◆ S 18th and Market Sts. 561.7500, 800/2.CROWNE; fax 561.4484. &. www.sixcontinentshotels.com/crowneplaza

Within the Crowne Plaza Philadelphia:

ELEPHANT & CASTLE PUB & RESTAURANT

$$ This British-style pub has vintage signs, bar trays, and faux beams just like those found in its London namesake. The menu offers such moderately priced dishes as shepherd's pie, Cornish pasty, and bangers, along with burgers and salads. The homey pub food doesn't get great reviews, but the place is popular—possibly because of its extensive beer list. ◆ British ◆ Daily, breakfast, lunch, dinner, and late-night snacks. 561.7500. &. www.elephantcastle.com

12 MILORD LA CHAMARRE

Philadelphians predictably called it "the Mummer," though French artist Jean Dubuffet named his 1973 sculpture-and-drawing installation *My Lord in the Fancy Vest*. ◆ Market St (between S 15th and S 16th Sts). www.philart.net/

13 THE CLOTHESPIN

This sculpture is exactly what it appears to be, a towering steel clothespin rising 54 feet above Center Square Plaza. It's the work of Swedish-born artist Claes Oldenburg, known for other famous pop art icons, such as *Bat Column*, a hundred-foot-high baseball bat in Chicago, and *Split Button* at the **University of Pennsylvania**. ◆ S 15th and Market Sts. www.philart.net/

14 COLLEGE OF PHYSICIANS AND SURGEONS

Founded in 1787 by John Redman, Benjamin Rush, and other prominent physicians, the college is the oldest existing honorary medical society in the US. It is also the home of the **F.C. Wood Institute for the History of Medicine** and an important library of medical literature, which has rare editions of Aristotle and paintings by Thomas Eakins, Charles Willson Peale, John Singer Sargent, and Gilbert Stuart. Completed in 1908, the building was designed by **Cope and Stewardson**. ◆ Free. M-F. 19 S 22nd St (between Chestnut and Market Sts). 563.3737. &. www.collphyphil.org

Liberty Place

Within the College of Physicians and Surgeons:

THE MÜTTER MUSEUM

This museum is a repository of frightful medical curiosities, including the tumor extracted from President Grover Cleveland's cancerous jawbone, the liver shared by famous 19th-century Siamese twins Chang and Eng Bunker, and a skeleton of a 7'6" giant alongside that of a 3'6" dwarf. Also housed here is the **Chevalier Jackson Collection of Foreign Bodies**. Chevalier Jackson (his real name, not a title) founded the **Temple University** department of broncho-esophagology in the early 20th century, and has been called the Father of Laryngology for his work; the collection consists of drawer upon drawer of objects extracted from people who had accidentally swallowed them.

Despite the squeamish delight that generations of Philadelphians have taken in these wonders, the exhibits were not collected for their shock value. When the distinguished Dr. Thomas Dent Mütter retired in 1856, medical science was growing out of its metaphysical stage, when doctors attributed diseases to various "ill humours." In the mid-19th century, medical education was based on gross anatomy and pathology, and diseases were observed by watching their clinical course in the patient, followed by autopsy. These exhibits were a boon to students of the era. Cleveland's jawbone, by the way, was replaced by a rubber prosthesis in a secret shipboard operation in 1893, leaving the nation none the wiser. ♦ Donation requested. Tu-F. 563.3737. www.collphyphil.org/muttpg1.shtml

15 LIBERTY PLACE

Philadelphia possessed a relatively low skyline until 1987, when developer Willard G. Rouse and Chicago architect **Helmut Jahn** completed this 60-story mixed-use complex, the first structure to exceed the height of the hat worn by *William Penn* on **City Hall**. (A gentlemen's agreement had previously limited the height of buildings in Philadelphia to that of the statue's hat.) The postmodernist **One Liberty Place**, with its blue-glass, neon-trimmed façade reminiscent of Art Deco skyscrapers (especially New York's Chrysler Building), may be the most important building erected in Philadelphia since World War II and is certainly one of the great examples of the current architectural era. Jahn also designed the tower's 58-story twin, **Two Liberty Place**, a less distinguished structure despite its similarity in design and material. The complex, which is the home of **The Shops at Liberty Place** and the plush **Westin Philadelphia** hotel, has transformed commercial life in the neighborhood. Unlike so many signature buildings of 1980s America, One Liberty Place is an integral part of its city environment: Every downtown corner provides a different view of the tower, and every change in the weather or time of day is reflected on its surface. ♦ S 17th St (between Chestnut and Market Sts). 851.9000

Within Liberty Place:

THE SHOPS AT LIBERTY PLACE

Seventy specialty shops, including a food court and stalls of craft merchandise, occupy the first and second floors of this upmarket urban mall with a breathtaking rotunda topped by a windowed dome. There's often piano music on the skylit rotunda floor; at Christmastime, troupes of Mummers march in with pageantry and song. ♦ M-Sa; Su, noon-6PM; extended hours during holiday season. ♦ 851.9055. ♿ www.shopsatliberty.com

Within The Shops at Liberty Place:

APRIL CORNELL

This store is devoted to linens and women's clothing. You'll find beautiful—and relatively inexpensive—pillowcases, tablecloths, and linens in country florals and vivid French Provençale prints. Care for a very feminine white blouse? This place carries several varieties in rayon, cotton, and linen, as well as those full white nightgowns worn by Victorian heroines. ♦ 981.0350. ♿ www.aprilcornell.com

Although the Native American Lenni Lenape people had no written language, many of their words live on as place names, like Manayunk (the Schuylkill River), Tioga ("the fork of the stream"), Tacony ("the empty place"), Passyunk ("the level place"), Wissahickon ("the catfish stream"), Wissinoming ("the place of fear"), Tulpehocken ("where the turtles are"), and, alas, Moyamensing, the Lenni Lenape word for "pigeon droppings."

The first women's suffrage book, Mary Wollstonecraft's *A Vindication of the Rights of Women*, was published in Philadelphia in 1792, almost as soon as it had come out in London.

Located just five blocks from the Philadelphia Museum of Art, the Eastern State Penitentiary was once the most expensive building in America. Built in 1829, it was the most famous prison in the world, designed not merely to punish, but to move the prisoner toward spiritual change, based on the Quaker-inspired system of isolation and labor. It counts Al Capone and Willie Sutton among its famous guests.

THE BEST

David Dye

WXPN World Cafe Host and Producer

Best-kept Philadelphia secrets:

1. The **Whispering Walls** next to **Memorial Hall** in **Fairmount Park**: Sit at one end of the bench and whisper to your loved one sitting 30 feet away at the other end of the curved bench. They'll hear you perfectly.

2. **Kelly Drive's bike path**: Keep going down Kelly Drive west, through **Manayunk** and all the way to **Conshohocken**, for an urban-into-suburban adventure.

3. Grilled octopus at **Dimitri's**: Bring a bottle of white. It's worth the wait.

4. **The Point** in **Bryn Mawr** and **North by Northwest** in **Mount Airy**, two lesser-known near-perfect spots for adults to hear music. **Downtown Tritone** is the newest hip spot for music lovers.

5. **Standard Tap** in **Northern Liberties**: The perfect bar of your dreams. Sure, it's a little like a stage set, but the pork sandwich makes it all worthwhile.

6. The Japanese teahouse in Fairmount Park.

7. **30th Street Station**: No secret, but if you flew into town, make a detour to stand in the grandeur of Philadelphia's most splendid space.

TreAnna's Adornments

Specialty and custom jewelry, related items, and gift certificates for all of the above are sold here. ◆ 569.2969 ♿

New World Coffee

This branch of the ubiquitous yuppie café provides a nice resting spot in between purchases. Try a latte, cappuccino, special blend, or iced coffee to pep you up. Pastries, soups, and gourmet sandwiches are also tempting. ◆ 587.9230. ♿. www.newworldcoffee.com

Caviar Assouline

You'll even find treats for the person who has everything at this branch of the locally based gourmet store, which sells everything from imported caviar and caviar spoons to foie gras, truffles, smoked salmon, and Valrhona chocolates. ◆ 972.1616; 800/521.4491. www.caviarassouline.com

Fire & Ice

This fascinating store is almost a museum of rocks, gems, minerals, fish fossils, and corals. Glass cases display handcarved soapstone from Kenya, malachite necklaces, earrings in sterling silver and onyx, and tiger-eye figurines. ◆ 564.2871

Rand McNally Map and Travel Store

Whether you're looking for a map of a newly formed Eastern European nation or a topographic map of your own backyard, it's probably here. The prices aren't discount, but the selection is good. You'll also find globes, guidebooks, travel-related toys, and games. This shop can be entered from S 17th Street, as well as from inside the complex. ◆ 563.1101. ♿. www.randmcnallystore.com

Brentano

In addition to the usual selection of best-sellers you'll find a nice collection of books of local interest and classics here. ◆ 557.8443 ♿

Westin Philadelphia

$$$$ This 290-room luxury hotel is furnished in European style, with 18th-century oil paintings, antiques, and hand-woven rugs. In the afternoon, a pianist plays classical music, and the evenings are given to jazz. Ask for an upper-floor room on the east side for great nighttime views of the **Liberty Place** rotunda and the frosted-glass Art Deco façade of the **Institute of Art**. Guests enjoy a fitness center and sauna, plus dual phone lines and 27-inch color TVs in all rooms. Enter the hotel from the Liberty Place shopping area or from S 17th Street, and take an elevator up to the third-floor lobby. ◆ S 17th St (between Chestnut and Market Sts). 563.1600; fax 564.9559. ♿. www.starwood.com/westin

Within the Westin Philadelphia:

The Grill

★★$$$ A clubby, masculine room provides a comfortable setting for lunch and dinner; prices are lower at lunch. Typical choices include tuna steak with fennel, peppered Gulf shrimp on fettuccine, and a chicken-breast club sandwich. Raspberry crème brûlée and Key lime pie are among the dessert choices. ◆ Contemporary American ◆ Daily, breakfast, lunch, and dinner. 563.1600 ♿

16 First Unitarian Church

In 1886, architect **Frank Furness** designed this two-story structure for his father, the Reverend William Henry Furness. Although the church's exterior has undergone much alteration, the sanctuary remains intact, with a ceiling of daffodils stenciled by the architect in gold leaf.

♦ Services: Su, 11AM. 2125 Chestnut St (between S 21st and S 22nd Sts). 563.3980; fax 563.4209. www.firstuuphilly.org

17 WHODUNIT

Creaky floors and dim lighting set the stage at this bookstore noir. At Art Borgeau's bookshop, mystery lovers can browse among thousands of new and used crime books, including some long-out-of-print items. ♦ M-Sa, 11 AM-6:30PM. 1931 Chestnut St (between S 19th and S 20th Sts). 567.1478. www.whodunitphilly.com

18 2300 CHESTNUT STREET MURAL

The 1983 painted trompe l'oeil mural by Richard Haas draws in a series of Philadelphia landmarks, seemingly placed in the building's interior: statues of William Penn and Benjamin Franklin, and behind them the ghost of architect **Frank Furness**'s long-demolished **Baltimore & Ohio Railroad Station**. At ground level, the parking lot seems to abut the Schuylkill River. ♦ At S 23rd St

19 BOYD'S FOR MEN

Holding forth in a 1907 Beaux Arts building that once housed the art school for the **Pennsylvania Academy of the Fine Arts**, this top-of-the-line men's store offers ready-to-wear labels and custom-made items. Though it may have the finest selection of men's clothes in the city, it's not really a store for browsers: The platoon of eager salesmen chills the atmosphere. White balustrades, marble columns, and prints enhance an already-elegant interior. **Cafe Emily**, a café in the store, serves gourmet sandwiches and such light entrées as grilled filet mignon on focaccia with sweet onion relish. ♦ M-Tu, Th-Sa; W, 9:30AM-9PM. 1818 Chestnut St (between S 18th and S 19th Sts). 564.9000. &. www.boydsphiladelphia.com

20 FREEMAN FINE ARTS

Not everything for sale at this auction house is a fine antique, and that makes the two-figure bidding all the more fun. The furniture on the floor of the cavernous salesroom can range from Mission buffets to Naugahyde-covered recliners, and some of the paintings are valuable only for their frames. Look for the quality stuff on the days before auctions, which take place every Wednesday beginning at 10AM. Glassware and paintings go first. Written bids are accepted. Cataloged auctions of antiques and paintings are held several times a year in the handsome third-floor gallery. ♦ M-F. 1808 Chestnut St (between S 18th and S 19th Sts). 563.9275. www.freemansauction.com

21 DAFFY'S

Find men's, women's, and children's name-brand fashions, at prices discounted 40%-75%. Leather items and Italian suits are best buys. ♦ Daily. 1700 Chestnut St (at 17th St). 963.9996. www.daffys.com

22 THE ART INSTITUTE OF PHILADELPHIA (WCAU BUILDING)

Built in 1928 for the **WCAU** radio station, this child of the Jazz Age uses all kinds of glass to show off its Art Deco charms. It was designed by **Harry Sternfeld** (who specialized in Art Deco) with his student **Gabriel Roth**, and renovated in 1983 by the local firm of **Kopple Sheward and Day**. Glass and metal chevrons run alongside the frosted-glass tower, which glowed blue at night when the station was broadcasting. The wall surface is composed of blue glass chips set in plastic. Inside, note the Deco brushed-metal elevator doors and mailbox. The institute, an independent art school, has occupied the premises since 1982. ♦ Daily. 1622 Chestnut St (between S 16th and S 17th Sts). 567.7080. &. www.artinstitutes.edu

23 PACKARD BUILDING

Early-20th-century artist Samuel Yellin, whose wrought-iron fixtures adorn several Philadelphia landmarks, designed the gates and lighting fixtures on the Chestnut Street side of this structure. Note the detailing above the 15th Street entrance. (Trivia buffs: The Packard's gates weigh 10 tons apiece.) ♦ S 15th and Chestnut Sts

24 SOFITEL PHILADELPHIA

$$$ The luxe French chain Sofitel set up shop in early 2000 at the former site of the **Philadelphia Stock Exchange** building. Amenities include a brasserie named for the French writer Colette; **La Bourse**, a sleek lobby bar; 306 soundproof rooms; 55 suites; and data ports offering high-speed Internet access. Eight private meeting rooms are ideal for conferences or dinner meetings. The only **Sofitel** where the French is spoken with a Philadelphia accent. 120 S 17th St. 569.8300, fax 564.7453. www.accor.com

25 DAVIO'S

★★$$ Located in the former **Provident Bank** headquarters, complete with polished wood floors, creamy walls, 24-foot ceilings, and towering pillars, Davio's puts an Italian spin on a good steak. Chef David Boyle cooks up one of the best veal chops in town—served with Reggiano cheese, prosciutto, spinach,

Restaurants/Clubs: Red | Hotels: Purple | Shops: Orange | Outdoors/Parks: Green | Sights/Culture: Blue

A PRIMER OF PHILADELPHIA ARCHITECTS

At more than 300 years old, Philadelphia is one of America's oldest cities. During the course of its 3 centuries, virtually every kind of architectural style has been employed in the city, and Philadelphia architects have played a prominent role in the evolution of various schools of American architecture.

In the 1700s, the two most influential architects in Philadelphia were Scottish-born **Robert Smith**, the colonies' foremost carpenter-architect, and designer of **Christ Church** steeple, **St. Peter's Church**, and **Carpenters' Hall**, and New Jersey-born **William Strickland**, architect of the **Second Bank of the United States**, a design that established the Greek Revival style in the US. A century later, architects such as **Benjamin Latrobe**, **Robert Mills**, and **John Haviland** were working in the Greek Revival style and introducing more classical details to American buildings.

Thomas Ustick Walter (1804–1887) gained national attention with his design of **Girard College** in 1833, a project that engaged him for the next 14 years. He also designed the expansion of the US Capitol Building, including the extension of the Senate and House wings, and the addition of the Capitol dome. Walter was a founding member of the **American Institute of Architects**.

In the middle of the 19th century, another Scottish immigrant, **John Notman** (1810-1865), introduced a number of sophisticated English architectural styles to Philadelphia and the US. The **Philadelphia Athenaeum**, for example, was the first Renaissance Revival building in America. One of the city's greatest architects was Philadelphia native son **Frank Furness** (1839–1912). After the Civil War, during which he won the Congressional Medal of Honor, Furness opened a Philadelphia office, first with **John Fraser**, then with **George Hewitt**. Furness and Hewitt gained national prominence with their design of the **Pennsylvania Academy of Fine Arts**.

Furness's personal style—Victorian Gothic—brought him fame in the many banks, residences, and railroad stations he crafted. When the Classical Revival style became popular, Furness's career declined. His accomplishments were virtually ignored for 50 years, a time when, sadly, many of his most important Philadelphia buildings, including the **Provident Life and Trust Company** and the **National Bank of the Republic**, were demolished.

The city's next prominent architect, **Wilson Eyre** (1858-1944), was born in Florence, Italy, and moved to Philadelphia around 1877. Eyre was one of the most creative and imaginative residential architects of his time, garnering national recognition for his work in Philadelphia's suburbs. He was the cofounder, with Frank Miles Day, of *House & Garden* magazine, and its editor between 1901 and 1905.

Paul Philippe Cret (1876-1945) was born in Lyons, France, and studied at the Ecole des Beaux-Arts in Paris. He came to Philadelphia at the age of 27 to teach at the University of Pennsylvania. His interest in city planning led to the original plans for **Benjamin Franklin Parkway** and redesign of **Rittenhouse Square**.

George Howe (1886-1955), of Worcester, Massachusetts, settled in Philadelphia in 1913. Howe favored the International style, a modern approach that reached its pinnacle in his design of the **Philadelphia Saving Fund Society Building**, still one of the finest examples of modern architecture in the country.

Philadelphia's contemporary architecture of the 1950s and 1960s was influenced strongly by **Edmund Bacon**, director of the city planning commission; **G. Holmes Perkins**, dean of the School of Fine Arts at the University of Pennsylvania; and Louis I. Kahn, who, as a teaching architect at Penn beginning in 1957, stressed the use of heavy materials, elaborate structural solutions, and natural light to form interior space.

---

and polenta, along with steaks, homemade pasta, and a killer crab cake. Choose from a wine list specializing in Italian vintages, or every Friday night, bring your own, with no corkage fee. ◆ 111 S 17th St (at Sansom St). 563.4810. www.www.davios.com

25 AMERICAN INSTITUTE OF ARCHITECTS BOOKSTORE

The tall store windows reveal a terrific variety of books on architecture, especially about Philadelphia and the region, as well as posters, mobiles, T-shirts, cards, bookmarkers, and other design-oriented gift items. Surely you know someone who would love a model airplane kit based on Leonardo da Vinci's drawings of flying machines, or

adult building blocks that teach architecture principles. ◆ M-Sa, 10AM-6PM; W, open til 8PM; Su, closed. 117 S 17th St (at Sansom St). 569.3188. &. www.aiabookstore.com

26 THE CLASSICAL GUITAR STORE

All kinds of guitars, many of them secondhand, are sold here. The mellow, nylon-stringed classical guitar is the house specialty. ◆ M-F, noon-6PM; Sa, 10AM-5PM. 2038 Sansom St (between S 20th and S 21st Sts). 567.2972. www.classicalguitarstore.com

27 INTERACT THEATRE COMPANY

This respected company, now housed in the former home of the **Wilma Theater**, has built a national reputation producing new and contemporary plays by and about people of different cultures. Billing itself as a genuinely multicultural professional theater, InterAct produces a main-stage season of four plays between September and May in the **Adrienne Theatre** across the street. The company's workshops for schools, corporations, and the community at large use theater as a tool for addressing pressing social problems. ♦ 2030 Sansom St (between S 20th and S 21st Sts). 568.8077. ⅆ. www.interacttheatre.org

28 FAT JACK'S COMICRYPT

A full line of superheroes, from Adam Strange to Zot, plus an extensive collection of back issues, is available in this shrine to the comic book. How about a few copies of *Love and Rockets*, a magazine of graphic short stories for adults? ♦ M-Sa; Su, 1PM-6PM. 2006 Sansom St (between S 20th and S 21st Sts). 963.0788

28 HOME SWEET HOMEBREW

What exactly is a zymurgist? Well, you could become one in George H. Hummel's shop, which has everything you need to make your own wine and beer ("except the time," Hummel advises): starter kits, labels, bottles, bottle caps, you name it. The store also offers mail-order service. ♦ Tu, Th, F, 11:30AM-6PM; W, 11:30AM-8PM; Sa, 11AM-5PM. 2008 Sansom St (between S 20th and S 21st Sts). 569.9469. www.homesweethomebrew.com

29 TRIA

★★$ Owner Jon Myerow couldn't find a cool place that served only boutique beers, wine, cheese, and small plates—so he opened this groovy wine bar and cheese lounge, a terrific addition to the neighborhood. Chef Chris Kujawa, last of **Striped Bass**, is also fromager, bringing in cheese from Murray's Cheese Chop in New York. Most menu items are $10 or less. And the wine list is in the $6-$10 range; beers like Allagash White out of Portland, Maine, Brooklyn Lager, and Belgian Saison Dupont run in the $4-$16 range. ♦ 123 S 18th St (at Sansom St). 972.8742

30 JOSEPH FOX BOOKSHOP

Descend the steps to this homey, sensitively stocked bookstore (with a superb art section) that boasts a devoted clientele. The family-run business, which opened in 1951, is refreshingly personal compared to the newer megabookstores nearby. ♦ M-Sa. 1724 Sansom St (between S 17th and S 18th Sts). 563.4184. www.foxbookshop.com

31 FIRST BAPTIST CHURCH

A brooding brownstone completed in 1899 and designed by **Edgar Seeler**, this church combines Byzantine and Romanesque features. The 12 panels in the dome are Byzantine stained glass. ♦ Daily, 11:30AM-2PM. S 17th and Sansom Sts. 563.3853. ⅆ. www.philadelphiabuildings.com

32 GROSS MCCLEAF GALLERY

Most of the artists who exhibit landscapes and representational paintings here hail from the Philadelphia region. They include Joe Sweeney, whose paintings have portrayed traditional scenes of Boathouse Row along the Schuylkill River; Bertha Leonard and her fanciful interiors; and Jacqueline Chesley, a neo-Impressionist who has used **Longwood Gardens** as a subject. ♦ M-Sa. 127 S 16th St (at Sansom St). 665.8138. www.grossmccleaf.com

33 SANSOM STREET OYSTER HOUSE

★★$$ Chef-owner Cary Neff took over David Mink's traditional fish house a few years ago, maintaining many of the favorite dishes while adding a few new twists, like sesame-crusted tuna served medium rare in a ginger-soy reduction and a variety of exotic farm-raised oysters. But you can also get fried and grilled seafood served with potato and veggies—no fuss, no muss. Mink's family collection of antique oyster dishes still hang on the walls, and the creamy rice pudding—a favorite of David Mink's father—is still the perfect way to end your meal. ♦ 1516 Sansom St (between S 15th and S 16th Sts). 567.7683. ⅆ. www.sansomoysyters.com

33 NODDINGHEAD BREWERY & RESTAURANT

★★$ You'll find savory comfort food in a casual atmosphere at this second-floor bar-restaurant located just steps away from **Rittenhouse Row** shopping. The ambiance is all polished wood and deep colors, dominated by the gleam of the copper brewing tanks that are at the heart of the

---

Restaurants/Clubs: Red | Hotels: Purple | Shops: Orange | Outdoors/Parks: Green | Sights/Culture: Blue

brewpub's allure. Master brewer Brandon Greenwood applies his degree in brewing, malting, and distilling science to the task of creating world-class brews like Angry Scotch Ale and Robust Porter. The food is above the usual pub fare, with dishes like polenta torte, jerked chicken, and lamb shank served with white beans and sausages. ◆ 1516 Sansom St. (between S 15th and S 16th Sts). 569.9525. www.noddinghead.com

34 Roy's

★★$$$ The Philadelphia location for chef Roy Yamaguchi's trend-setting Hawaiian fusion cuisine is set in the architecturally stunning former **Fidelity Bank**. The bilevel restaurant sports a spacious, tropical feel, accentuated by a palette of jewel tones and exotic artwork. A large open kitchen turns out Pacific Rim concoctions like crispy spicy tuna sushi roll, white sesame seed–crusted sea bass with a creamy miso sauce, and cilantro-seared Alaskan halibut in caramelized pineapple and black bean jus. Best bet is the dim sum "canoe"—priced at $25 and sporting generous portions of five different appetizers to introduce a wide range of flavors, including Szechuan-style ribs and Kahlua pork spring rolls. A five-course chef's tasting menu is also available. Choose from a wide range of sakes—including Roy's signature brand—or opt for a glass or bottle of wine from the exuberant wine list, including several spicy whites meant to be paired with exotic fare. Plan ahead for the melting-hot chocolate soufflé, which should be ordered with your entrée so it will be molten and ready at dinner's end. ◆ 124-134 S 15th St (at Sansom St). 988.1814. www.roysrestaurant.com

35 Loie

★★$$ Jeremy Duclut, last of **Le-Bec Fin**, whips up classic French bistro fare at this sexy little spot, from a Parisian-style burger à cheval, topped with a fried egg and grilled onions, to hearty French onion soup, crispy salted *frites*, and rotisserie chicken with garlic mashed potatoes. A DJ comes onto the scene around 10PM. ◆ 128 S 19th St (between Walnut and Sansom Sts). 568.0808

36 William H. Allen Bookseller

Countless used and antiquarian books have changed hands in these musty surroundings. The selection on classical history and literature is particularly fine. ◆ M-F; Sa, 8:30AM-1PM. 2031 Walnut St (between S 20th and S 21st Sts). 563.3398. 占. www.whallenbooks.com

37 Irish Pub

★$ Stained glass, high ceilings, and bars of carved cherry wood recall older pubs in Ireland, and portraits of Irish-American

celebrities grace the walls. The Dublin Irish stew is the best thing on the menu, which also includes chili, salmon, and steak, but people come here for the drinks and live-it-up atmosphere, not the cuisine. On many nights, a DJ spins records from 9PM on, and a high-decibel crowd takes over. ◆ Irish/American ◆ Daily, lunch and dinner. 2007 Walnut St (between S 20th and S 21st Sts). 568.5603. Also at 1123 Walnut St (between S 11th and S 12th Sts). 925.3311

38 Anthropologie

Now occupied by an ultrahip clothing and housewares store, this 1898 Beaux Arts building was once the home of Drexel heiress Sara Drexel Fell and Alexander Van Rensselaer. It's rich with columns, projecting bays, and a paneled dome at the top of the grand winding staircase. The best-preserved part of the **Peabody & Stearns** building is the first-floor **Doges Room**, formerly the dining room. Mrs. Van Rensselaer, born a Quaker, converted to Catholicism and decorated accordingly: The ceiling portraits include four popes and several Venetian magistrates surrounded by festoons, anthemia (relief floral forms), and cartouches. As for shopping, look for women's clothing on the first floor and hip housewares in the basement. ◆ M-Sa; Su, noon-6PM. 1801 Walnut St (at S 18th St). 568.2114

39 Helen Drutt Gallery

Owner Helen Drutt has helped elevate such crafts as ceramics, textiles, and jewelry to fine art. Her prestigious gallery features such prominent artists as goldsmith and painter Breon O'Casey, and Rudolf Staffel, who specializes in translucent porcelain vessels. ◆ W-F, 11AM-5PM; Sa, by appointment. 1721 Walnut St (between S 17th and S 18th Sts). 735.1625. www.helendrutt.com

40 The Latham Hotel

$$$ Located near Center City West shopping, this unpretentious first-class hotel has 138 sunny guest rooms and one suite. The staff is friendly and well-informed; some are said to have worked here since the former apartment building, erected in 1906, became a hotel in 1970. A $3 million renovation has outfitted the rooms with marbled bathrooms, in-room coffeemakers, cable TV, and, for a boon to business travelers, dual-line telephones with voice mail. Other amenities include same-day valet and laundry services and a fitness center. There is no restaurant, but the hotel serves a breakfast buffet each day, and there are dozens of restaurants within walking distance. ◆ 135 S 17th St (at Walnut St). 563.7474, 877/LATHAM1; fax 568.0110. 占. www.lathamhotel.com

41 URBAN OUTFITTERS

Clothing, accessories, and housewares for the impossibly young and hip line the stores of this funky and fun boutique. End-of-season sales are great for bargain hunters. Many of the items have a multicultural bent. ♦ 1627 Walnut St (between S 16th and S 17th Sts). 569.3131

42 ALMA DE CUBA

★★★$$$ A joint venture between New York chef Douglas Rodriguez (the godfather of Nuevo Latino cuisine) and Stephen Starr, this elegant tri-level restaurant serves food that pays homage to Cuban, Peruvian, Spanish, Brazilian, and Caribbean cuisine. The downstairs lounge drips with beautiful people sipping mojitos and looking fabulous. You'll enjoy the scene—but you'll come back for the food. ♦ 1623 Walnut St (between S 16th and S 17th Sts). 988.1799. www.almadecubarestaurant.com

42 NEWMAN GALLERIES

This Philadelphia institution has been in business since 1865—and the dated stock of landscapes and portraits clearly reflects it. Nevertheless, some noteworthy pieces can be found in the huge inventory here, including items of historic interest. Newman wasn't always a place for the affluent (as it is now); in the 1870s, the gallery exhibited art on the streets with a handsome horse-drawn Art Cart. ♦ M-Sa. 1625 Walnut St (between S 16th and S 17th Sts). 563.1779. ♿. www.newmangalleries1865.com

43 BRASSERIE PERRIER

★★★$$$ Chef and restaurateur Georges Perrier, who also owns **Le Bec-Fin**, the city's preeminent French restaurant (see below), added this star to the burgeoning Walnut Street Restaurant Row. The goal here was to offer modern French cuisine in a more casual atmosphere than that of Le Bec-Fin, and somewhat more reasonable prices. Although prices aren't exactly cheap, the light French cuisine is well worth it.

The décor rises to the occasion: a 65-seat bar, backed by shimmering, silvery-green cracked glass, is surrounded by barstools and chairs covered in Ultrasuede in shades of lilac, peri-winkle, mulberry, and aubergine; banquettes snuggle against the walls. The 88-seat main dining room is outfitted with more comfy banquettes and tables set with Italian glassware and Villeroy & Boch plates. Additionally, there are two private dining rooms on the second level. The menu? Start with oysters from the raw bar or seared-potato–goat cheese terrine; move on to a pasta dish like rabbit-pancetta canelloni with sage jus, or a major entrée: pistachio-crusted wild bass with butternut-squash risotto, or a classic sirloin. The signature dessert is a nouvelle tiramisù with frozen-chocolate liquid center. ♦ French ♦ M-F, lunch and dinner; Sa, Su, dinner. Reservations recommended. 1619 Walnut St (between S 16th and S 17th Sts). 568.3000. ♿. www.brasserieperrier.com

44 LE BEC-FIN

★★★★$$$$ Georges Perrier could have set up shop anywhere—but he opened his world-class French restaurant in Philadelphia more than 30 years ago and has stuck with the city ever since. While the classics still rule, chef Perrier has allowed subtle changes in the menu, a few modern French touches, and more of the Asian flavors that Perrier himself is so fond of. Le Bec-Fin remains the premier French dining experience, from the opulent surroundings—love that salmon Scalamandre silk—to the attentive European service and letter-perfect food. Prices are fixed at $135 for dinner, $45 for lunch—both include the sinfully famous dessert cart, which is, thankfully, still all you can eat. Sample food prepared by the same chef for less money downstairs in **Le Bar Lyonnais**; a popular watering hole for well-heeled singles, it also is an ideal spot for pre- and post-theater drinks and light meals. ◆ French ◆ M-F, lunch and dinner; Sa, dinner. Jacket and tie requested. Reservations required. 1523 Walnut St (between S 15th and S 16th Sts). 567.1000. www.lebecfin.com

45 PORTICO

★★★$$$$ Chef-owner Alberto DelBello insists that everything in his upscale Italian restaurant be authentic, made from scratch, and reflective of the cuisine found in Italy's Tuscan region. Game, mushrooms, truffles, and risotto are prominently featured on the menu—the homemade *pappardelle alla lepre*, pasta with rabbit, is about as authentic as it gets. DelBello isn't one to compromise—but you'll know that as soon as you taste the polenta with imported mushrooms, lobster salad with orange dressing, and rack of veal over fresh greens. ◆ 1519 Walnut St (between S 15th and S 16th Sts). 587.7000. www.il-portico.com

46 DREXEL AND COMPANY BUILDING

Originally the offices of the Drexel financial company, this Italian Renaissance palazzo, designed in 1927 by **Day and Klauder**, echoes the Strozzi Palace in Florence. Bas-relief panels above the ground-floor windows depict the signs of the zodiac. From the outside, the building seems impervious; its walls are solid granite, and the massive doors swing shut on hammered-steel hinges. The red canopy that the current owners have erected in front of the door compromises the overall effect, however. The entrance to a **Bally's Total Fitness** center is on 15th Street (464.2121); other tenants occupy office space. ◆ 135-143 S 15th St (at Walnut St)

47 MORTON'S OF CHICAGO

★★$$$ Although there are steak houses springing up everywhere around town, Morton's is the original—at least it's the oldest continuously operating beef house in town. Firmly ensconced in its new digs at the former **Stock Exchange** building, Morton's boasts a large bar with TVs tuned into sporting events, a clubby dining room that accommodates more than 100, and private dining for up to 100. And the crowds keep on coming for the perfectly prepared aged steaks, giant lobsters, and chops—not to mention the creamed spinach, 1-pound baked potatoes, and sautéed wild mushrooms. Don't leave without trying the Godiva hot chocolate cake, which should be against the law but—happily—isn't. ◆ 1411 Walnut St. 557.0724. www.mortons.com

48 HOLY TRINITY CHURCH

Scottish-born architect John Notman, who gave Philadelphians some of their prettiest churches (**St. Mark's** on Locust Street and **St. Clement's** on Cherry Street), designed this Romanesque Revival brownstone, which opened as an Episcopal church in 1859. Philadelphia architect **George Hewitt** completed the tower in 1868, the same year the church's rector, Phillips Brooks, composed "O Little Town of Bethlehem." ◆ Services: Th, 12:15PM; Su, 8:30AM, 11AM. 1904 Walnut St (between Rittenhouse Sq W and S 20th St) 567.1267. www.philadelphiabuildings.com

49 DENIM

★★$$ Twentysomethings flock to Denim for its late-night scene, bottle service, and red-hot DJs. People who love to eat come for chef Scott McLeod's menu of Latin-Asian specialties. Check out the sexy Red Lounge to sit up close and personal with your main squeeze, or if you're with a group of 6 to 8 intimate friends, reserve the Crystal lounge, with its gauzy white fabric, single chandelier, and violet lighting. ◆ 1712 Walnut St (between S 17th and S 18th Sts). 735.6700. www.denimlounge.com

50 PIETRO'S COAL OVEN PIZZERIA

★★$$ Crisp, thin-crusted pizzas, huge salads ideal for sharing, and numerous pasta entrées are the mainstays at this casual, affordable restaurant. Wine, beer, and other alcoholic beverages are served. ◆ Pizza ◆ Daily, lunch and dinner. 1714 Walnut St (between S 17th and S 18th Sts). 735.8090. Also at 121 South St (between Front and Second Sts). 733.0675. www.pietrospizza.com

51 SCHMIDT/DEAN GALLERY

You might see the works of stone sculptor Bradford Graves, who draws inspiration from primitive cultures; local artist Stephen Estock, who paints abstracts on linen; or photographer Linda Adlestein, who creates multilayered negatives of Rome and Venice. Everything shown here—prints, paintings, sculptures, and photographs—is contemporary. ◆ Tu-Sa, 10:30AM-6PM, or by appointment. 1636 Walnut St (between S 16th and S 17th Sts). 546.7212. Also at 1721 Spruce St (between S 17th and S 18th Sts). 546.9577

52 MAHOGANY

If you crave a good cigar after dinner, consider a stroll over to Mahogany, upstairs from **Holt's Cigars** on Walnut Street. Known for its large selection of vintage scotches, Mahogany gives patrons the chance to smoke excellent cigars and savor a cocktail in a clubby, comfortable atmosphere. Although light fare is available—the charcuterie platter is a favorite—most patrons prefer to savor a good smoke sans food. What might surprise you is the quality of the air here—although you won't get away from the smell of an imported cigar, an aggressive air-cleaning system keeps the air clearer than in the average bar. Sinatra on the stereo, comfy leather couches, single malt, and a good cigar—sounds like one definition of heaven. ♦ 1524 Walnut St (between S 15th and S 16th Sts). 732.3982

52 STARBUCKS COFFEE

With more than 500 coffee shops nationwide, the Seattle-based chain finally opened one in Philadelphia in May 1995. Take your coffee or tea and pastry to a table or windowside counter for some caffeine-laced people watching. ♦ Daily. 1528 Walnut St (between S 15th and S 16th Sts). 732.0708. ♿ Also at 347 South St (between S Third and S Fourth Sts). 627.4060; 1201 Market St (at N 12th St). 925.1580; 10 Penn Center (1801 Market St). 569.4223

53 SUSANNA FOO

★★★★$$$ Chef-owner Susanna Foo—one of the most acclaimed female chefs in the nation—sets her culinary imagination free in this bright and airy restaurant, decorated in both traditional and contemporary Chinese styles. Though basically Asian, the cuisine borrows heavily from other cultures, offering such unusual dishes as 100-cornered crab cakes (named for the croutonlike breading), sea bass with freshwater shrimp in balsamic sauce; grilled baby rack of lamb with rosemary in a lemongrass-and-soy marinade, and a crispy duck from which all signs of fat have been meticulously removed. Foo also owns Suilan in the Borgata in Atlantic City. ♦ Eclectic/Chinese ♦ M-F, lunch and dinner; Sa, dinner. Jacket and tie requested. Reservations recommended. 1512 Walnut St (between S 15th and S 16th Sts). 545.2666. www.susannafoo.com

53 STRIPED BASS

★★★★$$$$ One of Philadelphia's defining restaurants for more than a decade, Striped Bass is now new and improved, thanks to a redo by new owner Stephen Starr and a rejuvenated menu, courtesy of Alfred Portale (Gotham Bar and Grill) as consulting chef and Christopher Lee (Oceana Restaurant, Restaurant Jean Georges, The Fifth Floor), Chef de Cuisine. Portale's imaginative menu is swimming in seafood, including creations like wild striped bass ceviche and smoked eel with micro arugula and quail eggs, but his signature grilled gotham steak, a 13-ounce New York Strip cut, with bone marrow and Dijon custard, Vidalia onion rings, and bordelaise sauce, are also available. The room's dramatic interior has been enhanced by decadent chandeliers, chocolate-brown velvet seating, and brown calf leather banquettes. What we thought was perfect is now even better. ♦ 1600 Walnut St (at S 15th St). 732.4444. www.stripedbassrestaurant.com

54 TIFFANY & CO.

The jewelry is real, but the granite-and-marble building, closely modeled after the flagship store in New York, is faux. It was built in 1990 by local developer Richard Rubin. The statue of Atlas, hoisting the clock, is a replica of the 1853 original in New York by Henry Frederick Metzler. ♦ M-Sa. 1414 Walnut St (between S Broad and S 15th Sts). 735.1919. www.tiffany.com

55 ENGLISH VILLAGE

Built in 1923, Spencer Roberts's English Village was a successful experiment in urban design, with attached houses arranged around a well-tended flagstone court (no vehicles are allowed). Tall mansard roofs contribute to the Elizabethan flavor—a delightful throwback to a bygone age. ♦ S 22nd St (between Locust and Walnut Sts). www.philadelphiabuildings.com

56 THE RITTENHOUSE HOTEL

$$$$ Alexander Cassatt, president of the **Pennsylvania Railroad** and brother of early-20th-century Impressionist painter Mary Cassatt, lived in the house that once occupied the site of this deluxe hotel and condominium tower, designed by **Alesker, Reiff and Dundon**. The Rittenhouse project was begun in the early 1970s, but the development stalled, leaving the white, horizontal ziggurat designed by local architect **Don Reiff** an empty shell for 7 years. With time and good maintenance, this hotel has found its place among the square's other mammoth apartment towers, and it ranks as the best place to stay in this part of the city. Occupying the first 12 floors of the 33-story building are 138 spacious guest rooms, each with two floor-to-ceiling windows overlooking either the square or the city's west side. Marble baths, mahogany furnishings, duvet-style bedspreads, and minibars create a luxurious ambiance. Luxury suites are available for longer stays. Out-of-town stars are frequent guests (Denzel Washington and Tom Hanks called the hotel home while shooting Jonathan Demme's film *Philadelphia*, and Brad Pitt and Bruce Willis stayed here in 1995 during the filming of *Twelve Monkeys*). **Topper's Spa**, with an indoor pool and fitness machines, is open to guests (fee on weekdays; no charge on weekends). Works by local artists are showcased throughout the building, and each floor has a Philadelphia scene by painter Dan Cavaliere. The hotel goes out of its way to welcome

Restaurants/Clubs: **Red** | Hotels: **Purple** | Shops: **Orange** | Outdoors/Parks: **Green** | Sights/Culture: **Blue**

children, with kid-oriented events and family packages. Top-of-the-line services for the disabled also are offered. ♦ 210 Rittenhouse Sq W (between Locust and Walnut Sts). 546.9000, 800/635.1042; fax 732.3364. &. www.rittenhousehotel.com

Within the Rittenhouse Hotel:

LACROIX AT THE RITTENHOUSE

★★$$$ Internationally renowned Chef Jean-Marie Lacroix, Maîtres Cuisiniers de France and James Beard "Best Chef, Mid-Atlantic" (formerly of the **Four Seasons**), creates the sumptuous French cuisine for Lacroix at the Rittenhouse. Formerly **Treetops**, the newly retooled restaurant offers a fabulous view of Rittenhouse Square and a private dining room to accommodate 18 guests. ♦ Daily, breakfast, lunch, and dinner. 546.9000 &

SMITH & WOLLENSKY

★★★$$$$ This classic New York steak house came to Philadelphia in 2000, just in time for the Republican Convention. Known for its over-size dry-aged steaks, succulent seafood, and excellent service, Smith & Wollensky includes a more formal dining room upstairs and **Wollensky's Grill** downstairs, featuring a more casual menu and extended hours. The bar is cigar friendly. ♦ Daily, 11AM-2AM. 545.1700

CASSATT LOUNGE AND TEA ROOM

★★$ Right off the lobby, this delightful tearoom looks onto a courtyard with pastel garden murals. The dramatic walls of the **Holy Trinity Church** next door add further interest to the scene. Afternoon tea includes tomato-and-arugula finger sandwiches, smoked salmon on Viennese bread, and citrus scones. ♦ Tearoom ♦ Daily, afternoon tea, cocktails, and desserts. 546.9000 &

BOATHOUSE ROW BAR

This upscale pub adorned with **Schuylkill River** rowing memorabilia, including a scull owned by Olympic star Jack Kelly, serves light food. ♦ M-F, Su, 11:30AM-11:30PM; Sa, until 2AM. 546.9000 &

In 1776, the population of Philadelphia and its environs was 23,700.

William Penn's plan for Philadelphia was one in which all the streets would be wide and straight, intersecting one another in a rectangular grid pattern, and the houses laid out "so that there may be ground on each side, for Gardens or Orchards or fields, that it may be a green Country Towne, which will never be burnt, and always be wholesome."

57 MIEL PATISSERIE

Things just got a little sweeter in Center City, thanks to the opening of Miel Patisserie. Robert Bennett, former pastry chef at **Le Bec-Fin**, is back in town after opening the first location of his high-end French pastry shop in Cherry Hill, New Jersey, not far from where he lives. Gourmet desserts, sophisticated sweets and handcrafted specialty chocolates are on the menu. ♦ 204 S 17th St (between Chancellor and Walnut Sts). 731.9191 www.mielpastry.com

58 JANET FLEISHER GALLERY

Local artists whose works tend to have a visceral feel are displayed here. The gallery also offers the works of the legendary, anonymous "Philadelphia Wireman," found years ago in the trash of a gentrifying neighborhood. Constructed from wire and assorted debris, these small pieces are believed to have been used in African-American religious rites. ♦ M-Sa. 211 S 17th St (between Chancellor and Walnut Sts). 545.7562 &

59 RITTENHOUSE SQUARE

The most beloved of the five city squares laid out by William Penn and Surveyor-General Thomas Holme originally served as a pasture for stray cows, pigs, and chickens. Then the neighborhood's mid-19th-century gentrification graced it with great Victorian mansions. Now stately apartment buildings frame the square, which boasts a children's wading pool, wooden benches, overarching trees, and fine statuary. It's a perfect place to enjoy a sandwich and a cold drink, but refrain from bringing a beer: The park police strictly enforce the no-alcohol rule.

Much of the park's intimate ambiance is due to **Paul Philippe Cret**, founder of the famous architecture school at the **University of Pennsylvania**, whose designs for the small wading pool, central plaza, and entrances, reminiscent of European parks with fountains and statuary, were completed in 1913. The square (originally called **Southwest Square**) is named after 18th-century Philadelphia astronomer and mathematician David Ritten-house. (His orrery, a clocklike device that describes the positions of the planets as they orbit around the sun, is displayed at the **Van Pelt Library** on the University of Pennsylvania campus.)

People are always milling about in Rittenhouse Square, whether it be office workers or a break, shoppers resting their feet, or the elderly ladies who live in nearby apartments, out with their aides for a breath of fresh air. Whatever the current ills of the city, you're reasonably safe·walking through here any time of the day or night. On the west side of the square by Locust Street, parents of young children have staked out the "nursing circle": Infants nap under the trees and toddlers stretch their legs under the watchful gaze of *Billy* (1914), the goat statue by Philadelphia sculptor Albert Laessle. The classically sculpted *Duck Girl* (1911) presiding over the fun at the wading pool is by Paul Manship, a leading American sculptor of the first half of the 20th century, who also created the *Aero Memorial* outside the **Franklin Institute**. In the center of the square is *Lion Crushing a Serpent* by French sculptor Antoine Louis Barye, who cast the statue in 1832 as a commentary on the triumph of monarchy over the rabble of democracy (it was installed in 1892). In a less symbolic pose crouches Cornelia Van A. Chapin's stone carving, *Giant Frog* (1941). At the entrance, two nymphs hoist a sundial as a *Tribute to Evelyn Taylor Price* (1947), the community leader who helped beautify the square between 1916 and 1946. Beatrice Fenton, graduate of the **Pennsylvania Academy of the Fine Arts** and friend of famous painter Thomas Eakins, sculpted the classical bronze figures, which contrast nicely with their Art Deco-ish base. ◆ Bounded by Rittenhouse Sq and Walnut St and by S 18th St and Rittenhouse Sq W. www.ushistory.org/districts/rittenhouse

60 ¡PASION!

★★★$$$ Chef Guillermo Pernot mines his Argentine roots with dishes like ceviche, smoked rib eye served with *moros y cristianos* (black beans and rice), and *parillada*, an Argentinean mixed grill for two with five meats served on an ox-shaped hibachi. His new book, *¡Ceviche!*, won the World Gourmand Award for Best Latino Cookbook. ◆ 211 S 15th St (between Locust and Walnut Sts). 875.9895. www.pasionrestaurant.com

61 DEVON SEAFOOD GRILL

★★$$ This warm, moderately priced fishery on **Rittenhouse Square** is decked out like a 1920s speakeasy, but the menu is contemporary. Seafood, flown in daily from around the globe, includes tilapia from Costa Rica, grouper from Florida, mahimahi from Hawaii, and king salmon from Canada. A mesquite grill adds another dimension of flavor to both seafood and steaks. ◆ 225 S 18th St (between Locust and Chancellor Sts.) 546.5940. www.devonseafood.com

61 ROUGE

★★★$$$ A bilevel oval bar, intimate restaurant, and small outdoor café make up this comfortable bistro-lounge. Designed by prominent interior designer Marguerite

Rodgers, it's reminiscent of a 1920s French parlor, with its warm brown textured velvet settees, fully upholstered chairs decorated with bouillon fringe and cording, and walls draped floor to ceiling in shimmering dusty-rose fabric. The seasonally changing menu offers choices such as beet, endive, and baby arugula salad made with local greens and vegetables, prosciutto-wrapped Barnegat Light monkfish, and roasted Peking duck breast. During warm months, alfresco dining on Rittenhouse Square is delightful. ◆ American bistro ◆ Daily, lunch and dinner. Reservations recommended. 205 S 18th St (between Locust and Chancellor Sts). 732.6622

62 THE PRIME RIB

★★★$$ If you like your steak with a side of sophistication and glamour, the Prime Rib can oblige. One of the few "jacket required" restaurants in town (after 5PM), this restaurant is truly where the elite meet to eat meat. A motif of sexy Vargas babes, fresh flowers, and ebony paneling, with a jazz trio keeping the beat in the background, sets the stage for a first-class experience. From the garlicky clams casino to the oversize prime rib, perfectly cooked and big enough to feed a family of four, this restaurant is what steak-house dining for grown-ups is all about. ◆ 1701 Locust St. 772.1701. www.theprimerib.com

62 WARWICK HOTEL AND TOWERS

$$$ This hotel opened for business in 1926, the night of the Dempsey–Tunney fight in Philadelphia, and it still retains its Jazz Age glory, particularly the dazzling and spacious lobby, along with its status as a landmark in the National Registry of Historic Hotels. Designed in the English Renaissance style by local architect **Frank Hahn**, the 22-story building has 200 guest rooms and 150 apartments for longer stays. The third-floor rooms have been made especially accessible for disabled guests, and there are six floors for nonsmoking guests. Guests enjoy free use of a nearby fitness club and pool, as well as complimentary cable television service. There's a restaurant, **Circles off the Square**, open for breakfast, lunch, and dinner, as well as the **Prime Rib** and a coffee shop, **Capriccio's**. ◆ 1701 Locust St (at S 17th St). 735.6000

63 ST. MARK'S CHURCH

John Notman's striking 1851 church was self-consciously constructed in the medieval Gothic style revived by the Anglican reform movement. The interior is richly carved and decorated; note the silver altar in the **Lady Chapel**. ◆ 1625 Locust St (between S 16th and S 17th Sts). 735.1416. www.saintmarksphiladelphia.org

Restaurants/Clubs: Red | Hotels: Purple | Shops: Orange | Outdoors/Parks: Green | Sights/Culture: Blue

64 LOCUST STREET

Between 1848 and 1908, a number of wealthy Philadelphians hired prominent architects to design some of the city's finest town houses along a portion of this lovely street. Scottish-born John Notman, whose early Gothic Revival **St. Mark's Church** dominates the middle of the block, is also thought to be responsible for building **Nos. 1604**, **1620**, and **1622**. Italian-born Philadelphia architect **Wilson Eyre** renovated **No. 1618** (note the first-floor window and the human face hidden in the floral motif), and **Cope and Stewardson**, renowned for buildings on the **University of Pennsylvania** campus, designed the Georgian Revival houses at **Nos. 1631** and **1633**. **Horace Trumbauer**'s white limestone house at **No. 1629** represents the Beaux Arts school (Trumbauer also designed the **Free Library** on the parkway and famous mansions in the Philadelphia suburbs, New York City, Washington, DC, and Newport, Rhode Island.) ♦ Between S 16th and S 17th Sts

65 SANDE WEBSTER GALLERY

This 31-year-old gallery works hard to assemble innovative, varied shows featuring local artists. Contemporary abstract painters James Brantley, Moe Brooker, and Nanette Carter are among those they represent, along with sculptor Charles Searles and ceramicist Syd Carpenter. ♦ M-F; Sa, 11AM-4PM. 2018 Locust St (between S 20th and S 21st Sts). 732.8850. www.robertroesch.com/SANDE-WEBSTER.html

66 SHERATON RITTENHOUSE SQUARE

$$$ *Breathtaking* wasn't the word for the soaring skylit lobby of this new Sheraton property, with its magnificent 40-foot bamboos at the center, because this first environmentally smart hotel in the continental US was dedicated to giving you breath, starting with all that bamboo, which cleansed and oxygenated the air—alas, all that bamboo is now gone, a victim of corporate reality. The space is now a function room, but the air in the 193 guest rooms is still filtered round the clock, independent of the heating and cooling system, and the rooms still feature 100% organic draperies and bedding in their "organic sleep systems" (aka beds) of cotton and wool produced without any toxic bleaches or dyes. All paint, wallpaper, carpeting, and draperies contain no toxic chemicals. High technology is represented in the high-speed fiber-optic Internet connections in all rooms. There are several restaurants and a gym. ♦ 227 S 18th St (at Locust St). 546.9400; fax 875.9457. ㅊ. www.sheratonphiladelphia.com

Within the Sheraton Rittenhouse Square:

POTCHEEN

★★$$ The name of this 53-seat restaurant is derived from the Gaelic word for "potato whiskey." An upscale pub atmosphere is reflected in the whitewashed brick wall and winter-sea–blue walls and green columns. The bar features a fair selection of beer (and root beer) on tap, and the house special—Potcheen martini—is made with a clear Irish spirit dubbed Irish moonshine. Breakfast is served buffet style daily. Along with your favorite lunchtime drink—Irish or otherwise—try the excellent half-pound burger or a sandwich of smoked turkey, applewood bacon, and brie. Dinner entrées might include sesame-crusted tuna with a warm haricot vert salad or seared jumbo lump crabcake with tomato-risotto-basil beurre blanc. ♦ Eclectic ♦ Breakfast, lunch, and dinner daily. 546.9400

BLEU

★★$$ This azure bistro overlooks **Rittenhouse Square**, with the action spilling out onto the sidewalk when the weather is fine. Comfy blue rattan chairs and bright murals of Philadelphia sights make for a cheery spot to share a reasonably priced bottle of French wine. A three-course prix-fixe menu is on tap every night, with a choice of appetizer, main course, and dessert adding up to just $26. Chef David Wiederholt changes the menu daily, with choices ranging from a duo of salmon tartare to steamed PEI mussels, a romaine and endive salad, a 10-ounce strip steak, duck breast schnitzel, and kalamata-crusted rack of lamb. Desserts are worth waiting for, including a crème brûlée sampler, Oreo cookie cheesecake, and a lemon tartlet. ♦ Daily, lunch. Dinner: M-F, 11:30-1AM; Sa, 11-1AM; Su, 11AM-midnight. Reservations recommended. 227 S 18th St. 545.0342

66 THE CURTIS INSTITUTE OF MUSIC

What better place to study the world's great composers than under these frescoed and carved wood ceilings? Mary Louise Curtis Bok, daughter of *Saturday Evening Post* publisher Cyrus Curtis, founded the music school, which, since 1924, has counted Samuel Barber, Peter Serkin, and Benita Valente among its alumni. On summer nights, students sometimes serenade strollers in **Rittenhouse Square** from the windows on the upper floors of the main building. Free recitals are held 3 nights a week during the school year in the institute's **Curtis Hall**. (The hall

The Best

Clare Pelino

Professor of Culinary Arts, Drexel University

Dive bars: They are even more fun when you're traveling, because you can easily meet people. **Doobies** at 22nd and Lombard is classic, with a great jukebox and a very mixed crowd. Also, **Bob and Barbara's** on South Street, with great jazz jams and a dark atmosphere. Get the special—a shot of Jim Beam and a can of Pabst Blue Ribbon for $3.

Coffee: **La Colombe** on 19th Street near Sansom, not only for the best coffee on the planet (they sell to all the best restaurants) but also for the international clientele found any time of day. If the atmosphere is too smoky, take your coffee into **Rittenhouse Square** and pick a seat for great people watching.

Best tourist attraction: Top of **City Hall**—enter at the northeast corner and go to the top just under the statue of William Penn—strangely, it's a best-kept secret, but it is the *only* place for views of the city.

Best restaurants: It's next to impossible for me to choose—I like them all—but there are a few musts for foodies in every price range. Go to **Morimoto**, **Tangerine**, **Brasserie Perrier**, **Le Bar Lyonnais** (downstairs at **Le Bec-Fin**), **Bistro San Tropez**, **Django**, **Standard Tap**, **Tre Scalini**, anywhere in the **Reading Terminal Market**—especially the **Dutch Eating Place** for Amish food and the **Rib Stand**, a pork sandwich place.

Activities: Roller-blading on **West River Drive** on weekends; bike riding through **Wissahickon** and **Valley Green** any day.

---

also is used for faculty recitals, chamber music concerts, and occasional rehearsals of the **Curtis Symphony Orchestra**.) The three buildings that make up the institute were once four private houses built at the turn of the 19th century; the main building, for instance, was a mansion designed by **Peabody & Stearns** in 1893 for banker George Childs Drexel. The firm of **Cope and Stewardson** constructed the house at **1718 Locust Street** in 1903, and **Horace Trumbauer** designed **Knapp Hall**, where you'll find the library, in 1908. ♦ Free. Recitals M, W, F, 8PM. 1726 Locust St (at S 18th St). 893.5252. &. www.curtis.edu

67 Los Catrines & Tequila's Bar

★★$$ Formerly **Tequila's**, this handsome restaurant shines in its new location at 16th and Locust. Beloved for its upscale Mexican food in a city that is seriously challenged when it comes to authentic south-of-the-border eats, the new Tequila's is an eyeful, with its giant Day of the Dead wedding mural, ornate carved wooden archways, black-and-white photos of Pancho Villa and his men, and giant paintings of Mexican peasants working the land. Owner David Surro promises that only the space has changed—the *queso fundido*, *mole poblano*, and salsa Tequila's remain happily the same. ♦ 1602 Locust St. 546.0181. www.tequilasphilly.com

68 Fadó

★$$ This popular chain of Irish pubs made its Philadelphia debut a few years ago, and the crowds haven't thinned since. Pronounced "f'doe," an Irish expression meaning "long ago," the pub blends an atmosphere of Victorian Ireland with contemporary Irish music and cuisine. Head directly for the Guinness—**Fadó** uses a state-of-the-art gassing system that gives the brew its signature creamy head. For starters, have a toasted cheese and ham sandwich, or for something more substantial, try one of the boxtys, the pub's signature dishes, something like a burrito wrapped in a potato pancake instead of a tortilla. Shepherd's pie, fish and chips, and fresh salmon are also on the menu. Be advised: if an ear-splitting din and a smoky atmosphere bother you, Fadó is not for you—there is no no-smoking area within the restaurant. ♦ 1500 Locust St. 893.9700. wwwfadoirishpub.com

69 Monk's Cafe

★★$ This Belgian-themed bistro features mussels prepared five different ways, terrific Belgian beer and microbrews, a chatty local bar crowd, and a-cut-above-average pub fare. The fries with bourbon mayo dipping sauce are delish, salads are fresh and generously portioned, and the burgers are always good. You may have to wait for a table; just belly up to the bar and start globe-trotting through the beer selections. You really won't mind the wait. ♦ 264 S 16th St (between Latimer and Locust Sts). 545.7005. www.monkscafe.com/

70 Thomas Hockley House

Local architect **Frank Furness**, known for his eccentric buildings, designed (and 21 years later enlarged) this home for Thomas Hockley, a lawyer who was his friend and early supporter. It was completed in its earliest version in 1875. As in Furness's other

---

Restaurants/Clubs: Red | Hotels: Purple | Shops: Orange | Outdoors/Parks: Green | Sights/Culture: Blue

buildings, the variations in the cut and lay of the brickwork create a pattern of texture and silhouette, an effect strived for by later Philadelphia craftspeople. ♦ 235 S 21st St (between Rittenhouse Sq and Locust St)

71 D'ANGELO'S RISTORANTE ITALIANO

★★$$ Spread over three floors of a former residence, this lively restaurant has a bar on the first floor, and three airy dining rooms painted in light pastel colors. The food—Roman, Northern Italian, and Sicilian—is the outcome of several generations of owner Salvatore D'Angelo's family recipes. Choose from delicious dishes like pasta in marinara sauce with capers and olives; crabmeat-stuffed calamari in cognac sauce; and veal with mushrooms, prosciutto, and peas. ♦ Italian ♦ M-F, lunch and dinner; Sa, dinner. Reservations recommended. 256 S 20th St (at Rittenhouse Sq). 546.3935. www.dangeloristorante.com

72 PHILADELPHIA ETHICAL SOCIETY

This center for humanism holds talks on a variety of topics on Sunday mornings and in evening courses. ♦ 1906 Rittenhouse Sq (between S 19th and S 20th Sts). 735.3456. www.phillyethics.net

William Penn, founder of Pennsylvania and Philadelphia, was converted to Quakerism in Ireland as the result of a sermon he heard preached by Thomas Loe in Cork in 1667.

Because Quakers did not believe in naming places after people, Rittenhouse Square was known simply as Southwest Square. It was renamed in 1825 for astronomer and clockmaker David Rittenhouse (1732–1796), a descendant of William Rittenhouse, builder of the first paper mill in America in Germantown.

73 CREATIVE ARTISTS NETWORK (CAN)

The fabulous old **Barclay Hotel**, the first hostelry on **Rittenhouse Square** and long the neighborhood's grande dame, has turned into an all-condominium property, but it still houses this nonprofit organization, which presents group shows of artists who have an established body of work but haven't been discovered by a gallery—yet. CAN's prices usually run significantly lower than those at conventional galleries because it doesn't take a commission. ♦ M-F. Closed August. The Barclay on Rittenhouse, 237 S 18th St (between Manning and Locust Sts), suite 3-A. 546.7775. ♿ www.creativeartistsnetwork.org

74 RITTENHOUSE SQUARE B&B

$$$ This former **Rittenhouse Square** carriage house offers Old World elegance, European-style service, and 10 charming guest rooms and two suites. Continental breakfast is served in the café, which doubles as a private meeting room. Computer workstations and Internet access are available in every room. ♦ 1715 Rittenhouse Square (between Manning and Locust Sts). 546.6700; fax 546.8787, 877/791.6500. www.rittenhousebb.com

75 BLACK SHEEP

★★$$ Cozy up to the Mission-style fireplace at this warm and friendly Irish pub, blessed with amicable owners, a menu of above-average pub fare, and steady crowd of neighborhood locals. The fireplace is on the main floor, where guests can dine on satisfying dishes like steak salad or baby rack of lamb with garlic mashed potatoes and baby asparagus. The bar-restaurant is divided among three floors; the top tier is no-smoking during dinner. There's darts in the basement bar to keep things interesting—something also accomplished by the 10 beers on draft and 30 choices of bottled brew. ♦ 247 S 17th St (at Latimer St). 545.9473. www.theblacksheeppub.com

76 THE PRINT CENTER

Begun in 1915 as the **Print Club**, this center provides opportunities and a venue for printmakers and photographers from around the world to create, exhibit, and promote their work. Purchase prints, photographs, and books in the **Gallery Store**, which has the best selection of photo art books. ♦ Free. Tu-Sa. 1614 Latimer St (between S 16th and S 17th Sts). 735.6090. www.printcenter.org

77 BUCA DI BEPPO

★$$ *Mangia!* is the theme at this popular chain located in the heart of Center City not far from Rittenhouse Square. Buca is a kitschy southern Italian trattoria specializing in oversize portions and plenty of schmaltzy art on the walls. There's even a Pope's room that offers semiprivate dining in the shadow of the Pontiff's watchful eyes. The food is tasty—try the cheese ravioli—and a good value as long as you don't overorder. A small Caesar easily serves four; same goes for the signature Di Beppo "1893" salad, laden with imported mortadella, pepperoni, and peperoncini. There's pizza and familiar dishes like eggplant parm and spaghetti and meatballs. For dessert, try the quart-size bowl of rum and espresso–soaked tiramisù. Now that's *la dolce vita*. ♦ 258 S 15th St (at Latimer St). 545.2818

78 FRIDAY, SATURDAY, SUNDAY

★★$$ For two decades, this intimate town-house restaurant has endured while others have come and gone. The specials are written on a Day-Glo board between the two little downstairs dining rooms. Fabrics hang across the walls and form a ceiling of cloth to make the place seem bigger than it really is. A little bar—lined with a large fish tank—and an additional dining room are located upstairs. The meal-size salads, grilled swordfish, rack of lamb, poached salmon in sorrel sauce, and Cornish hen haven't changed much since the 1970s. ♦ Eclectic ♦ M-F, lunch and dinner; Sa, Su, dinner. Reservations recommended. 261 S 21st St (between Spruce St and Ritten-house Sq). 546.4232. www.frisatsun.com

79 PHILADELPHIA ART ALLIANCE

Ornate granite columns flank the entranceway of this mansion, built in 1906 for Samuel Price Wetherill. **Frank Miles Day**, an architect known for buildings at Princeton and Yale Universities, designed the house, which the Art Alliance purchased in 1926 to serve as a venue for art exhibitions, concerts, and readings. R. Tait McKenzie's terra-cotta bas-relief of the alliance's founder, Christine Wetherill Stevenson, enlivens the arch above the dining-room door. An outdoor sculpture garden is open in the summer. ♦ Free. Tu-Su. 251 S 18th St (between Manning St and Rittenhouse Sq). 545.4305. www.philartalliance.org

Within the Philadelphia Art Alliance:

80 MANGEL GALLERY

This well-regarded gallery presents a range of prestigious contemporary artists, from realist Alex Katz's images of high-society figures to Robert Motherwell's abstractions and Red Grooms's funky portrayals of everyday life. ♦ Tu-Sa. 1714 Rittenhouse Sq (between S 17th and S 18th Sts). 545.4343. www.artincontext.org/philadelphia_pa /mangel_gallery

81 TWENTY MANNING

★★★$$ Asian accents embellish New American fare at this stylish neighborhood bistro. Executive chef Kiong Bahn offers such inventive standouts as chewy lobster pot stickers, a shrimp cocktail martini, and chocolate-rum mousse. There's a four-course tasting menu every evening, different every day depending on what the chef gets in the market. It might go something like this: tuna, featuring tuna with udon noodles, tuna tartare, tuna in a spring roll, and grilled tuna as a main course. ♦ 261 S 20th St (at Manning St). 731.0900. www.twentymanning.com

81 ASTA DE BLUE

The unpredictable selection of trendy women's clothes in this tiny boutique might include a short-sleeved fly-away jacket with wide-legged trousers; a long, feminine floral sundress; and a denim sarong with a sleeveless vest, cowboy boots, and a baseball cap. Cutting-edge hats and shoes, expensive but hard to lay your hands on elsewhere, can be found here, along with pricey jeans that fit like a glove. ♦ M-Sa; Su, noon-5PM. 265 S 20th St (between Spruce and Manning Sts). 732.0550.

82 MELOGRANO

★★★$$ Snagging a table at this popular trattoria on the weekend can mean waiting an hour or more, all for the privilege of tasting chef Gianluca Demontis's inspired Italian cuisine from Tuscany, Umbria, and his native Rome. His homemade penne in pancetta-tomato sauce alone is worth the sidewalk time. ♦ 2201 Spruce St (at S 22nd St). 875.8116

83 SPRUCE STREET

Two fine blocks of brownstones were erected here during the second half of the 19th century; the mansard roofs and round-headed windows suggest their Second Empire influence. Brownstone has never been as

LIGHTS, CAMERA, ACTION: THE PHILADELPHIA MOVIE SCENE

For a low-profile city, Philadelphia has been the location of choice for a lot of movies. Here's a list of some films in which you can catch glimpses of the City of Brotherly Love. The **Greater Philadelphia Film Office** (1600 Arch Street, at N 16th Street; 686.2668) has designed a tour of the city for film buffs, featuring many locations immortalized on the big screen.

Local son **M. Night Shyamalan** has really put Philadelphia on the cinematic map in the past few years. His surprise blockbuster *The Sixth Sense* (1999), featuring Bruce Willis and Haley Joel Osment, did more for the city than any film since the Italian Stallion left town. In *Unbreakable* (2000), Bruce Willis and Samuel L. Jackson reunite, under the tutelage of Shyamalan, to figure out what might be making Willis's character indestructible. In *The Village* (2004), William Hurt and Sigourney Weaver hunt a mysterious creature with many scenes filmed in Philadelphia's countryside.

The book *In Her Shoes* by local author Jennifer Weiner was filmed in Philadelphia in the spring of 2004 for a 2005 release. Starring Cameron Diaz and directed by Curtis Hanson (*8 Mile*), the movie centers around party girl Maggie (Diaz) and her clashes with her conservative sister Rose (Toni Collette of *The Sixth Sense* and *The Hours*).

The Age of Innocence (1993)   Martin Scorsese's lush adaptation of Edith Wharton's Pulitzer Prize–winning novel tells the story of doomed love in the restrictive setting of upper-crust New York society a century ago. The opening opera scene was shot at the **Academy of Music**.

Birdy (1984)   In an army hospital, Nicolas Cage and Matthew Modine flash back to their teen years in working-class Philadelphia, including chasing pigeons at **46th** and **Market** near the **Arena**—the original home of *American Bandstand*.

The Blob (1958)   Shot at several locations—including **Phoenixville's Colonial Theater**, the now-defunct **Phoenixville Diner**, and the **Downingtown Diner** (formerly the **Cadillac Diner**)—this campy sci-fi classic features Steve McQueen in his first starring role, leading teens into battle to save their town from being swallowed by a giant blob from outer space.

Blow Out (1981)   In a Brian De Palma film, John Travolta plays a sound-effects man who records a car accident on **Lincoln Drive** that is a politically motivated murder. Travolta drives a Jeep through the narrow pedestrian passage of **City Hall's** courtyard and crashes into the window of **Wanamaker's** (now a **Lord & Taylor**).

Dressed to Kill (1980)   Brian De Palma returned to his hometown to film this thriller about a psychotic killer who stalks two women. One scene that purports to be inside a New York art museum was actually shot at the **Philadelphia Museum of Art**.

Eddie and the Cruisers (1983)   This story about a rock 'n' roll band starring Ellen Barkin and Tom Berenger was filmed on the campus of nearby **Haverford College**.

Fallen (1996)   Director Gregory Hoblit used scenes of **Manayunk** and elsewhere, including **St. Mark's Church**, **Pat's Steaks** in **South Philly**, and **30th Street Station**, in this murder mystery starring Denzel Washington and John Goodman.

Mannequin (1987)   Andrew McCarthy and Kim

common in Philadelphia as it is in New York City, but during the 1800s, it appealed to builders because it was relatively cheap yet handsome. The earthen tones of these elegant blocks offer a pleasing contrast to the brick and stucco façades of nearby houses. **No. 2111-13** and **No. 2132-34** are attributed to **Frank Furness**. Local architect **Wilson Eyre**, known for his picturesque residences, designed the Colonial Revival house at **No. 2123-25**. The Victorian on the corner at **No. 2100**, designed by Philadelphia architect **George Hewitt**, is complemented by the red-and-white brick building opposite at **No. 2044**. ♦ Between S 20th and S 22nd Sts

84 SCHUYLKILL RIVER PARK

Overlooking the waters of the lower **Schuylkill River**, this is a real recreational park, with a children's playground, tennis courts, basketball courts, and leased lots for local gardeners. ♦ Delancey Pl and S 25th St. www.srdc.net/

85 THE DRAKE TOWER APARTMENTS

Formerly the **Drake Hotel**, this 36-story tower (designed by **Ritter and Shay** and completed in 1929) is a sterling example of Philadelphia's first skyscrapers—its graduating tiers were ordered by the city's then-new zoning codes. Terra-cotta ornamentation recalls the travels of Sir Francis Drake, with images of sailing ships, globes, and domes; Pompeiian brick covers the building's steel frame. ♦ 1512-14 Spruce St (between S 15th and S 16th Sts). 545.6900. www.draketower.com

Cattrall star in this romantic comedy in which artist McCarthy crafts his dream-woman mannequin, Cattrall, who—you guessed it—comes to life. A good portion of the film was shot at the old Wanamaker's in **Center City**.

Philadelphia (1993)   Tom Hanks won an Oscar for his portrayal of a young lawyer with AIDS who sues his **Main Line** firm after it fires him. Scenes were shot inside **Mellon Bank Center** and **City Hall**. Denzel Washington is at the **University of Pennsylvania**'s **Fisher Fine Arts Library** when he decides to represent Hanks in his lawsuit, and after the birth of his daughter, he buys party fare at **Famous Deli** on Bainbridge Street. Hanks dies at **Mount Sinai Hospital**.

Pride of the Marines (1945)   John Garfield starred in this true account of a Marine blinded during a Japanese attack. In one scene shot at 30th Street Station, you can see the station as it used to be—with trains arriving at street level—as well as the Philadelphia Museum of Art in the background, unobscured by high-rises.

Rocky (1976)   Sylvester Stallone immortalized the steps of the Philadelphia Museum of Art, the **Italian Market**, and the streets of **Kensington** in this melodrama about a prizefighter's big chance at fame. A huge box-office hit, the movie also took home an Oscar for Best Picture. More Philadelphia sites can be seen in the next three sequels.

Stealing Home (1988)   Washed-up baseball player Mark Harmon experiences a flashback when he comes home to deal with the ashes of his old friend Jodie Foster, who killed herself. In one great scene, Harmon and a friend sneak into **Veterans Stadium** at night to relive their high-school baseball memories.

Taps (1981)   Timothy Hutton leads his fellow military-school students in an armed takeover to keep their school from being torn down. The film was shot in **Wayne** at the **Valley Forge Military Academy**.

Trading Places (1983)   Preppie Dan Aykroyd and hustler Eddie Murphy are switched by two scheming brothers in this hilarious comedy. There are good shots of 30th Street Station's interior. Aykroyd's character lives at **2014 Delancey Place**, and the building that houses "Duke and Duke" stockbrokers is the **Fidelity Bank Building**.

Twelve Monkeys (1995)   Bruce Willis and Brad Pitt star in this sci-fi thriller set in future-tense Philadelphia. Scenes were filmed at **Girard College**, **Memorial Hall**, **Eastern State Penitentiary**, and the **Pennsylvania Convention Center**.

Witness (1985)   Big-city cop Harrison Ford hides out on an Amish farm, where he and young widow Kelly McGillis take a liking to each other. The murder that opens the film takes place in one of the rest rooms at 30th Street Station.

The Young Philadelphians (1959)   Paul Newman plays an ambitious lawyer who risks losing it all when he stands up to the Main Line establishment. The film includes shots of a honeymoon suite at the **Bellevue**, plus the University of Pennsylvania and **Rittenhouse Square**.

Why no listing for ***The Philadelphia Story***, the 1940 film classic starring Cary Grant, Katharine Hepburn, and Jimmy Stewart? Because although the movie was set in Philly, its location shots are strictly Hollywood.

86 WARSAW CAFE

★★$$ Only 35 people fit into the dining room, which is decorated with Art Deco posters, etched-glass windows, and crimson Formica tabletops. Try fresh borscht; a Baltic Sea salad with fish, olives, and pasta shells; or cabbage leaves stuffed with ground veal, herbs, onions, rice, and mushrooms. The dishes are lighter than you might expect. ♦ Central European ♦ M-Sa, lunch and dinner. 306 S 16th St (between Pine and Spruce Sts). 546.0204

87 ROSENBACH MUSEUM AND LIBRARY

The nation's preeminent museum for rare books and manuscripts continues to expand its collection, providing an important resource to literary scholars. Rare-books dealer Dr. A.S.W. Rosenbach and his brother Philip H. Rosenbach, a local art dealer, lived on Delancey Street between 1926 and the early 1950s. Their Victorian mansion—with its Georgian interior—is furnished with early English, French, and American furniture and,

---

Restaurants/Clubs: Red | Hotels: Purple | Shops: Orange | Outdoors/Parks: Green | Sights/Culture: Blue

The Best

Thora Jacobson

Director, Samuel S. Fleisher Art Memorial

Place to buy good Italian bread: **Faragalli**, **Cacia**, and **Lanci** are my picks in South Philly. All different, all good!

Most beautiful block in South Philly: **700 Catharine Street** (year round).

Most beautiful blocks at Christmas: **18th and Colorado**; **10th Street south of Wharton**.

"Public art": the bodhisattva at the temple on **13th Street**; the human planters at **11th and Marvine**; the hero figures at **5th and Catharine**; and *Ray King's Torches* at **Broad and Washington**.

Most beyooteeful building south of South on Broad: the **High School for Creative and Performing Arts**, the former **Ridgway Library** building. It is a masterpiece of adaptive reuse and a glorious punctuation point on South Broad Street. Runner-up: **St. Rita of Cascia**—echoes of Venice.

Place for chamber music: the **Fleisher Sanctuary** (well, I am a *little* partial) is a wonderfully evocative space to fill the eyes and ears with music—vocal or violin—particularly when the **Philadelphia Chamber Music Society** or **Voces Novae et Antiquae** presents programs.

Place to send your kids for arts classes: South Philly, the arts education cabal—home of the **Rock School of the Pennsylvania Ballet**, **Settlement Music School** (**Curtis Branch**), **Fleisher Art Memorial**, and **Point Breeze Performing Arts Center**. Excellent, affordable programs that can take a kid from complete novice to polished professional.

Home of anachronism: **Passyunk Avenue**, where they still sharpen scissors, sell parochial-school uniforms, basket cheese at Easter, and use the same red sauce on every possible food item from veal and eggplant parmigiana to pizza and spaghetti and meatballs.

Most amazing food shopping: **Washington Avenue** between S Eighth and S 16th Streets for Asian delights; Ninth Street, where the **Italian Market** is still thriving.

---

of course, rare books and manuscripts. The Rosenbachs' most important holding was James Joyce's manuscript of *Ulysses*, which played a key role in the controversy over the novel's "corrected" edition (try to decipher Joyce's crabbed handwriting). Three-quarters of all Joseph Conrad's manuscripts are here, as are Bram Stoker's manuscript notes for *Dracula*, which he began while staying at the long-gone **Stratford Hotel** on Broad Street. Rosy, as his friends called ASW, also owned the 1519 editions of Erasmus's New Testament (with prints by Holbein); Cervantes's *Don Quixote de la Mancha* (1605); and the first title published in North America, *The Bay Psalm Book* (1640). Many books are on display, and there are often temporary exhibitions as well as a permanent installation re-creating the poet Marianne Moore's Greenwich Village apartment. Guides escort visitors through the museum on hour-long tours. ♦ Admission. Tu–Su, 11AM–4PM; last tour begins at 2:45PM. Open to scholars by appointment. Closed in Aug. 2010 Delancey Pl (between S 20th and S 21st Sts). 732.1600. www.rosenbach.org

88 Delancey Street

Like many Philadelphia streets, this one runs through the same neighborhood for several blocks, then disappears into a T-junction with another street, rematerializing a few blocks away as if there had been no break. Shady and well kept on most blocks, this street provides a pleasant place for a contemplative walk among fine houses. One recommended stretch runs between 18th and 20th Streets, where most of the houses hail from the mid-19th century. Late-19th-century architect **Frank Furness** designed the **Horace Jayne Mansion** (1900 Delancey Street), with its balcony, carved stone at the entrance, and cherubim and seraphim on pediments.

89 The Plays and Players Theatre

Founded in 1911, the oldest amateur theater group in the country performs here in its original building. Under the leadership of its first president, Maud Skinner, wife of actor Otis Skinner, the theater became a fixture of Philadelphia high society. It continues to produce about four shows a year—usually contemporary American plays such as *Miss Firecracker*—renting its space to other companies the rest of the time. Murals by local artist Edith Emerson enliven the walls of the auditorium, which seats 324 people. Children's productions often run concurrently. ♦ 1714 Delancey St (between S 17th and S 18th Sts). 735.0630. www.phillytheatreco.com

90 Fitler Square

🍴 An idyllic shaded park treasured by city residents, this square is charming for its small size, brick walkways, fountain, and bronze statues. In the summer, it tops the list of places in the city to read or eat lunch. First established in 1896, the park has been refurbished several times, most recently in 1980. It was named after Edwin W. Fitler, a wealthy cordage manufacturer who was Philadelphia's first mayor. ◆ Bounded by Pine and Panama Sts and by S 23rd and S 24th Sts. www.fitlersquare.org

91 THE CIVIL WAR LIBRARY AND MUSEUM

This little-known, historically rigorous museum devoted to Civil War memorabilia holds ample evidence of Philadelphia's role in the war between the states. During the war, General Ulysses S. Grant made his home at 20th and Chestnut Streets, whereas General George Gordon Meade, the commanding Union officer at Gettysburg, lived at the corner of 19th and Delancey Streets. There are rooms devoted to both generals' artifacts (including the head of Meade's horse). The museum's collection includes several life masks of Abraham Lincoln, as well as a lock of his hair and the nightdress in which his nemesis, Jefferson Davis, attempted to escape capture. For nonbuffs, the room containing belongings of ordinary soldiers may prove more interesting (note the soldiers' sewing kit, called a housewife). Scholars have access to the manuscript collection and 16,000-volume library. ◆ Admission. W-Su. 1805 Pine St (between S 18th and S 19th Sts). 735.8196. www.netreach.net/~cwlm

92 MERITAGE

★★$$ Wine is at the forefront of this newcomer, thanks to the expertise of co-owner James Colabelli, who is also sommelier and a Master of Wine candidate. The restaurant's menu mines classic European specialties, from lobster Thermidor to schnitzel Holstein. Chefs Grant Brown and Lenny Williams, both from New England, share the kitchen. ◆ 500 S 20th St (at Lombard St). 985.1922

93 ASTRAL PLANE

★★$$ The small dining rooms in this funky town house evoke the 1970s, which is when the restaurant opened. The décor is an artsy jumble, with discordant florals on the tables, mismatched dinnerware, and chandeliers that hang from parachute-silk ceilings. Menu choices include a simple filet mignon with brandy and garlic; salmon with pepper crust and lemon butter; and phyllo stuffed with spinach, mushrooms, and feta cheese. ◆ Eclectic ◆ M-F, lunch and dinner; Sa, dinner; Su, brunch and dinner. Reservations recommended. 1708 Lombard St (between S 17th and S 18th Sts). 546.6230. www.theastralplane.com

94 L2

★★$$ Some 15 years after Nathan Dolente closed down his 1950s theme restaurant **Linoleum** in this space, it was languishing as a Russian restaurant, **Café Republic** (iconic Stephen Starr's only restaurant misstep). Dolente returned to start a new eatery and named it L2 in honor of the old one. The red-velvet banquettes and distressed plaster walls give the restaurant a feeling of mystery and intrigue as well as Old World charm. To start, try the polenta cakes or five-spice duck rice-paper roll. Entrées include roasted half crispy duck, chicken Vermouth with fusilli, and trout sautéed in sage butter. In addition to a selection of beers and wines to accompany dinner, the usual alcoholic options are available. The bar area is in dire need of a smoke filter. ◆ American ◆ Tu-Su, dinner. 2201 South St (at S 22nd St). 732.7878. ⅊. www.l2restaurant.com

94 SOUTH STREET STAINED GLASS

Curious illuminations in transoms, skylights, and doorways enliven many house interiors in Philadelphia. Some of these date to the 19th century; others were custom-made last week at local stained-glass workshops such as this one owned by Forrest Smith. Miscellaneous works of glass are also for sale here. ◆ M-Sa. 2209 South St (between S 22nd and S 23rd Sts). 735.2415

Restaurants/Clubs: **Red** | Hotels: **Purple** | Shops: **Orange** | Outdoors/Parks: **Green** | Sights/Culture: **Blue**

BENJAMIN FRANKLIN PARKWAY/ FAIRMOUNT PARK

Extending to the northwest in a diagonal from **City Hall**, the **Benjamin Franklin Parkway** ("the Parkway") is a wide, tree-lined thoroughfare studded with palacelike neoclassical structures, flags, statues, and fountains. This boulevard was designed to imitate Paris's Avenue des Champs-Elysées: The **Free Library** is reminiscent of the twin palaces on the Place de la Concorde, and the striking gateway to the **Rodin Museum** is

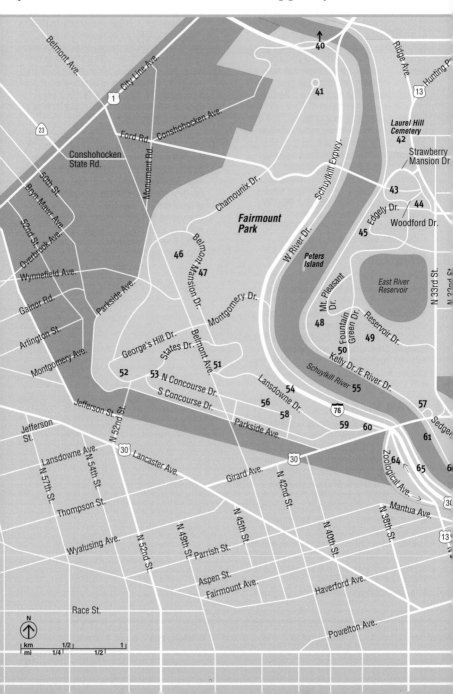

copy of the one at sculptor Auguste Rodin's home in Meudon, France, which in turn was based on the entrance to the Château d'Issy.

A group of society figures spearheaded the building of this stretch of road—a massive public works project in 1917—as a way of connecting **Fairmount Park** to the city's center. French landscape designer Jacques Greber proposed a design that would cut through existing neighborhoods, focus on **City Hall**, and be lined with impressive cultural institutions. The Parkway accomplished many of these goals: Its open expanses are a welcome release from the city's boxed-in precincts, and the **Philadelphia Museum of Art** and the **Franklin Institute** have earned world-class reputations. Nevertheless, few French visitors would mistake the Parkway for the Champs-Elysées, an urban boulevard of cafés and shops. In true American style, the Parkway caters to automobiles—and serves as a quick exit from **Center City**.

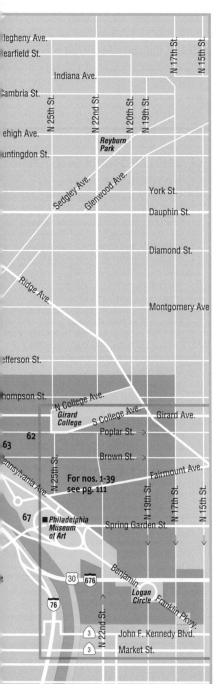

Once dimly lit, Benjamin Franklin Parkway is now brightly illuminated at night, with the completed installation of 354 new ornamental streetlights by the Center City District, along with pedestrian-friendly crosswalks around **Logan Circle**. More than 2.5 million visitors come to the Parkway every year to visit the extraordinary cultural and educational institutions that line Philadelphia's museum mile.

William Penn once praised the rocky bluff where the Philadelphia Museum of Art stands as the "Faire Mount." Thus, *Fairmount* was the logical name for what later became a vast landscaped park on both banks of the **Schuylkill River**. Both Penn and Benjamin Franklin saw the river as an important water resource, but it was not until 1843 that the city began purchasing property upstream of the **Fairmount Waterworks** to protect the supply. In 1867 the area was designated a public park. After rejecting a plan by Frederick Law Olmsted, who designed New York's Central Park, the city turned to its own Prussian-born junior engineer, Hermann Schwarzmann, to lay out the winding drives on either side of the river and landscape the grounds. The park's moment of celebrity came in 1876, when 10 million people crowded its west side to visit the Centennial International Exposition.

The park continued to gain territory, as well as a good deal of fine statuary, into the 20th century, but the greatest change came with the development of the **Schuylkill Expressway** and the increase in commuter traffic along **East River Drive** (now called **Kelly Drive**). The two highways separate the riverfronts from the park and leave much of it out of reach to anyone without a car. Visitors to the park's nether regions usually drive from sight to sight, through woods, and past fields, some of them unkempt. The well-maintained promenade along Kelly Drive, however, a lovely stretch of trees, rivers, and greenery, is the heart of the park, where visitors stroll, jog, roller-blade, or bicycle. Along the walkway are places to picnic and rent blades and bikes, and the **Ellen Phillips Samuel Memorial** sculpture garden is a serene spot to watch the sculling crews race their shells. Riding the **Fairmount Park Trolley** is a relaxing way to see the area; it takes visitors on a 17-mile loop, stopping at the early American mansions in the park. Just north of the Parkway, the gentrified neighborhood of Fairmount, with pretty shaded streets of restored row houses, offers the best restaurants to visit while touring the vicinity.

1 GIRARD COLLEGE

The richest man in America at the time of his death in 1831, French-born Stephen Girard kept his adopted country financially afloat during the War of 1812 and started the **Girard Bank**. He left the bulk of his $7 million estate to found this college for "poor white male orphans." Integrated since 1968, it now boards about 500 boys and girls from 1st to 12th grades. A collection of Girard's elegant furniture and household items is on display on campus in **Founder's Hall**, a Greek Revival temple noted for its Corinthian colonnade. Designed by **Thomas Ustick Walter**, the college was completed 16 years after Girard's death. His will stipulates that "no ecclesiastic, missionary or minister of any sect whatsoever, shall . . . be admitted for any purpose, or as a visitor, within the premises of (Girard) College." The rule is still enforced. ♦ Th, 1-3:30PM; other times by appointment. Bounded by Ridge and W College Aves and by S and N College Aves. 787.2600. www.girardcollege.com

2 REMBRANDT'S

★★$$ With a name like this, it's no surprise to find prints of the famous painter's work in the bar and rear dining room, a small library of books about him in many languages, and a dark wood interior that gives the restaurant the ambiance of Amsterdam. The eclectic menu achieves culinary artistry in its own right. Chicken wings, duck strudel with shiitake mushrooms, stuffed rainbow trout with scallop mousse, and salmon steamed in parchment are some of the better offerings. ♦ American ♦ M-Sa, lunch and dinner; Su, brunch and dinner. 741 N 23rd St (at Aspen St). 763.2228. www.rembrandts.com

3 EASTERN STATE PENITENTIARY HISTORIC SITE

The last prisoner walked out the gates in 1971, but this Gothic Revival monument to incarceration remains a ghostly presence in the Fairmount neighborhood. Though it is considered an architectural treasure, some nearby residents rue the dark, medieval shadow it casts on the area.

The massive fortress, completed in 1836, occupies 12 acres with its stone walls, crenellated towers, and radiating cell blocks. The design by **John Haviland** leans heavily on the 1787 radial plan of the English Utilitarian philosopher Jeremy Bentham, consisting of seven long cell blocks branching out from a central rotunda.

Completed in 1836, the prison is considered one of the most influential buildings in Philadelphia and is a National Historic Landmark: More than 300 prisons around the world were built along Haviland's design. At the time, it was the largest construction project in the country's history; the fact that it had central plumbing and heating further distinguished it. Each prisoner was put in solitary confinement—in cells 8 feet by 12 feet, with a single skylight and a toilet—and given the chance to study the Bible and reflect on his crimes. The layout was modified over the years to include four additional two-story cell blocks and other buildings. In 1988, the structure came close to demolition—plans called for a supermarket and parking lot in its place—but preservationists rallied to save it.

There is a museum and bookstore on site. Major events include a neighborhood Bastille Day celebration and a midnight Halloween tour. ♦ Admission. Sa-Su, Labor Day–Memorial Day; Th-Su, Memorial Day–Labor Day. Fairmount Ave (between Corinthian Ave and N 22nd St). 236.3300. www.easternstate.org

4 FIGS

★★$$ Moroccan-born chef-owner Mustapha Rouissiya's 47-seat restaurant features a mix of Mediterranean cuisine—dishes from Israel, Portugal, and Spain are on the menu. Entrées, priced in the $15-$20 range, include tuna with lobster ravioli and sautéed arugula, rack of lamb tagine served with crispy polenta, and duck breast served with sweet mashed

sautéed spinach and figs. Start off with kabobs—at $2.75 each. Choose from skewers of sushi, veal, chicken, vegetable, and shrimp. The restaurant's sunny interior, in hues of yellow, plum, and burgundy, is adorned with pictures of Rouissiya's country—altogether warm, inviting, and truly delicious. Cash only. BYOB. ♦ 2501 Meredith St (between N 25th and N 26th Sts). 978.8440

5 BRIDGID'S

★★$$ You can smell the garlic and herbs at work in this kitchen from many blocks away. It has two personalities—a shot-and-a-beer bar up front and a Belgian bistro in the back.

PARKWAY AREA

European music plays in the tiny rear dining room, where white tablecloths and candles adorn the tables. The menu features crispy duck with peppercorn sauce; duck stuffed with ground veal, pistachios, and raspberry sauce; and veal sautéed with shrimp and bay scallops in a lemon sauce. The bar boasts a large selection of Belgian beers. ♦ Belgian ♦ M-F, lunch and dinner; Sa, Su, dinner. 726 N 24th St (at Meredith St). 232.3232

6 BISHOP'S COLLAR

Let's just start by talking about the martinis at the Fairmount neighborhood bar. Best deal in town—$5 at last investigation—and if you ask, your vodka libation will come garnished with a bleu-cheese-stuffed green olive (don't knock it until you've tried it). Dine on homemade pub sandwiches. The teriyaki steak sandwich and turkey burger are favorites, and you can get any topping you want on your burger—no extra charge. Sandwiches start at $6, the beer includes imports and microbrews, there's live music Thursday through Saturday, and a new air-filtration system cuts way down on the smoke. What's not to like? ♦ 2349 Fairmount Ave (between 23rd and 24th Sts). 765.1616. www.thebishopscollar.com

7 LONDON GRILL

★★$$ In back, a terra-cotta–floored atrium looks out onto 23rd Street. Two additional low-lit dining rooms feature tiled floors and a marble bar. The grill offers a rib eye steak with shallot jam and a potato pancake, lamb with roasted pepper salad and couscous, and a molasses pork loin with stewed lentils. Roasted quail is stuffed with cornbread and accompanied by sweet-potato chips. Changing pasta entrées are available and the bar menu is top notch. ♦ American ♦ M-F, lunch and dinner; Sa, dinner; Su, brunch and dinner. 2301 Fairmount Ave (at N 23rd St). 978.4545. www.londongrill.com

8 JACK'S FIREHOUSE

★★$$$ One of those beautiful old firehouses that has outlived its purpose now draws diners to a desolate stretch across from the vacant **Eastern State Penitentiary Historic Site** (see page 110). The owner and chef, Jack McDavid, took over the building and established an upscale version of the down-home Southern cuisine he was known for at his place in the **Reading Terminal Market**. The dark wood interior features a brass fire pole, high ceilings, and a real **Schuylkill River** racing scull dangling from above. The setting alone is worth a visit. McDavid is said to churn his own butter, make his own ketchup, and grow his own herbs. It's best to avoid dishes that are too complicated and stick with traditional Southern choices. Some of the better selections are black-eyed pea and ham hock soup, pan-roasted lamb with figs and peppers, and pan-roasted trout. ♦ American ♦ M-Sa, lunch and dinner; Su, jazz brunch and dinner. Reservations recommended. 2130 Fairmount Ave (between N 21st and N 22nd Sts). 232.9000. www.jacksfirehouse.com

9 RELIANCE STANDARD LIFE INSURANCE COMPANY BUILDING

Formerly named after **Fidelity Mutual Life Insurance**, this building was renovated and renamed in 1983. Designed by **Zantzinger, Borie and Medary**, with sculptures by Lee Lawrie, this 1927 building stands as an Art Deco counterpoint to the neoclassical glories of the Parkway. At the main door, two sculpted dogs protect the company's assets. ♦ Pennsylvania and Fairmount Aves.

10 TAVERN ON GREEN

★$$ This busy neighborhood restaurant with wooden floors, red tables, and original prints looks out on pretty Green Street. In summer, outdoor tables allow for dining alfresco. The food is not spectacular, but you can eat simply at reasonable prices. The mainstays are pasta, burgers, stir-fries, chili, and nachos. ♦ Eclectic ♦ M-Sa, lunch and dinner; Su, brunch and dinner. N 21st and Green Sts. 235.6767. www.philadelphiabuildings.com

11 STATUE OF JOAN OF ARC

The work, dedicated 15 November 1890 by sculptor Emmanuel Frémiet and placed originally at the eastern approach to the **Girard Avenue Bridge**, is across from the **Philadelphia Museum of Art**, where it has stood since 1938. ♦ Kelly Dr and N 25th St. www.philart.net/

12 WILLIAM M. REILLY MEMORIAL

A trust fund established by the estate of a Pennsylvania National Guard general provided for this grouping of Revolutionary War heroes. The first four bronze figures, placed in the 1940s, depict European military officers who joined the colonists' cause: Polish general Casimir Pulaski, Prussian general Friedrich von Steuben, French major general Marquis de Lafayette, and Irish general Richard Montgomery. In later decades, memorials to John Paul Jones and General Nathanael Greene were added. ♦ On the terrace behind the Philadelphia Museum of Art

13 PHILADELPHIA MUSEUM OF ART

This museum houses one of America's greatest public collections of art in more than a half-million square feet of space. It displays a millennium of European art, as well as masterpieces from Asia and the Near East,

THE HISTORIC MANSIONS OF FAIRMOUNT PARK

Within the 8,900 acres of **Fairmount Park** are the vestiges of a bygone era of gentle living in the form of elegant 18th- and 19th-century mansions, and bucolic farms and farmhouses. They harken back to a time when Philadelphia's aristocratic families had the houses built as private residences and personal retreats from a busy, growing city, especially in the heat of summer. There are 23 houses on the east and west banks of the **Schuylkill River**. Seven of those houses are open for tours: **Lemon Hil**, **Laurel Hill**, **Mount Pleasant**, **Strawberry Mansion**, and **Woodford** in the East Park; **Sweetbriar** and **Cedar Grove** in the West Park.

Lemon Hill Built for Robert Morris, financier of the Revolutionary War, on 80 acres purchased in 1770 from the 350-acre estate of William Penn, it was the first farm that featured greenhouses. During the war, the house was destroyed by British forces. Henry Pratt, a successful Philadelphia merchant, built the present Adams-inspired Federal-style house in 1799 and began growing lemons and other rare plants in the greenhouses. ◆ Admission. W-Su, 10AM-4PM. Lemon Hill Dr (off Sedgely Dr). 232.4337, 684.7926

Laurel Hill Also known as the **Randolph House**, it is named for the laurel-covered hill on which it stands. It was built for Francis and Rebecca Rawle in 1760. The house's center portion, Georgian in style, is flanked by a kitchen built in 1767 by subsequent owner Samuel Shoemaker and a two-story octagonal wing added in the early 19th century. In 1900, it became the first Fairmount Park mansion to open to the public. ◆ Admission. W-Su, 10AM-4PM. Edgely Dr (at Randolph Dr). 235.1776, 684.7926

Mount Pleasant This house was the product of a fortune amassed by Scottish sea captain John MacPherson during the Seven Years' War (1756–1763). Constructed in 1761, at the height of the Chippendale craze in America, it is considered one of the finest examples of 18th-century building and carving. Benedict Arnold later bought the house but was convicted of treason before he could move in. ◆ Admission. Tu-Su, 10AM-5PM. Mount Pleasant Dr (off Reservoir Dr). 763.2719, 684.7926

Strawberry Mansion The largest in the park, this house was begun in 1783 by Quaker judge William Lewis. He completed the central portion in 1790 in the popular Federal style. Subsequent owner Judge Joseph Hemphill added the flamboyant Greek Revival wings in the 1820s. His son Coleman built a racetrack on the property, raised Dalmatians, and grew strawberries from plants imported from Chile. ◆ Admission. Tu-Su, 10AM-4PM. Strawberry Mansion Dr (off Dauphin Dr). 228.8364, 684.7926

Woodford This grand Georgian-style mansion was built as a one-story structure by Quaker judge William Coleman about 1756. After Coleman's death in 1769, Woodford became a Tory residence, first for Alexander Barclay, King George III's controller of customs at the Port of Philadelphia, and later for David Franks, crown agent for Philadelphia. Of special interest is the Naomi Wood collection of colonial furnishings and decorative arts, which has been called "one of the most important assemblages of its kind in America." ◆ Admission. Tu-Su, 10AM-4PM. Woodford Dr (off Strawberry Mansion Dr). 229.6115, 684.7926

Sweetbriar Built as a year-round residence for Samuel Breck in 1797, it was designed in the Federal classical style. Like many houses of the era, it was set close to the river, a major means of transportation to and from the city. ◆ Admission. W-Su, by appointment only. Sweetbriar Hill (off Lansdowne Dr). 222.1333, 684.7926

Cedar Grove Originally a Quaker farmhouse, it was built in the 1740s in a section of town called Harrowgate. The fine collection of Jacobean, William and Mary, Queen Anne, Chippendale, and Federal-style furniture in the house reflects the accumulations of five generations of the Morris family, who used the house as their summer residence between 1746 and 1888. In 1927, fifth-generation owner Miss Lydia Thompson Morris had the house moved, stone by stone, and rebuilt on its present site in the park. ◆ Admission. Tu-Su, 10AM-5PM. Lansdowne Dr (off N 41st St). 878.2123, 684.7926

and holds an important work by virtually every major 20th-century artist. Museum architect **C. Clark Zantzinger** and his colleagues, **Horace Trumbauer** and **Charles L. Borie Jr.**, presented their three Grecian temples to the public in 1928. Lawyer Eli Kirk Price Jr. led the museum effort, initiating the construction of both wings at once so that the city government could not back out of completing the project. For 30 years, the museum's first director, Fiske Kimball, aggressively pursued

great artwork, outbidding and out-hustling more established museums.

Minnesota Mankato and Kosota stone give the building a warm, golden cast; its roof is covered by 4 acres of blue tile and guarded by bronze griffins. The three temples are attached at right angles, with tall porticoes topped by pediments. C. Paul Jennewein's glazed terra-cotta figures on the right temple's pediment represent characters from classical mythology, with Zeus presiding.

Restaurants/Clubs: Red | Hotels: Purple | Shops: Orange | Outdoors/Parks: Green | Sights/Culture: Blue

PHILADELPHIA MUSEUM OF ART

Second Floor

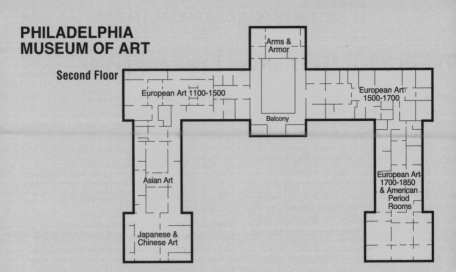

Arms & Armor

European Art 1100-1500

Balcony

European Art 1500-1700

Asian Art

European Art 1700-1850 & American Period Rooms

Japanese & Chinese Art

First Floor

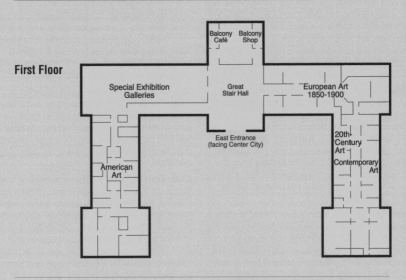

Balcony Café

Balcony Shop

Special Exhibition Galleries

Great Stair Hall

European Art 1850-1900

East Entrance (facing Center City)

American Art

20th Century Art

Contemporary Art

Ground Floor

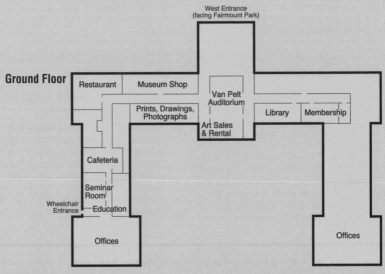

West Entrance (facing Fairmount Park)

Restaurant

Museum Shop

Van Pelt Auditorium

Prints, Drawings, Photographs

Library

Membership

Art Sales & Rental

Cafeteria

Seminar Room

Wheelchair Entrance

Education

Offices

Offices

Two cascading fountains follow the stairs going down to the Parkway, now sometimes called the "Rocky steps," after the film in which Sylvester Stallone triumphantly jogs up them. Sculptor A. Thomas Schomberg's statue of Stallone was placed at the top of the stairs for the filming of *Rocky III*. The statue was eventually removed to the **Spectrum**; two bronze footprints mark the place where Stallone—the statue and the man—once stood. From the rocky bluff at the rear of the museum is a splendid view of the **Schuylkill River**, the **Waterworks**, and **Boathouse Row**. In the springtime, the **Azalea Garden** blooms down the hill beyond the **Italian Fountain**. The entrance from the parking lot in the rear of the museum provides far easier access to the institution via the **West Foyer**, but walk to the front anyway. You'll get a great view of the city and see the vision realized by the Parkway's founders.

Just beyond the first-floor entrance, the **Great Stair Hall** is dominated by Augustus Saint Gaudens's 1892 statue of the nude huntress Diana, rescued from the demolished Madison Square Garden in New York. Directly above the entrance soars the mobile *Ghost*, by Alexander Calder. The museum counts among its treasures the **John G. Johnson Collection of European Painting**, which covers the 13th to the 19th centuries. Small but stunningly vivid is Flemish painter Jan van Eyck's early-16th-century *Saint Francis Receiving the Stigmata*, and Rogier van der Weyden's *Crucifixion with the Virgin and St. John* is considered one of the greatest masterpieces in American museums today.

In the gloried 20th-century rooms, one of Jasper Johns's most important works, *Painting with Two Balls* (1968), appears near Claes Oldenburg's 1970 *Three-Way Plug* suspended from the ceiling. German Anselm Kiefer ranks among today's greatest living artists; his stark, disturbing *Nigredo* suggests the burnt wasteland that is the legacy of the 20th century's world wars. The early modern collection is dominated by Marcel Duchamp, whose work here includes *Nude Descending a Staircase* and *The Bride Stripped Bare By Her Bachelors, Even*. The latter is composed of two large glass panels severely cracked after a showing at New York's Brooklyn Museum in 1926–1927; when the damaged work was returned to the artist, he declared that at last, it was finished. Don't miss Duchamp's final work, *Etant Donnés*, which at first appears to be little more than a barn door set in a darkened room. Approach the door and peek through two knotholes in the wood to get the full, grisly effect of the installation. The museum has equally provocative work by

Giorgio de Chirico, Pablo Picasso, Joan Miró, Salvador Dalí, and the largest group of sculpture by Constantine Brancusi outside of Paris.

Return to the Great Stair Hall and cross over to the **South Wing** to see the **American Collections**, which include Pennsylvania furniture and silver, Shaker art, and crafts. The museum has a prominent collection of work by neglected African-American artists, including Henry Ossawa Turner and Horace Pippin, whose 1943 *Mr. Prejudice* has received critical reappraisal. A comprehensive collection of work by Thomas Eakins is on display, including his 1877 painting of *William Rush Carving His Allegorical Figure of the Schuylkill River*. Rush is shown sculpting from a nude model as a chaperone looks on. In 1825, in fact, Rush completed two sculptures, which are fittingly located in the next room (fiberglass copies have been placed atop their original home, the Fairmount Waterworks just below the museum, beside the Schuylkill River). The rest of the first floor is set aside for special exhibitions, for which there is usually a separate admission charge.

The second floor is home to the museum's collections of Asian and European art. European art from 1100 to 1900 is arranged chronologically. Among the treasures are masterpieces by Rubens, Poussin, Delacroix, Ingres, Turner, Degas, and Toulouse-Lautrec. Note the evolution of European painting by two great paintings in adjacent rooms, Pierre Auguste Renoir's Impressionist *Bathers* (1887), and a work on the same subject, painted in 1906, heralding the dawn of abstract art, *The Large Bathers* by Paul Cézanne.

The Near Eastern, Asian, Chinese, and Japanese collections are excellent, tending toward huge reconstructions of ancient Asian sites that take up entire rooms. The Pillared Temple Hall from Madura in southern India is reconstructed from three 16th-century shrines to Vishnu. Another room, artificially lit as if by daylight, is occupied by the 14th-century Temple of the Attainment of Happiness, from Nara, Japan.

There's an inexpensive, cheerful cafeteria, an excellent restaurant, with a menu often inspired by a visiting exhibit, and a well-stocked museum shop on the ground floor, as well as galleries for prints, drawings, and photographs. On Friday evenings, the museum offers special programs, with gallery tours, talks, and films, and there's live jazz, wine, and snacks served in the early evening. ◆ Admission; free Su, 10AM-1PM. Tu, Th-Su; W, until 8:45PM. At the end of Benjamin Franklin Pkwy. 763.8100. &. www.philamuseum.org

---

Restaurants/Clubs: Red | Hotels: Purple | Shops: Orange | Outdoors/Parks: Green | Sights/Culture: Blue

14 PARKWAY HOUSE

Drawing from Art Deco and International styles, this pyramidal brick 1953 building with rounded bay windows was one of the first luxury apartment houses built after World War II. It was designed by **Gabriel Roth** and **Elizabeth Fleischer**. ♦ N 22nd St and Pennsylvania Ave. www.philadelphiabuildings.com

15 EAKINS OVAL

If you're walking to the **Philadelphia Museum of Art**, use the crosswalk at the oval, which is named for Philadelphia painter Thomas Eakins, the famous 19th-century artist noted for his expressive human figures. The enormous equestrian statue of George Washington sits on a base in the center of the oval, incorporating fountains that represent four great rivers: the Delaware, Hudson, Mississippi, and Potomac. German sculptor Rudolf Siemering designed the three-tiered monument, which was unveiled in 1897 in Fairmount Park and moved here in 1928. The monument of Washington and the fountains are flanked by two other fountains that memorialize John Ericsson, designer of the Civil War's ironclad ship *Monitor*, and Eli Kirk Price Jr., one of the civic leaders responsible for the Parkway's construction. ♦ N 24th St and Benjamin Franklin Pkwy. www.gptmc.org/culturefiles/attraction-e.htm

16 BEST WESTERN CENTER CITY HOTEL

$$ Free parking, a swimming pool, and a fitness center make this former **Ramada Inn** a good buy. The 183 renovated guest rooms feature such amenities as cable/satellite TV. There is a breakfast restaurant, the **Rodin Restaurant**, and a sports bar serving lunch and dinner. Overlooking the **Rodin Museum**, it is convenient to Parkway attractions but somewhat removed from other parts of the city. The good news is that public transportation is nearby. Walk over to 21st Street to catch the *No. 48* bus to the Society Hill area; the *No. 32* bus will take you to **City Hall** and south on Broad Street. ♦ 501 N 22nd St (at Pennsylvania Ave). 568.8300. ♿. www.bestwestern.com

17 BUTTONWOOD SQUARE

$$$ With 100 rooms—including 20 doubles—free parking, and a free shuttle service around Center City, this hotel is a great deal, even if it is slightly out of reach of Philadelphia's principal attractions. A cobblestone courtyard with modern sculpture, enormous brass doors, and a pleasant lobby help give the hotel a modicum of elegance. Stay on one of the upper floors for an extraordinary view of the Philadelphia skyline. The fitness facilities and outdoor pool are available to all guests. ♦ 2001 Hamilton St (at N 20th St). 569.7000. ♿. www.kormancommunities.com

Within Buttonwood Square:

TUSCAN TWENTY

★★$$ Savor the delights of contemporary Tuscan fare and brick-oven pizza in this stylish restaurant. Menu choices include linguine with whole baby clams and garlic, and scallops of veal pounded with fresh sage and prosciutto and layered with mushrooms and buffalo mozzarella. There is also a selection of wonderfully fresh salads. In season, dine outdoors in the garden courtyard. ♦ Italian ♦ M-Sa, lunch and dinner; Su, brunch and dinner. 569.7500

18 LONG'S GOURMET CHINESE COOKING

★$$ In a renovated strip of raised storefronts that was a former loading dock, a pastel dining room with well-spaced tables offers Chinese food and prices a notch above those in Chinatown. Daily specials usually feature fresh fish, such as salmon in an orange sauce. Try the crispy, boneless duck with Chinese vegetables, hot curried lamb, or baby shrimp with vegetables and peanuts. ♦ Chinese ♦ M-F, lunch and dinner; Sa, Su, dinner. 2018 Hamilton St (between N 20th and N 21st Sts). 496.9928

19 ROSE TATTOO CAFE

★★$$ A jungle of green plants hangs from the ceiling in this long-standing tenant of a dingy corner several blocks north of the **Free Library**. Try to snag a table in the rear room, which is lit by skylights. The menu offers possibilities from a cold grilled-chicken salad to jambalaya to veal tenderloins with cognac and apricot chutney. The ambiance is *très* romantic, making this an ideal date destination. ♦ American/continental ♦ M-F, lunch and dinner; Sa, dinner. 1847 Callowhill St (at N 19th St). 569.8939. www.rosetattoocafe.com

20 THE RODIN MUSEUM

This museum, which has the largest collection of Auguste Rodin's sculptures outside of France, opened in 1929. Two Frenchmen who already had much to do with designing Philadelphia, **Paul Philippe Cret** and **Jacques Greber**, were the architects of the French Renaissance–style building. The collection of statuary belonged to Jules Mastbaum, an early motion picture exhibitor. The sculptures he donated to the people of Philadelphia include *The Thinker* (which sits brooding at the front gate), *The Burghers of Calais*, *The Age of Bronze*, and *The Kiss*. Also, more than 100 drawings, paintings, and plaster studies are part of the collection.

In Rodin's time, the intensely expressive human figures represented a dramatic departure from the stiff, idealized statues of civic and cultural heroes that were the norm.

Rodin's *Monument to Balzac*, for instance, places the famous French author's craggy face above a flowing mass of loose robes. This depiction incensed the French Société des Gens de Lettres (which commissioned the work) when it was first exhibited.

Many of the sculptures are placed outdoors in the formal garden or near the reflecting pool. The cast of *Eternal Springtime* is the one Rodin gave to author Robert Louis Stevenson in 1885. Rodin worked for 37 years on *The Gates of Hell*, a tableau of about 190 writhing, miniature bas-relief figures. Left uncompleted at the time of the sculptor's death in 1917, its first bronze cast was made by Mastbaum and now stands at the museum entrance. ♦ Donation. Tu-Su. N 22nd St and Benjamin Franklin Pkwy. 763.8100. www.rodinmuseum.org

21 CALDER ON THE PARKWAY

In May 2002, the **Philadelphia Museum of Art** installed four Alexander Calder sculptures on the Parkway, part of an ongoing series of outdoor installations to celebrate the life of the famed artist, who lived and worked in Philadelphia. Located on the Parkway between 21st and 22nd Streets and across from the **Rodin Museum**, the sculptures include *Ordinary* (1969), a colorful stabile made of painted sheet metal, rods, and bolts and measuring 21 × 25 × 20 feet. www.phila.net/

22 CIVIL WAR SOLDIERS AND SAILORS MEMORIAL

The two marble pylons at the entrance to the tree-lined section of the Parkway were designed by Hermon Atkins MacNeil and installed in 1927. Important battles and naval engagements are listed on the sides facing the **Philadelphia Museum of Art**. Two sidewalks lead from here to the museum; take the one on the right, as it has a crosswalk at the end. ♦ N 20th St and Benjamin Franklin Pkwy. www.philart.net

23 THE FREE LIBRARY

Boasting a collection of 10 million items, the Philadelphia public library system is an important resource for students of all ages. In 1894, University of Pennsylvania provost Dr. William Pepper, with a $250,000 bequest from his uncle, George Pepper, and private subscriptions, began the Free Library in **City Hall**. The main branch was designed by architect **Horace Trumbauer** in 1917 as part of the Parkway project. Trumbauer's chief designer was **Julian Abele**, the first African-American graduate of the **University of Pennsylvania School of Architecture**. (Trumbauer and Abele also designed the **Philadelphia Museum of Art**.) The library's stacks are closed for browsing, but a computerized catalog and helpful librar-

ians make finding books relatively easy. Tours of the **Rare Book Department** can be arranged. The cafeteria on the fourth floor has lunch fare at bargain prices, and an outdoor terrace offers a lovely view of Center City. ♦ M-W, 9AM-9PM; Th-Sa; Su, 1PM-5PM. Closed in summer. Vine St (between N 19th and N 20th Sts). 686.5407. & www.library.phila.gov

24 SHAKESPEARE MEMORIAL

The 1926 monument by Alexander Stirling Calder was erected by the Shakespeare Society, which honored the Bard's original spelling of his name. The grouping depicts Hamlet and Touchstone, the court jester, and commemorates several of the actors who brought Shakespeare to the Philadelphia stage, including Thomas Wignell, John Drew, and Edwin Forrest. ♦ N 20th and Vine Sts

25 LOGAN CIRCLE

James Logan (1674-1751) was William Penn's agent and mayor of Philadelphia. In the middle of the busy traffic circle named for him is the **Swann Memorial Fountain**—one of the finest outdoor sculptures in America. Alexander Stirling Calder's spouting bronze figures, cast in 1924, represent the city's three main waterways—the male Native American stands for the **Delaware River**, and the two women for the **Schuylkill River** and **Wissahickon Creek**—whereas the swans play on the name of Dr. Wilson Cary Swann, president of the **Philadelphia Fountain Society**, in whose honor the fountain was constructed. Calder collaborated with Wilson Eyre Jr. on the fountain and pool. At night, the geysers and sprays glamorously reflect the city lights. During the day, the circle (one of the five original city squares) attracts lovers, readers, small children, and the homeless. Mind the traffic signals as you approach the fountain on foot, although new crosswalks are a help. ♦ N 19th St and Benjamin Franklin Pkwy

26 THE FRANKLIN INSTITUTE SCIENCE MUSEUM

Inspired as much by P.T. Barnum as by Benjamin Franklin, this is a great theatrical enterprise that will entertain, amuse, and exhaust you while it teaches you about science. The **Franklin Institute for the Promotion of Mechanical Arts** was founded in 1824 and became a major center for scientific study in the 19th century. The museum, designed by **John T. Windrim**, opened in 1934 and has been significantly enlarged with designs by **Geddes Brecher Qualls Cunningham**. As you enter, you'll see a rotunda that is the national memorial to Franklin. Anchoring it is an imposing 122-ton marble monument to scientist James Earle Fraser (who also designed the buffalo nickel). The museum is made up of several entities, and the admission fee depends on which you visit. Decide how much time you have and talk over the choices with the patient ticket sellers in the central atrium. The admission charges are higher than those of other museums in the city, so expect a fairly expensive outing, especially if you come with a herd of children. There are casual gift shops and restaurants to ensure that you are completely broke before you leave. ♦ Admission. Daily. N 20th St (between Race and Winter Sts). 448.1200. &. http://sln.fi.edu

Within the Franklin Institute Science Museum:

THE SCIENCE CENTER

The exhibits in this section—the original part of the museum—are fascinating and instructive. One of the real crowd pleasers is a newly renovated, two-story human heart: You walk through the arteries and ventricles while the heartbeat echoes in your ears. The **Mechanics Hall** contains levers, pulleys, and other mechanical devices that demonstrate the laws of Newtonian physics (as you operate them, docents are on hand to explain the principles). You can take a train ride (for about 12 feet) aboard a Baldwin locomotive. An entire room is devoted to trains and provides some of the best fun for kids in the museum. **Sports Challenge**, an exhibit that combines science with body mechanics, and **KidScience**, an eye-popping journey for 5- to 8-year-olds through scientific principles of light, water, earth, and air, are two of the other attractions to catch. ♦ Daily

MANDELL CENTER

This 20,000-square-foot space provides a home for traveling exhibitions, as well as **CyberZone**—a permanent exhibit on information technology. ♦ M-W, Su; Th-Sa, 9:30AM-9PM

By 1758, Philadelphia contained a number of Irish taverns, including the Faithful Irishman, the Jolly Irishman, and the Lamb.

Philadelphia, more than any other American city, showcases the history of architecture in the US. Its 300-year heritage of buildings includes examples of virtually every style found throughout the country.

The building that houses the restaurant Rembrandt's was once home to a tavern. Its owner, Harry A. Brogan, had a sign reading *HAB* hung at the front door. Though many believed the sign represented Brogan's initials, Rembrandt owner Jan Zarkin says the letters actually stood for *Have a Beer*.

TUTTLEMAN OMNIVERSE THEATER

The four-story dome contains a 79-foot-wide screen that wraps 180 degrees around the audience and is operated using an eight-track sound system and 56 speakers. The result is your complete immersion in a thrilling science film. The feature presentation is preceded by a superb short about Philadelphia. The features themselves—explorations of subjects that have ranged from Antarctica to the South American rain forest to outer space and the Rolling Stones live—are spectacular. ♦ Daily

FELS PLANETARIUM

Stars and other astral special effects are projected on the domed ceiling of this newly redone 350-seat planetarium. Theme and children's shows are offered, and on Saturday and Sunday afternoons, **The Sky Tonight** provides a well-narrated look at the sky du jour. Renovations improved the sound system and design to optimize the viewing experience. ♦ Show times vary. www.fi.edu

27 AERO MEMORIAL

Designed by Paul Manship and unveiled in 1948, this bronze sphere memorializes the Allied aviators who died during World War I. ♦ N 20th St (between Race St and Benjamin Franklin Pkwy). www.philart.net

28 PLEASE TOUCH MUSEUM

Interactivity is the name of the game at this children's museum. Park the stroller and head up a winding ramp where you'll be greeted by a real city bus with a working horn and steering wheel. Kids immediately climb into the driver's seat and demand spare change. A monorail that used to run through the **Grand Court** of the old **John Wanamaker Store** is here, along with miniature trains and a 30-foot replica of the **Delaware River**, complete with water, toy ferries, and cranes to load cargo onto little freighters.

One popular exhibit, **Supermarket Science**, features cash registers, stocked shelves, and shopping carts; after filling their carts, children unpack and "cook" in the designer kitchen next door. Other attractions include a mock television station with a working camera, and **Growing Up**, an exhibit that explores the four stages of childhood. The hottest exhibits are one that's based on the works of children's book author Maurice Sendak, and an outdoor interactive area, **Wachovia Science Park** (see page 119). The museum gets crowded on weekends, so arrive early or try a weekday, and bring your own lunch unless hot dogs from the cart out front will do. The gift shop has a fairly extensive selection of books,

THE BEST

Robert Driver
General Director, Opera Company of Philadelphia

White Dog Cafe—American cuisine, eclectic menu; great bar and atmosphere.

Girasole—fabulous Italian food.

Wilma Theater—classical and new theater in a great building on the **Avenue of the Arts**.

Philadelphia Museum of Art—one of the finest museums in the world.

Fairmount Park, West River Drive—a great place for summer, fall, and spring strolls.

Philadelphia Theatre Company—interesting, provocative productions.

Essene—superb health-food store and café.

Academy of Music—used for grand opera.

---

educational games, and toys. ♦ Admission; pay as you wish. Su, 9-10AM. Daily. 210 N 21st St (between Race and Winter Sts). 963. 0667. & www.pleasetouchmuseum.com

Within the Please Touch Museum:

WACHOVIA SCIENCE PARK

You may think this is just another playground, but it's really a joint venture of the **Please Touch Museum** and the **Franklin Institute** (see above). It lets kids, and the adults in their lives, learn about science through play—miniature golf teaches physics, a high-wire bike defies gravity, a swing set demonstrates energy transference, giant sound-amplifying dishes allow visitors to whisper to each other across the park. Over 30 interactive tools also include sundials, sand pendulums, hide-and-seek tunnels, and miniperiscopes. ♦ Included in admission to either Please Touch Museum or Franklin Institute Science Museum. Daily, May-Oct. 448.1200 &

29 CATHEDRAL OF SS. PETER AND PAUL

The seat of Philadelphia's Roman Catholic archdiocese was designed by **John Notman** and **Napoleon LeBrun** from plans drawn by the Reverends Mariano Maller and John B. Tornatore; the design was inspired by the Church of San Carlo al Corso in Rome. Notman is responsible for the Palladian Revival exterior, with the great copper dome and Corinthian portico. The inside of the dome was painted by Constantino Brumidi, who painted the frescoes in the Capitol dome in Washington, DC. Construction of the cathedral was completed in 1864; restoration and other new construction took place in the 1950s. The side chapels were turned into seven shrines, including one dedicated to Philadelphia's own blessed Katherine Drexel (1858-1955), a Catholic convert whose many charitable works have made her a candidate for sainthood. ♦ N 18th St and Benjamin Franklin Pkwy. 561.1313. www.archdiocese-phl.org

In front of the Cathedral of Ss. Peter and Paul:

STATUE OF THOMAS FITZSIMONS

The Irish-born signer of the Declaration of Independence served in the Continental Congress and the first three US Congresses.

30 WYNDHAM FRANKLIN PLAZA HOTEL

$$$ A city unto itself, this 758-room hotel offers comfortable accommodations, a pool, a sauna, a fitness club, squash courts, outdoor tennis courts, and a jogging track (there are extra charges for some facilities). **Geddes Brecher Qualls Cunningham** designed the hotel, which was completed in 1980; in 1994, Texas-based **Cullen & Associates** renovated the public spaces and meeting and guest rooms to the tune of $6.5 million. The massive atrium lobby includes an 1869 tower clock imported from Manchester, England. It's a 10-minute walk to either the **Pennsylvania Convention Center** or the shopping areas of Walnut and Chestnut Streets. Valet parking and a shuttle service from **Philadelphia International Airport** are available. ♦ N 17th and Race Sts. 448.2000, 800/996.3426; fax 448.2864. & www.wyndham.com/franklinplaza

Within the Wyndham Franklin Plaza Hotel:

SHULA'S STEAK HOUSE

★$$$ This steak house in the hotel offers king-size portions of certified angus beef in a football-themed men's club atmosphere. Fresh seafood, lamb, and live lobster are also offered. Memories of the winning Dolphins' coach are everywhere—the menu is even printed on a pigskin. ♦ American ♦ M-F, lunch; daily, dinner. Lobby level. 448.2700

THE TERRACE

★$$ An open dining area overlooking the massive lobby caters primarily to out-of-towners who don't feel like venturing outside.

Restaurants/Clubs: Red | Hotels: Purple | Shops: Orange | Outdoors/Parks: Green | Sights/Culture: Blue

The menu—grilled chicken sandwiches, fried shrimp, and pasta primavera—isn't too adventurous either. ♦ American ♦ Daily, breakfast, lunch, and dinner. First floor. 448.2000

THE LOBBY BAR

This bar stays open late—a good thing too, because there isn't much nightlife in the immediate area. A cigar lounge is an added feature. ♦ Daily, 3:30PM-1AM. Lobby level. 448.2000

31 THE GALLERIES AT MOORE

Located within **Moore College of Art and Design**, which was founded in 1848 and is the only 4-year visual arts college for women in the US, these galleries are on the ground floor. The **Goldie Paley Gallery** showcases emerging American and European artists, and the **Levy Gallery** focuses exclusively on African-American artists from Philadelphia. ♦ Tu, Th-F; W, 10AM-7PM; Sa, Su, noon-4PM. N 20th and Race Sts. 965.4027. ₺. www.thegalleriesatmoore.org

32 THE ACADEMY OF NATURAL SCIENCES

This is the place for dinosaurs. In addition to being the oldest natural history museum in the country, it also boasts one of the finest collections of re-created dinosaurs and mounted animals in the US. Founded in 1812 by druggist John Speakman and his friends, the academy began as a discussion group that met in a Market Street coffeehouse. It moved to its present site in 1876, bringing with it the beginning of its spectacular dinosaur collection, including the first bones ever attributed to dinosaurs. The bones of the Hadrosaurus were discovered in nearby Haddonfield, New Jersey, in the 1830s; in 1868, academy curator Joseph Leidy used them to assemble the world's first mounted dinosaur skeleton. Now, many of the creatures stand in the **Dinosaur Hall**, a hit among young children. At a fascinating permanent exhibit, **The Dig—A Dinosaur Adventure**, visitors (on weekends only) can dig for fossils and help chip out a dinosaur

---

The term *United States of America* was used for the first time on 6 July 1776 when the Declaration of Independence was published in Philadelphia's *Pennsylvania Evening Post.*

On a visit to Philadelphia in March 1830, the normally staid Ralph Waldo Emerson is said to have spewed, "If all the world was Philadelphia, suicide would be extremely common." But by 1864, Emerson had warmed to the city enough to write, in a letter to his friend Lucretia Mott, "I delight in that city and reckon it a good hospital."

---

skeleton from a pit filled with a concrete matrix. You can't keep your finds—the emphasis is on learning what paleontologists do, so every "treasure" is labeled and cataloged. Among the other exhibits is one on the ancient Egyptian process of mummification—with a real mummy, a high priest named Petiese, out of his wraps. Lifelike dioramas of mounted animals—lions, gorillas, wild yaks, buffalo, and polar bears—are shown in their natural settings. Mounted zebras drink from a stream in a re-creation of a Serengeti water hole. In the highly recommended third-floor children's museum, **Outside In**, kids can touch living animals, perhaps a tarantula or bunny, and play on a sandy beach. On the weekends, the museum has special events and sponsors field trips for adults as well as children. Typical exhibits include a look at beautiful but deadly reptiles and bugs from around the world. On display in the museum's library, which includes more than 150,000 volumes, is a folio copy of John James Audubon's *Birds of America.* ♦ Admission. Daily. 1900 Benjamin Franklin Parkway. 299.1000. ₺. www.acnatsci.org

33 FOUR SEASONS HOTEL

$$$$ This gracious and sophisticated hotel ties with the **Rittenhouse Hotel** for the two best hotel experiences in the city. The lobby opens onto a series of sitting rooms, with comfortable niches from which to watch the well-dressed and well-heeled go by. Designed by **Kohn Pederson Fox Associates**, the 365-room hostelry and the neighboring 30-story **One Logan Square** office tower feature a pool and health club facilities, as well as a dry cleaners and a beauty salon. Rooms are furnished in the Federal style with mahogany secretaries, marble baths, and minibars stocked with Belgian chocolates and Perrier. Free town car service is available within Center City. ♦ 1 Logan Sq (between Benjamin Franklin Pkwy and N 19th St). 963.1500, 800/332.3442; fax 963.9562. ₺. www.fourseasons.com

Within the Four Seasons Hotel:

FOUNTAIN RESTAURANT

★★★★$$$$ Change is a good thing. At the Fountain, longtime chef Jean Marie Lacroix exited, with Martin Hamann taking over as executive chef and David Jansen promoted to chef d'restaurant. The restaurant's interior was spruced up with additional wainscoting, shades of gold, and newly installed intimate lighting that bathes each diner in a warming glow. An evening at the Fountain Restaurant has *special occasion* written all over it, from the arrival of the *amuse bouche*—a scallop topped with salty gems of ossetra caviar—to the savoring of a creamy Mont Briac cheese paired with a fig tartlet in an aged balsamic vinegar. Every flavor note resonates, and the service and surroundings make every single diner feel like a VIP. Best bet—the Spontaneous Taste menu, six inspired courses for $110—or really splurge and add wine, for $185. The wine list is extensive, and the service is refined without being snooty. ◆ American/continental ◆ Daily, lunch, brunch, and dinner. Jacket and tie recommended. Reservations recommended. 963.1500

SWANN LOUNGE AND CAFE

★★$$ A light menu is offered in this airy, elegant room overlooking the Parkway. Recent renovations have introduced fabrics and finishes in a palette of salmon, terra-cotta, thyme green, and cream and added a wood-burning fireplace. Comfortable sofas and chairs make the Lounge a pleasant choice for afternoon tea or lunch. Choose from croissant sandwiches, pasta, or a daily special. On Friday and Saturday nights, there's a prix-fixe all-you-can-eat Viennese buffet—an elaborate dessert table with tortes, cakes, mousses, tarts, and fruit. Sunday brunch is wonderful and pricey, but a cut above every othr hotel spread. ◆ American ◆ M-Sa, lunch, afternoon tea, and dinner; Su, brunch and dinner. Viennese buffet: F, Sa, 9PM-1AM. Reservations recommended for afternoon tea and Su brunch. 963.1500 ఈ

34 EMBASSY SUITES HOTEL

$$$ This cylindrical 28-story hotel was remodeled from a 1963 apartment house designed by **Stonorov & Haws**. Each of the 288 newly renovated two-room suites has two balconies that overlook either the Parkway or Center City. It's an ideal place for families—there's a children's playroom right in the hotel, as well as a health club and sauna. ◆ 1776 Benjamin Franklin Pkwy (at N 18th St). 561.1776, 800/EMBASSY; fax 963.0122. ఈ. www.embassy-suites.com

Within the Embassy Suites Hotel:

T.G.I. FRIDAY'S

$ The burgers, salads, and bar food at this popular chain may be pedestrian, but the view from the busy deck bar keeps the crowds coming. ◆ American ◆ Daily, breakfast, lunch, and dinner. 665.8443 ఈ

35 UNITED FUND HEADQUARTERS

Designed by **Mitchell/Giurgola** in 1969, this building is perhaps the finest example of that firm's work in the city. Each of the three main façades addresses its urban context, as well as its compass orientation: A monumental vertical scale crafted in concrete faces the angled Parkway, horizontal concrete sunscreens front Logan Circle, and a curtain wall of gray glass faces north on Race Street. It's a remarkable response to the design limitations imposed by the Parkway, one of which is a trapezoidal site. ◆ Benjamin Franklin Pkwy (between N 17th and N 18th Sts). www.unfpa.org

35 STATUE OF KOPERNIK

Commissioned by local Polish-Americans to mark the 500th anniversary of Nicholas Copernicus's 1473 birth, Dudley Talcott's abstract sculpture recalls the astronomer's accomplishments and his original Polish name: Mikolaj Kopernik. The monument features a 16-foot stainless-steel circle that symbolizes the earth's orbit around the sun, with soil from Copernicus's birthplace—Torun, Poland—placed beneath it. ◆ N 18th St and Benjamin Franklin Pkwy. www.philart.net

36 ST. CLEMENT'S EPISCOPAL CHURCH

Looking as if it belongs amid serene graveyards and rolling English countryside instead of nondescript office buildings and row houses, this 1859 church is yet another John Notman project. When 20th Street was widened in 1929, this gracious Romanesque brownstone was moved 40 feet without sustaining any damage. The wrought-iron gates of the 1870 **Lady Chapel** are the work of Samuel Yellin, who, in the early part of the 20th century, fashioned exquisite ironwork for the homes of the Rockefellers and Vanderbilts. ◆ M-F, 10AM-3PM. Services daily; evensong daily, 5:30PM. N 20th and Cherry Sts. 563.1876. www.s-clements.org

37 THREE-WAY PIECE NUMBER 1: POINTS

Henry Moore's 1964 bronze sculpture, which weighs in at 1 ton, has been said to resemble many different things, including a hefty animal (with three points for paws), a gnawed bone, and a hunched bird. ◆ Benjamin Franklin Pkwy (between N 16th and N 17th Sts)

38 VERIZON TOWER

This office tower, designed by the hometown firm of **Kling Lindquist**, houses the corporate headquarters of Verizon. Its faceted sides and ziggurat top—illuminated at night—are wrapped in red granite and accentuated by polished brass trim at the base. ◆ N 18th and Arch Sts

39 *LOVE* SCULPTURE

Erected in 1976 for the city's bicentennial, the painted aluminum sculpture is located on the axis of the Parkway in Kennedy Plaza. This particular arrangement of the four letters of

FAIRMOUNT PARK

If you find yourself viewing any sizable patch of green in Philadelphia, chances are it's part of this park. The park system encompasses 8,700 acres—about 10% of all the land in Philadelphia—and is said to be the largest urban park in the world. The claim is very arguable. The Fairmount Park Commission manages all that green space, including **Rittenhouse Square**, the **Wissahickon Valley**, all the green areas lining the **Parkway**, and even the front yard of the **Cathedral of Ss. Peter and Paul**.

Most Philadelphians would agree that **Fairmount Park** proper consists of the large, contiguous expanse of green extending about 4 miles from behind the art museum to **Falls Bridge** near the neighborhood of **East Falls**. It's roughly the shape of South America, and the park's territory reaches eastward and westward from both sides of the river drives. The park is so vast that the park commission has had to make choices as to which sections should be given priority for upkeep. But large expanses are well maintained, and Philadelphia's inhabitants consider the park their backyard. This is where they picnic, grill hamburgers, drink beer (alcohol has traditionally been permitted almost everywhere in the park, with a growing list of excepted areas), read, stroll, and play with their kids. There are playing fields, tennis courts, biking trails, children's playgrounds, outdoor sculpture, and some of the nation's finest examples of early American residences in this urban oasis of breathable air and open spaces. A map is a must if you plan to explore the land off the river drives, as the circular roads tend to take you back to where you started—that's if you're lucky. Maps are available at the **Independence Visitor Center** on John F. Kennedy Boulevard in Center City West, 1 N Independence Mall W (at 6th and Market Sts) in Old Philadelphia.

the word *love* made its original appearance in a painting by Robert Indiana in 1964 and has been reproduced in jewelry, posters, plates, and even a US postage stamp. Once a haven for skateboarders, the park was redesigned; plants and trees were added, and skateboarders have gone elsewhere. ♦ John F. Kennedy Blvd and N 15th St

40 VERGE

★★ There's new energy in East Falls, as the opening of this new restaurant will attest. Chef Shawn Dolan is in the open kitchen, preparing an array of modern American fare in the $10-$22 range. Verge is part of the ongoing development of East Falls by Mark Sherman (www.shermanproperties.com), a native of the Schuylkill-bound neighborhood currently in the process of renovating 260,000 square feet of space and 31 buildings into an artist's co-op, loft living, and stylish retail and dining spaces. You might say he's on the Verge of an East Falls revolution. ♦ 4101 Kelly Dr (at Midvale Ave). 991.7601

41 CHAMOUNIX MANSION

$ Built in the early 19th century, and an inexpensive hostel since 1964, the mansion offers elegant period furnishings on the ground floor and dormitory facilities on the second floor, with separate accommodations for men and women. Several common rooms, a kitchen, laundry facilities, and free parking are available. The mansion sleeps about 25, and another 25 beds are in the 1856 Gothic Revival carriage house. Take the *No. 38* bus to reach the hostel. There is no restaurant on the premises. ♦ At the end of Chamounix Dr. 878.3676, 800/379.0017. &. www.philahostel.org

42 LAUREL HILL CEMETERY

🅟 "It's really a sculpture garden: a forest of looming obelisks, Greek-temple mausoleums, odd statues, and stone crypts festooned with doodads and decorative detail," Ron Avery, of the *Philadelphia Daily News*, wrote of this Victorian cemetery-cum-park. When the 99-acre nonsectarian cemetery was created in 1836 from designs by noted architect **John Notman**, burial grounds were places of rest for the dead and recreation for the living. Elaborate monuments and sculptures marked the graves of prominent Philadelphians. Families brought picnics to this hilly serene spot above the **Schuylkill**. Some of the more moving sculptures include James Thom's *Old Mortality* (inspired by Sir Walter Scott's book of the same name) near the entrance and the tomb of the coal magnate and philanthropist William Warner. Carved by Alexander Milne Calder, Warner's sarcophagus is shown being opened by a draped angel to allow his winged soul to escape. For a time, the cemetery was such a popular place for the living that its owners were forced to control the numbers of visitors with tickets for admission. It still gets visits from the curious and is reachable from Center City by taking the *No. 61* bus. Maps and guidebooks are available, as are burial plots. It's the first National Historic Landmark cemetery in the US. ♦ Tu-Sa, 9:30AM-1:30PM. 3822 Ridge Ave (at Nicetown La). 228.8200

43 STRAWBERRY MANSION

This stuccoed brick mansion was built in the 1790s along simple Federal lines. The Greek Revival wings added in the early 1820s converted a relatively modest country house into a massive mansion. It was owned by Judge Joseph Hemphill, whose son Coleman cultivated strawberries from roots imported from Chile. Coleman Hemphill was an optimist: He invited Daniel Webster to a political banquet meant to make peace between northern and southern Democrats. Webster arrived, eyed the company, offered a toast to the strawberries, and escaped out the ballroom window. A restaurant famed for its strawberries-and-cream dessert, in fact, operated here later in the century. An antique-toy exhibit is displayed inside. Such a grand mansion contrasts sharply with the struggling neighborhood (of the same name) that fronts the park here. ◆ Admission. Tu-Su. Strawberry Mansion Dr (off Dauphin Dr). 228.8364. www.phila.gov/fairpark

44 WOODFORD

By all accounts, Fairmount Park was a hotbed of treason during the Revolutionary War. While George Washington and his men suffered through the winter of 1777 in Valley Forge, British General William Howe was being lavishly entertained by crown agent David Franks at Woodford. Franks's daughter Rebecca was the toast of the redcoats. The oldest part of the Georgian country house dates to 1756. Its exterior brickwork is Flemish bond, and the 9-foot-high entrance doors, flanked by Tuscan columns, lead to a beautifully furnished interior. ◆ Admission. W-Su. Woodford Dr (off Strawberry Mansion Dr). 229.6115. www.philaparks.org/ewaawo.htm

45 LAUREL HILL (RANDOLPH HOUSE)

This Georgian brick mansion was completed by Francis Rawle in 1760. After he died in a hunting accident, his widow Rebecca married Quaker pacifist Samuel Shoemaker. Their home was confiscated when Shoemaker was convicted of treason during the Revolutionary War, providing General Joseph Reed, president of the Supreme Council of Pennsylvania, with a summer retreat. In 1784, Rebecca Rawle Shoemaker bought back the mansion, and it later became the home of Dr. Philip Syng Physick, the father of American surgical practice. ◆ Admission. W-Su. Edgely Dr (at Randolph Dr). 235.1776

46 BELMONT MANSION

Erected in 1746, with frequent subsequent additions, this mansion became the home of Judge Richard Peters, a supporter of the American Revolution and friend of George Washington. The three-story building, surrounded by a colonnade, is one of the first fully developed Palladian structures to be built in the American colonies and is noted for the fine plaster moldings, representing musical instruments, of the ceilings. It became a café in its later life. Restored in 1997, with a new banquet and meeting facility, it is now operated by the **American Women's Heritage Society**, which takes visitors through the building. ◆ Tours, Tu-F; Sa, Su, by appointment. Belmont Mansion Dr (off Wynnefield Ave). 878.8844. www.philaparks.org/ewaabm.htm

47 BELMONT PLATEAU

The Philadelphia skyline vista as seen from the top of the **Philadelphia Art Museum** steps is well known, but the view from here is even more spectacular. You get a sweeping north–south panorama of the area from the **Philadelphia Inquirer Building** at Broad and Callowhill Streets to the **Walt Whitman Bridge**. At night, when the distant city pulses with light, the panorama is electrifying, and it's a particularly popular spot on warm evenings. The plateau is also the site of busy playing fields and a kite launch. To reach it from Center City, take the Schuylkill Expressway or W River Drive to Montgomery Drive, and then make a right at Belmont Mansion Drive. ◆ Belmont Mansion Dr (off Montgomery Dr). www.phila.gov/fairpark

48 MOUNT PLEASANT

When John Adams visited Captain John MacPherson's home in 1775, he reported to a friend that the former privateer possessed "the most elegant Seat in Pensilvania" and "a clever Scot Wife." The central projecting pavilion, which is topped by an imposing pediment, and the use of stucco make this mansion the most distinctive home in the park. MacPherson sold the home, a Georgian-style country house, to Benedict Arnold. It was confiscated before the famous traitor could move in. The house is furnished and maintained by the Philadelphia Museum of Art. ◆ Admission. Tu-Su. Mt. Pleasant Dr (off Reservoir Dr). 763.2719. www.philamuseum.org/collections/parkhouse/mtpleasant.shtml

49 SMITH MEMORIAL PLAYGROUND

Children have been visiting this old-fashioned 6-acre playground for more than a century and finding it to their liking. Though the equipment is now very dated, the appeal hasn't lessened in the video-game era. A gift from wealthy Philadelphian Richard Smith, who died in 1894, the playground is stocked with old-time metal swings, merry-go-rounds, and climbing equipment. A 12-foot-wide enclosed sliding board lets 10 kids slide down it at once. A mansion converted into a playhouse is

---

Restaurants/Clubs: Red | Hotels: Purple | Shops: Orange | Outdoors/Parks: Green | Sights/Culture: Blue

specially designed for preschoolers, with lots of doll strollers, small cars, and a play kitchen. The basement is home to a kiddie driving course, with pedal cars, a pretend gas pump, and a working traffic signal.♦ M-Sa. Reservoir Dr (between N 33rd St and Mt. Pleasant Dr). 765.4325. www.smithplayhouse.org/

50 MONUMENT TO ULYSSES S. GRANT

The equestrian statue memorializing the 18th president of the United States guards the entrance to Fountain Green Drive. Designed by Daniel Chester French and Edward C. Potter, it was dedicated in 1899. ♦ Kelly and Fountain Green Drs

51 JAPANESE HOUSE AND GARDENS

Exquisitely out of place and time, the 16th-century-style teahouse is a zone of quiet contemplation—even with many visitors about. Designed by **Junzo Yoshimura** and assembled by four craftsmen imported from Japan, the house is set in a garden near a stream and surrounded by Japanese trees. A gift of the American-Japan Society of Tokyo, it was first exhibited in the Museum of Modern Art in New York in 1957. Age and the elements have left the house untouched. During the spring and summer, events include tea ceremonies and origami demonstrations. ♦ Tu-Su, 11AM-4PM, May–mid-Oct. Horticultural Dr (off Belmont Ave). 878.5097. www.shofuso.com

52 MANN MUSIC CENTER

From mid-June through July, the **Philadelphia Orchestra** plays three concerts each week under the stars; other nights through the summer are dedicated to pop concerts. ♦ George's Hill Dr (off Belmont Ave). 546.7900. ᪮. www.manncenter.org/

53 CATHOLIC TOTAL ABSTINENCE UNION FOUNTAIN

Designed for the centennial by Herman Kim, this marble monument to the temperance movement is shaped like a Maltese Cross; on each axis are statues of prominent Catholics. Looking at this dry, cracked fountain makes you yearn for a drink. ♦ N Concourse Dr and States Dr

54 CEDAR GROVE

This Quaker farmhouse was originally located in the Frankford section of Philadelphia. The house was inherited by the family of Isaac and Sarah Morris in 1793. Five generations of Morrises lived here until it was given to the Fairmount Park Commission, which moved it to the present location, with many of the original furnishings intact. The kitchen is stocked with

utensils, including a huge brass caldron. ♦ Admission. Tu-Su. Lansdowne Dr (off N 41st St). 878.2123. www.fairmountpark.com

55 SCHUYLKILL RIVER

Notoriously difficult to spell, *Schuylkill* means "hidden river" in Dutch. Stretching 100 miles from its headwaters in the anthracite belt in Schuylkill County to the **Delaware River** in South Philadelphia, the river is a former industrial giant and a major reason for Philadelphia's growth in the 18th and 19th centuries. Here behind the art museum, its role is aesthetic and recreational; it is both the centerpiece of **Fairmount Park** and the subject of hundreds of landscape portraits. In the 1800s, excursion boats trolled the waters Today it is famous for its scullers, who work out even in cold months. The annual Dad Vail Regatta in May draws rowing teams from around the country and fills the bleachers along Kelly Drive. Still, one of the best activities on the banks of the Schuylkill is a sedentary one: sitting quietly, contemplating the water.

56 MEMORIAL HALL

The only large building remaining from the Centennial Exhibition sits atop a rise in the park, its square glass-and-cast-iron dome visible for miles. **Hermann Schwarzmann** designed the Beaux Arts structure—which was conceived as an art museum for the centennial and later became the **Pennsylvania Museum of Art**—after a trip to Vienna. The three arched doorways lead to a grand central rotunda. On the dome, which is illuminated at night, *Columbia* hoists a laurel wreath. The winged horses at the entrance, Vincent Pilz's *Pegasus*, originally guarded the Vienna Opera House. The building, which late inspired the design of the New York Metropolitan Museum of Art as well as the German Reichstag, is now occupied by the Fairmount Park Commission offices. ♦ N Concourse Dr (between N 41st St and Belmont Ave)

57 STATUE OF COWBOY

America's romance with the Wild West was transformed into art by Frederic Remington, whose 1908 equestrian statue, his only large-scale bronze, perches on the rock above the drive. A dramatic apparition that continues to startle commuters, Remington's cowboy pulls the reins just as his mount is about to leap into traffic. ♦ Kelly Dr (at Brewery Hill Dr)

58 SMITH MEMORIAL ARCH

The two giant Doric columns with statues of Major General George Gordon Meade by Daniel Chester French and Major General John Fulton Reynolds by Charles Grafly can be seen from nearly anywhere in the park. They're on

THE FIRST CONTINENTAL CONGRESS

he First Continental Congress convened in **Carpenter's Hall** in Philadelphia on 5 September 1774 with 56 delegates from 12 colonies in attendance. (Georgia sent no representatives but agreed to support any plans made.) Although the Second Continental Congress 1775–1781) was responsible for the Declaration of Independence, that document might never have come to be without the actions of the First Continental Congress.

he First Continental Congress was convened to serve s the sounding board for a long list of colonial grievances, including 11 separate acts of taxation mposed on the colonies by the British Parliament. In a old move, the First Congress established the ontinental Association, which bound the colonists not o trade with Great Britain or use British goods until ritish taxation policies were amended.

he First Congress adopted the Declaration of Rights on 4 October 1774. This document declared that as British subjects, the colonists were not bound by laws o which they had not consented by means of elected epresentatives.

Delegates, including Thomas Mifflin, Edward Biddle, Samuel Rhoads, John Morton, Charles Humphreys,

George Ross, John Dickinson, and Joseph Galloway, declared the common law of England to be their birthright, including the rights of trial by jury, public meetings, and petition. Finally, delegates protested the British policy of maintaining standing armies in America without the full consent of the colonies.

When news of the First Congress and its proceedings reached London, the colonists had the attention of the British Crown. In retaliation to this first step in rebellion, the British Parliament passed an act that restrained the commerce of all the New England provinces, forbidding them from fishing on the banks of Newfoundland, which, in short order, was extended to New Jersey, Pennsylvania, Maryland, Virginia, South Carolina, and the lower counties on the Delaware River.

The War of Independence began on 19 April 1775, commencing in Massachusetts with the famous "shot heard 'round the world." By that time, the Second Continental Congress was in session, for it had become increasingly clear that total separation from Great Britain was inevitable.

top of two triumphant arches at the entrance to the 1876 centennial fairgrounds (though the arches weren't completed until 1912). Thirteen sculptors collaborated on the monument, which was made possible by the bequest of Richard Smith, a typesetter and Civil War hero. The figures, busts, and equestrian statues depict several of Pennsylvania's fighting men—and Smith himself. Don't miss the whispering bench near the memorial. If you sit at one end and whisper, a friend sitting at the opposite end can hear you. ◆ N Concourse Dr (at N 41st St)

59 SWEETBRIAR

Congressman Samuel Breck built this Federal-style country house in 1797. Breck was a gracious host to foreign visitors like Lafayette and Talleyrand and an arts and science enthusiast. The congressman helped establish the Philadelphia school system. Inside, floor-to-ceiling windows overlook the river and the **Fairmount Waterworks**. The chandelier is from a palace owned by the Aga Khan. Breck's own 1834 sketch of Talleyrand shows the French diplomat in his old age. ◆ Admission. W-Su, by appointment only. Sweetbriar Hill (off Lansdowne Dr). 222.1333

60 LETITIA STREET HOUSE

This small dwelling is the oldest surviving brick house in America. Carpenter John Smart built the two-room, two-story house in 1713 on what is now Market Street. It was later moved to its present location and supplied with period furnishings. The house is not open for tours. ◆ Lansdowne Dr (off W Girard Ave). www.philadelphiabuildings.org

61 ELLEN PHILLIPS SAMUEL MEMORIAL

The three terraces of allegorical statuary fronting the river are the gift of a Philadelphia philanthropist who died in 1913. Seeking to encourage the art form of sculpture, Phillips established a fund that sponsored three international exhibitions. These served to bring many great artists, along with great artwork, to Philadelphia. Some of the best pieces originally intended for the memorial ended up elsewhere in the city. The selection process was interrupted by the Depression and World War II, and it was not until 1961 that the last piece in the group was dedicated. The grouping is called **The Emblematic History of the United States**.

Restaurants/Clubs: Red | Hotels: Purple | Shops: Orange | Outdoors/Parks: Green | Sights/Culture: Blue

PHILADELPHIA ZOO

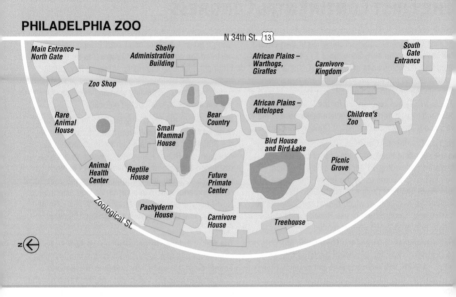

N 34th St. 13

Main Entrance – North Gate
Shelly Administration Building
African Plains – Warthogs, Giraffes
Carnivore Kingdom
South Gate Entrance
Zoo Shop
Rare Animal House
Bear Country
African Plains – Antelopes
Children's Zoo
Small Mammal House
Bird House and Bird Lake
Picnic Grove
Animal Health Center
Reptile House
Future Primate Center
Zoological St.
Pachyderm House
Carnivore House
Treehouse

South Terrace: Starting where it all began is Wheeler Williams's *Settling of the Seaboard* (1942), celebrating the taming of the continent by Europeans and the drive for independence. *The Puritan and the Quaker* (1942) by Henry Rosin reminds US citizens that their nation was founded by religious dissenters.

Central Terrace: Conceived in the late 1930s, the grouping of *The Immigrant*, *The Plough*, *The Slave*, and other heroic figures depicts the workers who built the country from muscle and sweat. The terrace is dominated by the most abstract piece in the memorial, *The Spirit of Enterprise* by Jacques Lipchitz, who cast the bronze in 20 separate pieces between 1950 and 1960.

North Terrace: Four granite figures from the 1950s suggest that in the 20th century, the US finally achieved civilization. These tributes to *The Poet*, *The Preacher*, *The Scientist*, and *The Laborer* are all by foreign émigrés. ◆ Kelly Dr (between Poplar and Brewery Hill Drs)

62 NORTH STAR BAR

★★$ This popular night spot will satisfy your hunger for an eclectic range of live bands, from roots to folk, world beat to rock 'n' roll, and the sandwich menu, which tops out at about $8, will also hit the spot. ◆ 2639 Poplar St. 684.0808. www.northstarbar.com

63 LEMON HILL

Set in the nucleus of Fairmount Park, this residence and surrounding estate was originally occupied by financier Robert Morris. The greenhouses are stocked with lemon trees,

which gave the mansion its name. Later sold to merchant Henry Pratt, the mansion is furnished with period artifacts and is open to the public. The house currently serves as a chapter headquarters of the **Colonial Dames of America**. ◆ Admission. W-Su. Lemon Hill Dr (off Sedgely Dr). 232.4337

64 PHILADELPHIA ZOO

Though the Philadelphia Zoo's original charter dates back to 21 March 1859, opening day was delayed for 15 years due to the Civil War. Opening its gates to about 3,000 visitors on 1 July 1874, it is the oldest zoo in America, with more than 1,800 animals in residence. It's also one of the newest, given that it constantly and vigorously reconfigures itself. A leader in animal conservation projects and captive breeding programs, the zoo protects more than 50 endangered species. In 1994, the zoo became the first in the Western Hemisphere to exhibit white lions, of which there are fewer than 20 in the world. Jezebel and Vinkel, the zoo's first two white lions, also gave birth in 1994 to cubs, two of them white. In recent years, the zoo has put many of its animals into open environments that are meant to approximate the wild. After one of the worst zoo fires in American history led to the deaths of 23 primates in 1995, the zoo began work on a new $21 million primate center that opened on 1 July 1999, the zoo's 125th anniversary.

In **Bear Country**, polar bears swim in a 200,000-gallon tank with glass walls—ideal for viewing their incongruously graceful strokes. The **Carnivore Kingdom** is home to otters, red pandas, a jaguar, and a snow leopard, who live amid a tableau of boulders. The **Bird House**, opened in 1916 to designs of **Mellor, Meigs and Howe**, is one of the most unusual spots in the zoo: Many of the avians fly freely among the visitors. In the **Carnivore House**, the zookeepers throw lions and tigers fresh meat—a crowd-pleasing activity since the time of the Roman Empire. The **Reptile House** is a dark, tomblike series of rooms with glass cases holding tree frogs, turtles, and ungainly boa constrictors. Don't miss the alligators in the back. "Cobras!" is the latest exhibit in this slithering neighborhood.

The zoo operates both a small **Children's Zoo** and the **Treehouse**, designed by **Venturi, Scott Brown and Associates**, The former offers elephant, camel, and pony rides; educational talks by zookeepers; and opportunities to pet the animals. Inside the latter, small children climb and scramble over giant play sculptures of frogs, caterpillars, and other creatures. There is a separate admission charge for the Treehouse, as well as for the aerial monorail tour and the Channel 6 Zoo balloon, which soars 400 feet overhead. **Solitude**, an 18th-century mansion near the flamingos, was built by John Penn, grandson of William Penn. The Victorian zoo-entrance pavilions with wrought-iron gates were designed by **Frank Furness** and **George Hewitt**. The best place to eat is at the tables alongside the **Impala Fountain**, a terrific water sculpture of exuberant, leaping impalas by Henry Mitchell. McDonald's now runs the food concessions at the zoo. ♦ Admission. Daily. 3400 W Girard Ave (at N 34th St). 243. 1100. www.phillyzoo.org

65 THE RIVER DRIVES

Ⓟ The serpentine roadways that parallel the **Schuylkill** are among Philadelphia's most picturesque thoroughfares. **Kelly Drive**, formerly **E River Drive**, runs along the east side of the river from the **Philadelphia Museum of Art**, to **Lincoln Drive** above **East Falls**. **West River Drive** follows the other side of the river. For the unaccustomed motorist, the drives' sharp curves and distracting scenery can be hazardous. Contiguous pathways forming an 8-mile loop are a prime attraction for cyclists and walkers. By taking these pathways and the **Wissahickon Valley Trail**, it is possible to bike from the museum to the Montgomery County line, about 24 miles round-trip. ♦ Kelly Dr is closed to car traffic for special events. River Dr is closed to cars Sa and Su, Apr-Oct: from the Girard Ave Bridge to Eakins Oval, 7AM-noon; north of Sweetbriar, 7AM-5PM. From the Philadelphia Museum of Art to Falls Bridge. www.phila.gov/fairpark

66 BOATHOUSE ROW

Ⓟ At nighttime, you can see the outline of these delightful late-19th- and early-20th-century Victorian boathouses with their turrets and gables. Lined with pinpoint lights, they create a fairy-tale image visible from the other side of the river. The 10 structures were built by private groups and then occupied by rowing clubs. The clubs, known as the **Schuylkill Navy**, have kept the sport an important part of Philadelphia life. **No. 13**, the **Undine Barge Club**, was erected in 1883 by Philadelphia's famed **Frank Furness**. ♦ Kelly Dr (between Poplar and Brewery Hill Drs). www.boathouserow.org

On Boathouse Row:

LLOYD HALL

Ⓟ This public recreational facility houses a gymnasium and rest rooms, plus concessions for the rental of bikes, skateboards, and in-line skates. ♦ 1 Boathouse Row (at Kelly Dr). 685.0000 ♿

67 FAIRMOUNT WATERWORKS

"Philadelphia is most bountifully provided with fresh water, which is showered and jerked about, and turned on, and poured off everywhere. The Water Works, which are on a height near the city, are no less ornamental than useful, being tastefully laid out as a public garden, and kept in the best and neatest order." Charles Dickens extended this praise during a visit to Philadelphia in 1840, when the Waterworks already had completed 25 years of service. **Frederick Graff** designed the structures that housed steam engines, which in 1815 began pumping 4 million gallons of water daily to a reservoir at a site now occupied by the **Philadelphia Museum of Art**. From there, the water was fed by gravity to hydrants and residential taps. The cost of the steam engines prompted the city to dam the river and shift to hydropower in 1822, through a set of waterwheels housed in the **Old Mill House**. By 1835, construction and extensive landscaping of the **South Garden** and the **Esplanade** drew visitors from throughout the US and Europe. The architect's son, **Frederick Graff Jr.**, introduced the first turbines in 1862, which eventually replaced the waterwheels. Pollution on the **Schuylkill** closed the system in 1909. For 50 years, the site housed an aquarium, before falling into decline. A massive $12 million restoration of this National Historic Landmark began in 1998; catering facilities and events for groups are now an option. ♦ Tours daily, 1-3:30PM, mid-June-mid-Oct; group tours by appointment. Aquarium Rd (off Fairmount Ave). 685.4908. www.parkalacarte.com

---

Restaurants/Clubs: Red | Hotels: Purple | Shops: Orange | Outdoors/Parks: Green | Sights/Culture: Blue

UNIVERSITY CITY

Exactly as the name suggests, University City is an area dominated by college campuses and the hum of student life, a 2.2-square-mile district just west of downtown. Within the neighborhood extending from the **Schuylkill River** to **52nd Street** are the **University of Pennsylvania** (better known as **Penn**) and **Drexel University**, temporary homes to more than 30,000 students, who cram in lectures and laboratories by day and local ethnic restaurants by night.

In fact, University City has an international flair and thriving commercial district all its own. Many of the changes in the neighborhood, from a new school to renovated housing and new retail, have been underwritten by Penn, a smart investment which in turn has vastly improved the quality of life for the people who live and work here. A new movie theater and a large grocery store with garage parking, along with the WXPN World Café Live! performance space and studios, are further testimony to this neighborhood's dynamic evolution.

For visitors, the Penn campus holds the most interest. Founded as a small academy for men in a single brick building in 1749 by Benjamin Franklin and a group of fellow

civic leaders, the coed campus now sprawls over 250 acres and contains 100 academic departments. Some of Philadelphia's leading architects had a hand in shaping the university, with its juxtaposition of ivy-covered 19th-century buildings and impressive modern structures. Noteworthy architectural highlights include the **Anne and Jerome Fisher Fine Arts Library**, built in 1891 by **Frank Furness**; the **University of Pennsylvania Museum of Archaeology and Anthropology**, designed by **Wilson Eyre** with **Frank Miles Day** and **Cope and Stewardson** and built in 1893 (the museum's vast galleries filled with archeological finds from around the world are a must-see); and modern master **Louis I. Kahn**'s seminal **Alfred Newton Richards Medical Research Building**, completed in 1961. Other cultural treasures on campus are the cutting-edge **Institute of Contemporary Art (ICA)** and the **Annenberg Center**, a performing arts complex that hosts drama, music, and dance performances throughout the year.

Stop for lunch at one of the ethnic restaurants concentrated west of **38th Street** and save a late afternoon for studying the Victorian tombstones at the **Woodlands**, an 18th-century estate that was converted into a park and cemetery in the 1840s. And be sure to peek into the wonderfully restored neoclassical **30th Street Station**, the second-busiest train station in the country.

These days it's easy to reach the area west of the Schuylkill River by car, train, subway, or foot. But in the early 1800s, the only way across the water was over the **Permanent Bridge**, a simple wood structure built in 1805 and destroyed 70 years later. The bridge received heavy use from the beginning—in a single night in 1806, some 5,000 people were said to have crossed it to fight a fire on the western side. Today, bridges at **Spring Garden Street**, **John F. Kennedy Boulevard**, **Market Street**, **Walnut Street**, **South Street**, and **Gray's Ferry Avenue** span the waterway—and few people who use them even notice they are crossing a major river.

1 LEMON GRASS

★★$$ This Thai eatery has a steady following. And no wonder. Start out with the traditional *mieng cum*—toasted coconut chips, lime, ginger, and peanuts served on lettuce with a plum sauce. Then move on to a Thai salad of grilled beef, dried red peppers, onions, lime juice, and basil, or Young Girl on Fire, a roasted Cornish game hen stuffed with pineapple and raisins and flamed with Thai whiskey. The large vegetarian menu includes Musaman Curry (bean curd with mixed veggies in a red curry peanut sauce with coconut milk, onions, and potatoes). Mangos with sticky rice and sesame seeds make a fine ending. ◆ Thai ◆ M-F, lunch and dinner; Sa, Su, dinner. Reservations recommended. 3630 Lancaster Ave (between N 36th and N 37th Sts). 222.8042. www.phillylemongrass.com

2 ZOCALO

★★★$$ Pinpoint lights frame the large first-floor windows, and Mexican art decorates the walls in this handsome restaurant that creates delicious contemporary Mexican cuisine. Try the grilled chicken salad with tomato vinaigrette, seared shrimp tacos with red bell peppers and poblano pepper, or any of many vegetarian dishes. In warm weather, there's dining on the terrace as well. ◆ Mexican ◆ M-F, lunch and dinner; Sa, Su, dinner. Reservations recommended. 3600 Lancaster Ave (at N 36th St). 895.0139. www.ucnet.com/Zocalo

3 30TH STREET STATION

As you cross the Market Street Bridge or John F. Kennedy Boulevard leaving Center City, look for the majestic Corinthian columns of this monumental train station. You might expect such a palatial building to have a cold, impersonal interior, but its main concourse is actually one of the warmest, most romantic public spaces in the city. Though it is less of a tourist attraction than Union Station in Washington, DC, the station merits a visit even if you don't have to catch a train. Few travelers who pass through here forget its beauty.

Restaurants/Clubs: Red | Hotels: Purple | Shops: Orange | Outdoors/Parks: Green | Sights/Culture: Blue

This was the country's first major station designed for electric trains, and smokeless engines made it possible for it to be built right over the tracks. The first section opened in 1933, and the rest was built gradually over the next 17 years. The neoclassical design is the work of the Chicago architectural firm of **Graham, Anderson, Probst, and White** (also responsible for Philadelphia's **Suburban Station**). Over the years a coat of grime obscured the stone columns, gilt ceilings, and classical sculptures, but in 1991 a $100 million restoration uncovered the structure's original beauty.

Though a hub of **Amtrak**'s northeast corridor and of regional commuter rail lines, the station rarely feels crowded. The main concourse is so cavernous that pigeons fly about beneath the 10-story coffered ceiling. (Note the ceiling's orange and red detailing.) Roman travertine stone walls and low-lit bronze and glass fixtures give the concourse—featured in the movies *Witness* and *Blow Out*—a lovely aura. The **Pennsylvania Railroad War Memorial**, a bronze winged angel holding the limp body of a soldier, commands the east end of the room. American artist Walter Hancock created the 39-foot monument, installed in 1950 as a tribute to the 1,300 railroad employees killed in World War II. Viennese artist Karl Bitter's work *Progress of Transportation*, a bas-relief completed in 1895 and moved here from the city's old **Broad Street Station** in the 1930s, adds drama to a waiting area located beside the Amtrak ticket counters. The piece is an ode to several different modes of transportation: oxen and wagon, steam locomotive, steamboat, and airplane.

If you're in the neighborhood at lunchtime, investigate the offerings at any of the refurbished storefront take-out shops and restaurants on the south side of the main concourse—there are several to choose from. There's also a candy store, bookstore, bakery, and flower stall. ♦ N 30th St (between Market and Arch Sts). ♿ www.30thstreetstation.com

Within 30th Street Station:

CUCINA ITALIANO

$ Tasty Italian dishes, including shrimp with pasta, scallions, and sun-dried tomatoes in anchovy sauce, are available to eat in the station or take home. ♦ Italian deli ♦ Daily, breakfast, lunch, and early dinner. No phone.

ALL AMERICAN BUFFET

$ This stand proffers gourmet burgers, rotisserie chicken, assorted vegetable dishes, meat loaf, beef stew, Buffalo wings, and chicken teriyaki, as well as a number of Chinese dishes. ♦ American ♦ Daily, lunch and dinner. 386.3449

BUCKS COUNTY COFFEE CO.

In addition to coffee in all its popular forms (espresso, cappuccino, and *latte*), they'll provide you with a muffin, cookies, popcorn, and an assortment of nuts for your train ride. ♦ Daily. 382.2550

4 INTERNATIONAL HOUSE

$ This landmark high-rise, made of brownish gray concrete and designed by the architectural firm of **Bower and Fradley** in 1970, is a residence for international students, a cultural center, and a hotel for visiting academics. If you have an academic affiliation—perhaps you're attending a conference or visiting a university—you can stay in one of the 379 dormitory-like rooms, most of which have single beds, a desk, a chair, and a dresser, at bargain-basement prices (the bathrooms are communal). More than 400 students from 50 or so countries live here, some staying for several years and others for just a few weeks. Founded in 1918, this nonprofit corporation is affiliated with 12 similar organizations around the world. ♦ 3701 Chestnut St (at S 37th St). 387.5125 ♿

Within the International House:

CAFÉ BON APPÉTIT

★$ Soups, salads, and sandwiches, plus chicken, turkey, beef, and pasta entrées, are the satisfying staples at this warm and friendly dining room. ♦ American ♦ M-F, lunch and dinner. 222.5520

5 SANSOM COMMONS

This lively corridor of shops and restaurants includes a food court, the outstanding **Penn** bookstore, a fitness center, record store, and more. ♦ Sansom St (between 34th and 38th Sts)

6 SHERATON UNIVERSITY CITY

$$$ Located across the street from the **Penn** campus, this hotel has 374 newly renovated sunny rooms, as well as a restaurant, a fitness room, an outdoor pool, and reasonably priced overnight parking. ♦ S 36th and Chestnut Sts. 387.8000, 800/325.3535; fax 387.7920. www.businessservices.upenn.edu/public/sheraton.html

Within the Sheraton University City:

SHULA'S STEAK 2

★★$$ Ex–Miami Dolphins football coach Don Shula tackles the lunch and dinner crowd with this casual, comfortable steak place, filled with more than 500 pieces of sports memorabilia. Serious steak eaters will enjoy the 347, a 14-ounce rib eye named in honor of Shula's total career wins as a professional coach. Salads, sandwiches, all-beef burgers, and pasta dishes round out the menu. ♦ American ♦ Daily, lunch and dinner. 386.5556

7 DREXEL UNIVERSITY

In 1891, financier Anthony J. Drexel founded the **Drexel Institute** as a technical school for working-class young people. The school, which changed its name in 1970, is now the city's third-largest university, with 11,000 students in six colleges. The university excels in engineering, business, and computer studies, and it has one of the oldest cooperative education programs in the country (most undergraduates must alternate their studies with full-time work). It was also the first university to require all students to have a personal computer. The **Main Building**, completed in 1890 following designs by the **Wilson Brothers**, has one of the city's finest interior spaces, a skylit atrium of red tile, pink marble, white enameled brick, and wrought-iron balustrades. ♦ S 32nd and Chestnut Sts. 895.2000. &. www.drexel.edu

8 NEW DELHI

★★$ Philadelphia's oldest Indian restaurant is set in a quiet, low-lit dining room accented with soft multicolored lights that glow warmly from behind ceiling-height valances of graceful arches. Try chicken tandoori, lamb *tikka* (broiled cubes of lamb flavored with a touch of garlic), shrimp curry, various vegetable dishes, and an assortment of tandoori breads, baked to order in the restaurant's tandoor (Indian clay oven); or try a little of everything, at fantastically low prices, from the buffet table. ♦ Indian ♦ Daily, lunch and dinner. Students with ID receive a 20% discount. 4004 Chestnut St (between S 40th and S 41st Sts). 386.1941. wwwindoamerica link.com/RestaurantUS/RESTPA/Philadelphia REST.htm

8 TANDOOR INDIA

★$ Another of several Indian restaurants in the neighborhood, this place is distinguished by its pleasant interior. Hanging plants, skylights, traditional Indian art, and cases filled with currency from around the world serve as décor. *Nan* (unleavened bread) from the large tandoor comes with each meal. A buffet is usually available, with selections that vary daily, plus these staples: red-skinned tandoori chicken marinated in homemade yogurt and freshly ground herbs, *saag paneer* (minced spinach cooked with fried cheese in spices and a light cream sauce), and *gulab jamun* (soft milk balls dipped in honey syrup). ♦ Indian ♦ Daily, lunch and dinner. 106 S 40th St (between Sansom and Chestnut Sts). 222.7122

9 NAN

★★$$ This dazzling Thai–French restaurant features the handiwork of chef Kamol Phutlek, highbrow dishes like sweetbreads sautéed and served in puff pastry on a bed of creamed leeks with port-wine sauce, and New Zealand rack of lamb, roasted with a Dijon mustard crust and a half Peking duck breast. Flo Mayes, a retired homemaker who now serves as hostess and pastry chef at Nan, prepares the most delicious seasonal desserts; you'll be lucky to taste her strawberry-rhubarb tart, but the warm chocolate cake is always on the menu. ♦ Thai–French ♦ 4000 Chestnut St. 382.0818. nanrestaurant.tripod.com

10 THE RESTAURANT SCHOOL AT WALNUT HILL COLLEGE

★★$$ The kitchens and dining rooms at the restaurants on this pretty campus are staffed by students of the school, who also create the menus; their willingness to please and the bargain prices more than make up for any rough edges. Graduates of this culinary school have gone on to work at such notable local restaurants as **Le Bec-Fin**, the **Striped Bass, Sonoma**, and the **Fountain**. Major changes here have added considerable charm to the setting: A 3,000-square-foot atrium, soaring 45 feet, has been transformed into a European courtyard with seating for 50, complete with a cobblestone street, fountains, trees, an open-to-the-public gourmet shop, and café tables. Street vendor carts offer crepes and fresh flowers to diners. Just off the courtyard are two themed restaurants, the 28-seat **Italian Trattoria** and a 20-seat American restaurant, **The American Heartland**; each offers a three-course prix-fixe dinner for $15-23. There is also the **French Pastry Shop and Café**, off the courtyard. The first floor of the Italianate 1854 **Allison Mansion** has become **The Great Chefs of Philadelphia**, a 34-seat dining room that offers a three-course prix-fixe dinner for $55, based on a menu prepared by 10 of Philadelphia's most distinguished cuisiniers. At the 30-seat rooftop **Courtyard Restaurant**, looking out on the courtyard, you can mix and match your own composition from both the American and Italian menus, from earthy soups inspired by Italy's Campagna region to chicken potpie and smoked brisket. ♦ Eclectic ♦ Tu-Sa, dinner. Reservations recommended. 4207 Walnut St (between S 42nd and S 43rd Sts). 222.4200. &. www.therestaurantschool.com

11 THE INN AT PENN

$$ This six-story modern hotel on **Penn**'s campus is geared toward visitors to the

UNIVERSITY OF PENNSYLVANIA

university. Done out in Arts and Crafts style, the 238 rooms include amenities like dual-line phones and Internet access. There is a comfy lobby bar and a restaurant, **Penne** (832.6222), where executive chef Roberta Adamo creates legendary pasta dishes—her ravioli is divine, her gnocchi nirvana. Ask to sit at her pasta bar, where you can watch her work her magic up close and personal. The spacious restaurant serves top-rate Italian fare with an emphasis on freshness and seasonal produce. ♦ Sansom Common, 3600 Sansom St. 222.0200; fax 222.4600. www.theinnatpenn.com

11 POD

★★$$ The Jetsons collide with Japanese pop culture at this *trés*-chic eatery, with its white walls, shiny red foam couches, light-up bar stools, and lizard lounge music. Best of all are the three elevated egg-shaped rooms that let diners change the mood lighting with the push of a button. Then there's the conveyor-belt sushi bar and glowing cocktails. The food's good, but the show's even better. ♦ 3636 Sansom St (between S 34th and S 36th Sts). 387.1803. www.podphiladelphia.com

12 BLACK CAT

The offbeat collection of housewares and knickknacks at this "alternative gift store" adjoining the restaurant includes everything from copper cookie cutters and paper lamp shades to chairs made of twisted twigs and iron lamp stands, plus jewelry and men's ties. ♦ Daily. 3426 Sansom St (between S 34th and S 36th Sts). 386.6664. www.whitedog.com/blackcat.html

13 WHITE DOG CAFÉ

★★$$ Madame Helena Blavatsky, a Russian noblewoman who founded the Theosophical Society and lived in this row house more than 100 years ago, is the inspiration behind the enormously popular restaurant that now occupies the site. A perennial favorite with campus graduate students and **Penn** faculty, the White Dog combines owner Judy Wick's socially enlightened politics with her passion for regional cuisine and locally grown produce, for an eclectic dining experience that includes signature items like oven-roasted local organic free-range chicken with balsamic–rosemary glaze, juicy duck steaks barbecued with New Mexico red chili and

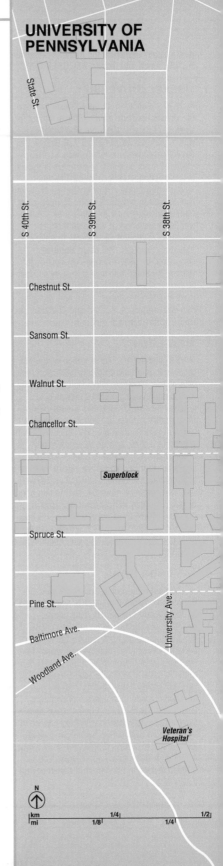

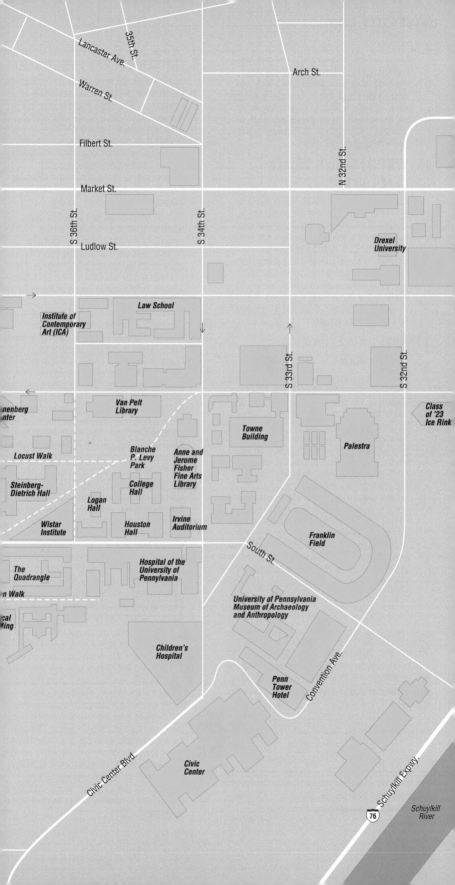

honey sun-dried cherry glaze, and pan-fried Pocono Springs rainbow trout in Brazil-nut crust with dark rum sauce. Take a walk next store to the **Black Cat** for cool cards and gift ideas. Eclectic ◆ M-F, lunch and dinner; Sa, Su, brunch and dinner. Reservations recommended. 3420 Sansom St (between S 34th and S 36th Sts). 386.9224

14 WXPN RADIO & WORLD CAFÉ LIVE!

Opened in the fall of 2004, WXPN Radio & World Café Live! is a new live performance space and home to the popular grassroots radio station WXPN, with its nationally syndicated World Café music and interview program. The new space, a $15 million renovation of the existing Hajoca building, will house the radio station's offices, along with studio space and a small restaurant. ◆ 3035 Walnut St (between S 30th and S 31st Sts). 898.6677. www.xpn.org

15 ABYSSINIA ETHIOPIAN RESTAURANT

★★$ Have a glass of water ready and waiting before you dig into the food at this Ethiopian restaurant, where you're in for what may be one of the hottest meals of your life. Scoop up spicy stews with *injera*, the moist Ethiopian flat bread. Order the Shefensen Special for two, a sampling of every major item on the menu, and you'll have traveled along Ethiopia's culinary road map: You'll get *key wat* (beef chunks with garlic, pepper, and onion), *timt'mo* (a mixture of lentils and herbs that will make your nose burn), *doro wat* (chicken braised with pepper, onions, tomato, and garlic, served under a hard-boiled egg), and *hamli* (sautéed onion with broccoli leaves and collard greens). The restaurant occupies two row houses. ◆ Ethiopian ◆ Daily, lunch and dinner. No credit cards accepted. 229 S 45th St (at Locust St). 387.2424

When William Penn left the city for the last time in 1701, there were about 2,000 people living in modest brick homes near the Delaware River. Most were Quakers of English, Dutch, Welsh, and German ancestry.

Keep thy shop and thy shop will keep thee.
—Benjamin Franklin,
Poor Richard's Almanac

The University of Pennsylvania's Wharton School of Commerce and Finance, established in 1881, was the nation's first collegiate business school.

16 UNIVERSITY OF PENNSYLVANIA

"It has long been regretted as a misfortune to the youth of this province that we have no academy in which they might receive the accomplishment of a regular education," Benjamin Franklin lamented in 1749. A few months later, he and his friends—including 10 future signers of the Declaration of Independence, 7 of the Constitution, and 21 members-to-be of the Continental Congress—formed the **Academy** in the brick **Charity School Building** on Fourth Street.

Franklin became the first president of the board of trustees and created a core curriculum of mathematics, geography, history, logic, and science. The Academy established the country's first medical school in 1765 and became the University of Pennsylvania—known today simply as **Penn**—in 1792. The university grew rapidly, opening the country's first law school, first teaching hospital, and first business school (the **Wharton School of Finance and Commerce**, which moved to larger quarters at Ninth and Chestnut Streets in 1829). Early pioneers of science associated with the university included astronomer David Rittenhouse, naturalist Joseph Leidy, and Alexander Dallas Bache, a professor of chemistry who directed the Coast and Geodetic Survey. Architect **Paul Philippe Cret**, who designed Philadelphia's **Rittenhouse Square** and the **Rodin Museum**, brought prestige to the university's school of architecture.

In 1872, the trustees decided to relocate the university to an open space west of the **Schuylkill River**. Until 1940, it was mainly a regional school, with students and faculty commuting from the Philadelphia area. At the end of World War II, the G.I. Bill began offering free college education to veterans, and the enrollment of Penn expanded dramatically. Today the university includes more than 100 academic departments and 13 graduate and professional schools, occupies 260 acres, and has over 22,000 students.

During the 1960s, the campus was altered and enlarged as part of the University City redevelopment. Many old structures between the river and 44th Street were torn down and replaced with new buildings. Streets bisecting Penn's campus were closed, and surface trolley cars were replaced by a subway line. The changes gave the school a small college green and a more cohesive setting. Though it's not a grassy, idyllic campus, Penn has a series of garden courtyards that link a number of beautiful buildings representing an extraordinary range of architectural styles. ◆ Bounded roughly by S 33rd and S 40th Sts and by Civic Center Blvd and Chestnut St. ♿ www.upenn.edu

On the University of Pennsylvania campus:

FRANKLIN FIELD

Noted architect **Frank Miles Day** gave this stadium a distinctly Philadelphian brick exterior and an innovative **U** shape, providing good seats on all three sides. The athletic facility opened in 1895 with tennis courts, running tracks, and playing fields; it was enlarged for collegiate football in 1922, in time for the **Penn–Navy** game attended by President Harding. The **Philadelphia Eagles**, who played their home games here until the **Vet** opened in 1971, won their last NFL championship here in 1960, defeating Vince Lombardi's Green Bay Packers 17-13. It's still the home of Penn football and the **Penn Relays** track meet held every April. The quarter-mile track opens to the public when athletic practice permits; call for the schedule. ♦ Box office: M-F. 233 S 33rd St (at South St). 898.6151

UNIVERSITY OF PENNSYLVANIA MUSEUM OF ARCHAEOLOGY AND ANTHROPOLOGY

When this museum opened in 1889, archeology and anthropology were in their infancy. Though both fields have since become widely familiar through books and television documentaries, the museum's vast galleries, filled with rare artifacts from around the world, still capture that original excitement. Though its mummies are the biggest crowd-pleasers, this world-class museum has 30-plus galleries, full of archeological finds from ancient Egypt, Mesopotamia, Mesoamerica, Asia, Greece, and Rome, as well as from traditional cultures in Africa, Polynesia, and North America. Two 17th-century cloisonné lions flank the entrance to the **Chinese Rotunda**, which also houses one of the largest crystal balls in existence. (Experts believe the 55-pound ball belonged to the last Empress Dowager of China.) In the **Lower Egyptian Gallery**, you can see a 12-ton granite Sphinx of Rameses II, circa 1293–1185 BC, as well as grand-scale architectural remnants from the Palace of Merneptah, son and successor to Rameses II. Elsewhere are rare Benin bronzes from Nigeria, native garments of the Inuit (Eskimo) people, and histories in stone of the ancient Maya of Guatemala. Visitors enter via the newly renovated **Stoner Courtyard** garden, 3260 South Street, featuring a central fountain, cobblestone walkway, park benches, and plantings from three continents. The two capitals in the courtyard came from Roman ruins in Amman, Jordan, and were donated by the Kingdom of Jordan. Alexander Stirling Calder, Philadelphia's premier early-20th-century sculptor, made four inward-looking statues atop the gated entrance. The statues represent four continental regions—Asia, Africa, Europe, and the Americas—where museum researchers work.

Inside, the rotunda—measuring 90 feet high and 90 feet in diameter—is composed of concentric circles of overlapping terra-cotta tiles without any supporting beams. **Mitchell/Giurgola** designed the modern glass-and-reinforced-concrete addition to the museum, which was completed in 1971. **Atkin Olshin Lawson-Bell Architects** designed the newest **Mainwaring Wing** for collection storage and study, completed in 2002. That new wing serves to enclose the refurbished Stoner Courtyard main entrance.

About one million objects are housed here, and many were collected through archeological and ethnographic expeditions sponsored by the museum and the university. Renowned archeologists such as Leonard Woolley, who excavated the 4,500-year-old Royal Tombs of Ur in what is now Iraq, and William Farabee, who between 1913 and 1916 investigated little-known South American tribes, were affiliated with the university. More than 30,000 clay tablets inscribed with cuneiform writing are housed here, almost all recovered by museum expeditions at the turn of the 20th century; a selection of these tablets is on display on

The Philadelphia Committee of Observation, Inspection, and Correspondence convened a Congress of the Thirteen Colonies in September 1774 to formulate statements on colonial rights and grievances.

In 114 years of trying, the Philadelphia Phillies have just one World Series Championship. It came in 1980 against American League Champions the Kansas City Royals, four games to two. The Phillies also played, but lost, in the World Series of 1915, 1950, 1983, and 1993.

Restaurants/Clubs: Red | Hotels: Purple | Shops: Orange | Outdoors/Parks: Green | Sights/Culture: Blue

BENJAMIN RUSH: PHILADELPHIA'S OTHER FAMOUS BENJAMIN

Benjamin Franklin is certainly Philadelphia's all-time best-known citizen. But there was another man named Benjamin around at the same time who, though not as famous, was nevertheless one of the most influential people in the American colonies' push for independence from Great Britain. That man was **Benjamin Rush** (1745–1813), the most famous physician in colonial America and a largely behind-the-scenes founding father.

Thomas Jefferson said no man was "more benevolent, more learned, of finer genius, or more honest" than Benjamin Rush. However, Rush also had his detractors, including writer William Cobbett, who, writing under the name Peter Porcupine, called him a quack who had slaughtered thousands related to his belief that bloodletting and purging with calomel (mercurous chloride) could cure a variety of maladies. An angry Rush sued Cobbett for libel and won.

Rush's greatest gift was his unassuming yet forceful personality, an attribute which he used to build support for American independence among fellow patriots, such as George Washington and Thomas Paine. Rush convinced Paine to write and publish his powerful essay *Common Sense*, which reasoned for immediate independence from England. In his autobiography, Rush praised Paine's "wonderful talent of writing to the tempers and feelings of the public." In fact, Rush became so involved in the project that it was he who suggested the title (over Paine's suggested title of *Plain Truth*). After reading it, no less a luminary than George Washington remarked, "I find *Common Sense* is working a powerful change in the minds of men."

Rush's medical career began in 1760 when he graduated from the **College of Princeton** at the age of 15. He then served a 5-year apprenticeship in Philadelphia with Dr. John Redman. Following that, he sailed for Edinburgh, Scotland, home of the most prestigious medical school in Europe. There he earned his MD degree, and returned to Philadelphia and the **College of Philadelphia**, now the **University of Pennsylvania**.

In 40 years there, Rush taught some 3,000 students, helped distinguish Philadelphia as the medical capital of the United States, and explored virtually every avenue of medical science. His book, *Medical Inquiries and Observations Upon the Diseases of the Mind*, earned him the title Father of American Psychiatry. He also studied veterinary medicine and pediatrics.

In 1776 he joined the Philadelphia militia as a volunteer physician, and in April 1777 became physician-general of the Middle Department of the Continental Army, despite openly criticizing George Washington. That criticism resulted in the abrupt end of his military service later that year, but not before he had written the Pennsylvania Packet of 22 April 1777 in which he outlined his *Directions for Preserving the Health of Soldiers*. It was considered such a valuable document that it was reprinted numerous times during the Civil War and as recently as 1908. Rush served as treasurer of the **US Mint** from 1797 to 1813, helped found the first American antislavery society and **Dickinson College**, and was a member of the Continental Congress and a signer of the Declaration of Independence.

the third floor. A permanent exhibition, *Canaan and Ancient Israel*, features more than 500 rare artifacts dating from circa 3000 to 500 BCE, principally excavated by museum archeologists in Israel, Jordan, and Lebanon. ♦ Admission. Tu-Sa, Memorial Day–Labor Day; Tu-Su, after Labor Day–after Memorial Day. 3260 South St (at S 33rd St). 898.4000. www.upenn.edu/museum

Within the University of Pennsylvania Museum of Archaeology and Anthropology:

MUSEUM CAFE
★$ Dine in a room with floor-to-ceiling windows looking onto both the new and old façades of the museum. This cafeteria serves sandwiches, soups, and salads, as well as wine and beer. ♦ American ♦ Tu-Sa, lunch and snacks, Labor Day–Memorial Day; Tu-Su, lunch and snacks, Memorial Day–Labor Day. 898.4890

MUSEUM SHOP
Arts, crafts, books, CDs and cassettes, clothing, a wide selection of jewelry from around the world, and fine museum reproductions are found here. The shop closes 15 minutes before the museum. ♦ 898.4040

PYRAMID SHOP
Stop here to check out children's books, games, crafts, puzzles, dolls, toys, and jewelry from around the world. ♦ 898.4022

PENN TOWER HOTEL
$$ This hotel, owned by the **University of Pennsylvania**, is popular with those visiting the campus (only a block away) or patients at one of the hospitals across the street. The lobby has a 1970s look, with a round tiled fountain and potted palms, but it's bright and comfortable. Choose from 175 spacious and

fully equipped rooms or 10 suites. Amenities include a restaurant and day-care service provided by the nearby **Penn Children's Center**. *One caveat:* The location is somewhat undesirable, given the traffic on 34th Street. ♦ 300 S 33rd St (at S 34th St). 387.8333, 800/356.7366; fax 573.2040. ᘒ. www. upenn.edu/penntower

IRVINE AUDITORIUM

Horace Trumbauer (architect of the **Free Library** and several local hospitals and hotels) designed this 1929 auditorium to resemble a medieval French cathedral. Its exterior is distinguished by a steeply sloping roof, spires, turrets, and gargoyles; its interior adorned with colorful Gothic designs. The auditorium plays host to concerts, convocations, and awards ceremonies and houses one of the largest pipe organs in the world. ♦ 3401 Spruce St (at S 34th St). ᘒ. www.upenn.edu/curtisorgan/irvine.html

TOWNE BUILDING

Headquarters of the university's **School of Engineering and Applied Science**, this building displays part of the original ENIAC (Electronic Numerator Integrator and Computer)—the world's first electronic computer. The computer was developed at **Penn** and unveiled in 1946. ♦ Call for hours. 220 S 33rd St (between Spruce and Walnut Sts). 898.7244; tours, 898.7246

ANNE AND JEROME FISHER FINE ARTS LIBRARY

Usually referred to simply as the **Furness Building**, this is one of the great masterpieces of **Frank Furness**, the architect who adorned Philadelphia with his idiosyncratic Victorian designs. Housing the library of the **Graduate School of Fine Arts**, the building is an energetic, unforgettable structure, "both serene and hysterical," as described by Paul Goldberger, architecture critic for the *New York Times*. The building was almost torn down in the 1950s, when it was out of fashion, but is now here to stay, having undergone a $16.5 million restoration under the direction of the Philadelphia firm of **Venturi, Scott Brown and Associates**. Completed in 1891 as the university's main library, the building has a coarsely textured, deep red façade of brick, fieldstone, and terra-cotta. The north side looks ecclesiastical, with a semicircular churchlike apse; the south side, where you'll find the library stacks, looks somewhat like a train shed (not surprising, given the architect's many railroad commissions). The building's most dramatic space is the four-story reading room, which resembles an exterior courtyard or a railroad waiting room with skylights, gargoyles, and exposed iron beams. The reading room's brick-and-limestone walls have two-story terra-cotta arches above squat columns that seem about to spring upward. On the west wall is a massive stone fireplace with a tile roof, arched dormer, and

Anne and Jerome Fisher Fine Arts Library (Furness Building)

Curry Favors

Although not quite as densely populated as New York's Indian Row, West Philly does have a grouping of East Indian restaurants, modest purveyors of curry and tandoori, located on 40th and 38th Streets, close to Chestnut. Follow the exotic smells of cardamom and coriander to the **New Delhi Indian Restaurant** (4004 Chestnut Street; 386.1941), **Panghad Indian Restaurant** (4015 Chestnut Street; 662.1777), **Sitar India Restaurant** (60 S 38th Street; 662.0818), and **Tandoor India Restaurant** (106 S 40th Street; 222.7122), family-run establishments frequented by a casually dressed student crowd drawn to Indian food fo its heady blend of spice, vegetarian options, and rock-bottom prices.

steel-faced clock. As you tour the library, look for the inscriptions on the leaded-glass windows: "Talkers are no great doers," "Men should be what they seem," and "Self-love is not so vile a sin as self-neglecting." ♦ Daily. 220 S 34th St (between Spruce and Walnut Sts). 898.8325 ♿

Within the Anne and Jerome Fisher Fine Arts Library:

Arthur Ross Gallery

This intimate gallery specializes in one-of-a-kind exhibits on art history and ethnography. Women in ancient Egypt, Guatemalan textiles, and the restoration of the Parthenon, with renderings of work by Greek architect Manolis Korres, have been featured. Retrospectives of works by faculty, including Maurice Lowe's semi-abstract figures, also take place. ♦ Free. Tu-Su. 898.4401. ♿. www.upenn.edu/ARG

College Hall

An example of what is commonly referred to as Collegiate Gothic architecture, this is quintessential Ivy League. Some say the building may have been the inspiration for the house portrayed in Charles Addams's famous *Addams Family* cartoons. The first building on **Penn**'s West Philadelphia campus, it housed lecture halls when it opened in 1872. Now the university's administrative offices are located here. The exterior, topped by a French mansard roof, is made of serpentine rock quarried in Chester County. The building originally had towers at each end. Next door is **Logan Hall**, the second building on campus (completed in 1874) and initially the home of the university's medical department. Philadelphia architect **Thomas W. Richards** designed both buildings. ♦ Blanche P. Levy Park (off Walnut St, between S 34th St and S 36th St Walk)

Benjamin Franklin Statue

One of three statues of the university's founder on the **Penn** campus, this 1899 bronze of a wizened Franklin seated on a granite base is the work of John J. Boyle, a prominent turn-of-the-19th-century Philadelphia sculptor. (The other Ben Franklin statues are on S 33rd Street near Spruce Street and on a bench off the western end of Locust Walk.) ♦ Blanche P. Levy Park (off Walnut St, between S 34th St and S 36th St Walk)

Split Button Sculpture

Inspired by the thought that John J. Boyle's paunchy Benjamin Franklin across Levy Park might pop a button, sculptor Claes Oldenburg and artist Coosje van Bruggen created this 4-foot-high painted aluminum button in 1981. ♦ Blanche P. Levy Park (off Walnut St, between S 34th St and S 36th St Walk)

Locust Walk

Streetcars used to run right through campus on Woodland Avenue, which intersected the former Locust Street on what is now Levy Park. Both this portion of Locust Street and Woodland Avenue were closed to traffic by 1960 and now serve as the main pedestrian way through the campus. ♦ From Blanche P. Levy Park to S 40th St

The Quadrangle

They just don't make dorms like this anymore. Archways, gargoyles, bay windows, sculptures, and gables surprise and delight throughout this rambling complex, reminiscent of the college buildings at Cambridge and Oxford. **Cope and Stewardson**, the firm that planned similar Jacobean Revival buildings at Princeton University and other American colleges, is responsible for the redbrick-and-white-limestone design. One of the first dormitory complexes on such a grand scale in the country, the four-story quad is actually a collection of 39 contiguous buildings enclosing a large quadrangle and smaller courtyards. Construction began in 1895, and the last building was completed in the 1950s. ♦ 3700 Spruce St (between S 36th St Walk and University Ave) ♿

Alfred Newton Richards Medical Research Building

When constructed in 1961, this laboratory building became a seminal structure of the late 20th century, establishing **Louis I. Kahn** as one of the century's most influential architects. Kahn was a **Penn** professor, a genius known for breathing new life into modern architecture. In contrast to the glass and steel of prevailing skyscrapers, this building and the adjoining **Goddard Laboratories** (built a short time later) are geometric designs constructed of heavy masonry. The engineering was extremely novel: the frames of both buildings are of rigid reinforced concrete with post-tensioned beams held in place by steel cables, a design that eliminates the need for interior structural columns. Elevators, stairs, and heating ducts—what Kahn referred to as the "servant areas"—are in separate brick towers alongside the labs, lit naturally through large geometric windows. (Today's scientists within have covered up many of these windows to ensure their privacy or protect their experiments from exposure and heat.) The brick-and-concrete façades and adjoining stair towers ingeniously reflect the brick-and-stone chimneys and turrets of the 19th-century dormitory buildings across the walkway. Behind the laboratories is a small botanical garden with a pond and pathways. ♦ 3700 Hamilton Walk (off University Ave)

ANNENBERG CENTER

Walter Annenberg, newspaper publisher, philanthropist, and former ambassador to Great Britain, donated the money for construction of this brick performing arts center on the **Penn** campus. Drama, music, and dance performances are held in the center's three theaters: the 970-seat proscenium **Zellerbach Theatre**, the intimate 200-seat **Harold Prince Theatre**, and the 120-seat **Studio Theatre**. The **Philadelphia Festival Theater for New Plays** and **Philadelphia Dance Company** perform here. Events throughout the year include an annual series of avant-garde music and a dance series that features nationally known groups, such as the Mark Morris Dance Group and the Paul Taylor Dance Company. The **Annenberg Center Theatre Series** presents a variety of classical and new plays. (David Mamet's *Oleanna*, Spaulding Gray's *Gray's Anatomy*, and a production of Shakespeare's *Macbeth* have been among them.) Each May, the **Philadelphia International Theater Festival for Children**, a 5-day event with puppeteers, storytellers, singers, and jugglers from around the world, takes center stage. ♦ Box office: M-F. 3680 Walnut St (at S 37th St Walk). 898.6791. www.annenbergcenter.org

INSTITUTE OF CONTEMPORARY ART (ICA)

Founded in 1963, this institute is a major exhibitor of avant-garde art and an important force in keeping Philadelphia on the art-world map. It was the first museum in the US to show Andy Warhol's art (in 1965), and it premiered the works of performance artist Laurie Anderson and painter David Salle in 1986. The museum also organized the traveling exhibit of Robert Mapplethorpe's sexually explicit photographs, which caused a storm of protest in some parts of the country. Since 1991, the institute has been housed in this sleek geometric building designed by **Adele Santos**, a former architecture instructor at the **University of Pennsylvania**. Galleries on each floor, boasting ceilings as high as 32 feet, comprise the main exhibition spaces. ♦ Admission. W-Su. 118 S 36th St (between Walnut and Chestnut Sts). 898.7108. ♿. www.icaphila.org

SUPERBLOCK

The largest construction project undertaken by the university, this $41 million high-rise dorm complex provides accommodations for 3,500 undergraduates. The aloof, fortresslike buildings include a dining hall and parking garage. ♦ Bounded by Spruce and Walnut Sts and S 38th and S 40th Sts ♿

17 Rx

★★$$ This restaurant is good for what ails you. Located in a former neighborhood apothecary in University City, **Rx** (pronounced "Rex") is a collaborative effort between owner Greg Salisbury and chef Luis Melendez, formerly of Le Mas Perrier. A menu featuring new cuisine of the Americas includes specialties like a *mofongo* appetizer of fried green plantains filled with shrimp and chorizo sausage in spicy tomato sauce. Melendez's experience in the country French classics is put to good use as well—just taste the morel mushroom sauce that tops the Green Meadow Farm grass-fed rib eye with truffled potatoes. Desserts are stellar, including an organic Granny Smith apple cobbler made by the chef's mom. Rx doesn't take reservations, so to avoid a long wait, get there before the rush of locals and **Penn** professors eat up all the specials. 4443 Spruce St. 222.9590. www.caferx.com

18 GENJI

★★$$$ Fine sushi is prepared in this basement restaurant with a tatami (sit-on-the-floor) area and blond-wood tables, popular with both locals and the university crowd. Order your sushi à la carte—the best way to go—or choose from an assortment of Japanese appetizers and dinner entrées. Salmon broiled in teriyaki sauce, noodles with shrimp, vegetable tempura, and tofu with assorted vegetables are all prepared at your

---

Restaurants/Clubs: Red | Hotels: Purple | Shops: Orange | Outdoors/Parks: Green | Sights/Culture: Blue

table. ♦ Japanese ♦ M-F, lunch and dinner; Sa, Su, dinner. 4002 Spruce St (at S 40th St). 387.1583. Also at 1720 Sansom St (between S 17th and S 18th Sts). 564.1720. www.genjionline.com

19 THE CARROT CAKE MAN

Vernon Wilkins and his sister, Valarie Collier, make 100 different renditions of carrot cake in this corner bakery-café at the edge of the University City neighborhood. Variations from this innovative kitchen include the Very Berry Carrot Cake (with blackberries, strawberries, blueberries, and raspberries), chocolate-chip carrot cake, and walnut-pineapple carrot cake (one of the most popular). *Philadelphia* magazine has given its Best of Philly award to the tiny shop several times for its miniature loaf cakes, which can be iced to order while you wait. ♦ Daily. S 47th St and Cedar Ave. 729.3018

20 DICKENS AND LITTLE NELL

The world's only statue of Victorian novelist Charles Dickens (portrayed with Little Nell, one of his most famous characters) stands here in Clark Park. As the story goes, the statue was made for the 1895 World's Fair by local sculptor Frank Elwell, who was unaware that Dickens's last request to his family was that no statues ever be made of him. ♦ S 43rd St and Baltimore Ave

21 FIREHOUSE FARMERS' MARKET

Thanks to community action, an abandoned firehouse has gotten a new lease on life as the home of a neighborhood farmers' market. Almost a miniature **Reading Terminal Market**, it includes a bakery, fish market, produce stand, butcher shop, deli, flower shop, coffee store, and grill. ♦ Tu-Sa. S 50th St and Baltimore Ave. 724.7660. www.firehousefarmersmarket.com

22 GABLES

$ This meticulously restored redbrick Victorian mansion with a wraparound porch and a garden provides 10 antiques-filled rooms and

Gables

a full breakfast, all for a reasonable price. ♦ 4520 Chester Ave (at S 46th St). 662.1918. www.gablesbb.com

22 THE WOODLANDS

Originally the splendid estate of William Hamilton, grandson of lawyer Andrew Hamilton, who designed **Independence Hall**, today this site is both a park and a historically significant—and still operating—cemetery. Hamilton, a country gentleman who fully indulged his interests in architecture and botany, cultivated one of the most extensive gardens in colonial America. (Thomas Jefferson and George Washington were said to have visited the grounds.) His mansion, a National Historic Landmark currently undergoing restoration, reportedly served as an inspiration to Jefferson when he was building Monticello. Completed in 1790, the Federal-style house is noteworthy for its novel layout: The first floor (the only part of the building open to visitors) has rooms of five distinct geometric forms, including two large ovals. Secret passages honeycombed throughout the house allowed the servants to circulate and yet remain out of sight.

After Hamilton's death, the property was acquired by the Woodlands Cemetery Company, which offered the 78 acres of grounds for "removing the dead from the midst of the dense population of our cities, and placing them in operation with the beautiful works of nature." The cemetery boasts a fascinating collection of Victorian tombstones, many of them imposing obelisks. Among those buried here are artists Thomas Eakins and Rembrandt Peale, 1812 naval hero Commodore David Porter, noted Philadelphia Beaux Arts architect Paul Philippe Cret, Drexel University founder Anthony J. Drexel, and his father, local financier Francis M. Drexel. Today the cemetery is run by a nonprofit group. The **Woodlands Heritage National Recreation Trail**, operated by the National Park Service, wends its way through the cemetery grounds. ♦ Free. Cemetery: daily. House: M-F. 4000 Woodland Ave (between University Ave and S 42nd St). 386.2181. www.uchs.net/Woodlands/woodlandshome.html

John Batram House

24 JOHN BARTRAM HOUSE AND GARDENS

Carolus Linnaeus, the renowned Swedish botanist, once called John Bartram (1699–1777) "the greatest natural botanist in the world." Bartram is certainly recognized as the New World's first botanist, and this 44-acre site was one of the first botanical gardens in the country. He (along with his son William, author of *The Travels of William Bartram*) traveled throughout the American wilderness collecting plant samples, sending many of them to Europe, and is credited with introducing more than 200 plants to European gardeners, including the sugar maple. Some of his handiwork still flourishes here, including pawpaws, ginkgo, persimmons, and oaks. His 18th-century Pennsylvania stone house—a National Historic Landmark—has been faithfully restored, and a guided tour of both house and garden is offered. ♦ Garden open daily, 10AM-5PM. Tours offered and shop open Tu-Su, Mar-Dec. Off Lindbergh Blvd (between Grays Ave and S 56th St). 729.5281. ㄐ. www.ushistory.org/tour/tour_bartram.htm

km   1/2   1
mi   1/4   1/2
N

1 Morris
Arboretum

Germantown Pike

Ridge Pike

Barren
Hill Rd.

Hillcrest Ave.

Stenton Ave.

Paper Mill Rd.

Bethlehem Pike

2

Norwood Ave.

Hampton Rd.

Germantown Ave.

3
Andorra
Natural
Area

4

5 Crefeld Ave.

Manor Rd.

Northwestern Ave.

Bells Mill Rd.

Wissahickon Ave.

Oldline Rd.

Forbidden Dr.

CHESTNUT HILL
For nos. 21-50,
see pg. 150

Seminole Ave.

Pastorius
Park

Willow Grove Ave.

422

Spring La.

Manatawna Ave.

Hagys Mill Rd.

Henry Ave.

Wissahickon Creek

St. Martins La.

Hartwell La.

Huron St.

Mermaid La.

9
UPPER
ROXBOROUGH

Summit Ave.

Valley Green Rd.

Cherokee St.

6 Valley Green Rd.

McCallum St.

Port Royal Ave.

Shawmont Ave.

Wise's Mill Rd.

Wigard Ave.

Fairmount
Park

Attens La.

Wissahickon Ave.

Hollow Rd.

Ridge Ave.

Livezey St.

Sherwood St.

Silverwood St.

Domino La.

Umbria St.

Parker Ave.

ROXBOROUGH

Gorgas
Park

Fountain St.

Venice
Island

76

Leverington Ave.

Manayunk Ave.

Manayunk Green La.

Walnut La.

MANAYUNK
For nos. 51-67,
see pg. 155

Shurs La.

23

Conshohocken State

N. Woodbine Ave.

Manayunk Rd.

Rock Hill Rd.

Belmont Ave.

Main St.

Schuylkill River

Ridge Ave.

Lincoln Dr.

8

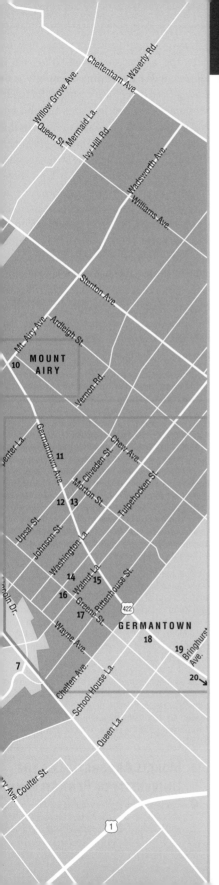

Philadelphia is home to 1,400 rugged acres of undeveloped land known as the **Wissahickon Valley**, which is characterized by winding roads, craggy cliffs, stone bridges, and waterfalls. It is thickly forested and steep, with **Wissahickon Creek** flowing between Precambrian rock from one of the earth's oldest rock formations. Many houses are made from Wissahickon schist, stone that bears a distinct glimmer. In 1700, mystic Johann Kelpius chose the valley, now part of **Fairmount Park**, as the place where he and his followers would await the end of the world. Edgar Allan Poe spent time here, memorializing the area in his poem *The Elk.*

Colonists first ventured into northwest Philadelphia in the 1700s, setting up paper mills, farms, and country retreats. Later, as the railroads connected the area with the original city, separate communities emerged. Today, such towns as **Chestnut Hill**, **Manayunk**, and **Germantown** retain their own personalities, each offering a wealth of interesting shops, restaurants, and historic sites.

The Battle of Germantown, a pivotal event in the Revolutionary War, was fought on a Germantown estate, and you can still see the pockmarks patriot cannonballs made in the walls of **Cliveden**, the mansion owned by Pennsylvania's Loyalist chief justice Benjamin Chew. George Washington set up temporary offices at what is now known as the **Deshler-Morris House** during the summer of 1792 to escape the yellow fever epidemic in Philadelphia. In the 1840s, middle-class families began building picturesque villas and Victorian mansions in the town. Two streets—**Tulpehocken Street** and **Walnut Lane**—are particularly vivid examples of this period. SEPTA trains *R8* and *R1* run from Center City to Germantown, stopping at Tulpehocken Street, **Queen Lane**, and **Chelten Avenue**.

In contrast, Chestnut Hill developed only after the railroad expanded farther out in the 1850s. It quickly became a fashionable address; today the entire community is on the National Historic Register. Its shady streets are graced by English cottages, Italianate villas, and Tudor mansions, as well as modern homes designed by **Louis I. Kahn** and **Robert Venturi**. In recent years, **Germantown Avenue**, the long cobblestone road that comprises Chestnut Hill's main retail district, has really taken off. Though old-timers disdain the arrival of chain stores like Banana Republic and The Gap, the street's revival has also attracted a high concentration of good restaurants and one-of-a-kind shops. SEPTA runs commuter trains to the station at the top of the hill on Germantown Avenue.

Manayunk (pronounced "Man-ee-*yunk*") had very different origins. Its position on the **Schuylkill River** and the construction of the Schuylkill canal system led to its emergence as a textile manufacturing town in the early 1800s. Blue-collar families have long resided in the row houses that seem to tumble down the community's steep hills. Although it eventually lost its industrial base, the town has found a new identity as an artsy enclave. Although upscale chain stores have made inroads, **Main Street**, popular for its mix of restaurants, galleries, and shops, is refreshingly devoid of slickness and hype. The small row houses that line the street are now home to shops selling everything from secondhand jeans and designer shoes to 1950s mementos and avant-garde furniture. SEPTA's *No. 61* bus provides the best access from Center City to Main Street.

WISSAHICKON VALLEY

Though it runs along the spine of densely populated neighborhoods—Germantown, **Roxborough**, **Mount Airy**, and Chestnut Hill—this valley is virtually cut off from urban life. Most of its 1,400 acres are part of Fairmount Park and comprise one of its most popular sections. The valley's recently refurbished 5-mile gravel and dirt path, known as both **Forbidden Drive** and **Wissahickon Drive**, is a haven for joggers, cyclists, walkers, and horseback riders. (It's closed to automobiles—hence the name *Forbidden Drive*.) This is a great place to stroll in any season. On the hottest days of summer, it's relatively cool, and after a snowstorm, the woods are enchanting.

Forbidden Drive wends along the creek, passing waterfalls, an old covered bridge, an inn, massive cliffs, and secluded benches. The busiest area is in the vicinity of the **Valley Green Inn**, where ever-vigilant ducks in the creek feed on almost anything that is tossed to them. Forbidden Drive can get congested on weekends, but the park has dozens of trails off the well-beaten path. Trail maps are sold at several locations, including the Valley Green Inn (see page 146), the **Andorra Natural Area** (see page 145), and **O'Donnell's Fine Stationery** (8331 Germantown Avenue, between E Southampton Avenue and E Gravers Lane, Chestnut Hill; 247.7345).

Parking is available on the Chestnut Hill side of the creek on **Valley Green Road**, which forks off the southern end of **Springfield Avenue**, and off **Bells Mill Road**, between **Ridge** and Germantown Avenues. About three fourths of a mile south of Bells Mill is the only covered bridge in a US city, and to the north is the serene Andorra Natural Area. At the southern end of the valley, the drive meets a 2-mile paved pathway that parallels the creek as it hooks hard toward the Schuylkill. It's a pleasant, less crowded alternative for a bike ride, especially recommended during the fall foliage season for its striking panoramas. The only drawback here is the noise of traffic from Lincoln Drive.

Mobster Al Capone was arrested only three times in his life. Once was in Philadelphia in 1932 for carrying a concealed weapon. He was held at Eastern State Penitentiary.

Edgar Allan Poe lived at six different addresses in Philadelphia. The longest period was in a house at 530 N Seventh Street, a property that has been preserved in his memory. It's believed he wrote substantial parts of *The Raven*, *The Bells*, and *Annabel Lee* while living there.

1 MORRIS ARBORETUM OF THE UNIVERSITY OF PENNSYLVANIA

Ⓟ Few pleasures in Philadelphia are as wonderful as a stroll through these 92 acres, which include meadows, sculpture, an English rose garden, stunning Asian trees, a pond with swans, a Tuscan love temple, and rolling hills. The estate of brother and sister John and Lydia Morris, built in 1887 and known as **Compton**, was given to the university in 1932. The Morrises—from a wealthy Quaker family—had collected plant specimens from around the world that would thrive in the area's temperate climate. The university was charged with converting their exotic garden into a public facility and research center. Over the years, the university, which tore down the Morris mansion in the 1960s, has augmented the plant collection, making trips to China, Korea, and Taiwan.

Today more than 6,000 trees and shrubs flourish on the grounds, among them a spectacular Katsura tree, a Japanese camellia, a purple European beech, a Chinese elm, a weeping hemlock, witch hazels, hollies, pines, and hundreds of rhododendrons and azaleas. The Morrises drew on various styles for their gardens: The statue of Mercury in a loggia on the northern end of the arboretum is typical of Victorian English landscaping; the **Hill and Cloud Garden**, on the north side of the pond, is a miniature Asian garden with small hills and valleys; the formal **Rose Garden**, a collection of old and new species surrounded by a stone wall, blooms from May into October. Winners of the All America Rose Selections are displayed in the garden before they are introduced to the public in commercial catalogs. (These new varieties are to the left of the circular stone steps at the entrance of the Rose Garden.)

In 1983, the arboretum's board of managers agreed to gradually acquire a fine arts collection, and a number of modern sculptures are scattered throughout the grounds. One of the most impressive is *Two Lines*, by American artist George Rickey. Marking the location of the demolished Morris mansion, its two scissor-like stainless steel arms, each 30 feet long, rotate at the top of a 32-foot rod according to the movements of the wind. ♦ Admission. Daily. Guided tours Sa, Su, 2PM. 9414 Meadowbrook Ave (between Stenton and Northwestern Aves). 247.5777. ⅃. www.business-services.upenn. edu/arboretum

2 WOODMERE ART MUSEUM

Charles Knox Smith worked his way up from humble beginnings as a grocer's boy in the Kensington section of the city to become the owner of his own oil company. During the late 1800s he amassed a large collection of European and American paintings, porcelains from around the world, carved ivories, laces, and Oriental art. Smith's will specified that his Victorian mansion be converted into a

museum. Its doors first opened in 1940. Eight galleries and salons display Smith's collection, along with contemporary works by regional artists. Benjamin West's dramatic oil painting *The Fatal Wounding of Sir Philip Sydney* is part of the permanent collection, as are Frederic Church's *Sunset in the Berkshire Hills* and Jasper Cropsey's *The Spirit of Peace*. Several rooms are decorated with Smith's furnishings, including Oriental rugs and a large Meissen chandelier and mirror frame. The **Helen Millard Gallery** exhibits art for children created by children. The museum also hosts art classes, an annual members' exhibition, and a juried show for regional artists. ♦ Suggested donation. Tu-Su. 9201 Germantown Ave (at E Bells Mill Rd). 247. 0476. ⅃. www.woodmereartmuseum.org

3 ANDORRA NATURAL AREA

This 210-acre preserve of steep rocky paths and native forest continues **Fairmount Park**'s greenway along Wissahickon Creek. Follow the rocky path from the parking area to the **Tree House**, a 19th-century wooden house that serves as the preserve's headquarters and contains displays on wildlife, plants, and local history. A naturalist is usually on hand to talk about the valley or lead walking tours along some of the more than 5 miles of trails. Trail maps and program calendars are kept on the porch. ♦ Trails: daily, dawn to dusk. Tree House hours vary; call for schedule. Off Northwestern Ave (between Ridge and Germantown Aves). 685.9285. wwwphila.gov/fairpark

4 HIGH HOLLOW

Only a veteran voyeur can make out anything but the cobblestone courtyard and steeply pitched roofs of this private stone mansion overlooking **Fairmount Park**. Hidden by trees and located at the end of a descending driveway, the house was designed in 1914 by and for **George Howe** in the evocative style that Howe called Wall Street Pastoral, based on traditional English and French houses. Critics consider this house a minor masterpiece of American domestic architecture. ♦ 101 W Hampton Rd (at Crefeld Ave). www.phila.gov/fairpark

5 PEPPER HOUSE

Rough Wissahickon stone, a simple tower, and an austere façade make this one of many houses in Chestnut Hill that blend seamlessly into the area's natural setting. Built in 1920, the English country-style house was designed by **Willing and Syms**, a prominent Philadelphia architectural firm of the 1920s and 1930s. ♦ 9120 Crefeld Ave (at W Hampton Rd)

Restaurants/Clubs: Red | Hotels: Purple | Shops: Orange | Outdoors/Parks: Green | Sights/Culture: Blue

6 VALLEY GREEN INN

★$$ Legend dates this inn to the 1600s, but it probably wasn't built until the 1850s, sometime after the advent of **Wissahickon Drive**, the gravel path running right out front. The green-shuttered building provides a lovely setting for a meal. After renovation in the spring of 2002 to accommodate an additional 100 diners, there is a porch overlooking the creek and three homey dining rooms displaying old photos, antique clocks, and cooking utensils. People have always come here more for the surroundings than the food, though. Try the grilled salmon with creamy pesto sauce or the pork chops stuffed with apples in Calvados cream sauce. ♦ American ♦ M-Sa, lunch and dinner; Su, brunch and dinner. Reservations suggested. Wissahickon Dr (between Valley Green and Wise's Mill Rds). 247.1730

7 HISTORIC RITTENHOUSE TOWN

Right off Lincoln Drive in a pretty, woodsy niche of **Fairmount Park** is the site of the first paper mill in North America—and one of the area's lesser known tourist attractions. Wilhelm Rittenhausen came to the US from Holland in 1690 and built a mill here on the Monoshone Creek, a tributary of the Wissahickon. It manufactured fine white paper and remained one of this country's most important paper mills for 100 years. Seven 18th-century houses that were grouped around the mill are still standing.

The visitors' center has a working model of a colonial paper mill, and a studio offers frequent papermaking workshops by local artists. Be sure to call ahead to inquire about special events. ♦ Admission. Individual visitors: Sa, Su, Apr-mid-Oct; other times by appointment. Groups: M-F by appointment. Don't try to enter from Lincoln Drive; instead, turn right off Lincoln Drive onto Rittenhouse Street, then left onto Wissahickon Avenue. After crossing Lincoln Drive, enter the first driveway on the left. ♦ 206 Lincoln Dr (at Wissahickon Ave). 438.5711

8 LINCOLN DRIVE

Ⓟ One of Philadelphia's most scenic roadways links Germantown, Mount Airy, and Chestnut Hill with the rest of the city. The southern portion of the road—formerly known as Wissahickon Drive—winds along Wissahickon Creek and its rocky ravines. In the words of former *Inquirer* columnist Clark DeLeon: "It was a road that resembled its name, with a curve for every syllable. If your car tires had ink on them they could almost spell Wissahickon in cursive just by traveling the route." The upper part of the road, which leads to Mount Airy and Chestnut Hill, was called Lincoln Drive. In 1984, the city renamed the entire highway Lincoln Drive so that the road would be more easily identified under one name. The speed limit in the old Wissahickon Drive section is 25 miles per hour, and though Philadelphians are notorious for disregarding it, you'd be wise to take it easy. ♦ From Kelly Dr to Cresheim Rd

UPPER ROXBOROUGH

9 SCHUYLKILL CENTER FOR ENVIRONMENTAL EDUCATION

Ⓟ Located at the extreme northwestern edge of the city, this is one of Philadelphia's quieter hiking areas, with 40 acres of rolling hills, woodlands, ponds, walking trails, and a native animal population that includes deer and foxes. The center has an excellent bookstore and gift shop where you can buy the latest field guides on insects, climate, geology, and botany; an exhibit area geared toward children, with a tame corn snake that can be petted, a working beehive enclosed in glass, and hands-on activities like making nature rubbings; a library; and a vast collection of local insect specimens. If you visit between May and September, be sure to wear long pants on the hiking trails, where Lyme disease, transmitted by deer ticks, has been contracted. ♦ Admission. Daily. 8480 Hagys Mill Rd (between Port Royal Ave and Spring La). 482.7300. ♦ www.schuylkillcenter.org

MOUNT AIRY

10 UMBRIA

★★$$$ Run by the mother–daughter team of Donna and Lisa Consorto, this tiny, narrow storefront is one of the best finds in Mount Airy, the neighborhood between Germantown and Chestnut Hill. Known for its consistently good food, the restaurant serves such appetizers as grilled sweet Italian sausage in a spicy fig sauce or grilled Portobello mushrooms with tomato, garlic, almond, and pepper sauce. Entrées include sweetbreads with Marsala wine and shiitake mushrooms and fillet of salmon in basil sourdough crust. Look for the long list of nightly specials on the blackboard. Bring your own wine. ♦ Eclectic/Italian ♦ Tu-Su, dinner. Reservations recommended. 7131 Germantown Ave (between Mt. Pleasant and Mt. Airy Aves). 242.6470

GERMANTOWN

In 1683, William Penn deeded a tract of land to 13 German families led by Francis Daniel Pastorius, and this town was born. An independent community long before it became part of Philadelphia, it was laid out along both sides of an Indian trail, now **Germantown Avenue**, and the early German settlers made it a center of papermaking and printing.

As far back as the 1700s, the community was a refuge from the city for wealthy British colonists. The yellow fever epidemics of 1793, 1794, and 1797, which killed one seventh of the city's population, sent more Philadelphians to Germantown to escape the plague.

In the early 19th century, Germantown began its growth as a textile manufacturing center. Railroad lines connected it with Philadelphia in the 1840s, making it a full-fledged suburb, and in 1854 it was officially incorporated into the city. As early as the 1930s, Germantown began to suffer from urban problems, and by the 1950s its middle-class and affluent families started to leave for the suburbs. Though it still contains pockets of poverty, Germantown's historical war sites and mansions are national treasures, and the community boasts an outstanding collection of Victorian residential architecture. Many of the historic sites are closed between October and April and have limited hours the rest of the year. The best way to tour Germantown is by car. Germantown Avenue is cobblestoned, so be prepared for a bumpy ride.

11 NORTH BY NORTHWEST

This Mount Airy Woolworth's-turned-restaurant-and-jazz-and-blues-club is a welcome addition to the Mount Airy–Chestnut Hill scene. The cavernous space is filled with tables from shop windows to stage, with a range of music genres represented nightly, beginning around 10PM. A reasonably priced menu focuses on Southern specialties. ♦ 7165 Germantown Ave. 248.1000. www.nxnwphl.com

12 UPSALA

Built in 1798 out of Wissahickon schist, this Federal mansion was the estate of John Johnson, great-grandson of an early German settler and a leading Germantown citizen in the early 19th century. George Washington's troops camped here during the Battle of Germantown when staging their assault on British troops occupying **Cliveden** across the street. The dignified house has a square façade with a marble belt and marble lintels above the windows. The library is decorated in beautiful shades of peach, mustard, and maroon and has a mantel carved with swags, rosettes, and shields.

Some of the furniture was owned by the Johnson family, and there are many notable 18th- and 19th-century antiques, including a walnut tall-case clock made by Philadelphia clockmaker John Wood Jr. and a maple high-post bed built by cabinetmaker Jacob Super. ♦ Admission. Th-Sa, or by appointment, Apr-Dec. 6430 Germantown Ave (between Johnson and Upsal Sts). 842.1798. www.ushistory.org/germantown/upper/upsala.htm

13 CLIVEDEN

Benjamin Chew, a leading figure in the early history of the Pennsylvania colony, prominent lawyer, and chief justice of the Supreme Court of Pennsylvania, purchased 11 acres here in 1763 and constructed a stone country estate of simple grandeur. On 4 October 1777, when the house stood empty, British soldiers took it over and fended off an attack of patriots. More than 50 American patriots were felled on the front lawn here during the Battle of Germantown. George Washington's troops were unsuccessful in routing the British from the house, which they occupied for about a week. (Though the colonists lost the battle, French observers at the scene were so impressed by their fighting skills that they returned home and convinced King Louis XVI to support the rebellion.) You can still see the scars made by cannons in the building's façade, damaged statuary on the front lawn, and a bullet hole inside Chew's first-floor office. The house's symmetrical exterior has a stately center pavilion and pedimented front door. A belt course divides the first and second stories of the stone façade, and five limestone urns on brick pedestals crown the roof. Inside, Tuscan columns stand in the large entrance hall. The estate contains an outstanding collection of early American furniture, including a mahogany camelback sofa crafted by the famous Chippendale furniture maker Thomas Affleck and covered in yellow damask. The sofa is believed to have been purchased by Chew from William Penn's family in the early 1700s. The elegant chest-on-chest in the second-floor back bedroom also is attributed to Affleck. Other interior highlights include the immense carved wood mirrors made by James Reynolds in the 1700s and, in the dining room, mahogany knife cases purchased by Benjamin Chew Jr. in London in 1789.

In a back study on the first floor are a collection of Chew's English law books and a map depicting the Mason–Dixon line in 1767, a boundary that Chew adjudicated. After the Revolutionary War, Chew, who did not favor military rebellion, escaped the harsh treatment accorded to other loyalists and was appointed presiding judge of the state's high court of appeals. Seven generations of Chews lived in the house, which is a National Historic Landmark. ♦ Admission. Th-Su, noon-4PM, Apr-Dec. 6401 Germantown Ave (at Johnson St). 848.1777. www.cliveden.org

---

Restaurants/Clubs: Red | Hotels: Purple | Shops: Orange | Outdoors/Parks: Green | Sights/Culture: Blue

ROBERT MORRIS: A FALL FROM GRACE

The more things change, the more they remain the same: Take the case of Robert Morris, who went from chief financier of the Revolutionary War, signer of the Declaration of Independence and Constitution, member of the Continental Congress, and member of the Senate to a term of 3 years, 6 months, and 10 days in Philadelphia's debtor's prison—just slightly longer than he had served as the country's leading fund-raiser and money manager.

Born in Liverpool, England, in 1734, Morris came to the American colonies at the age of 13. By the time he married Mary White in 1769, he was already a successful businessman who relished the good life. On the eve of the revolution, he wrote, "It is known that besides our capital in trade, we possess valuable landed estates and that we are totally free from encumbrances."

Throughout the war, the fledgling nation turned repeatedly to Morris for financial help. He found sources of revenue time and again, once raising $50,000 requested by George Washington for the general's famous surprise Christmas-night counterattack at Trenton in 1776 by borrowing silver, promising to repay in gold, and vowing to collect the gold "in the best manner I can."

Measures such as this left the new nation in dire straits, with Congress declaring the country bankrupt in March 1780. In 1781, Morris was elected to the position of superintendent of finance at an annual salary of $6,000. He succeeded in reducing the cost of the war from an annual high of $20 million to about $5 million a year.

All the while, Morris had been speculating in land and growing deeper in debt. In the years after the war,

Morris lost his considerable wealth. The wave of economic expansion that enveloped the new nation after the revolution didn't come soon enough to rescue him from financial disaster. Of Morris's land speculation, historian William Graham Sumner wrote, "He piled one form of credit upon another, and it is plain that he soon became entirely lost, so that he did not know the amount or forms of his liabilities."

Ultimately, Morris owed an estimated $3 million, and there was a good deal of public sentiment against him because his firm, Willing & Morris, had profited from the war, securing several contracts for obtaining arms and gunpowder when Morris served as chairman of the Secret Committee of Commerce, which was charged with obtaining war matériel. Also, as owner of a fleet of privateers (privately owned warships licensed to attack and plunder shipping and permitted to keep a portion of the proceeds), he earned a reported $1 million while agent of marine, a position comparable to today's secretary of the navy.

Despite these accusations, a committee of Congress, which investigated Morris at his request, found that he had "acted with fidelity and integrity and an honorable zeal for the happiness of his country." Regarding contracts with Willing & Morris, the committee stated, "The purchases made by them for the public account were done on the best terms."

Still, on 15 February 1798, the man once regarded as the richest in America was sent to debtor's prison. Released in 1801, Morris died 5 years later in comparative penury, and was buried at **Christ Church Burial Ground**.

14 WEST TULPEHOCKEN STREET

Once a family farm, **Tulpehocken Street** was developed into a road of stately mansions during the late 1800s. Many of the homes have remained intact, complete with gingerbread woodwork, varied trellises, and towers. The Victorian Gothic house at **No. 9** and the house across the street at **No. 20** are known respectively as the **Queen's House** and the **Ladies in Waiting House**; they were built for Queen Maria Cristina of Spain in case she was forced to leave her country because of political upheaval. The Italianate houses at **Nos. 112**, **120**, and **128**, built in 1858, were culled from an architect's design book, with individual features added to differentiate them. **No. 240** is an eclectic villa in pink stucco and brick designed by the noted architect **Frank Miles Day** in 1893. ◆ Between Green St and Germantown Aves

15 WYCK

One of the oldest houses in Philadelphia, this mansion is situated on an estate purchased in 1689 by Hans Millan, a Swiss Mennonite. His son-in-law built a house that later was incorporated into the existing building, which was used as a hospital by the British army during the occupation of Germantown in 1777. In the 1800s, the estate was owned by the Haines family; in 1824, Reuben Haines engaged architect **William Strickland** to unify the additions to the house, and when the Marquis de Lafayette visited during his tour of the US in 1825, it looked much as it does today. It was occupied by the Haines family until it was given to the Germantown Historical Society in 1973. Haines was a founder of the Pennsylvania Horticulture Society, and his wife, Jane, planted the box-bordered rose garden, which today has 37 varieties of antique roses and is one of the oldest gardens in the country still growing according to its original plan. ♦ Admission. Tu, Th, Sa, Apr-Dec; other times by appointment. 6026 Germantown Ave (at W Walnut La). 848.1690. &. www.wyck.org

16 EBENEZER MAXWELL MANSION

In the late 1950s, this Victorian house was on the verge of destruction, but neighborhood residents rallied to save it. Over the years, volunteers have spent thousands of hours restoring the building. The result is a delightful example of 19th-century residential architecture and interior design. If you're into Victorian wallpaper, furniture, marbling, or stenciling, this is a great place to visit.

The stone house was built in 1859 to the designs of **J.C. Hoxie** by Ebenezer Maxwell, a textile merchant and real-estate speculator. It was enlarged in the 1870s by its second owners. The eclectic exterior has an Italianate tower, Flemish gables, French steep mansard roof, and Gothic embellishments. The building is full of faux decorative details, providing a classic example of how middle-class home owners of the period tried to imitate the dwellings of the very rich. The wallpaper in the entranceway looks like marble; the mustard-and-magenta floor made of linoleum (invented the year the house was built) imitates mosaic tiles; a fine grain was painted on the cheap door frames; and a sand-encrusted paint was applied to the exterior window frames to make them look like stone.

Nearly all the furniture was donated and is authentic to the period. Note the ornate brass gas-lit chandelier in the dining room with tiny foxes reaching for bunches of grapes beneath its globes. One of the house's best features is the ceiling stenciling in the second-floor bedrooms. The lush gardens—a rarely seen re-creation of Victorian landscaping—include a "ribbon bed" with a scalloped edge and plantings arranged to suggest the swags on the bottom of a Victorian woman's dress. ♦ Admission. Th-Sa, Apr-Dec. Call first, because group tours sometimes preempt tours for individual visitors. 200 W Tulpehocken St (at Greene St). 438.1861. www.maxwellmansion.org

17 WEST WALNUT LANE

This lovely street of eclectic residential architecture dates to the second half of the 19th century. The ornate European-style houses tell of the aspirations of the modestly affluent families who lived here. Built in 1864, **No. 116** has a Palladian window and eyebrow windows on the roof. **No. 125** is a combination of Flemish bond brick and Tudor half-timbering with a Flemish gable. **No. 143**, constructed in 1856, was renovated in the 1880s for the Button family, which owned steam-powered mills. The stone English Gothic-style house at **No. 200**, with its steeply pitched gable roof, blue trim, and crenellated tower, was the home of Joseph G. Mitchell, a founder of the Presbyterian church at Greene and Tulpehocken Streets. ♦ Between Wayne and Germantown Aves

18 DESHLER-MORRIS HOUSE

In the summer of 1792, President George Washington came to Germantown to escape Philadelphia's yellow fever epidemic and carried on the country's business from this house. Thomas Jefferson, Alexander Hamilton, and Henry Knox attended cabinet meetings here. Aside from its historic importance, this is a notable example of 18th-century Georgian architecture. The original structure, built between 1750 and 1772, consisted of just two rooms; a substantial enlargement in 1770 added a spacious dining room, a living room, and more bedrooms. With low ceilings and wooden floors, it is typical of small English manors from the same era. The Chippendale camelback sofa belonged to Washington. A large, tranquil garden behind the house has pachysandra, a ginkgo tree that dates back to Washington's time, and a small herb garden. ♦ Nominal admission. Tu-Sa, Apr-Dec. 5442 Germantown Ave (between Coulter St and School House La). 596.1748

19 GRUMBLETHORPE

Wine importer John Wister, a German immigrant, made this his summer home from 1744 until his death in 1781. A British general used the house as his headquarters and died here from wounds suffered in the Battle of Germantown in 1777. The house has two front doors—a typical feature of early Pennsylvania German architecture. Wister's grandson, Charles Jones Wister, also lived in the house. A scientist and inventor, Charles observed the movement of the planets from his observatory on top of the smokehouse on the property. Descendants of Wister occupied the house until 1940. ♦ Admission. Tu, Th, Su, or by appointment. 5267 Germantown Ave (at Bringhurst Ave). 843.4820. www.us history.org/germantown/lower/grumblethorpe .htm

20 STENTON

The county seat of James Logan, one of the early Pennsylvania colony's greatest intellects and civic leaders, is named after the Scottish village where Logan's father was born. Logan was an Irish Quaker who came to Pennsylvania as William Penn's secretary. When Penn returned to England, Logan managed the colony until after Penn's death. During the fledgling years of the colony, he served as secretary of the province, president of the Pennsylvania Provincial Council, and chief justice, among other things. He spoke the language of the Lenni Lenape and was Penn's Indian negotiator, made the first translation of Cicero's *Cato* published in America, and was an amateur astronomer and botanist in his spare time. Today his extensive library is housed in the **Library Company of Philadelphia**. The somewhat austere 1728 Georgian brick building, a National Historic Landmark, resembles a small Irish manor house. It's furnished with pieces dating from 1730 to 1830. ♦ Admission. Tu, W, by appointment; Th-Sa, 1-4PM, Mar-Dec. 18th St and Windrim Ave. 329.7312. www.stenton.org

CHESTNUT HILL

CHESTNUT HILL

Until the commuter railroad was extended here in the 1850s, Chestnut Hill was a modest village of farmers, millworkers, and shopkeepers. Once it was linked to the city, Henry Howard Houston, a director of the **Pennsylvania Railroad**, exploited Chestnut Hill's scenic setting along the Wissahickon Valley to create a fashionable suburb. Houston commissioned architects **George** and **William Hewitt** to help him build an enormous inn and church, constructed nearly 100 houses (including his own), and donated land for the **Philadelphia Cricket Club**, the country's first.

Houston's son-in-law, George Woodward, continued development of the western section of the community into the 1930s. Between 1890 and 1905, the population of Poffrabia, a village in Northern Italy, dropped from 2,200 to 1,000 when its stoneworkers left for Chestnut Hill to build its stone estates. The eclectic architecture represents the work of nearly every significant late-19th- and early-20th-century Philadelphia architect, and the entire community is now a National Historic District.

Chestnut Hill is the highest elevation point in Philadelphia, rising from 294 feet at **Mermaid Lane** to 446 feet at **Summit Street**. **Germantown Avenue**, the cobblestone former Indian trail that also runs through Germantown, is the neighborhood's principal street. One of the great things about visiting Chestnut Hill is the parking. The local merchants' association had a brilliant idea when they decided to open little parking lots and staff them with friendly retirees. The attendants will give you a ticket when you leave your car; you will receive a discount on parking if you have it stamped wherever you eat or shop. The lots are located off Germantown Avenue on **Southampton Avenue**, **Highland Avenue**, and **Bethlehem Pike**.

21 PRICE HOUSE

Reminiscent of an Italian villa, this cream-colored mansion built in 1854 with flat roofs and arched windows has an elegant central bell tower. As you walk or drive through the area, you'll notice quite a few other palazzo-like mansions that were constructed around the same period. ♦ 129 Bethlehem Pike (between E Chestnut Hill Ave and Lynnebrook La). www.philadelphiabuildings.org

22 ANGLECOT

The whimsical sundial above the front entrance and the eyelid dormer in the attic are some of the delightful details in this house designed by **Wilson Eyre**, who was born in Italy and moved to Philadelphia in 1877. Eyre is known for energizing the city's suburban architecture. This delightful structure, built in 1883, represents his use of the Queen Anne style, characterized here by a complexity of gables and odd-shaped

windows. The brick and wood building and the carriage house out back have been restored and converted into condominiums. ♦ E Evergreen and Prospect Aves. www.philadelphiabuildings.org

23 POST LIGHT

American country lighting fixtures in wrought iron, wood, and brass fill this small store. The cut-paper shades and traditional country furniture are particularly nice. ♦ M-Sa. 51 Bethlehem Pike (between Summit and Newton Sts). 242.3810 &

24 WATSON HOUSE

"Cottages and villas, surrounded by neat grounds, trees, shrubbery, and flowers, many of them costly and handsome, all comfortable and pretty. . . . The same spectacle is to be seen on every lane near Germantown all the way up to Chestnut Hill. . . . They are the results of the railroads which enable anyone to enjoy the pleasures of the country life and at the same time attend to business in town." So wrote Sidney George Fisher, a chronicler of events in the area in the latter half of the 19th century. This was one of the first grand houses in Chestnut Hill. Built in 1856, the stucco house, now in a state of disrepair, looks like an Italian villa with a tower. And though the architect is unknown, the style shows the influence of Philadelphia architect **Samuel Sloan**, who brought Italianate design to Chestnut Hill. ♦ 100 Summit St (between Bethlehem Pike and Prospect Ave). www.philadelphiabuildings.org

25 GRAVERS LANE STATION

This small railroad station built in 1883 seems fairly uninteresting when you pull up in front. But walk around to the tracks and you'll see the signature details of architect **Frank Furness**, who loved to use Victorian ornament. The cone-shaped ticket tower and the complex of dormers, heavy brackets, and trusses in the shed that overhangs the outside waiting area are quintessential Furness. ♦ E Gravers La and Anderson St

26 ROLLER'S

★★$$ A fiercely loyal clientele frequents owner-chef Paul Roller's bright café tucked in a corner of **Top of the Hill Plaza**, a low-slung shopping center off Germantown Avenue. Formerly an ice-cream parlor, the restaurant has an open kitchen, terra-cotta floors, café chairs, blond-wood tables, and large windows with half-curtains. It's better suited to lunch or brunch than dinner, when

---

Restaurants/Clubs: Red | Hotels: Purple | Shops: Orange | Outdoors/Parks: Green | Sights/Culture: Blue

THE BEST

Ellen Yin

Owner, Fork Restaurant, Old City

Because I live on the east side of town, I would suggest starting the day with a coffee at **LaCigale** on **Washington Square** and sitting out in the park to enjoy the morning.

Then make your way to the **Reading Terminal Market** and spend the rest of the morning looking at food, shopping for food, and eating! Get some cheese from

Downtown Cheese, some bread from **Metropolitan Bakery,** and a bottle of wine from the new wine superstore at **1218 Chestnut Street** for lunch in **Fairmount Park**.

While up there, walk through the **Rodin Museum** and take in a few exhibits at the **Philadelphia Museum of Art**.

Then walk back through **Rittenhouse Square**, stop for a cocktail at **Rouge**, maybe window-shop on **Walnut Street** at **Joan Shepp**. For dinner, have appetizers at a few places—have the Fruit de Mer at **Blue Angel** with champagne and then sit at the sushi bar at **Morimoto**.

---

the tight quarters seem less agreeable. The nouvelle American cuisine is simply prepared using fresh seasonal produce, and the menu changes daily. On Sunday, excellent pancakes and French toast are served for brunch. All desserts are homemade, and standouts include the pecan pie, chocolate cake, and lemon soufflé tart. There's outdoor dining in summer. ♦ American ♦ Tu-Sa, lunch and dinner; Su, brunch and dinner. 8705 Germantown Ave (at Bethlehem Pike). 242.1771. www.rollersrestaurants.com

26 ROLLER'S MARKET

Buy the desserts offered at **Roller's** restaurant next door, as well as take-out pasta, salads, and entrées. ♦ Tu-Su. 8705 Germantown Ave (at Bethlehem Pike). 248.5510 ら

27 OSAKA

★★$$ The second Osaka in the area (the first is in Wayne on the Main Line), this friendly neighborhood Japanese restaurant wins fans for quality sushi (live scallops, Hong Kong dragon roll) as well as its creative cooked fare, including a hefty lump crab cake and a high-brow appetizer of kobe beef and foie gras. ♦ 8605 Germantown Ave (between W Evergreen Ave and Rex Ave). 242.5900

28 BEST OF BRITISH

★★$ An authentic taste of Britain may be enjoyed at this delightful combination shop, bakery, and restaurant. Try afternoon tea and sample the British-American menu in the second-floor dining room. The first floor offers the largest selection of British foods—crumpets, anyone?—on the East Coast, as well as English china, miscellaneous gifts, and baked goods to go. ♦ British ♦ M-Sa, lunch and afternoon tea; Su, afternoon tea. Closed in July and Aug. 8513 Germantown Ave (between E Highland and E Evergreen Aves). 242.8848. Also at 5820 Lower York Rd (at Peddler's Village), Lahaska. 794.6855. www.britishinamerica.com/pa.html

28 ANTIQUE GALLERY

Though it all looks expensive, some of the wonderful estate jewelry here is quite afford-able. There's a large selection of Scottish agate jewelry, as well as Art Deco and Art Nouveau decorative pieces in porcelain, bronze, and pottery. ♦ Tu-Sa; other times by appointment. 8523 Germantown Ave (at E Evergreen Ave). 248.1700. www.antiquegal.com

29 ROBERTSON FLORISTS

Though this is essentially a flower shop, a visit to the wonderful glass conservatory in the back, with ivy-covered walls, fountains, and pampered flowering plants, is like taking a walk through springtime. ♦ Daily. 8501 Germantown Ave (at E Highland Ave). 242.6000. ら. www.robertsonsflowers.com

29 CHESTNUT HILL CHEESE SHOP

The scent of ripe cheese and fresh coffee beans lingers outside the door of this shop with fairly steep prices but an exceptionally knowledgeable staff and a first-rate selec-tion. ♦ Daily. 8509 Germantown Ave (between E Highland and E Evergreen Aves). 242.2211. ら. www.chcheeseshop.com

30 PHILADELPHIA PRINT SHOP

This is a wonderful place to browse through old prints and maps. In addition to affordable works by lesser-known artists are maps by Blaeu and Ortelius; flora and fauna by Audubon, Catesby, Besler, and Thornton; art of the American West by Moran and McKenney and Hall; scenes of Philadelphia; and 1920s French fashion prints. ♦ M-Sa. 8441 Germantown Ave (at E Highland Ave). 242.4750. ら. www.philaprintshop.com

31 EL QUETZAL

Women's peasant clothing from India, Ecuador, and Indonesia; carved animals from Kenya; hand-painted trays and figurines from Mexico; and T-shirts sporting aboriginal Australian designs fill the racks and baskets in this Third World–style boutique. ♦ M-Sa. 8427 German-town Ave (between E Gravers La and E Highland Ave). 247.6588

32 2 SUSANS

Unstructured women's clothes in natural silks, knits, and linens are available in this little boutique. There's a nice selection of sweaters, scarves, and costume jewelry. ♦ M-Sa. 8428 Germantown Ave (between W Gravers La and W Highland Ave). 242.0533

32 THE CANDLE SHOP

Traditional tapers in a variety of colors, novelty candles, beeswax candles, and other wax wares are included in the ample candle collection. ♦ M-Sa. 8432 Germantown Ave (between W Gravers La and W Highland Ave). 248.1459

33 INTERMISSION

Devotees of the performing arts stock up on books about Woody Allen and Marlon Brando, movie scripts, librettos, Broadway CDs, and film posters here. ♦ Daily. 8405 Germantown Ave (between E Gravers La and E Highland Ave). 242.8515. ♿ www.intermissionshop.com

34 ROLLER'S EXPRESS-O

★$ Restaurateur Paul Roller's eatery is part café, part espresso bar. The sleek, brightly lit luncheonette serves egg dishes, pancakes, and French toast for breakfast, and soups, salads, sandwiches, and hot entrées for lunch. Be sure to try the homemade ice cream. ♦ American ♦ No credit cards accepted. Tu-Su, breakfast and lunch. 8341 Germantown Ave (at E Gravers La). 247.7715

35 CHESTNUT HILL HOTEL AND THE CENTRE AT CHESTNUT HILL

$$ If you want to stay overnight in Chestnut Hill, this is your only option. The 28-room hotel shares a large 19th-century building with two restaurants and various shops. The rooms are not luxurious, but most are neatly furnished with four-poster beds and homey antiques. The Centre at Chestnut Hill, a small complex of restaurants and shops, is not affili-ated with the hotel, though they share the same building. ♦ 8229 Germantown Ave (at E Southampton Ave). 242.5905, 800/628.9744. ♿ www.chestnuthillhotel.com

Within Chestnut Hill Hotel and the Centre at Chestnut Hill:

THE MELTING POT

★$$ Philadelphia's only all-fondue restaurant is a quiet little spot colored cool green and light purple, accented with lots of blond wood—perfect for a couple looking for a chance to dip into a different dining experience. ♦ Fondue ♦ Daily, lunch and dinner. 242.3003. ♿ www.meltingpot.com

CHESTNUT HILL FARMERS MARKET

More than a dozen vendors sell produce, flowers, fresh coffee beans, pasta, meats, and fish in a shedlike building that's part of the Centre at Chestnut Hill. It's a good place to stop to get a cup of coffee and a sweet roll in the morning for takeout. ♦ Th-Sa. No phone. www.localharvest.org/farmers-markets

36 THE LABRADOR CAFE

★$ Salads, sandwiches, and great desserts fill the bill of fare at this small café just a few steps from the shops of Germantown Avenue. A lovely garden with Adirondack chairs makes a good place to take a break after antiquing. ♦ American ♦ M-Sa, breakfast and lunch; Su, brunch. No credit cards. 6 E Hartwell La (at Germantown Ave). 247.8487

37 BREDENBECK'S BAKERY AND ICE CREAM PARLOR

Skip the baked goods here and have a cone topped with Bassetts or Häagen-Dazs ice cream to go. ♦ 8126 Germantown Ave (between W Abington Ave and W Hartwell La). 247.7374. www.bredenbecks.com

38 CITRUS

★★$$ This minuscule bistro-bakery specializes in modern seafood and vegetarian fare—meat is never an option, just so you know. But you won't miss it; the cooking is sophisticated, light, and often boasts an Asian influence. The desserts, featured in a prominent showcase, are so tempting you may want to skip dinner and get right to it. The restaurant doesn't take reservations, which means there is often a wait for one of the few tiny tables. Pita and PETA are served here—there is a no-fur policy that has ruffled more than a few feathers. ♦ 8136 Germantown Ave (between E Hartwell Ln and E Abington Ave). 247.8188

39 MARGARET ESHERICK HOUSE

The elegant simplicity of this house, designed in 1960 by famous modern architect **Louis I. Kahn**, who was a professor at the **University of Pennsylvania**, blends in well with the lush, leafy neighborhood. The structure is essen-tially two stuccoed concrete blocks with vertical and horizontal windows, a narrow chimney shaft, and natural cedar shutters. Its simple lines benefit by contrast with Chestnut Hill's more sumptuous houses. ♦ 204

Restaurants/Clubs: **Red** | Hotels: **Purple** | Shops: **Orange** | Outdoors/Parks: **Green** | Sights/Culture: **Blue**

Sunrise La (off Millman St). www.philadelphia buildings.org

40 BAKER STREET BREAD CO.

Against one wall of this small bakery is a rack full of freshly baked baguettes, brioches, and scones; in the rear is an open area where the loaves are prepared and baked. There are more than 25 varieties, including roasted red pepper focaccia, sun-dried tomato boule, and stuffed spinach ricotta bread, and homemade pizza. The warm, welcoming smell of bread just out of the oven lends a homey atmosphere. ♦ Daily. 8009 Germantown Ave (between E Willow Grove and Woodale Aves). 248.2500. www.bakerstreetbread.com

41 VANNA VENTURI HOUSE

Unfortunately, you can barely make out the striking geometry of this famous building in the summertime, when the view is obscured by trees. The house, designed in 1962 by **Venturi, Scott Brown and Associates** for Robert Venturi's mother, is considered a classic of Postmodern design. The most striking feature is the sloping gabled roof divided by a deep recess with an arched window. ♦ 8330 Millman St (between W Hartwell and W Gravers Las). www.vsba.com/projects/fla_archive/10.html

42 PASTORIUS PARK

There are no fancy ball fields, playgrounds, or tennis courts here, just green meadows, large shade trees, benches, and lots of quiet. It's a great place for a picnic. ♦ Bounded by W Abington Ave and Millman and Roanoke Sts

43 HOUSTON-SAUVEUR HOUSE

Henry Houston built this house in 1885 in the Queen Anne style, characterized here by an exuberantly busy exterior of half-timbered gables, dormers, porches, odd-shaped windows, a steeply pitched roof, and railings. The house was designed by Houston's principal architects, **George** and **William Hewitt**. ♦ 8205 Seminole St (at W Hartwell La). www.philadelphiabuildings.org

44 CINCIN

★★$$ A sister restaurant to **Yangming** in suburban Bryn Mawr, this new eatery presents Chinese cuisine with a French twist. Service in the contemporary, pink-and-green dining room is attentive, and the menu offers a broad range of choices. Its grilled fish is especially noteworthy. An extensive wine list includes sake and plum wine. ♦ Chinese ♦ Daily, lunch and dinner 7838 Germantown Ave (at Springfield Ave). 242.8800. www.chestnuthillfood.com/cincin

45 SULGRAVE MANOR

"The adulation of things colonial and Revolutionary blended at times into out-and-out Anglophilia, a worship of English roots that seems on its face unfaithful to the intent of the American Revolution," **Temple University** professor Morris J. Vogel has written of Philadelphia culture. He noted this house, built in 1926 for the city's Sesquicentennial Celebration, as a prime example. With its steep slate roof and stone façade, it was meant to be a replica of an English manor once occupied by George Washington's ancestors. Believe it or not, it was moved from the **Sesquicentennial Fairgrounds** in South Philadelphia to this idyllic spot. ♦ 200 W Willow Grove Ave (between Seminole St and Lincoln Dr). www.philadelphiabuildings.org

46 NIGHT KITCHEN

The rich, crumbly chocolate shortbread cookies cinnamon buns loaded with nuts, and cakes topped with creamy frosting as opposed to fluffy white icing set this bakery apart. The breads, scones, muffins, soups, and small pizzas are also good. ♦ Tu-Su. 7725 Germantown Ave (between E Mermaid La and E Moreland Ave). 248.9235. www.nightkitchenbakery.com

47 YU HSIANG GARDEN

★$$ This Chinese restaurant is decorated with Oriental screens and has decent spareribs and scallion pancakes. ♦ Chinese ♦ M-Sa, lunch and dinner; Su, dinner. 7630 Germantown Ave (between Cresheim Valley Dr and W Mermaid La). 248.4929. www.yuhsianggarden.com

48 ST. MARTIN-IN-THE-FIELDS EPISCOPAL CHURCH

Henry Houston commissioned **George** and **William Hewitt** to build this lovely stone Gothic church with arches and a four-story tower, completed in 1888. Situated next to the playing fields of the **Philadelphia Cricket Club** and across the street from the prestigious **Chestnut Hill Academy**, the church adds to the picturesque English setting. The beautiful west window was crafted by Louis C. Tiffany. ♦ W Willow Grove Ave and St. Martin's La. www.stmartinec.org

49 CHESTNUT HILL ACADEMY

This rambling castlelike structure was once the **Wissahickon Inn**, a vacation spot for city dwellers. It was designed with rich exterior woodwork, corner bay windows, and half-timbered dormers by **George** and **William Hewitt** in 1884. The inn had 250 rooms and was situated on a so-called lake, created by the damming of a nearby creek. It didn't last long as a resort and has been a prestigious boys' prep school since 1898. ♦ W Willow Grove Ave and Huron St. www.chestnuthill academy.org

50 DRUIM MOIR

It's name being the Gaelic phrase for "great crag," this stone structure was built for developer Henry Houston in 1886. It was designed in the style of a Scottish baronial castle by **George** and **William Hewitt**, the architects responsible for most of Houston's buildings. In the 1940s, alterations removed turrets and gables, leaving the house much less elaborate than it once was. It overlooks a magnificent walled garden designed by Robert Rhodes McGoodwin after World War I. Next door is the privately owned **Brinkwood**, a stone and cedar-shingled house built by Houston for his son in 1887. ♦ W Willow Grove Ave (at Cherokee St). www.philadelphiabuildings.com

MANAYUNK

Manayunk has been called a workingman's San Francisco, and though that is a bit of a stretch, its steep hills overlooking the Schuylkill River and row houses ascending like stairs do seem familiar. Called **Flat Rock**

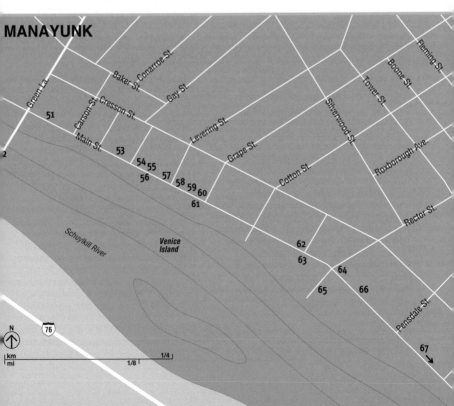

by the English settlers who first came to this area in 1683, it remained a small village until 1822, when the Manayunk section of the Schuylkill canal system was built. The canal made this rough, churning portion of the river navigable and greatly enhanced the village's economic fortunes. After acquiring its current name (an Indian expression meaning "place to drink"), the town became a textile manufacturing center, and English, Irish, German, Italian, and Polish immigrants built row houses up the narrow streets on the hills along the river.

Boom times hit in the 1880s, and Manayunk was flush with mills and commerce. **Main Street**, which runs parallel to the river, was lined with stores, hotels, restaurants, and banks. A few factories remain, but the area is no longer a symbol of industrial might. In the late 1970s, a towpath and boardwalk were built along the old canal, and in 1983 Main Street became a National Historic District. Today Main Street flourishes once again, attracting people to its wealth of shops, restaurants, and art galleries. www.manayunk.com

51 US HOTEL BAR AND GRILL

★$$ In 1903, the **US Hotel** was granted a permit to construct a bar next door. Eleven years later, when the hotel was ripped down and a movie theater took its place, the bar was spared. The long, narrow saloon retains much of its original interior, including the lovely green and white tiles, a tin ceiling, and a cherry bar with shelves and glass fronts. The dining area is a cramped row of tables lining the long wall opposite the bar. Steaks, crab cakes, barbecued baby back ribs, a fish of the day, and black pepper gnocchi are highlights of the brief menu. The blue crab corn chowder is not to be missed. A raw bar with clams, shrimp, and oysters is located in the rear. ◆ American ◆ Daily, lunch and dinner. 4439 Main St (between Carson St and Green La). 483.9222. www.ushotelbar-grill.com

52 CARMELLA'S

★$$ Located on Venice Island on the Schuylkill River, this Italian steakhouse features traditional Southern Italian favorites—all in *mangia*-size portions—along with an expansive bar and open-air deck area, which gets crowded after work and when the weather is nice. Live music is featured on weekends. Parking is free and ample, a real plus in Manayunk. ◆ Italian ◆ Daily, lunch and dinner. 1 Leverington St (at Flat Rock Rd) 487.1400

53 KILDARE'S IRISH PUB

★$ A rollicking bar, fueled by a fine selection of ales and whiskies from the old sod, make this new Main Street pub a popular spot. The menu includes fish and chips, hand-carved roast beef sandwiches, tasty salads, and pasta entrées. There is live Irish music on the weekends. ◆ 4417 Main St (between Gay and Conarroe Sts). 482.7242. www.kildarespub.com

54 SONOMA

★★$$ The noise in this sophisticated restaurant filled with skylights, floor-to-ceiling windows, and wall panels of metallic silver and Pacific blue can be unbearable when the place is jammed—as it always is on weekend nights—but it's a small price to pay for the excellent food. Owner-chef Derek Davis describes his cuisine as "Italiafornian," and it's well represented in the roast chicken with rosemary, grilled chicken breast with pesto, and garlic rib eye steak. Entrées are served with roasted potatoes, dense, crusty bread, and salad or Italian greens in oil. Pizzas are made with a wonderful thin, flaky crust in a wood-burning oven. One pie is topped with grilled rock shrimp, tomatoes, hot peppers, leeks, fontina cheese, and basil. Try one of the reasonably priced wines from the restaurant's all-California list. A circular staircase leads up to the second-floor greenhouse bar, where scores of vodka bottles from all over the world are chilled in an ice trough between the bartender and customers. Complement your cocktail with such appetizers as baked

THE BATTLE OF THE KEGS

No, not beer kegs, although that sounds more plausible in a city that once had more than its share of breweries. This was actually a battle that involved powder kegs set afloat in the Delaware River in an effort to disrupt and destroy British shipping the night of 5 January 1778.

Patriots released a number of these kegs charged with gunpowder into the river. Like modern mines, they would explode on contact. And because the river was choked with British ships lying just off the port of Philadelphia, the patriots were certain some of the kegs would find some of the ships. When one of the kegs exploded that night, the patriots thought their plan was working. It did some serious damage, killing some sailors and injuring others, and sparked a general alarm. Soon the docks were filled with soldiers who spent much of the next day firing at anything floating in the river, but the kegs were hard to see and harder to hit. Mother Nature threw a twist into the story, for that very night, the winter's first hard frost forced the British to bring their ships into port. With the ships out of the river, effects of the kegs were negligible, even laughable, it seems, according to newspaper accounts of the day.

This city hath lately been entertained with a most astonishing instance of activity, bravery and military skill of the royal army and navy of Great Britain. The affair is somewhat particular and deserves your notice. Some time last week a keg of singular construction was observed floating in the river. The crew of a barge attempted to take it up, it exploded, killed four of the hands and wounded the rest.

On Monday last some of the kegs of a singular construction made their appearance. The alarm was immediately given. Various reports prevailed in the city, filling the royal troops with unspeakable consternation. Some asserted that these kegs were filled with rebels, who were to issue forth in the dead of night, as the Grecians did of old from the wooden horse at the siege of Troy, and take the city by surprise. Some declared they had seen the points of bayonets sticking out of the bungholes of the kegs. Others said they were filled with inflammable combustibles which would set the Delaware in flames and consume all the shipping in the harbor. Others conjectured that they were machines constructed by magic art and expected to see them mount the wharves and roll, all flaming with infernal fire, through the streets of the city.

"In truth, not a chip, stick or drift log passed by without experiencing the vigor of the British arms. The action began about sunrise and would have terminated in favor of the British by noon had not an old market woman, in crossing the river with provisions, unfortunately let a keg of butter fall overboard, which as it was then ebb tide, floated down to the scene of battle. At sight of this unexpected re-enforcement of the enemy the attack renewed with fresh forces, and the firing from the marine and land troops was beyond imagination and so continued until night closed the conflict.

"The rebel kegs were either totally demolished or obliged to fly, as none of them have shown their heads since. It is said that His Excellency, Lord Howe, has dispatched a swift sailing packet with an account of this signal victory to the Court of London. In short, Monday, January 5, 1778, will be memorable in history for the renowned battle of the kegs."

oysters in a vodka cream sauce served with caviar. There's also valet parking—a nice touch, given the difficulty of parking in this area. ♦ Italian/Californian ♦ Daily, lunch and dinner. Reservations accepted for parties of six or more. 4411 Main St (at Gay St). 483.9400. www.mainstreetrestaurants.com

55 BEANS BEAUTY SUPPLY

Those expensive shampoos and conditioners you usually find in hair salons are available here at reasonable prices. ♦ Daily. 4405 Main St (between Levering and Gay Sts). 487.3333. www.beansbeauty.com

56 MAINLY SHOES

Cork platforms, tooled leather boots, suede pumps, and classical calf flats are sold in one of the city's better shoe stores. Designer brands include Clergerie, Charles Jourdan, Vittoria Ricci, Kelian Studio, and Espace. ♦ Daily. 4410 Main St (between Cotton St and the Green La Bridge). 483.8000

57 CHARLES TILES

One of the larger and more handsome storefronts on **Main Street** displays a large selection of imported tiles for floors and walls. Spanish and Portuguese wall tiles, French limestone floor tiles, Mexican terra-cottas, and bas-reliefs are laid out in this lovely space with large windows and decorative woodwork. ♦ Tu-Sa. 4401 Main St (at Levering St). 482.8440. www.charles-tiles.com

58 JAKE'S

★★★$$$ It's hard to miss this popular restaurant: A humorous piece of pop art—a

Restaurants/Clubs: Red | Hotels: Purple | Shops: Orange | Outdoors/Parks: Green | Sights/Culture: Blue

dinner table and wine bottle splashing its contents into a glass—juts from the building's façade at the second story. Eschewing the white-wall minimalism of many of its contemporaries, this dining room has textured green walls with rainbow lighting and a clever collection of modern artwork and sculpture. The kitchen has its own smoker, and a different hickory-smoked fish appetizer is available daily. Try the smoked duck salad with strawberries and a balsamic vinegar dressing, or the smoked chicken with arugula and angel-hair pasta in a sun-dried tomato vinaigrette. Entrées range from a simple grilled beef fillet with potato purée to barbecued salmon in a sauce of apple cider, soy, and garlic, served with fried yams. Crab cakes are a house specialty. The wine list is extensive. ◆ New American ◆ M-F, lunch and dinner; Sa, dinner; Su, brunch and dinner. Reservations recommended. 4365 Main St (between Grape and Levering Sts). 483.0444. www.jakesrestaurant.com

59 PAT KING'S

The women's clothing you'll find in this boutique ranges from silk floral dresses you could wear to a wedding to odd fringed vests that resemble upholstery. ◆ Daily. 4357 Main St (between Grape and Levering Sts). 487.7890

59 PACIFIC RIM

Dark, intricately carved woods from faraway lands line the walls of this shop. Among the other exotica: a wooden puppet from Java, ceremonial swords, Indonesian masks, water buffalo bells, Thai gongs, and a carved wooden banana tree. They'll ship purchases anywhere. ◆ Tu-Su. 4351 Main St (between Grape and Levering Sts). 482.0498

59 OWEN PATRICK GALLERY

This contemporary art gallery sells paintings, jewelry, sculpture, glass, metal, and ceramics made by artists from the US and abroad. It specializes in art furniture and lighting. ◆ Tu-Su. 4345 Main St (between Grape and Levering Sts). 482.9395. 占.
www.owenpatrickgallery.com

60 VESPA

Local Italian businessman Vincenzo Mercuri opened this eye-catching Vespa showroom a couple of summers ago, home to the original Italian motor scooter in all colors of the rainbow. With everything from vintage models to custom scooters, this stylish boutique will get your wheels spinning. ◆ 4373 Main St (between Grape and Levering Sts). 508.3600. www.vespaphiladelphia.com

61 NICOLE MILLER

Here you'll find Philadelphia high style with an emphasis on chic evening wear, simply elegant bridal gowns, and barely there little black dresses. Sales consultants help match clients with the perfect party or prom dress, but be aware that perfection doesn't come cheap. ◆ 4249 Main Street. 930.0307. Also in Center City at 200 S Broad St. 546.5007. www.nicolemiller.com

62 AMERICAN PIE CONTEMPORARY CRAFTS

Contemporary folk art, such as mirrors with wood frames painted in bright greens and pinks, hand-painted ceramic tiles, and Bohemian glass earrings, fills this boutique. ◆ Daily. 4303 Main St (at Roxborough Ave). 487.0226. Also at 327 South St (between S Third and S Fourth Sts). 922.2226. www.americanpiecrafts.com

63 LE BUS MAIN STREET

★$ A cavernous dining room with a stone wall, wooden beams, and enormous windows offers a great setting in which to while away an hour. The casual menu is promising, but the quality of the items on it vacillates. Comfort foods, like meat loaf and mashed potatoes, chicken entrées, a decent burger, and creative salads earn the highest marks. Appetizers include a garlicky hummus, and the homemade breads are good. ◆ Eclectic ◆ M, dinner; Tu-F, lunch and dinner; Sa, Su, brunch and dinner. 4266 Main St (between Rector and Cotton Sts). 487.2663. 占. Also at Reading Terminal Market, N 12th St (between Filbert and Arch Sts). 592.0422; and 135 S 18th St. 569.8299. 占. www.lebusbakery.com

64 MAINLY DESSERTS

★★$ Decorated with floral swags and china teapots, this storefront serves cappuccino and decent treats, particularly a strawberry shortcake with white chocolate and a triple chocolate mousse cake. Bassetts ice cream is served alone or on top of brownies with chocolate sauce. The restaurant also offers sandwiches, salads, and homemade soup for lunch. ◆ American ◆ W-Sa, lunch and dinner; Su, brunch and dinner. 4247 Main St (at Rector St). 487.1325. http://www.philly restaurants.com/mainly/index.cfm

65 BOURBON BLUE

★★$$ Located in a former Smith and Hawkens, this New Orleans–style restaurant includes a bright team in the kitchen, executive chef Brian Watson and sous chef Brenda McGrew. The pair have crafted the Southern/ Louisiana menu to include terrific appetizers, main courses, and pasta dishes. Try the blackened filet tips tossed with sea scallops and sun-dried tomatoes over homemade gnocchi in a lemon garlic cream sauce or the French-cut 12-ounce pork chop served with asparagus and shrimp mashed potatoes. ◆ 2 Rector St (at the river). 508.3360

66 SPORTS WORKS

This is the place to go for chic athletic togs, sports accoutrements, and the latest must-have yoga and Pilates duds. You'll also find high-style sneaks and athletic footwear. ◆ 4320 Main Street (between Pensdale and Rector Sts). 487.0220

66 CATHERINE STARR GALLERY

Colorful figurative and primitive paintings, sculpture, and ceramics are sold here. Owner Catherine Starr likes to call it "a happy collection." ◆ Tu-Su. 4235 Main St (between Pensdale and Rector Sts). 482.7755

67 MANAYUNK BREWERY & RESTAURANT

★★$$ In addition to seven handcrafted ales and lagers, this casual, friendly pub-atmosphere eatery, on the banks of the historic **Manayunk Canal**, comes through with some tasty selections. Try the slow-smoked baby back ribs, lobster ravioli, Tuscan chicken penne, Harry's cedar plank–roasted salmon, and can't-miss shrimp scampi. There is a patio for outdoor dining in fine weather. ◆ American. ◆ Daily, lunch and dinner. 4120 Main St (near Lock St). 482.8220. www.manayunkbrewery.com/

67 RESTORATION HARDWARE

Okay, so it's a chain store, but it's a good one. Restoration Hardware offers an eclectic line of home furnishings and accessories, with terrific end-of-season and after-Christmas sales. Whether you're looking for a rich leather chair, that satin-nickel fitting for the bath, or 464-thread-count bed linens, it's all here. ◆ 4130 Main Street. 930.0300. www.restorationhardware.com

67 POTTERY BARN

This ubiquitous home and furniture gallery features everything for the well-appointed yuppie household, from flatware and glasses to garden statuary and sectional sofas. ◆ 4230 Main St. 508.6778. www.potterybarn.com

GAY PHILADELPHIA

The City of Brotherly Love hasn't always been brotherly or lovely since its founding in 1682, but these days the US's fifth-largest city is on the whole a comfortable place for its gay and lesbian citizens. With a diverse history of gay rights activism that goes back at least to the 1950s and an even older queer culture, this town has evolved into a cosmopolitan home to a vibrant gay and lesbian community and a reasonably gay friendly political establishment. Starting in 2003, the city kicked off a marketing campaign to reach out to gay tourists in a big way, with The Greater Philadelphia Tourism Marketing Corp. committing $100,000 annually through 2006 to promote the city's historical attractions and its small but increasingly hip gay district to gay travelers. Advertising slogans have raised a few eyebrows, but also attracted a growing share of gay tourism dollars from around the region and beyond. There is even a gay section of the city's tourism website: www.gophila.com/gay.

Tough battles have been fought here, and a fair number of them won, including one of the first municipal equal-rights laws in the country in 1982, a civilian review board to cut down on police gay-bashing in 1991, and a "rainbow curriculum" teaching tolerance in the city schools. In 1996, Democratic mayor Ed Rendell, now the state's governor, signed an executive order extending domestic partnership benefits to some city employees, which has now been extended to all city employees.

The social scene here is compact; gay and lesbian nightspots number fewer than 20, and the most visible gay district consists of a 15-square-block area downtown. There's plenty to do, but if you absolutely need a high-energy party scene, this town won't meet your needs. Many of the city's top-notch restaurants are gay-owned, but not all of them necessarily have queer atmosphere.

Homo life here is not as in your face as it can be on the Castro in San Francisco or New York City's Eighth Avenue. Same-sex hand-holding and public displays of affection are more the exception than the rule—not that it's dangerous; it's just not done. This low-key, somewhat conservative outlook is at least partly a result of the town's Quaker heritage and somewhat WASPish social traditions. The upside is that attitude (or "atty tood," as the locals render it) is at a minimum. The natives—gay and straight—are mostly down-to-earth and friendly (and sometimes restless, but in a good way—the scene is small, so new faces are very welcome).

Geographically, Philadelphia fagdom means **Center City**—the downtown area bordered by the **Delaware River** to the east, the **Schuylkill River** to the west, **South Street** to the south, and the **Vine Street Expressway (Interstate 676)** to the north. Homo central is **Washington Square West**, site of Colonial-era brick homes, charming cobblestone streets, and many of the city's queer dance palaces and homo-friendliest nosheries. Equally gay is **Rittenhouse Square**, one of the nation's loveliest urban plazas and a traditional cruising ground for men. All around are tony high-rise apartment buildings and stately fin-de-siècle town houses. There's also a significant gay presence just south of Center City in **Queen Village**—no punchline; it just happens to be named after Sweden's 18th-century Queen Christina, who was reportedly ambiguous in her proclivities (and was brought to the screen in 1933 by another ambiguous Swede, Greta Garbo). The **Art Museum** section to the north of Center City has its fairy contingent, and **Mount Airy** to the northwest is an enclave favored by lesbian couples for its sprawling stone houses. **Narberth** to the west is also populated with lesbian couples. The working-class

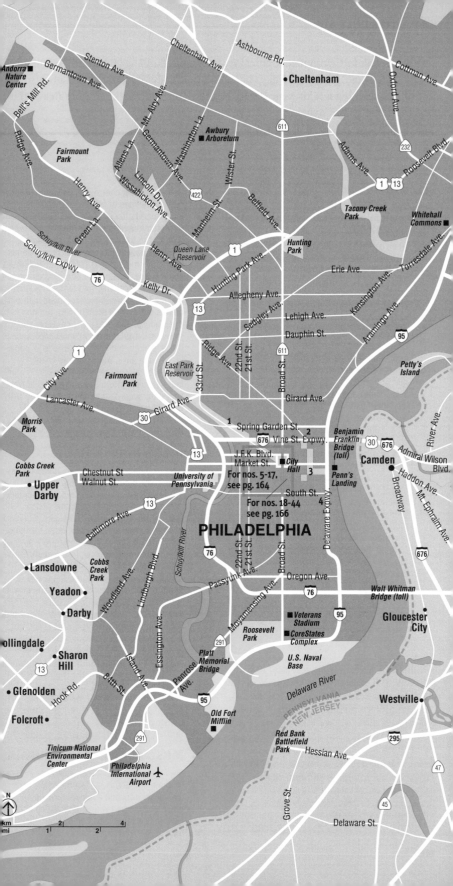

neighborhoods farther south of Center City (such as **Bella Vista** and **South Philadelphia**) are home to some lesbians and gays but aren't especially welcoming to visitors, so step out of the downtown with care. Otherwise, strap on your walking shoes (leave those heels at home, as brick sidewalks can be murder on the feet) and enjoy.

SYMBOLS

♂ predominantly/exclusively gay-male-oriented

♀ predominantly/exclusively lesbian-oriented

♂
♀ predominantly/exclusively gay-oriented, with a male and female clientele

1 PHILADELPHIA MUSEUM OF ART

One of the finest and most comprehensive art collections in the country calls this 1928 Greek Revival temple home. Climb the notorious steps that Stallone pranced up in *Rocky* to see such highlights as vast European holdings (including van Gogh's *Sunflowers*) and masterpieces from Asia and the Near East. Then too, there are many works by artists of queer interest, including local 19th-century master Thomas Eakins, whose paintings of boys rowing on the **Schuylkill River** set an early standard for homoerotic imagery; Marsden Hartley, whose abstract works with military emblems are an homage to his lover, a German officer killed in World War I; Jasper Johns; and Marcel Duchamp, the cross-dressing French modernist whose pieces here include the landmark *Nude Descending a Staircase* (a male nude, by the way) and *The Bride Stripped Bare By Her Bachelors, Even.* ♦ Admission; free Su, 10AM-1PM. Tu, Th-Su; W, 10AM-8:45PM. At the end of Benjamin Franklin Pkwy. 763.1800. &. www.phila museum.org/

Bessie Smith, celebrated bisexual blues singer of the early 20th century, lived in two houses on the 1100 block of Kater Street in the 1920s and early 1930s during Philadelphia's own jazz age. In those days, South Street was home to many black jazz clubs where Smith performed. Even though she sang in one of her numbers, "There's two things I don't understand—that's a mannish-acting woman and a lisping, swishing, womanish-acting man," she grasped the concept very well. Smith in fact earned much notoriety in these parts for her carousing and many affairs with chorines.

2 SHAMPOO

♂
♀ Remember that cheesy 1970s Warren Beatty flick? If the idea of a funky, two-floor dance club named after it tickles you, come hither. Retro furniture and pop art themes mix with plenty of retro tunes from the 1970s and 1980s. But with eight bars and three dance floors, this megaclub is far from nostalgia—in some spaces, alternative and progressive grooves predominate, and in the industrial-looking basement space (complete with old boilers, pipes, and stone walls), hip-hop, deep house, and acid jazz rule. Gays and lesbians leaven the mix all three nights the place is open, but Friday is especially popular with the guys, when hip homos and wannabes alike flock to Shaft, a dance party featuring well-known DJs and a bevy of New York drag queens sometimes led by the Lady Bunny herself. ♦ Cover. Th-Sa, 9PM-2AM. 417 N Eighth St (entrance on Willow St). 922.7500. www.shampooonline.com

3 INDEPENDENCE HALL

Sure, a bunch of guys in wigs made history here a few hundred years ago, but this 1748 Georgian building is also a landmark in the struggle for gay independence—though you won't see any plaques. Almost 2 centuries after the birth of a nation on this site, queer America made one of its earliest high-profile appearances in the country's history—well before the Stonewall riots of 1969. The so-called Annual Reminder (a polite but no less revolutionary early form of "We're here, we're queer, get used to it!") was a demonstration attended by thousands each 4 July between 1965 and 1969 and organized by the Eastern Regional Conference of Homophile Organizations. (The gay-rights gang in those days was known as the homophile movement.) The march is reenacted in the 1995 film *Stonewall*. After Stonewall, this national march moved permanently to New York. ♦ Free. Daily. Chestnut St (between S Fifth and S Sixth Sts). 597.8974. &. www.nps.gov/inde

4 MUSTARD GREEN RESTAURANT

★★$$ Yes, mustard greens really are included on the menu at this fag favorite—along with firecracker pork and a limited selection of other unusual and yummy specialties from Hunan, Szechuan, and Canton provinces. The clean, simple setting (white walls, wood floors) highlights the food, and the cute waiters are very gay-friendly. ◆ Chinese ◆ Daily, dinner. 622 S Second St (between Bainbridge and South Sts). 627.0833

4 JUDY'S

♂
♀ ★★$$ This is the queerest restaurant in town, hands down—from its staff of divas, both male and female, to the clientele, which is gay and lesbian, with a few token straights. Here, couples hold hands and even smooch a little, under a painting of two men holding hands. The look is post-minimalist with touches of neon and glass brick, whereas the menu is an eclectic mix that might pair spicy-cool gazpacho with buttery salmon in pesto sauce or veal and pork meat loaf with spinach and provolone in a mushroom gravy. With all this to offer, no wonder it's always crowded. ◆ International ◆ M-Sa, dinner; Su, brunch and dinner. Reservations recommended. 627 S Third St (at Bainbridge St). 928.1968

5 FOUR SEASONS HOTEL

$$$$ Generally hailed as the best hotel in Philadelphia, this hostelry is also known in certain circles for its gay and lesbian—and gay-friendly—staff, especially at the concierge desk. The 371 luxurious rooms are tastefully furnished in Federal style and stocked with Godiva chocolates and Perrier. English tea at the **Swann Lounge** is veddy, veddy lovely, and the **Fountain Restaurant**, featuring fine American and continental fare, is ranked as one of the city's (even the country's) best. ◆ 1 Logan Sq (between Benjamin Franklin Pkwy and N 19th St). 963.1500, 800/332.3442; fax 963.9562. &. www.fourseasons.com

6 THE PENNSYLVANIA ACADEMY OF THE FINE ARTS

Home to a small museum of 19th-century American art, this structure is most notable for its ornate High-Victorian building designed in

1876 by local architect **Frank Furness** and for giving the boot in 1886 to its most famous teacher, painter Thomas Eakins. As the story goes, Eakins's "sin" was that he allowed nude male models to pose in front of female students (boys posing for boys was evidently not a problem). Works on display includes Eakins's *The Cello Player*, paintings by Benjamin West, and sculpture by Louise Nevelson. ◆ Admission; free W, 5-7:30PM. M, Tu; Th-Su, 11AM-5PM; W, 5-7:30PM. 118 N Broad St (at Cherry St). 972.7600. &. www.pafa.org

7 PRINCE MUSIC THEATER

Named for Broadway great Harold Prince, this is a venue for new musical theater and cabaret acts, showcasing the talents of such luminaries as Lou Rawls, Andrea Marcovicci, Lee Breuer, Philip Glass, and Adam Guettel, grandson of the great Richard Rodgers. ◆ 1412 Chestnut St (between S Broad and S 15th Sts). 972.1000, 569.9700

8 BORDERS

Yes, this is the same chain bookstore found across the country. But this shop, by virtue of its prime location near **Rittenhouse Square**, is surely one of the gayest, going out of its way to cater to the community with author readings and musical acts. Located in a former upscale women's dress shop, the sprawling store offers three levels, including a first-floor magazine area and second-floor coffee bar that are prime cruising zones for guys. ◆ M-F, 7AM-10PM; Sa, 9AM-9PM; Su, 11AM-7PM. 1 Broad St (at Penn Sq S). 568.7400 &

9 THE RITTENHOUSE HOTEL

$$$$ Denzel Washington and Tom Hanks must have chosen these upscale digs during the filming of *Philadelphia* to get into character: many guests and more than a few of the staffers are "like that," so the queer quotient is high indeed. Don't think, though, that they're the only celebs to crash in one of the 98 lovely rooms (all featuring floor-to-ceiling windows) or enjoy a meal at **Lacroix**, a luxe dining spot with continental cuisine. For the financially challenged, there's **Boathouse Row Bar**, a less pricey eatery featuring American fare, and the **Caassah Tea Room**, a lobby-level tearoom. **Adolf Becker** features an indoor pool and workout equipment. ◆ 210 Rittenhouse Sq W (between Locust and Walnut Sts). 546.9000, 800/ 635.1042; fax 732.3364 &

10 RITTENHOUSE SQUARE

One of the US's most beautiful parks, this stretch of green is known for more than fine

---

Restaurants/Clubs: Red | Hotels: Purple | Shops: Orange | Outdoors/Parks: Green | Sights/Culture: Blue

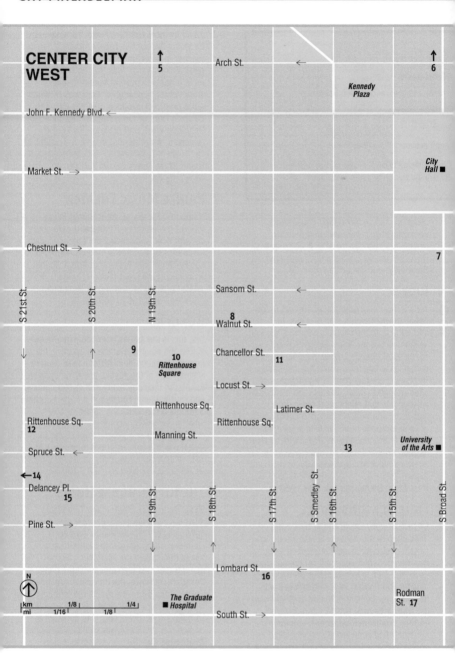

CENTER CITY WEST

Arch St.

Kennedy Plaza

John F. Kennedy Blvd.

Market St.

City Hall ■

Chestnut St.

7

S 21st St.   S 20th St.   N 19th St.   Sansom St.

8
Walnut St.

9   10
Rittenhouse Square   Chancellor St.   11

Locust St.

Rittenhouse Sq.   Latimer St.

Rittenhouse Sq.
12   Rittenhouse Sq.

Manning St.

University of the Arts ■

13

Spruce St.

←14
Delancey Pl.
15

S 19th St.   S 18th St.   S 17th St.   S Smedley St.   S 16th St.   S 15th St.   S Broad St.

Pine St.

Lombard St.
16

N

The Graduate ■ Hospital

Rodman St. 17

South St.

km   1/8   1/4
mi   1/16   1/8

statuary and stately trees: Here men have met men, and women women, for generations. Before police commissioner (and later mayor) Frank Rizzo cracked down on the surrounding coffeehouses in the late 1950s, it was also the center of "bohemian" life. Today this melting pot of urban types is still a major (and cruisy) meeting spot, ideal for lunch, dinner, or a late-night post-bar stroll. ◆ Bounded by S 18th St and Rittenhouse Sq W and by Rittenhouse Sq and Walnut St

11 LITTLE PETE'S

★$ If it looks like a diner, smells like a diner, and sends your cholesterol through the roof, it gotta be this favorite hangout—known for superlative fries and milk shakes and its big-haired waitresses (in spirit if not always in fact). Given its location in the heart of Center City West, this eatery attracts a wacky cross-section of patrons that grows gayer as the night grows long. ◆ Diner ◆ Daily, 24 hours. 219 S 17th St (at Chancellor St). 545.5508 ᴪ

12 FRIDAY, SATURDAY, SUNDAY

★★$$ One of the key spots in Philadelphia's restaurant renaissance of the 1970s still exudes *beaucoup de* charm in its romantic dining rooms with billowing cloth ceilings, tiny white lights, and specials on a blackboard. The crowd is mixed, but the upstairs bar with its colorful fish tank can get especially gay late at night. The menu is American nouvelle (grilled swordfish, rack of lamb, poached salmon in sorrel sauce, and meal-size salads), and the luscious cheesecake and blueberry pie are to die for. ♦ New American ♦ M, Sa, Su, dinner; Tu-F, lunch and dinner. Reservations recommended. 261 S 21st St (between Spruce St and Rittenhouse Sq). 546.4232. www.frisatsun.com

13 1521 CAFE GALLERY

★$ Artists staring dreamily into space; grad students writing in their journals; friends dishing over dishes of pasta, salads, sandwiches, and heavenly gelato—that's the panorama at this Euro-style coffeehouse. The crowd is mixed but definitely gay- and lesbian-friendly, with professionals and students from the nearby **University of the Arts** attracted by the spartan but homey black-and-white décor—and the ever-evolving display of art. ♦ Coffeehouse ♦ Tu-Sa, 11AM-midnight; Su, 11AM-7PM. 1521 Spruce St (between S 15th and S 16th Sts). 546.1521

14 SCHUYLKILL RIVER PARK

Overlooking the waters of the **Schuylkill River**, which forms the western boundary of Center City, this long, skinny green space (which continues north toward the **Philadelphia Art Museum**) is affectionately known by locals as Judy Garland Park because on summer days, it turns into a gay (some lesbians flock here too) beach (no swimming, though). At night (and days year-round), many come for the cruising, but the "fuzz" have been known to make surprise raids at the behest of residents of the upscale surrounding neighborhood. There have also been some incidents of bashing, so if you must cruise, cruise cautiously—preferably in packs. ♦ Delancey Pl and S 25th St. www.fairmountpark.com

15 ROSENBACH MUSEUM AND LIBRARY

The nation's preeminent museum for rare books and manuscripts has a gay twist: It's rumored that one of the two founding Rosenbachs (Philip, an art dealer) was, well, a confirmed bachelor. (Check out his jeweled, custom-made Tiffany eyeglass case and draw your own conclusions.) Besides a wonderful collection, including original manuscripts of James Joyce's *Ulysses* and Lewis Carroll's *Alice in Wonderland*, the museum offers a window into Philadelphia intellectual life in the early 20th century. ♦ Admission. Tu-Su, 11AM-4PM (last tour begins at 2:45PM); closed in Aug. 2010 Delancey Pl (between S 20th and S 21st Sts). 732.1600. www.rosenbach.org

16 ASTRAL PLANE

★★$$ Ceilings draped in parachute cloth, cheerfully mismatched china and silverware, and walls plastered with vintage headshots of movie stars and just plain folks all make for a romantic and very gay restaurant experience (though it's so dim, they should consider glow-in-the-dark menus). Service can be snippy or smooth, but the self-described "comforting food" is deliciously rendered (salmon with a pepper crust and lemon butter; phyllo stuffed with spinach, mushrooms, and feta cheese), and the heavenly dessert table takes center stage. The crowd is a mix of gays, lesbians, and straights and includes neighborhood types, folks celebrating special occasions, and syrupy first-date couples. ♦ New American ♦ M-F, lunch and dinner; Sa, dinner; Su, brunch and dinner. Reservations recommended. 1708 Lombard St (between S 17th and S 18th Sts). 546.6230. www.theastralplane.com

17 ALEXANDER INN

$$ Large, with 49 rooms, but boasting the intimacy of a bed-and-breakfast, this hostelry comes highly recommended by local vendors as a gay-friendly place to lay your head at the end of a long day of visiting. It is well equipped for business travelers, with fax and modem ports in all rooms, and newly furnished in Art Deco style. There's no restaurant, but a deluxe continental breakfast buffet is included. ♦ 301 E 12th St (at Spruce St). 923.3535; fax 923.1004. www.alexanderinn.com

18 READING TERMINAL MARKET

Situated in the former **Reading Train Shed**, this sprawling, cheerfully chaotic market built in 1892 is anything but your typical food court. Sure, there are stalls aplenty offering all manner of tempting edibles—from the quintessential Philly hoagie to authentic Pennsylvania Dutch treats (including the very best soft pretzels on earth), but fresh produce, meats, fish, and fabulous baked goods are also on sale. This is a favorite Saturday destination for guppie male and female couples doing their week's food

---

Restaurants/Clubs: Red | Hotels: Purple | Shops: Orange | Outdoors/Parks: Green | Sights/Culture: Blue

shopping or brunching at the aptly named **Down Home Diner**. Gay-owned **Salumeria** features Italian deli delights and prepared food, and lesbian-owned **Vorspeise** has wonderful—and heavily vegetarian—goodies. ◆ M-Sa. N 12th St (between Filbert and Arch Sts). 922.2317. ♿. www.readingterminalmarket.org

19 AIDS INFORMATION NETWORK LIBRARY

People with AIDS and interested parties have come here since 1987 to take advantage of one of the world's largest (and free) collections of HIV/AIDS books, periodicals, videos, and brochures. Together with its Oasis database, all these media provide a wealth of information on political issues, drug research, service providers, referrals, prevention/education, nutrition, and more. Many books and videos can be taken out on loan. The Oasis database is also available to those outside Philadelphia by dialing 561.1941. ◆ M, F; Tu, Th, Sa, noon-5PM; W, noon-7PM. 1211 Chestnut St (between S 12th and S 13th Sts), seventh floor. 575.1110; fax 575.1123. www.critpath.org/docs/33resource.html

20 SPARACINO MENS

This shop features cool, retro men's duds, including a line by Ben Sherman, the godfather of '60s fashion, and lines by Park and

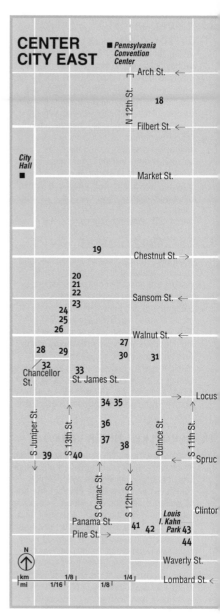

CENTER CITY EAST

■ *Pennsylvania Convention Center*

> Back in Philly, it was rough. If you were a queen and you wanted to carry a purse, you'd better have a .38 in it.
>
> —John Bowman
> former Philadelphia resident

Mark Segal, now publisher of *Philadelphia Gay News*, made his own news in the 1970s by crashing Walter Cronkite's *CBS Evening News* broadcast. Upset about the character Lamont's limp-wristed fag act in the hit comedy *Sanford & Son*. Segal actually sat on Walt's desk with a sign that read, "Gays protest CBS bigotry." He was immediately arrested and fined $400, but thanks to his courage, CBS began consulting gay activists when presenting homo topics, and the news division increased its coverage of the gay and lesbian community.

In 1959, gay real estate developer Mel Heifetz sued the city and police commissioner Frank Rizzo for closing down Philadelphia's "bohemian" coffeehouses.

> The most beautiful thing there is, is a naked man.
> —Thomas Eakins
> 19th-century Philadelphia painter

Ronen, and Verge. ◆ M-Sa, 11AM-8PM; Su, 11AM-6PM. 115 S 13th St (between Sansom and Chestnut Sts). 922.4211

21 OPEN HOUSE

Shop here for innovative home, garden, and body accoutrements—the kind of great stuff you won't find at every chain home décor store in town. ◆ M-F, 11AM-7PM; Sa, 11AM-8PM; Su, noon-5PM. 107 S 13th St (between Sansom and Chestnut Sts). 922.1415

22 CAPOGIRO

The creamiest gelato is made here fresh daily in 27 flavors both traditional and original, from nutello and pistachio to bitter chocolate, spearmint, and blood orange. It's habit-forming. ♦ M-Th, 7:30AM-11:30PM; F-Sa, 8AM-1AM; Su, 1PM-9PM. 119 S 13th St (between Sansom and Chestnut Sts). 351.0900

23 EL VEZ

★★★$$ El Vez is a trendy take on regional Mexican food. Tableside guacamole-making, a huge margarita menu, and delicious rare tuna tostadas owe it all to the deft talents of chef José Garces in the kitchen. The bar scene is happening, the margaritas are shaken, never stirred, and seating is first come, first served. ♦ 121 S 13th St (at Sansom St). 928.9800

24 LOLITA'S

★★$$ Lesbian chef Marcie Turney, who used to be in the kitchen at Valanni, is now creating contemporary Mexican dishes at this intimate café, done up in sultry red and black against a backdrop of exposed brick walls. Specialties include grilled salmon with apple-wood-smoked bacon and chipotle-garlic grilled beef tenderloin. This BYOB is also BYOT—as in bring your own tequila. For $10, you'll get a pitcher of freshly squeezed margarita mix to add to your agave juice of choice. Turney owns the restaurant with her partner Valerie Safran. The pair also own **OpenHouse** (see page 166). ♦ Su-Th, 5PM-10:30PM; F-Sa, 5PM-11PM. Cash only. 106 S 13th St (between Walnut and Sansom Sts). 546.7100

25 CLUB BODY CENTER

♂ If a night at **Woody's** (see opposite) doesn't yield a date, sample some of the tasty local morsels in circulation at this very 1990s bathhouse, conveniently situated one block away. On four levels are 57 small, private rooms (a few with TV/VCRs); two video lounges; a masseur; a snack room with sodas, munchies, and microwaved burgers for sale; a sauna and steam room; lockers; and free condoms. Oh, and a workout area whose Universal equipment and free weights do actually see some use. The crowd peaks on weekend nights (when you're also more likely to see some young'uns; otherwise, the regulars tend toward the "big daddy" types, 40 and up). ♦ Admission. Daily, 24 hours. 120 S 13th St (between Walnut and Sansom Sts), second floor. 735.7671. www.clubbodycenter.com/philly.htm

26 HOLIDAY INN EXPRESS MIDTOWN

$$ Sure, this is a typical Holiday Inn, but think location: It's steps away from **Woody's** (see below) and much of the bar scene and really convenient to restaurants, theaters, and shopping. It's especially popular during Pride, circuit parties, and other such blowouts. Besides 166 rooms, the property offers an outdoor pool, valet parking, and workout privileges at nearby **Bally's** health club. There's no restaurant. ♦ 1305 Walnut St (between S 13th and S Juniper Sts). 735.9300; fax 732.2682. ♿ www.holidayinn.com

27 12TH STREET GYM

♂ It's not easy being beautiful, as the lean and ♀ (occasionally) mean prove at this popular workout spot. A former Turkish bathhouse has been transformed into a modern eight-level facility with a full Hammer Strength Body Circuit, an indoor pool, sauna, steam room, massage center, tanning beds, classes galore, and of course, a café. The clientele and atmosphere are as gay and lesbian as the day is long, and the roof deck in summer has more Speedos than the US Olympic swim team does. Daily, weekly, and monthly rates are available (lockers included). ♦ M-F, 5:30AM-11PM; Sa, Su, 8AM-7PM. 204 S 12th St (between St. James and Walnut Sts). 985.4092. www.12streetgym.com

28 KEY WEST

♂ Once one of Philadelphia's most happening ♀ clubs, in recent years this place has been eclipsed by **Woody's** (see below). On weekends, though, it's still a busy part of the loop, with a convenient location just off the **13th Street** queer zone. The five-bar complex features a game room, a large dance floor, and **Key West For Her**, a women's space with a cheesy pseudo-tropical motif (a bit of neon and some stuffed parrots). The crowd is more diverse than elsewhere, with a higher percentage of African-American patrons and a less pretentious attitude. ♦ Cover. M-Sa, 4PM-2AM; Su, 2PM-2AM. 207 S Juniper St (between Chancellor and Walnut Sts). 545.1578

29 WOODY'S

♂ Lots of guys who know nothing else about the scene in Philadelphia have heard of this place, and lots of locals agree that this is gay ground zero. They come from miles around for the crowds and the cruise quotient, whereas others avoid the joint for the very same reasons. *Mobbed*, in fact, is the word for the downstairs bar, where the boys play pool and

---

scarf down such all-American delights as meat loaf. Upstairs, the video bar doles out campy clips, and there's a cybercafé (free!), while the city's largest gay disco, done in a catchy Greco-Roman motif (faux frescoes and all), positively throbs with shirtless gods in the flesh. Spring chickens predominate, especially on Wednesday, all-ages night (18+), but there's a good helping of hot older dudes too. ♦ Disco: cover. M-Sa, 11AM-2AM; Su, noon-2AM. 202 S 13th St (between Chancellor and Walnut Sts). 545.1893. www.woodysbar.com

30 MILLENNIUM COFFEE

★$ In the very heart of Philadelphia's gayest nabe, the clientele at this popular café is as stylish as the postindustrial décor. That doesn't translate to cozy, comfy seating—but who cares? In good weather, the French doors open for fab people watching (and plenty of it, with the **12th Street Gym** on one side and **Afterwords** on the other). There's a good range of caffeinated brews, along with fresh-squeezed juices, tasty sandwiches (try the goat-cheese-and-roasted-pepper variety), soups, and baked treats. ♦ Café ♦ M-F, 7:30AM-midnight; Sa, Su, 10AM-midnight. 212 S 12th St (between St. James and Walnut Sts). 731.9798

31 BIKE STOP

♂
♀ Don't let the Harley hanging front and center fool you: The scene here is more grunge than tough. Grunge before it was hip, in fact, and these days, grungier still. The place attracts a mostly male crowd to its first-floor bar and second-floor sports bar (complete with pool table and dartboard). On the third floor is a medium-size disco that attracts some women as well. Hipsters and boys with too much cologne should head straight to **Woody's** (see

page 167)—the scene here is more Budweiser and Camels than Stoli and Ecstasy. ♦ Bar: M-F; Su, noon-2AM; Sa, 1PM-2AM. Disco: F, Sa, 9PM-2AM. 206 Quince St (between Locust and Walnut Sts). 627.1662. www.thebikestop.com

32 SISTERS RESTAURANT & NIGHTCLUB

♀ Philadelphia's only full-time women's club attracts every kind of lesbian—from lipstick to butch and beyond—with a few men thrown in for good measure. The main bar-restaurant serves good salads, sandwiches, and snacks under fluorescent Warholesque paintings of Annie Lennox, k.d. lang, Marlene Dietrich, and other female icons. The Sunday brunch is a real steal. Upstairs is a wooden dance floor flanked by two large bars; down in the basement, the ladies shoot pool and play video games. ♦ M-Sa, 4PM-2AM; Su, noon-2AM. 1320 Chancellor St (between S 13th and S Juniper Sts). 735.0735. sistersnightclub.com

33 PURE

♂ This after-hours club offers some of the city's hottest dancing, but no booze. Not that that bothers the buff twentysomething crowd, many of whom are high on Ecstasy and couldn't drink anyway. Unfortunately, this is a private club with a strict membership policy, so if you want to join the party, make a friend somewhere else (or hang out by the door) so he can sponsor you. A note for history buffs: once upon a time, this dark and narrow space housed a chi-chi supper club where Ol' Blue Eyes himself performed. ♦ M-Th, Su, midnight-3AM; F, 10PM-3AM; Sa, 11PM-3AM. 1221 St. James St (between S Camac and S 13th Sts). 735.5772

34 UNCLES UPSTAIRS INN

♂
♀ $ What it's upstairs from is a neighborhoody gay men's bar that's done up in *Miami Vice* colors and glass bricks. This pleasant bed-and-breakfast for gays and lesbians has six rooms tastefully appointed in soothing shades of hunter green, cream, and burgundy; some offer fireplaces and all have private baths, air conditioning, and cable TV. The continental breakfast is complimentary. Noise from the bar is not a big problem, but the extra-sensitive might note that the third-floor rooms are the quietest. ♦ Bar: daily, 11AM-2AM. 1220 Locust St (at S Camac St). 546.6660; fax 546.1653. www.unclesinn.com

35 BUMP

♂ Philadelphia's newest bar is a luxe lounge with an after-hours restaurant and juice bar on Friday and Saturday nights and a "beef

Local daughter and Homophile Action League member Barbara Gittings made an early mark by founding the first East Coast chapter of the Daughters of Bilitis in New York in 1958 and later editing the group's newsletter, *The Ladder* (illustrated with photos by her pseudonymous lover, "Kay Tobin"). Gittings also helped organize the Annual Reminders and was a cofounder of the National Gay Task Force, now the National Lesbian and Gay Task Force.

In 1975, the state of Pennsylvania became the first government to establish a committee to address the concerns of sexual minorities, and in 1982, Philadelphia passed one of the very first civil rights ordinances in the US covering sexual orientation.

THE BEST

Ed Hermance

Owner, Giovanni's Room

Philadelphia is a beautiful old city best seen on foot. On a fine day, take a walk to **Independence Hall** (where the first national demonstrations for "homosexual rights" took place every 4 July starting in 1965). Next, head to **Franklin Court**, with his bookstore on the street, the printing plant in the first courtyard, and the steel outline of the house with underground museum behind—a typical arrangement for fine colonial living. Then go to **Christ Church Cathedral**, which, together with Independence Hall, is the most beautiful colonial building in town. If you walk the block of **Church Street** to **Third Street**, you will be in the center of **Old City** and its dozens of art galleries. The neighborhood will give you some feeling of what life was like in the 19th century.

Another walk is to **Pennsylvania Hospital**, the first hospital in British North America. The central early-19th-century pavilion has a truncated dome covered with glass, under which is the country's first operating theater. The theater was the scene of some of Thomas Eakins's most famous paintings. Across the street is a beautiful brownstone mansion with a garden along the west side. This house is the setting for the wonderful gay novel *Closing Distance*. Pick up a snack to eat in **Louis I. Kahn Park**, named after the architect. For a more substantial lunch, you might try **More Than Just Ice Cream**—it's famous for its gigantic desserts.

Quince Street is one of the many tiny streets that give Philadelphia its distinctive flavor. On Quince is the **Mask and Wig Club**, a jewel-box, gilt-and-red-plush theater that has hosted drag performances by **University of Pennsylvania** students since the 19th century. Continuing on Quince and crossing **Spruce Street**, you'll be among an exceptionally fine collection of trinities (three-story houses, each floor a single room). Originally housing the simplest citizens, trinities have sometimes been doubled and survive as middle-class homes on very serene streets. Another block along Quince takes you past the **Bike Stop**, the city's principal leather bar and its café.

Rittenhouse Square is the city's fanciest and most beautiful urban address. It has been called the most successful public park in the country because of the wide variety of people who use it at all hours. You'll need a Philadelphian to tell you gay stories about the square. A famous spot for high tea is the **Rittenhouse Hotel**, directly across the square. From the square, head to **Delancey Place** and you'll be in the heart of high-society Philadelphia as it was just after the Civil War. These handsome town houses conform with Philadelphia's Quaker modesty, yet they are huge. To see the interior of one of these houses, you can visit the **Rosenbach Museum and Library**.

For a rainy day, start at the **Reading Terminal Market** for lunch—try the gay-owned **Salumeria**, the lesbian-owned **Vorspeise**, or the fine foods of the **Down Home Diner**. For a snack, have a soft pretzel at the Amish stand toward the north end.

Then dash to the **Pennsylvania Academy of Fine Arts**, a very fine example of post-Civil War architecture and the home of the first art museum in the country—the **Museum of American Art**. The museum has a special connection to Thomas Eakins, creator of those gay icons, *The Swimming Hole* and his rowing pictures. You can see his portrait of *Walt Whitman* at the **Philadelphia Museum of Art**.

On a nice day, take the ferry across the **Delaware River** to **Camden, New Jersey**, and visit the **Walt Whitman House**. Many people took the ferry to visit Walt, among them Oscar Wilde, Edward Carpenter (the first person to advocate gay rights in the English language), and Thomas Eakins. Walt too liked to ride the ferry, watching the boatmen, then ride the street cars along **Chestnut Street** in Philadelphia.

and drag" brunch on Sundays featuring drag queens and body builders. Tuesday-through-Friday happy hour features a $2 martini menu and lots of after-work eye candy. ♦ Tu-Su, 5PM-2AM. 1234 Locust St (between S 12th and S Camac Sts). 732.1800

36 TAVERN ON CAMAC

♂ One of the city's oldest gay bars, this cozy spot features show tune singalongs and a friendly crowd of mostly older martini drinkers. For those not in the mood for Broadway, head upstairs, where you'll find alt entertainment, from drag queen cabaret to disco dancing with go-go boys. ♦ Daily, 11:30AM-2AM. 243 S Camac St (between Spruce and Locust Sts). 545.0900

37 THE INN PHILADELPHIA

★★$$ Historic is the mood (and the crowd, some would say) in this colonial-ish charmer on one of old Philadelphia's quaint back streets. The well-heeled gay and straight crowd swears by chef Harlan Russell, who serves up a mouth-watering rack of lamb, not to mention wonderful Louisiana crab cakes. The service, by the warm fireplace or under the stars, can be as starched as the white linen tablecloths, but the bar is a friendly spot that becomes gayer by the hour, especially on weekend nights when there's live piano music featuring show tunes and pop classics. ♦ Continental/American ♦ M-Sa, dinner; Su, brunch and dinner. 251-53 S Camac St (between Spruce and Locust Sts). 732.2339. www.innphiladelphia.com

Restaurants/Clubs: Red | Hotels: Purple | Shops: Orange | Outdoors/Parks: Green | Sights/Culture: Blue

A GAYTRIP TO NEW HOPE

Who said *gay* and *country* don't go together? For quiet getaways, Philadelphia's pink-triangle crowd flocks to the **Bucks County** enclave of **New Hope**—funky, artsy, but definitely not hot like Provincetown or Fire Island. Once the weekend playground of New York sophisticates like Dorothy Parker, Oscar Hammerstein, and Moss Hart, New Hope is splendidly set along the leafy banks of the **Delaware River** about a 45-minute drive north of **Center City** on **I-95** and **Route 32**. Even its hard-core fans wouldn't call it exciting—and some mean queens have gone so far as to dub it No Hope because the gay and lesbian doings here are pretty much limited to two main venues. In fact, same-sexers are just one part of the picture in this square-mile village, sharing the pretty streets, shops, restaurants, and guest houses with suburbanites away from the kids for the night, teenagers hanging out down on **Main Street**, and assorted city slickers taking a break from the slick city.

With only four major streets (Main, **Bridge**, **Ferry**, and **Mechanic**), New Hope is delightfully strollable. Unfortunately, most weekends the streets are packed with tourists. (The best time to beat the hordes is in the winter and early spring.) Bring lots of plastic, as shopping and eating are the two top activities in town (not counting snuggling). For the former, there's a whole range of possibilities, from potpourri and other conventional country kitsch to the more outré. Check out, for example, **Mystickal Tymes** (127 S Main St, south of E Mechanic Street; 862.5629; www.mystickaltymes. com), a positive witchcraft shop with a welcoming

rainbow flag out front. No eye of newt here, but there are some lovely copper cauldrons, candles, jewelry, essential oils, and the like. (They claim, incidentally, that New Hope is the "most positively charged vortex" in the world.) From wicca to Whitman, it's just a hop and skip down the street to **Farley's Bookshop** (44 S Main Street, at Ferry Street; 862.2452), a cluttered, cozy emporium with more than 70,000 titles in stock. Tomes overflow onto the timeworn floor, and the homo-friendly staff will point you to the lavender section. **Book Gallery** (19 W Mechanic Street, between S Main and New Streets; 862.5110) is much smaller but also has a good assortment of authors gay and lesbian. The congenial **Ember Glo** shop (27 W Mechanic Street, between S Main and New Streets; 862.2929) sells gay and lesbian cards, homo supplies, and rainbow everything, from jewelry to windsocks.

For the second favorite pastime, it's good to know that most local eateries are queer-friendly, even if their clientele is mostly straight. Gay-favorite spots include **Karla's** (★$$; 5 W Mechanic Street, between S Main and New Streets; 862.2612), a romantic, sunny bistro with rattan chairs, cute waiters, and lots of plants. Lunch here is burgers and sandwiches, whereas dinner features an interesting mélange of world cuisines. After a night at the bars, it's *the* place to be seen; breakfast is served on Friday and Saturday between 12:30AM and 4AM. **Martine's** (★$$; 7 E Ferry Street, at S Main Street; 862.2966) offers pasta, filet mignon *au poivre*, and succulent duckling in a cozy, Old Worldish setting, whereas **Wildflowers** (★$; 8 W Mechanic Street;

---

37 VENTURE INN

★$ Discreetly tucked away in a narrow alley, this place has history—not just as the oldest gay bar in town but also for its earlier incar-

In 1685, Philadelphia had seven licensed taverns. The oldest was the Blue Anchor, the first building William Penn saw when his barge landed on the low, sandy beach at the mouth of Dock Street on the Delaware River.

The first female employee of the federal government was hired in Philadelphia in 1795.

Fox Chase Farm in the Fox Chase section is the city's last working farm. The 115-acre farm is owned by the city and is open to the public at certain times of the year. For more information, call 671.0440.

nations as home to the legendary Barrymore show business clan and as a 19th-century stop on the underground railroad. While evil queens do refer to this joint as the "denture," for a clientele that allegedly remembers those days well, it really does attract a (mostly male) crowd of all ages for its friendly bar and restaurant menu of pot roast, shrimp scampi, and filet mignon. The ambiance, especially at the bar, is dark and clubby. ♦ American ♦ Restaurant: M-Sa, dinner; Su, brunch and dinner. Bar: daily, noon-2AM. 255 S Camac St (between Spruce and Locust Sts). 545.8731. www.gayreading.com/Travel /Camac/VentureMenu/venturemenu.htm

38 12TH AIR COMMAND

Butch boys cruise the downstairs bar amid leftover mirrors and lighting from the joint's previous life as **Hepburn's** lesbian nightclub. (In the 1970s, it also housed the storied club **Equus**, which disco queens of yore may

862.2241) serves bargain lunches and homey dinners like chili and meat loaf) in a kitschy dining room or outside overlooking **Ingham Creek**. Fish gotta swim, birds gotta fly, and cabaret queens gotta flock to **Odette's** (S Main Street and Route 232; 862.3000) for fabulous (and often nationally known) acts. More than a few homosexuals also patronize the venerable **Bucks County Playhouse** (70 S Main Street, at E Mechanic Street; 862.2041), which stages old warhorses like *Annie Get Your Gun*, *Funny Girl*, and *My Fair Lady* in a former grist mill. (If you're lucky, you'll catch Loretta Swit—Hot Lips from *M*A*S*H*—or some other sitcom luminary.) It was this theater, in fact, that helped trigger the influx of gays to the area when it was built in 1939.

For snuggling with that someone special (or your pillow), try the **Fox & Hound** ($$; 246 W Bridge Street, between Main Street and Highway 202; 862.5082, 800/862.5082; fax 862.5082), set in an 1850s stone farmhouse with a barn and lush formal garden. The setting is homey but not too fussy, and gay innkeeper Dennis Cianci is a known pusher of homemade brownies. He also offers five rooms—some with fireplaces, all with private bath. Breakfast is served in a pleasant dining room with French doors. Another option—modern and comfortable yet charming—is a stroll across the **Lambertville–New Hope Free Bridge**: the **Inn at Lambertville Station** ($$$; 11 Bridge Street, at the Delaware River; 609/397.4400, 800/524.1091; fax 397.9744) boasts 45 rooms nicely furnished with antiques.

Just down the street from the Fox & Hound is a bunkhouse of a rather different sort. One of two gay

complexes in town, the **Raven Hall** ($; 385 W Bridge Street; 862.2081) bundles a 1950s-style motel with a restaurant (★$$), several bars, and an outdoor pool. The 17 motel rooms may be charmless, but they have all the essentials, as well as a social, even cruisy scene. The atmosphere in the dark-paneled main bar is heavy on the male hormones, with a loud, boozy, but friendly crowd. Outdoors, the scene's still cruisy but quieter, with the boys in their Speedos eyeing each other by the poolside bar. B-movie queen Arlene Dahl and talk show maven Sally Jessy Raphael have been known to pop in to the Victorian-style dining room, warmed by fireplaces and overlooking a pleasant garden and aviary. Lesbians join the boys here for the likes of roasted garlic–rosemary ravioli and pork sundance with corn salsa.

A few miles away, the **Cartwheel** center (437 Old York Road/Highway 202; 862.0880) offers good dining and the area's most hopping nightlife. **Café Mo** (★$), located in a 300-year-old farmhouse at the front of the complex, has an eclectic menu amid a Southwest motif. Here the food ranges from comfort (chicken-fried steak) to passably creative (fresh baked salmon with crispy potato crust). Dishing it up at the large bar and dance floor is a mixed gay and lesbian crowd, along with a few straights. There's also an outdoor deck and the intimate **Q-Lounge**, with an unusual terrazzo-like stone floor.

For more information, and even last-minute room reservations, stop at the **New Hope Information Center** (1 W Mechanic Street, at S Main Street; 862.5880, 862.5030; fax 862.5245). It's open daily.

---

recall.) Adjacent is a compact café serving dinner, and upstairs is a nondescript disco with more mirrors and a mix of dance and house tunes. ◆ Daily, 4PM-2AM. 254 S 12th St (between Spruce and Locust Sts). 545.8088. ₿. www.12thair.com

39 WILLIAM WAY LESBIAN, GAY, BISEXUAL, AND TRANSGENDER COMMUNITY CENTER

♂
♀ The center's spacious new home in the former **Engineers' Club** offers plenty of room for all sorts of events and services, groups, coffee hours, and concerts featuring lesbian and gay performers. Bookworms will love the new library and archives, and for slow nights, there's even gay bingo. ◆ M-Th, 6-10PM; F, for scheduled events; Sa, 11AM-5PM; Su, 5-9PM. 1315 Spruce St (between S 13th and Juniper S Sts). 732.2220. ₿. www.waygay.org

40 WESTBURY BAR

♂ Brick walls and a fireplace make for a cozy watering hole for the thirtysomething-to-fortysomething set. The sandwiches, soups, and Sunday brunch are decent, but the real draw is a comfy place to hang with the neighborhood boys. It's not cliquish, though, and a tourist face is always welcomed. The fab jukebox ranges from disco divas to country queens, with the requisite videos on several television monitors. ◆ M-Sa, 10AM-2AM; Su, 11AM-2AM. 261 S 13th St (at Spruce St). 546.5170. ₿. www.thewestburybar.com

41 GIOVANNI'S ROOM

♂
♀ Nationally known as one of America's best and largest gay and lesbian bookstores—or as owner Ed Hermance puts it, "the grandest"—this shop offers a varied selection of fiction and nonfiction, CDs, tapes, and magazines.

Restaurants/Clubs: Red | Hotels: Purple | Shops: Orange | Outdoors/Parks: Green | Sights/Culture: Blue

A WALT WHITMAN PILGRIMAGE

After a stroke that left him partly paralyzed, poet Walt Whitman, who wrote so stirringly of the "love of comrades" in his celebrated and controversial *Leaves of Grass*, moved in 1870 to **Camden, New Jersey**, a small (and today rather depressed) city across the **Delaware River** from Philadelphia. Between 1884 and his death in 1892, he lived in a modest wood-frame row house (330 Mickle Boulevard, between S Fourth and S Third Streets; 609/964.5383) that is now open to the public. Here, old Walt entertained celebrities of the time, including the flamboyant Oscar Wilde. Edward Carpenter, one of the earliest gay rights advocates, also stopped by to pay homage—though Whitman himself preferred to beat around the bush regarding his own sexual orientation, at least publicly.

On display at the house are original furniture (including Whitman's rocking chair), many of his letters, and the earliest known photo (1848) of the great man. A half-century after his passing, he sparked controversy yet again when local officials decided to name a new bridge spanning the Delaware in his honor. Some Catholics protested, citing Whitman's anticlerical philosophy and celebration of the body. The authorities held their ground, and the **Walt Whitman Bridge** opened in 1957.

To reach the house, drive over the **Benjamin Franklin Bridge**, or follow the route of Walt's old ferryboat on the **Riverbus** (S Columbus Boulevard, between Spruce and Chestnut Streets). Get off at the **Aquarium** stop and walk three blocks east on **Mickle Boulevard**. The house is open Wednesday through Saturday, 10AM to noon and 1 to 5PM, and Sunday, 1 to 4PM; there's no admission charge.

Ensconced in two town houses since 1979, today it's a series of cozy rooms with 20,000 titles on seemingly every topic, from travel to erotica, coming out to feminism, theater to spirituality. Big-name authors like Urvashi Vaid, Kathleen Forrest, Martin Duberman, and Greg Louganis stop by regularly for readings, and it can also be an excellent place to find out what's up in gay Philadelphia. ♦ M-Tu, Th, 11:30AM-9PM; W, 11:30AM-7PM; F, 11:30AM-10PM; Sa, 10AM-10PM; Su, 1PM-7PM. 345 S 12th St (at Pine St). 923.2960. www.giovannisroom.com

41 ANTIQUE ROW BED & BREAKFAST

$ The six homey rooms (some with private bath) and small apartment at this bargain spot offer such amenities as Oriental rugs, air conditioning, telephones, and TVs—as well as a full breakfast and a friendly welcome from owner Barbara Pope. Hanging out in her cozy, book-lined living room is encouraged, but those on the make, take note: Tricks spending the night aren't. ♦ 341 S 12th St (between Pine and Spruce Sts). 592.7802; fax 592.9692. www.antiquerowbnb.com

42 MORE THAN JUST ICE CREAM

★$ The wrought-iron chairs can be murder on the back, but that doesn't keep the boys (and some girls) away from this charming, old-fashioned ice-cream parlor. Skip the standard sandwiches and entrées in favor of the sweet treats, especially the humongous homemade apple pie à la mode (big enough for you, your current squeeze, and a few exes). Or hit the take-out counter and take your goodies out to nearby **Louis I. Kahn Park** (see page 173). ♦ Café ♦ M-F, 11AM-11:30PM; Sa, 10AM-11:30PM; Su, 9AM-11:30PM. 1141 Pine St (between Quince and S 12th Sts). 574.0586

B-3: An addition to the gay-borhood—Marketing types working for hotshot New York developer Tony Goldman, who helped turn around SoHo and South Beach, have branded the neighborhood B-3, as in "blocks below Broad," but the name hasn't quite made the popular lexicon. No matter what you call it, B-3 is the trendiest neighborhood in town, and it's just up the street from Woody's. Loosely defined as a grid of streets between 11th and Broad Streets, E/W, and Chestnut to Locust Streets, N/S, B-3 is home to snazzy retail, a handful of restaurants and cafés, and newly redone loft apartments that are drop-dead gorgeous.

The Philadelphia Live Arts Festival and the Philly Fringe (413.1318, 410.9000; www.pafringe.org) is an audaciously in-your-face festival held at the beginning of September, featuring avant-garde performances, some 700 in all, many with a decidedly queer perspective. Spoken word, cabaret, dance—it's all performed both in traditional venues and on street corners, in cars, galleries, cabarets, and restaurants. Gay artists make a prominent contribution every year.

43 LOUIS I. KAHN PARK

Named in honor of the local renowned architect, this tiny urban green space is a pleasant oasis in the heart of the gayest 'hood—and therefore popular with the boys and girls. With its benches and tables, it's more of a hangout for friends sharing treats from **More Than Just Ice Cream** (see page 172) than a spot to cruise. Despite that, the mobile "scenery" can be breathtaking. ♦ S 11th and Pine Sts. ♿. kahnpark.homestead.com

44 ABOUT THE BEAT RECORDS

The display window festooned with disco balls of various sizes says it all: For club queens who boogie around the clock, this is the place to buy dance music of all stripes, from high-energy to house to progressive. Co-owner Brian Norwood is a professional DJ who is making a name for himself on the gay party circuit. There's also a kaboodle of industrial sunglasses, bags, T-shirts, and other must-have accessories for the painfully hip. ♦ M-Sa, noon-9PM; Su, noon-6PM. 1106 Pine St (between S 11th and Quince Sts). 351.2328. www.aboutthebeat.com

Restaurants/Clubs: Red | Hotels: Purple | Shops: Orange | Outdoors/Parks: Green | Sights/Culture: Blue

DAY TRIPS

Philadelphia's cultural and historical breadth extends far beyond the Liberty Bell and Independence Hall, into the rolling green hills of the surrounding countryside. A host of must-see attractions are within a 90-minute drive in any direction from downtown.

West of Philadelphia is the famous **Main Line**, more a way of life than a tourist attraction. Upscale incomes support the area's beautiful homes, fine boutiques, new-concept retail stores, and the largest mall on the East Coast. A cultural highlight is the notoriously eccentric **Barnes Foundation**, which holds one of the world's largest private collections of Impressionist paintings and decorative African art and artifacts.

The Main Line is of particular interest to history buffs as well: It was from here that George Washington's spies monitored British activity in Philadelphia while the Revolutionary army was encamped at **Valley Forge**. Today, the quiet **Valley Forge National Historical Park**—marked by statues, memorials, and open fields where visitors are free to roam—is one of the region's most popular recreation areas.

Farther west and northwest of Philadelphia are **Lancaster County** and **Reading**, a shopaholic's idea of bliss, with 300-plus discount outlet stores. Lancaster offers much more than a change of scenery—it's almost a change of century, with Amish and Mennonite farm families dressed in traditional garb and living without electricity or indoor plumbing. Amish country provides a rare chance to examine an iconoclastic culture in the backyard of a big city.

Head east for the glitter and pizzazz of **Atlantic City**, the Las Vegas of the East Coast and a real hoot whether you're a gambler or just an admirer of over-the-top kitsch. This New Jersey resort town bops 24 hours a day, and it's never too early or late for a champagne cocktail or a roll of the dice. Big-name stars perform in the nightclubs, and virtually everyone strolls on the boardwalk, which at midday can seem as crowded as Calcutta. In addition to the casino life, the seaside city and its environs offer some of the East Coast's broadest sand beaches and excellent ocean swimming. And if you'd rather not take your chances with Lady Luck, consider a peaceful weekend unwinding in **Cape May**, a windswept resort town known for its lacy Victorian architecture.

To the south of Philadelphia lie the rolling hills and horse farms of the **Brandywine Valley**, a suburb both of Philadelphia and of Wilmington, Delaware. The valley's genteel estates, mannered country gardens, and subtle natural beauty inspired many of the paintings of N.C., Andrew, and Jamie Wyeth. The world-famous du Pont family also left its mark on the area: Their formal **Longwood Gardens** rival those of Versailles, and their collection of 18th- and 19th-century American furnishings at the **Winterthur** mansion is among the foremost in the country.

To the north, the wooded seclusion of **Bucks County** offers escape from the hectic pace of both Philadelphia and New York City. Once the favorite country getaway of Oscar Hammerstein, the Algonquin's roundtable gang, and many other famous names in the arts, the county's chic country-politan atmosphere still attracts the literati. Towns such as **New Hope** and **Lambertville, New Jersey**, successfully blend lovely riverside settings with fine dining and deluxe bed-and-breakfast inns. Bucks is a great place to gallery-hop, and the country nightlife is just as hip as in the big city. For the kids, the county offers **Sesame Place**, the world's only amusement park inspired by educational television.

THE MAIN LINE

...ke L.A.'s Bel-Air and Cleveland's Shaker Heights, the ...ain Line is American suburbia at its most luxurious. ...osh modern homes and "George Washington Slept ...ere" estates share the quiet, tree-shaded streets of this ...0-mile stretch just west of the city.

...he Main Line is so named because of its location along ...hat was once the main line of the **Pennsylvania** ...ailroad. Today, **SEPTA** runs the trains on what remains ...ne of the busiest segments of commuter railroad in the ...ountry. Known officially as the *Paoli Local*, the Main ...ne train can be boarded in Philadelphia at the **Market ...ast Station** (N 11th and Market Sts), **Suburban ...tation** (John F. Kennedy Blvd, between N 16th and N ...7th Sts), or the stately, refurbished **30th Street ...tation** (N 30th St, between Market and Arch Sts). The ...aoli Local generally runs twice an hour both into and ...ut of town. Call 580.7800 for specific schedules or ...sit www.septa.org.

...or decades, an old-fashioned mnemonic device has ...een used for the names of the communities (and train ...ations) that make up the Main Line: The first letters of ...e words in "**O**ld **M**aids (substitute **M**en if this offends) ...ever **W**ed **A**nd **H**ave **B**abies, **P**eriod" correspond to the ...wns of **O**verbrook, **M**erion, **N**arberth, **W**ynnewood, ...rdmore, **H**averford, **B**ryn **M**awr, and **P**aoli. (Nowadays, ...ome trains make a few additional stops.)

... you're venturing out to the Main Line by car, take ...terstate 76 West from downtown Philadelphia to ...ighway 1 South, then take **Highway 30 West** ...ancaster Ave), which runs parallel to the rail line.

Because of its proximity to Philadelphia, the Main Line differs from the more far-flung wealthy suburbs of other metropolitan areas. This proximity has kept old money near the center of the city, helping Philadelphia maintain a thriving urban core and keeping charity funds flowing to Center City cultural institutions. (The late Main Line communications mogul Walter Annenberg endowed a graduate school at the **University of Pennsylvania**, a research institute downtown, and a gallery at the **Philadelphia Museum of Art**.)

THE BARNES FOUNDATION

The Main Line is relatively light on tourist attractions per se. In fact, the area's biggest draw was never intended to be open to the public. The Barnes Foundation (300 N Latches La, between Old Lancaster and Raynham Rds; 610/667.0290; www.barnesfoundation.org) in **Merion**, a 5-minute walk from the Merion train station, was the private art collection of the late Dr. Albert C. Barnes, an eccentric man who amassed his fortune by inventing an eyewash. Housed in a building designed by **Paul Philippe Cret**, more than 1,000 major works by artists such as Renoir, Cézanne, Matisse, and van Gogh make

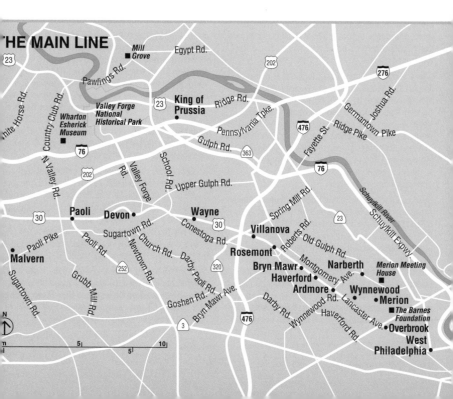

this one of the world's finest displays of 19th- and 20th-century painting. Barnes wanted to keep his masterpieces from the eyes of critics and the public, so he permitted only a select group of students to view his collection. But in 1961, a court order claiming that tax breaks were given to the foundation as an educational institution led the way to limited public access. A $10 million renovation of the building's internal systems improved security, fire protection, and environmental controls. Additions include an audio tour, elevators, and a visitor orientation room explaining the collection's unique history. Call for the gallery schedule; be advised that tickets and parking must be reserved in advance. The **Arboretum** of the Barnes Foundation, which surrounds the main building, is a remarkable 12-acre collection of more than 290 types of plants. The arboretum was designed in 1933 by University of Pennsylvania Professor of Landscape Architecture Frank Schrepfer. It's particularly notable for its Asian specimens, including the Korean boxwood, the paperback maple, and the rare handkerchief tree. Radios and sports equipment are forbidden in the gardens. The admission charge to the gallery includes the arboretum. There is talk about the collection moving to a freestanding museum on the Benjamin Franklin Parkway, a hotly disputed issue now being considered in court.

Nearby is the pale yellow **Merion Meeting House** (615 Montgomery Ave, at Meeting House La; 610/664.4210; www.pym.org), a 1695 structure where colony founder William Penn once attended worship. A Quaker meeting is still held every Sunday at 11AM and is open to the public.

A few stops beyond Merion, the view from the **Bryn Mawr Station** platform will give you a general idea of the lifestyle in this area. **Bryn Mawr**, along with the other towns on the *Paoli Local* line, is not marked by the generic suburban sprawl that characterizes so much of America; it's more like a small village, with a central civic and business area surrounded by outlying residential areas. The station overlooks a little green public square that houses a dentist's office, a service station, a bank, and a post office.

After a stroll through town, stop for lunch or dinner at **Tango** (39 Morris Ave, between Lancaster and Montgomery Aves; 610/526.9500), directly across from the train station. Once a baggage depot, this chic watering hole is now home to a contemporary American menu, a comfortable dining room done up in warm tones of adobe and Aztec red, and a cozy bar that is always a lively scene. A fireplace in winter and outside seating in summer are added bonuses. Another, for oenophiles, is 100-plus wines by the glass.

Head up Lancaster Avenue to **Borders Books & Music** (Rosemont Sq, 1149 Lancaster Ave, Rosemont; 610/527.1500; also at 80 E Wynnewood Rd, Wynnewood; 610/642.0362; www.borders.com). This national chain's first multimedia store has more than 30,000 square feet filled with books and CDs. Although the pop music section is well stocked, locals flock to the store for its extensive catalog of jazz, classical, and international music. Borders also has an espresso bar and two event spaces—for children and adults—where various authors and musicians present free programs several times a week.

If you're ready for lunch, you're just a few blocks away from **Toscana Cucina Rustica** (24 N Merion Ave, between Lancaster and Montgomery Aves, Bryn Mawr; 610/527.7700), whose menu includes a wonderful antipasto platter and Northern Italian entrées. The setting is so artfully decorated that you'll feel like you've found a Tuscan villa in the heart of the Main Line.

SAVONA

One of the best restaurants in the region, including Center City, is **Savona** in **Gulph Mills** (100 Old Gulph Rd, at Rte 320; 610/520.1200; www.savonarestaurant.com), where the Mediterranean sun is always shining. Chef-owner Dominique Filoni offers a culinary tribute to the French and Italian Rivieras. Take a peek downstairs at the glass-enclosed wine cellar, which stores more than 1,000 international selections—the wine list is 31 pages long.

Finally, don't miss the magnificent **Anthropologie** (201 W Lancaster Ave, at Bellevue Ave, Wayne; 610/687.4141; www.anthropologie.com), the flagship of a growing national chain of eclectic emporiums. The brain child of local entrepreneur Dick Hayne, creator of the Urban Outfitters stores, this stunning Art Deco boutique is housed in a former auto dealership and is decorated with wood planks, granite slabs, and terra-cotta tiles. Coins tossed into the bubbling mosaic fountain are donated to the **Women's Resource Center**. Displays include beds in unusual shapes stacked high with pillows, and chic, politically correct housewares, candles, picture frames, and women's clothing. Spend as little as $3 for a cake of rainbow-hued soap or thousands for an elaborate dried-flower arrangement.

If you're hungry and tired, treat yourself to a gourmet lunch or dinner at **Restaurant Taquet** in the awning-festooned **Wayne Hotel** (139 E Lancaster Ave, between Aberdeen and N Wayne Aves, Wayne; 610/687.5005; www.taquet.com). Fine French cuisine is served at this brasserie; in warm weather, you can dine alfresco. Afterward, you might want to get dessert at **Sweet Daddy's** (N Wayne and Lancaster Aves, Wayne; 610/688.4500), with delectable cakes and candies, as well as a tempting selection of homemade ice creams, sorbets, and gelati.

Georges Perrier, famed chef-owner of Philadelphia's world-renowned **Le Bec-Fin** French restaurant, has gone a little bit country with **Le Mas Perrier** (503 Lancaster Ave, Wayne; 610/964.2588; www.lemasrestaurant.com), an upscale Provençal French eatery in the Main Line. You'll pay top dollar, but the food is divine and the setting drop-dead gorgeous. The bar menu offers the best value, and there's entertainment on weekends.

As you drive back to town, take note of the many educational institutions along **Lancaster Avenue**. **Villanova University**, **Haverford College**, and **Bryn Mawr College** with its Louis I. Kahn–designed **Erdman Hall** dormitory (1960–1965), can be seen along the way.

VALLEY FORGE

Located just 18 miles from downtown Philadelphia, the **Valley Forge National Historical Park** (Rte 23 and N Gulph Rd; 610/783.1077; www.nps.gov/vafo) offers a challenge to the imaginations of tourists and amateur historians alike. During the famed winter encampment of 1777–1778, Washington's Continental Army of 12,000 used virtually all of the 3,500 acres for entrenchments, livestock pens, parade grounds, and 1,000 log cabins.

Today, the area is a vast, rolling blanket of green; the **Visitors' Center**, **Washington's Headquarters**, soldiers' huts, and a handful of simple monuments are the only hints of that momentous winter. Valley Forge tourism peaks in the summer months, when weather conditions are least similar to those faced by Washington's men.

The wide vistas and fields of Valley Forge provide a welcome opportunity for relaxation and play. Kite-flying, sunbathing, playing Frisbee, and playing touch football are common activities here, so don't hesitate to bring along your sporting equipment. The **National Park Service** has even created special jogging and biking paths, used much more by natives than tourists.

The best way to reach the park is by car. Take the **Schuylkill Expressway (Interstate 76)** west from Philadelphia and watch for the signs. **Exit 26B** will put you on **North Gulph** Road for 1.5 miles, leading to the Visitors' Center. Valley Forge can also be reached by SEPTA *Bus 125*, which departs from N 16th Street and JFK Boulevard; however, with stops and a transfer, the trip can take close to 2 hours. Call 580.7800 for bus information.

The Visitors' Center (610/783.1077), a contemporary building that reflects the grassy landscape, includes a modest display of colonial artifacts, a ranger station, and an excellent travelers' reference desk with detailed maps and information on attractions and special events throughout the Philadelphia area. The information is updated frequently, so check them for antiques shows, auctions, or art festivals that coincide with your visit. An expanded gift shop was recently added.

The center's 18-minute film presentation shows the vast expanse of the park in winter and describes the failing health of Washington's poorly clothed and fed troops. The film is especially helpful for children trying to comprehend the historical significance of Valley Forge, as are the costumed reenactments of army training procedures occasionally staged by local organizations. Costumed interpreters at Washington's Headquarters are available 7 days a week to provide information and answer questions.

A self-guided 10-mile driving look whisks around the park's memorial sites, including equestrian statuary; the **National Memorial Arch**, a handsome, quote-covered tribute to the Continental Army; the re-created huts of the Muhlenberg Brigade; and **Wayne's Woods**, a stand of tall pines retrofitted with tables and benches for picnicking. **Washington's Headquarters**, built in 1774 and still standing in its original form, was converted from farm use to serve the general's needs during the war. There is a nominal fee for a brief tour of the interior, which is furnished with period reproductions.

Changes are afoot in the park. The **Valley Forge Historical Society Museum** is to be replaced by the **American**

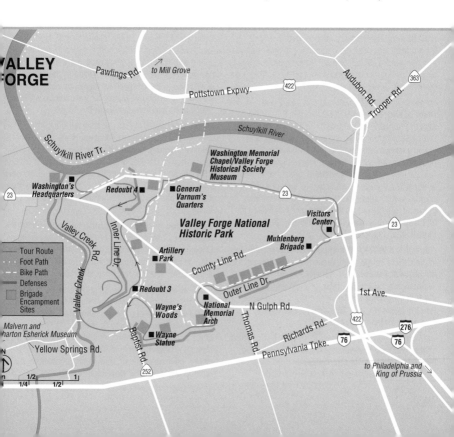

Revolution Center (opening in 2006). A public-private partnership between the National Park Service and the National Center for the American Revolution, this museum will hold more than 11,000 artifacts, weapons, manuscripts, and more—the largest collection of Revolutionary War artifacts in the world. It will be located adjacent to the Visitors' Center.

Washington Memorial Chapel, (610/783-0120; www.libertynet.org/chapel), which commemorates the life of George Washington with rich decorative carvings and stained glass, is the site for free carillon concerts held on Sunday after services. Two miles from Valley Forge is **Mill Grove** (Audubon and Pawlings Rds, Audubon; 610/666.5593; www.montcopa.org/historic sites), a small museum and wildlife preserve on the 130-acre estate of famed colonial-era naturalist John James Audubon. Audubon's informal, naturalistic drawing style—which broke with traditionally formal wildlife art—grew from his observations of birds on the grounds of his father's house, which is now the site of the museum. More than 175 species of birds have been identified here. The museum and grounds are open Tuesday through Sunday; a donation is requested.

Another noteworthy artist's homestead is the **Wharton Esherick Museum** (Horseshoe Tr, off Country Club Rd, Paoli; 610/644.5822; www.levins.com/escherick.html), which comprises the 20th-century master's unique studio and residence. Although formally trained as a painter in Philadelphia, Esherick drew inspiration from his woodland surroundings, first carving elaborate frames for his pictures, then moving on to sculpt the dramatically contoured wooden furniture that made him famous. Located 2 miles west of Valley Forge, Esherick's studio is preserved as it was during his lifetime, with no signs or plaques to detract from the moving sense of the artist at work. The museum may be visited only on guided tours (reservations required); it is open Saturday through Sunday, March through December. Tours available for groups of five or more on weekdays. There's an admission charge.

For those in need of a history break, **The Plaza** and **The Court** at **King of Prussia** (160 N Gulph Rd, at Hwy 202, King of Prussia; The Court: 610/337.1210; The Plaza: 610/265.5727; www.kingofprussiamall.com), the nation's largest retail mall, is just 10 minutes away. Anchored by Macy's, JCPenney, Bloomingdale's, Lord & Taylor, Neiman Marcus, Nordstrom, Sears, and Strawbridge's department stores, this mall includes an additional 400 specialty shops and 35 restaurants, including familiar chains like Bennigan's, Houlihan's, and T.G.I. Friday's, Maggiano's Little Italy, Sullivan's Steakhouse, and more.

Although the **Valley Forge Music Fair** is long gone, top-name entertainment is still presented at venues such as the **Keswick Theatre** (291 Keswick Ave, off N Easton Rd, Glenside; 572.7650; www.keswicktheatre.com) and the **Bob Carpenter Center** (University of Delaware, Newark, Delaware; 302/831.4367). Call 610/644.5000 for more information.

For more serious entertainment in a lovely rustic setting, try the nationally recognized and critically acclaimed **People's Light and Theatre Company** (39 Conestoga Rd, between Hwys 30 and 202, Malvern; 610/644.3500; www.peopleslight.org), which presents an impressive array of drama, from the classics to the cutting edge.

LANCASTER COUNTY

A 90-minute drive west from Philadelphia up **Interstate 76** and the **Pennsylvania Turnpike** leads straight to the heart of Amish country. The hypnotic winding of even the major highways draws you into the Lancaster area, where the air is farm-country fresh and Amish people ride in horse-drawn buggies. Please note that the sect's most traditional factions regard photographs as graven images, forbidden by the Bible. Always ask permission before taking pictures.

To begin your tour of Pennsylvania Dutch Country, take Turnpike exit 286 to Route 272 and begin your exploration of what is known by antiques collectors and enthusiasts countrywide as **"Antiques Alley."** Along this 10-mile stretch of road, you'll find numerous antiques shops—everything from huge antiques malls to small mom-and-pop shops. www.udel.edu/bcc

The area's largest tourist station, the **Pennsylvania Dutch Convention and Visitors' Bureau** (501 Greenfield Rd, a Hwy 30; 717/299.8901; www.padutchcountry.com), is open daily, and offers a multi-image presentation that gives a good overview of local attractions.

For answers to serious questions about the Amish religion and lifestyle, stop at the **Mennonite Information Center** (2209 Millstream Rd, between Strasburg Pike and Lincoln Hwy E, Lancaster; 717/299.0954). The center, which is open daily, offers referrals to Mennonite bed-and-breakfasts in the community and also provides a one-of-a-kind tour guide service. For a fee, a Mennonite guide will accompany you in your car as you drive through the community. There's no need to make advance reservations; the center will set it up while you watch a 20-minute video about the Amish.

Outlet shopping is big in the Lancaster area. Among the biggest and best deep discount spots are the 120-store **Rockvale Square Outlets** (Lincoln Hwy E and Rte 896, Lancaster; 717/293.9595), where everything is 30% to 70% off, and **Tanger Outlet Center** (Hwy 30 E, between Rtes 896 and 462, Lancaster; 717/392.7260), whose 53 shops offer 25% to 65% off retail. Both are open daily.

Around the corner, the new **Lancaster Quilt and Textile Museum** (37 Market St; 717/299.6440; www.quiltand textilemuseum.com) exhibits antique Amish quilts and other textile arts. It's open Monday through Saturday, 10AM-5PM, and Sunday, noon to 5PM.

If and when shops and shopping become too much, head for downtown Lancaster (follow Rte 462) for a refreshing change of pace. The **Lancaster Cultural History Museum** (King and Queen Sts; 717/299.6440) offers a look at the heritage and history of the county through exhibits of furniture, Pennsylvania long rifles, clocks, paintings, folk art, and much, much more. It's open May through mid-November, 10AM-4PM.

stick to **Route 272** to pack as much variety as possible into your 1-day outing. Just 1.5 miles north of the turnpike, stop in Adamstown to tour the award-winning **Stoudt's Brewery** complex (Rte 272, between Main St and Rte 897, Adamstown; 717/484.4385). Throughout the year, about 10 different small-batch brews are created and sold fresh in champagne-style bottles. Pasteurized versions of a golden variety and an Oktoberfest-style variety also are sold throughout the region in conventional 12-ounce bottles. Tours are given Saturday at 3PM and Sunday at 1PM. On Wednesday, Friday, and Sunday nights, there is country dancing in an Oktoberfest-style beer hall. The Stoudt family also operates the **Black Angus** restaurant on-site, where all the beers and an amazing selection of wines are served with locally raised steaks for dinner only. A mall of antiques shops at the complex is open Sunday only.

Continuing south, you can't miss **Doll Express** (Rte 272, between the Pennsylvania Turnpike and Church St; 717/336.2414) in **Reamstown**, a cooperative of more than 100 dealers of collectible dolls, dollhouses, and miniatures who display their wares in a complex including actual freight train cars. It's open Monday, Tuesday, and Thursday through Sunday.

Train enthusiasts should take a detour from Route 272 to the town of **Strasburg**, home of the nation's oldest short-line railroad. At the **Strasburg Railroad** (Rte 741, between Paradise La and Fairview Rd; 717/687.7522), passengers take a 45-minute steam engine train ride on a 9-mile route through the scenic countryside. The train runs daily April through October, and Saturday and Sunday from November through March. Afterward, stop in across the street at the **Railroad Museum of Pennsylvania** (Rte 741, between Paradise La and Bishop Rd; 717/687.8628), a gem for railroad buffs of all ages. The museum has 85 pieces of rolling stock, including two dozen steam locomotives. It's open daily April through October, and Tuesday through Sunday from November through March. There's an admission charge.

Other railroad attractions that are sure to please the kids include the **National Toy Train Museum** (300 Paradise La, between Rte 741 and Fairview Rd, Strasburg; 717/687.8976), with a collection of model trains from 1880 to the present, and the **Red Caboose Restaurant** (312 Paradise La, between Rte 741 and Fairview Rd, Strasburg; 717/687.5001), where you can eat in a Victorian dining car, complete with simulated railroad motion. The museum is open daily May through October, and on Saturday and Sunday in April and November to mid-December. There's an admission charge.

Sight & Sound Theatres, just outside Strasburg (300 and 202 Hartman Bridge Rd, Ronk, 717/687.7800;

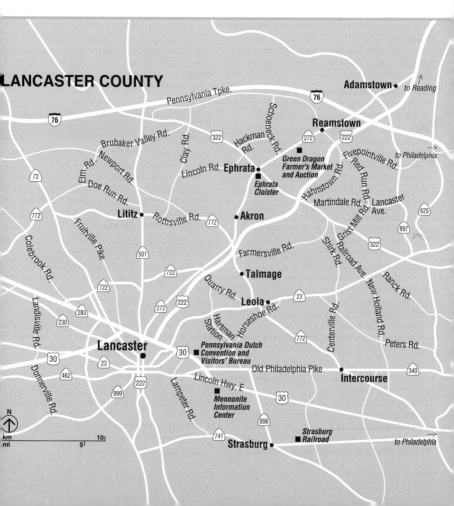

www.bibleonstage.com), put on theatrical renditions of familiar Bible stories, interpreted through a Christian perspective. Shows like *The Miracle of Christmas, Abraham and Sarah: A Journey of Love* and *Noah, The Musical* draw huge crowds. The production value is top rate, including lots of multimedia special effects, drawing an average of 800,000 visitors annually, many of them arriving in group tour buses. Tickets are in the $15 range for kids and $29 for adults, and reservations are a must. For those in search of theatrical inspiration, these shows will fill the bill. There's an on-site restaurant if you're feeling peckish.

The **Green Dragon Farmers' Market and Auction** (955 N State St, at Garden Spot Rd; 717/738.1117), north of **Ephrata**, is a town-size combination of flea market, farmers' market, and livestock sale and auction. It's a great place to browse and a good reason to schedule your Lancaster trip for a Friday—the only day the market is open. More than 10 varieties of local bologna (sweet or savory, and not remotely like the supermarket kind) are sold here. You'll also find every imaginable cut and cooked variety of beef and pork, and some you won't want to imagine. One local favorite is tongue souse, best described as a cross between olive loaf and Jell-O.

Other Green Dragon highlights include listening to the mile-a-minute patter of auctioneers hollering prices of farm equipment; browsing through stalls of books written in the Pennsylvania German language; tasting **Michael's Breads** (cloud-soft and flecked with onion or cinnamon); and cooling off with a cone at **Lapp's Ice Cream**—the bonneted Amish women who serve you were milking dairy cows earlier in the week.

Nearby is the **Ephrata Cloister** (632 W Main St, at Rte 272, Ephrata; 717/733.6600), a compelling historical site with 20 buildings (including the **Academy**) that housed one of America's earliest communal societies. Founded by German Pietist Conrad Biessel in 1732, the group reached its peak population of about 300 in 1750. A fascinating tour and slide show focuses on the group's haunting original music and medieval Germanic architecture. The site is open daily; there's an admission charge.

If you're planning to stay overnight in Amish country, consider **Doneckers** (100 N State St, between Locust St and Mohler S Church Rd, Ephrata; 717/738.9502), Ephrata's village-within-a-town. Given the rural surroundings, this is a surprisingly upscale complex that includes an inn with 35 rooms and suites, as well as art galleries, fashion boutiques, a catalog outlet center, and restaurants housed in finely refurbished turn-of-the-19th-century buildings. Lodging prices are reasonable, especially given the antiques-filled rooms featuring Jacuzzis and other modern amenities. If you're tired of snacking and want some serious cuisine, try **The Restaurant at Doneckers**, where the prices at lunch are especially reasonable.

Branch off to the northwest at Route 772 and drive about 5 miles to the town of **Lititz**, home of the **Sturgis Pretzel** (219 E Main St, between N Locust St and Rte 501, Lititz; 717/626.4354) since 1861. Here you can take a guided tour of the small factory, watch the process of making pretzels by hand, and even do a little twisting of your own. Sturgis cranks out an impressive variety of pretzels, from a horse-and-buggy-shaped pretzel to a jalapeño-flavored

version. The factory is open Monday through Saturday; there's a nominal admission charge.

Heading south on Route 772, venture deep into farm country, the location of such towns as **Talmage** and **Leola**. Watch for local families in the traditional Amish dress of dark suits and broad-brimmed hats for men and modest, apron-draped dresses for women. Children, dressed much the same as the adults, play outside one-room schoolhouses and in family yards (many Amish are firm advocates of homeschooling). The Amish shun modern technology, and many homes don't have electricity or telephones. In the fields, some farms do use tractors, but many farmers can be seen working the fields with seven-mule teams hooked to their plows.

Teenagers love T-shirts from **Intercourse**, and yours will probably want one too. But this charming Amish town will appeal to the whole family. Among the spots to visit is the **Amish Experience** and **Amish Homestead** at Plain and Fancy Farm (Rte 340, between Bird-in-Hand and Intercourse; 717/768.3600, Ext. 10; www.amishexperience .com), with a multimedia presentation, a replica of a modern Amish home, buggy rides, and a Pennsylvania Dutch family-style restaurant.

With so much to explore, you may want to spend an additional day in Lancaster County. A good, centrally located family hostelry with a swimming pool is the **Eden Resort Inn** (222 Eden Rd, near junction of Hwy 30 and Rte 272, Lancaster; 717/569.6444, 800/528.1234). Couples may prefer **King's Cottage** (1049 E King St, between Cottage and Ranck Aves, Lancaster; 717/397.1017; www.kingscottagebb.com), a deluxe mansion converted to a romantic bed-and-breakfast. Located just 11 blocks from the heart of Lancaster, they serve an excellent afternoon tea.

READING

Once a boomtown and the headquarters of the legendary **Reading Railroad**, the city of Reading began a serious economic decline in the 1950s as manufacturing moved overseas and train travel became nostalgic rather than necessity. Located in Berks County just northeast of **Lancaster**, Reading was made virtually obsolete by modern highway systems and air travel.

Local boosters proved resilient, however, offering favorable lease terms and attractive incentives to draw retailers and manufacturers into the Reading area to open discount stores. As name-brand companies from Wrangler to Coach and Body Depot took Reading's bait, the discount phenomenon snowballed, pulling in tourists from far away and bargain hunters from nearby. Now billing itself as "the original Outlet Capital of the World," rather than riding the rails, Reading is riding the sales.

Shopping is only part of the picture. Reading is also home to the **Sovereign Center**, home of the Reading Royals professional hockey team, and the **Reading Eagle Theater**. The arena has also played host to pop stars like Elton John and Cher. The **Sovereign Performing Arts Center** is housed in a restored historic theater, home to the Reading Symphony and other cultural and theatrical events.

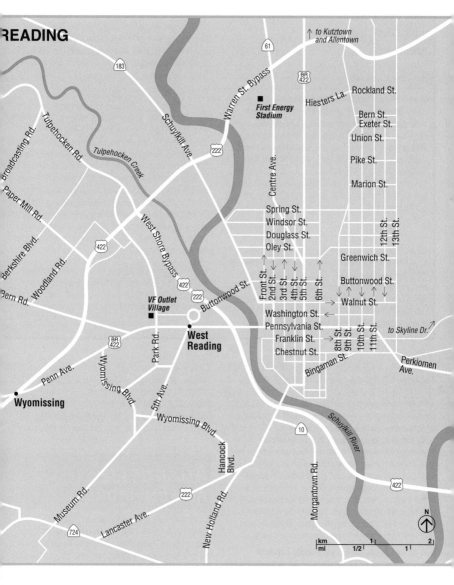

READING

To Kutztown and Allentown

First Energy Stadium

West Reading

Wyomissing

The city has several designated historic districts, including the beautiful Victorian **Centre Park** area. The 90-minute drive to Reading from Philadelphia is a scenic one along I-76 and highway 422. Festivals, from jazz to holiday, abound, so visit www.reading berkspa.com for timely info.

When you drive into Reading, head up **Skyline Drive** to **he Pagoda**. The Pagoda (Skyline Dr at Buryea Dr, 610/375.6399) is modeled after a Filipino structure, painted a striking yellow with red roof tiles and trim. Completed in 1908, it was intended to be a hotel but never opened and was eventually sold to Reading for $1 (probably the city's first bargain). Today, it's the headquarters of the **Berks Arts Council** and is used for exhibitions and other events. Climb to the top of the seven-story building and you'll be rewarded with a perfect panorama of the city and surrounding farmland.

To shop most efficiently, hit the outlet malls, which feature a half-dozen to several dozen retailers under one roof.

Start your conspicuous consumption at the very largest discount complex, the **VF Outlet Village** (N Park Rd and Hill Ave, Wyomissing; 610/378.0408), owned by the parent corporation of apparel companies as diverse as Vanity Fair, Wrangler, Jantzen, and Jansport. Almost all merchandise here is priced at a full 50% off recommended retail. The outlet's pamphlets, available at virtually every Reading and Lancaster County visitors' center, include a certificate for $10 off any combined purchase of more than $100 from mall stores. Coach, Nautica, London Fog, and others are located in the VF Outlet Village. There are also outlets on Hiesters Lane and at the **Fairground Square Shopping Mall**.

THE BEST

Aaron Posner

Cofounder and Artistic Director,
Arden Theatre Company

The performing arts are thriving in Philadelphia these days. So go to the theater! And not only the great adult and children's productions at the **Arden** (eclectic/great stories), of course, but also try the **Wilma** (funky/dark European), **Philadelphia Theatre Company** (American Realism), **1812 Productions** (offbeat comedy), **Pig Iron** (Experimental Movement Theatre), and a host of others, small and large. There is a lot of vital new work in town, and it's all much cheaper (and often more interesting!) than in New York.

Spend a day in **Old City**, Philly's own SoHo-esque neighborhood of art galleries, theaters, boutiques, historic sites (**National Constitution Center**, **Liberty Bell**, **Independence Hall**, **Betsy Ross House**, and many more), and excellent restaurants of every kind. If you haven't been in this historic area of Philadelphia in the past five years, you might hardly recognize it. It is green, clean, and inviting, with a huge variety of things to do for the whole family. At night it is the busiest, hopping-est place in town. There are superb restaurants like **Fork**, **The Plough and The Stars**, **The Continental**, **Tangerine**, and dozens more, with new ones opening practically every week.

There are excellent and affordable Vietnamese, Chinese, Japanese, Thai, and Korean restaurants all over **Center City**. And of course Italian in **South Philly**, and wonderful funky little hip comfort-food neighborhood eateries like **Sabrina's** and **Morning Glory** and **Sarcone's** down around the **Italian Market**. And for the best cheese shop just about anywhere, there is **DiBruno Brothers** on 9th Street in the heart of the Italian Market. On a nice day, just walk around town. Look up just about anywhere, and you will be struck by some elegant architectural surprise. Even after 15 years this happens to me all the time. And if you stroll along the many back alleys that criss-cross the city, you will see even more.

There is so much more, too. The **Reading Terminal Market**. **The Philadelphia Museum of Art**. Ballet. Opera. Philadelphia is a world-class city, but definitely with an energy and a personality all its own.

Name brands have nothing to do with the shopping at **Renningers Antique & Farmers Market** (740 Noble St, between Trexler Ave and Main St; 610/683.6848), held on Saturday in nearby **Kutztown**. Considered one of the top flea markets in the world, this indoor–outdoor extravaganza draws up to 1,200 dealers from 42 states in the peak summer. Depending on one's perspective, wandering through here is either like discovering a treasure chest or falling into your weird uncle's junk drawer. In a day's browsing, you can come across medieval armor, a fresh-baked shoofly pie, or a handful of World War II insignia pins. Beer-can collectors, Shaker-furniture dealers, and booksellers all compete for your dollars here. Don't be afraid to haggle; many of the vendors don't hesitate to overcharge outrageously.

Also of note in Kutztown is the **Rodale Institute Research Center** (611 Siegfriedale Rd, between Hwy 222 and Rte 863; 610/683.1400; www.rodaleinstitute. org). The center is a nonprofit arm of Rodale Press, a major publisher of magazines, such as *Prevention*, and books on gardening and alternative health. The institute maintains this 333-acre facility to explore and develop the fields of organic farming and gardening. The inexpensive, 1.5-hour guided tours are very informative.

Reading is one of the few towns where a minor-league baseball club plays right near its big-league affiliate. The **Reading Phillies** are the AA farm team of the **Philadelphia Phillies**, so they benefit doubly from the locals' home-team spirit. **First Energy Stadium** (1900 Centre Ave, between Spring St and Warren St Bypass; 610/375.8469) has great sight lines and an intimate feel. Also, because tickets cost a fraction of big-league prices ($3.50 to $9), this is a great place to take children to their first ball game.

If you're staying overnight, the **Inn at Reading** (1040 N Park Rd, at Hwy 422, Wyomissing; 610/372.7811) is a good bet. It's modern, well located, and has a tourist information center on the premises. There is also the **Sheraton-Reading** and the **Wyndham Reading**, the latter a historic renovation of the **Lincoln Plaza** hotel.

ATLANTIC CITY AND ENVIRONS

The first US city outside Nevada to legalize casino gambling, **Atlantic City, New Jersey**, entered the big leagues in 1978 with the opening of **Resorts**, the first of today's dozen glitzy gaming palaces. It's an easy drive from central Philadelphia to what the locals call simply A.C. Just take **Interstate 95** and the **Benjamin Franklin Bridge** or the **Walt Whitman Bridge** into New Jersey, then pick up the **Atlantic City Expressway**, which is well marked. In about an hour, you'll find yourself in this exciting city by the sea. Virtually all the casino-hotels offer parking at their garages for a small fee. If you are among the thousands of visitors who prefer to use public transportation, take the casino-underwritten bus services that stop daily in most Philadelphia neighborhoods. The fee is less than $20 round trip, and the casinos usually give passengers most of that amount back in coupons for free food and quarters for gambling. Consult Philadelphia newspaper ads or call a casino directly for bus schedules. You also can reach Atlantic City by convenient **New Jersey Transit** trains (215/569.3752); they depart several times a day from Philadelphia's **30th Street Station** for the **Atlantic City Rail Terminal**, four blocks from the main casino strip.

Perhaps the town's most endearing feature is the **Board-walk**, a 4-mile elevated walkway flanked by casinos, hotels, and shops on one side and wide sandy beaches on the other. Made of wooden planks laid out in a herringbone pattern and supported by a steel structure, today's Boardwalk had its genesis in 1870, when the city council wanted to find a way to keep visitors from tracking sand into hotels and railway cars.

Before 10AM, cyclists and joggers enjoying the ocean breeze dominate the Boardwalk. By noon, however, pedestrian traffic is thick with visitors strolling from casino to casino. On fair summer days, this is people-watching heaven, as high-rolling New Yorkers, foreign tourists, and charter bus groups from as far away as Kentucky mingle with one another and stop by dozens of essentially identical video arcades and junk souvenir shops.

Siganos Plaza on the Boardwalk at Martin Luther King Jr. Boulevard has a selection of newer, nontypical Boardwalk shops such as a surf shop, a women's boutique, and a place to make your own teddy bears, as well as **Opa**, an upscale eatery.

Favorite Boardwalk snacks include the many flavors of saltwater taffy from **James's** or **Fralinger's**, both of which have several shops along the casino trail. Though James's taffy will give your jaw a challenging workout, Fralinger's melts in your mouth. Also recommended are **Steel's Fudge**, corn dogs, and excellent fresh lemonade served at the stands along the Boardwalk.

Each of the 12 Atlantic City casino-hotels has more than 600 guest rooms and vast, carpeted gambling areas where guests can play their favorite games of chance 24 hours a day. The smoky gambling floors have no clocks or windows, which can lead you to lose track of time.

Although all the casinos claim to outdo one another in deluxe accommodations, they are actually quite similar. Interior design runs toward rococo gilded moldings and crystal chandeliers. All have overpriced luxury restaurants, 24-hour coffee shops, and much-ballyhooed all-you-can-eat buffets. If you prefer to dine away from the casinos, try the **White House Sub Shop** (2301 Arctic Ave, at Mississippi Ave; 609/345.1564), which is great for cheap eats and a sense of history. Autographed celebrity photos sing the praises of White House sandwiches. Cheesesteaks and hoagies are even

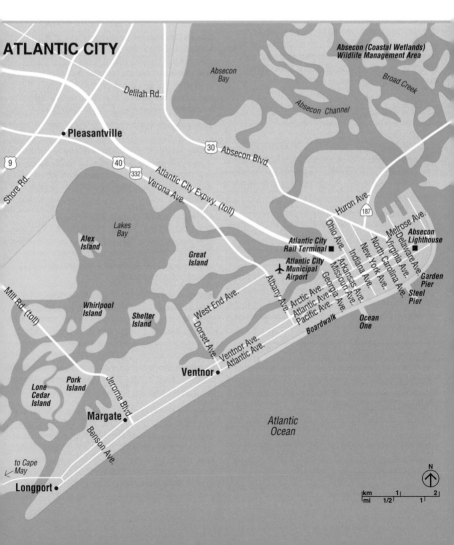

better here than in Philly because of the wonderfully chewy Italian rolls baked right in the neighborhood.

The casinos also offer lots of live entertainment, much of it free with a two-drink minimum. These complimentary lounge shows range from sultry female jazz vocalists to 1950s rock 'n' roll cover bands to the occasional stand-up comedian. Quality varies significantly too, but if you wander from lounge to lounge, you'll likely discover at least one act that you would happily pay to see again. If you're willing to pay top dollar ($30 and up), you can catch major headliners in any of the casinos' big theaters, where stars such as Liza Minnelli, Jerry Seinfeld, and Cher regularly perform. **Boardwalk Hall** at Mississippi Avenue and the Boardwalk is the city's premier entertainment arena and regularly hosts top concert tours, sporting events, ice shows, the circus, and other family shows. During the summer, Atlantic City's four beach bars provide a mix of live entertainment and DJs, and there are frequently free, live concerts at Kennedy Plaza on the Boardwalk in front of Boardwalk Hall. Call individual casinos or consult Philadelphia newspapers to find out who's playing.

Hotel-casinos located on the Boardwalk include the following:

Atlantic City Hilton (Boston Ave and the Boardwalk; 609/347.7111, 800/257.8677; fax 609/340.4879; www.hiltonac.com), classy as far as casinos go and tops for serious gambling, as it tends to be less hectic and distracting than the other large casinos a few blocks away.

Historic Gardner's Basin, located in the inlet area of Atlantic City, has been the heart of the seaside resort's fishing industry since the turn of the 19th century.

Natives pronounce *Lancaster* with the accent heavily on the first syllable, often as "*Lank*-ister" instead of "Lan-*cas*-ter."

Celebrated residents of Bucks County have included lyricist Oscar Hammerstein, anthropologist Margaret Mead, novelist Pearl Buck, playwright George Kaufman, and painter Edward Hicks, famous for his *Peaceable Kingdom.*

Washington Crossing Historic Park in Bucks County commemorates the spot from which George Washington and the Continental Army crossed the Delaware River to defeat 1,400 Hessians at Trenton on Christmas night in 1776.

The only space on Parker Brothers' Monopoly board that doesn't correspond to a real Atlantic City site is Marvin Gardens, which is actually in nearby Margate and is correctly spelled *Marven Gardens.*

Tropicana (Brighton Ave and the Boardwalk; 609/340.4000, 800/257.6227; fax 609/343.5254; www.tropicana.net), which, in addition to the usual trappings, features the **Top of the Trop**, a 20th-floor lounge (evening piano music) affording sweeping views of Atlantic City. **The Quarter**, Tropicana's Havana-themed $275 million expansion, debuted in 2004. The dining/retail venue includes **The Sound of Philadelphia**, a 300-seat restaurant and live entertainment venue inspired by Philly Sound icons Gamble & Huff and owned by the Bynum Hospitality Group (**Zanzibar Blue**, **Warmdaddy's**); along with more than 60 restaurants, entertainment, shopping, and spa options including **Ri Ra Irish Pub and Restaurant**, **Red Square**, **Cuba Libre Restaurant and Rum Bar**, **Barron's Gentlemen**, **bluemercury** spa and apothecary, **MONDI**, **Melonie de France**, **Zinman Furs**, **White House/Black Market**, and more. Visit www.tropicana.net for more information.

Trump Plaza (Mississippi Ave at the Boardwalk; 609/441.6000, 800/677.7378; fax 609/441.2729; www.trumpplaza.com), one of tycoon Donald Trump's three Atlantic City casinos, but originally built for Playboy Enterprises, Inc. Wags have speculated that the peculiar architecture—a sleek glass tower with a wider, knoblike top—is intentionally phallic.

Caesars (Arkansas Ave and the Boardwalk; 609/348.4411, 800/443.0104; fax 609/343.2611; www.caesars.com), a sister hotel of Caesars Palace in Las Vegas. Glutted with pink marble and oversize reproductions of classic sculpture (Michelangelo's *David* weighs 17 tons), it's truly a faux Roman monstrosity. Among the hotel's eateries is **Bacchanal**, a seven-course orgy of haute cuisine.

Bally's Atlantic City (Park Pl and the Boardwalk; 609/340.2000, 800/772.7777; fax 609/340.2595; www.ballysac.com), which, in addition to having mercifully spare modern décor, is worth noting for **The Spa**, a well-equipped gym where day-trippers are welcome to pay a small fee to work out, sit in the whirlpool, or get a massage.

Sands (Indiana Ave and the Boardwalk; 609/441.4000, 800/AC.SANDS; fax 609/441.4630; www.acsands.com) has a high-tech skywalk called the People Mover that glides you over a courtyard between the Boardwalk and the hotel past a memorabilia display from old-time Atlantic City.

Resorts Atlantic City (1133 Boardwalk; 609/344.6000, 800/336.6378; fax: 609/340.6349; www.resortsac.com), Atlantic City's original casino-hotel, formerly **Merv Griffin's Resorts**, boasts a new hotel tower with the city's largest rooms, a variety of casual and gourmet restaurants including the Zagat-award-winning **Capriccio**, the Northern Italian gourmet room, a rooftop swimming pool, and the 1,400-seat **Superstar Theatre**, site of year-round, big-name entertainment.

Trump Taj Mahal (Virginia Ave and the Boardwalk; 609/449.1000, 800/225.7777; fax 609/449.5501; www.trumptaj.com), the biggest, most ostentatious casino in town, is topped with onion domes and minarets. Staffers wear turbans and caftans, and exotic place names are used with abandon (the **Bombay Cafe**, for instance). The facility's **Mark Etess Arena**, hosting major pop concerts

nd championship boxing matches, is the largest casino-
wned hall in the country.

howboat (Delaware Ave and the Boardwalk; 609/
43.4000, 800/621.0200; fax 609/343.4057;
ww.harrahs.com/our_casinos/sac), which has a
isneyesque décor that has turned the large lobby area
to a New Orleans–style town square.

addition to the casino-hotels, a Boardwalk trek leads
ast **Boardwalk Hall** (Boardwalk, between Mississippi
nd Florida Aves; 609/449.2000), where the Miss
merica Pageant has been held annually since 1940.

lore Boardwalking passes **Ripley's Believe It or Not!**
New York Ave on the Boardwalk; 609/347.2001;
ww.ripleys.com), where a replica of Australia's Sydney
arbor Bridge, constructed with 160,000 matchsticks, is
n display, and the **Ocean Life Center** (Gardner's Basin;
09/348.2880, 609/348.7100; www.oceanlifecenter.
om), an interactive aquarium at which visitors may
xplore the marine environment through wet exhibits and
eld study programs. Gardner's Basin is also the site of
everal large festivals, casual restaurants, and fishing
nd sightseeing boat excursions, as well as two amuse-
ents piers—**Steel Pier** at Virginia Avenue and **Central
ier** at Tennessee Avenue. **Garden Pier** at New Jersey
venue houses the **Atlantic City Historical Museum**
nd **Atlantic City Art Museum**, both free and open daily
ll year. Off-Boardwalk attractions include **Absecon
ighthouse** at Rhode Island Avenue between Atlantic
nd Pacific Avenues, the tallest light in New Jersey with
28 steps to a panoramic view, and a **Civil Rights
arden** on Martin Luther King Jr. Boulevard just off
acific Avenue.

tlantic City has three other casino-hotels, **Harrah's**
1725 Brigantine Blvd, at Absecon Inlet; 609/441.5000,
00/427.7247; fax 609/344.9740; www.harrahs.com)
nd **Trump's Marina** (Huron Ave and Brigantine Blvd;
09/441.8300, 800/777.8477; fax 609/441.8541;
ww.trumpmarina.com), both situated by the calm waters
f Absecon Inlet near the Farley State Marina a couple of
iles from the Boardwalk. These hotels share a sense of
erenity and relaxation away from the constant hustle and
re highly recommended for those serious about gambling
r looking for a more tasteful ambiance.

ne glitzy $1 billion **Borgata Hotel Casino and Spa**
609/317.1000; www.theborgata.com), is the hippest
d on the casino block, with 2,002 rooms and suites, a
asino, a European-style spa, upscale shopping,
eeting, and entertainment facilities, and a large
utdoor event arena. More Vegas than any of its sister
roperties, the Borgata boasts sophisticated dining and
exy nightclubbing options, including **Siulan**, owned by
hiladelphia's Susanna Foo, as well as **Mixx**, **Specchia**,
mbra and **Metropolitan**. Coinless slots make the casino
lightly less deafening than the norm, but only slightly.

tlantic City's post-midnight hot spot is **Studio VI** (12 S
t. Vernon Ave, off Atlantic Ave; 609/348.0192), a high-
nergy disco that attracts a comfortable mix of gays and
traights who dance until dawn, along with the casino
orkers, musicians, and occasional celebrity entertainers
ho come here to unwind after their evening's work. Other

late-night hot spots include **Déjà vu** (225 S New York
Ave, 609/348.4313), **The Casbah** at Trump Taj Mahal,
Mixx at the Borgata, and **The Wave** at Trump Marina.

If you're visiting Atlantic City in summer and are interested
in the beach as much as the casinos, the beaches have
been widened through a beach replenishment program
and enhanced with protective dunes. They are available
to the public free of charge and guarded in the summer by
the country's oldest and most experienced professional
lifeguard squad. Or, drive a few miles south to the
communities of **Ventnor**, **Margate**, and **Longport**, where
many Philadelphians have second homes. The beaches
here attract a family-oriented crowd. After you settle in,
beach patrols will approach and ask for $5 per person for
a pin-on beach badge. This usage fee covers the costs of
maintenance and of hiring professional lifeguards.

While in Margate, don't miss **Lucy the Margate Elephant**
(9200 Atlantic Ave, at S Benson Ave; 609/823.6473), a
National Historic Landmark and an excellent example of
whimsical Victorian architecture. Built in the 1880s to lure
prospective land buyers to the shore, Lucy is a 65-foot-
high, metal-clad wooden structure in the shape of an
elephant. She eventually fell into weathered disrepair
and was scheduled for destruction in the late 1960s,
but local housewife Josephine Harron began a "Save
Lucy" campaign, which led to the splendid restoration of
the unusual edifice you see today. Current plans are in
the works to make Lucy ADA compliant, without compro-
mising her Victorian charm. For a nominal fee, you can
explore the structure inside and out. It's open daily
between mid-June and Labor Day, and on Saturday and
Sunday between early September and late October and
between late April and mid-June.

A mere stone's throw from the pachyderm is **Ventura's
Greenhouse** (106 S Benson Ave, at Atlantic Ave; 609/
822.0140), a casual restaurant and bar known for its
garlicky white pizza and spacious outside deck overlooking
the beach. Crowded every summer afternoon with sun
worshipers sipping daiquiris and cold beers, the deck
here is the place to be seen in Margate in the daytime.

Once you've had your fill of the excitement in Atlantic
City, venture 40 miles south to **Cape May**—the perfect
antidote to the clanging racket of hundreds of slot
machines. Treat yourself to a few nights in one of the
sumptuously restored Victorian bed-and-breakfasts and
spend the day puttering around the antiques shops or
taking long walks along the beach. The 19th-century
architecture of this tiny resort town is inspiration enough
to carry a camera around at all times; the bright-colored
shingles, white picket fences, and other details beg to be
captured on film.

BRANDYWINE VALLEY

Painter N.C. Wyeth once described his home turf in the
Brandywine Valley as a place of "succulent meadows"
and "big, sad trees." This sweeping sun-dappled valley of
horse farms, country estates, and rolling hillsides runs

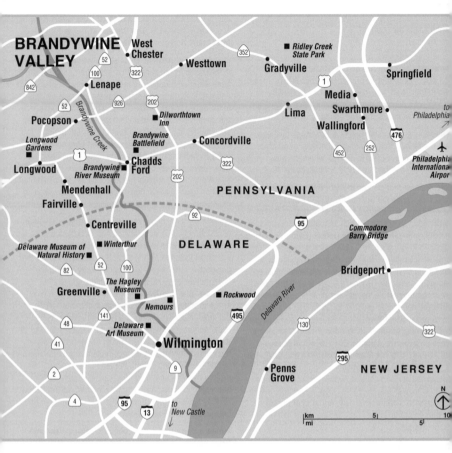

alongside **Brandywine Creek** for about 30 miles, starting west of Philadelphia and ending just below **Wilmington, Delaware**. Rich in history and filled with visitor attractions, yet surprisingly underused by Philadelphians, the Brandywine Valley is still dominated by Wilmington's industrial dynasty, the du Ponts, Huguenots who came to this country more than 200 years ago.

The most popular Brandywine sights, particularly the several du Pont estates, are huge, so allow plenty of time to explore them by focusing on only a few of the major attractions. Also, consider packing a picnic to enjoy in one of the area's many gardens rather than using up a chunk of the day in a restaurant.

Although Amtrak provides service between Philadelphia and downtown Wilmington several times a day, virtually every place you'll want to hit is outside the city proper, making a car the best way to take in the terrain. From Philadelphia, drive about 20 miles south on **Interstate 95**, then exit according to your specific itinerary. All the major sights in the valley are close together, despite the fact that you'll be crossing the Pennsylvania border and going into Delaware in some instances.

Without question, Brandywine Valley's one must-see attraction is **Longwood Gardens** (Hwy 1, just west of Rte 52, Longwood; 610/388.1000; www.longwoodgardens.org), 30 miles from Philadelphia. The gardens are open daily; there's a $12 admission charge. Internationally regarded

as the country's foremost horticultural institution, Longwood is laid out to encourage leisurely walking and observation. You'll feel shortchanged if you allot less tha 2 hours for a visit.

Once the country residence of Pierre S. du Pont, the 1,000-acre estate has 11,000 plant species in its fertile soil. The 5-acre **Fountain Garden** was completed in 1931, inspired by a similar display at the 1893 Chicago World's Fair. Several evenings each summer, classical concerts synchronized with the fountains and colored lights are held here. The **Terrace Restaurant**, a lovely lunch spot, serves very good salads.

Though outdoor displays vary according to season (April and May offer the widest profusion of blooms, rose gardens highlight the summer months, and chrysanthemums as wide as Frisbees are among fall favorites), the gardens' greenhouse conservatories grow orchids and other tropical plants year-round. At Christmastime, the greenhouses are festooned with colored lights and poinsettias. Another indoor highlight is the **Cascade Garden**, where waterfalls and Brazilian foliage evoke the homeland of designer Roberto Burle Marx.

The du Ponts set the tone for much of Brandywine Valley life, but William Penn's Quakers also left an important historical legacy. Near the entrance gates to Longwood Gardens is the **Chester County Information Center** (610/388.2900, 800/228.9933), housed in a simple

GOING DUTCH: A GLIMPSE OF THE AMISH

Chances are you'll encounter the Amish (also referred to as the Pennsylvania Dutch) on a visit to the Philadelphia area; if you visit **Lancaster County**, about an hour and a half west of the city, you're bound to see them riding through the streets in their horse-drawn buggies. Some 25,000 Amish—members of an Anabaptist sect that originated in 17th-century Germany and Switzerland when it separated from the Mennonites—live in the rural county.

Named after Jacob Amman, a Swiss Mennonite bishop, the Amish believe that true Christians should not bear arms, use force, or hold public office. They left their homelands because of war and persecution, arriving in Philadelphia in 1737. The agrarian group found the fertile soil of Lancaster County, now home to the nation's largest Amish community, particularly attractive and well suited to their lifestyle. The Amish live simply and dress modestly. Women wear bonnets and long dresses with aprons and shawls; married men and those over 40 are required to grow untrimmed ear-to-ear beards, with the upper lip shaven, and wear black hats and suspenders (they do not use belts or zippers). The Amish don't own cars, and they eschew modern farm machinery and electricity.

Sect members also are expected to intermingle only among themselves, except in matters of commerce. Their farm products—fresh vegetables, poultry, jellies, preserves, and relishes—are immensely popular with Pennsylvanians and tourists, as are their patchwork quilts. (The quilts, which are assembled continuously from leftover scraps of cloth, play two important roles in Amish life—decorative and functional.)

Though the Amish maintain an uneasy relationship with modern society, that hasn't kept them from prospering. One reason for this is their birthrate: The average family has 6.6 children, most of whom remain in the community. Approximately 90,000 Amish live in North America, primarily in the US and Canada.

Although Lancaster County's gently rolling farmland has been good to the sect, it hasn't provided them much protection from the outside world. The Amish have been a consistent source of curiosity for visitors, journalists, and Sunday drivers for decades. In the 1980s, the community suffered the ultimate invasion when the Pennsylvania Bureau of Motion Pictures and TV Development (yes, there really is such a thing) persuaded Hollywood to shoot a movie about the Amish in Lancaster County. The filming of *Witness*, starring Harrison Ford, stirred deep controversy among members of the group, who not only shun publicity but likewise oppose film and photography. Infuriated Amish leaders threatened to uproot the community and move elsewhere. Ultimately, the state commerce department reached an agreement with them, pledging that it would never again promote the sect as a feature film subject.

---

clapboard structure that served as a Quaker meeting-house until 1940, and open daily. The meetinghouse was also a gathering point for the area's active slavery abolition movement. The valley became a hotbed of abolitionist activity in 1786, as Quaker merchants and farmers participated in the Underground Railroad, which helped southern slaves escape to the North. In support of the cause, local Quakers hosted such speakers as Susan B. Anthony and Sojourner Truth.

If you'd like to add a bit of spice to your visit to Longwood, drive a few miles east to the **Chaddsford Winery** (632 Baltimore Pike/Hwy 1, Chadds Ford; 610/388.6221; www.chaddsford.com). Run by Eric and Lee Miller, this operation has been producing wine since 1983. Eric's expertise in wine making is showcased on the weekend tours, when he guides visitors through a 30-minute look at the crushing, fermenting, aging, and bottling processes. After the tour, tastings let you sample the winery's fine table reds and whites before purchasing some to take home. A popular novelty is Chaddsford's Apple-Spice wine, a great autumn drink when served warm. During the week, visitors may take a self-guided tour. The `winery is closed Mondays, January through April; there's a fee for tasting the wines. In the summertime, live music is often featured on weekend evenings.

Nearby, the **Brandywine River Museum** (Station Rd, off Hwy 1, Chadds Ford; 610/388.2700; www.brandywinemuseum.org) is as notable for its building as for its art holdings. The museum is a project of the **Brandywine Conservancy**, a local interest group involved in shaping policies for water resources and historic preservation. It's housed in a converted Civil War gristmill, where the original rough-hewn beams and wide wooden floorboards enhance the ambiance of the exhibit galleries. The second-floor lobby features a curved, cobblestone floor that leads to dramatic bowed glass walls, where you can look down through the trees for a spectacular view of the **Brandywine River**. Antique stables in front of the building are used for crafts fairs and occasional live entertainment. It is open daily; there's an admission charge.

Focusing on local artistic heritage, the museum holds an impressive collection of paintings by three generations of the Wyeth family: N.C., Andrew, and Jamie. Although the works on display are changed regularly, visitors can count on seeing some of N.C.'s classic book illustrations, Jamie's popular pig paintings, and many of Andrew's most famous works (the controversial Helga series is the major lure). Maxfield Parrish, Rockwell Kent, and Horace Pippin are among the other significant American artists whose works are shown here. After touring the galleries, be sure to step out behind the museum, where there is a

Bishop William White: Chaplain to the Revolution

Bishop William White, a close friend of George Washington and Benjamin Franklin, served as a chaplain to the volunteers of the Continental Army. He later became the presiding bishop of the American Protestant Episcopal Church and chaplain to the US Senate.

The leader of Philadelphia's clergy, White believed life was a celebration, as long as the celebrating didn't violate the Ten Commandments. In keeping with his philosophy of tempered enjoyment, White smoked cigars, drank wine, played cards, read novels, took part in fox hunts, and even went to the theater. He was also a one-man ecumenical movement. Parading on the Fourth of July, he would walk arm in arm with the rabbi from **Mikveh Israel** and the priest from **Old St. Mary's**. It's said his house, which still stands at **309 Walnut Street** and is part of Independence National Historical Park, was open to one and all, day and night, especially those in need.

White is best remembered for the courage he demonstrated the day he took an oath of allegiance to the patriot cause, especially because, as a minister of the Church of England, he had pledged loyalty to the English throne. It seems that as patriots entered the State House, a British loyalist stood outside recording the names of all who entered. When the bishop walked by, the man placed his hands around his own neck, mimicking a hangman's noose. Once he had signed his pledge, White returned, saying to the tattletale: "I perceived, by your gesture, that you thought I was exposing my neck to great danger by the step I have taken. But I have not taken it without full deliberation. I know my danger, and that it is greater on account of my being a clergyman of the Church of England. But I trust in Providence. The cause is a just one, and I am persuaded that it will be protected."

White was rewarded with the post of chaplain, a position he held until the fighting ended at Yorktown in 1781. After that, he devoted the rest of his life to the American Anglican Church, transforming it ultimately into the American Protestant Episcopal Church. He was consecrated as its first bishop in London in 1786. White was founder or supporter of a number of Philadelphia institutions—the **Episcopal Academy**, **Episcopal Hospital**, **Philadelphia School for the Deaf**, the **Society for the Alleviation of Misery in Public Prisons**. Bishop White died in his Walnut Street home on 17 July 1836. He was 88 years old.

---

small wildflower garden and a pleasant walking trail along the riverbank.

Also along Highway 1 is the **Brandywine Battlefield** (Hwy 1, between Hwy 202 and Rte 100, Chadds Ford; 610/459.3342), which, unlike Valley Forge, was the site of actual fighting during the American Revolution. It was here that Washington's army was handed a defeat by the troops of British general William Howe in a raging battle that proved a turning point in the war (the famous French general Lafayette, who witnessed the battle, was so impressed with the rebels' tenacity that he decided to join forces with Washington). On the battlefield are a visitors' center and two restored Quaker farmhouses that served as headquarters for Washington and Lafayette. The battlefield is open Tuesday through Sunday; there's an admission charge to the farmhouses.

With a history that predates the revolution, it's not surprising that the Brandywine Valley is an antiques-collector's paradise. Many of the best shops and stalls (some of the greatest finds pop up at sporadic, flea market–style weekend events) can be found in and around **West Chester**. This charming town of less than 20,000 was a major beneficiary of America's mid-19th-century fascination with Greek Revival architecture. West Chester has become a restaurant mecca in recent years, with dozens of eateries and nightspots lining the town's main streets of Market and Gay. A few standouts include upscale Mexican at **Coyote Crossing** (102 Market St at Walnut St, 610/825.3000; www.coyotecrossing.com) and innovative French fare at **Gilmore's** (133 Gay St. between Matlock and Walnut Sts; 610/431.2800).

A tour of the **QVC** studios is a popular West Chester attraction (1200 Wilson Dr, West Chester; 800/600.9900; www.qvctours.com). The world's largest electronic retailer is open for a behind-the-scenes walking tour Monday through Sunday, between 10AM and 4PM; there is an admission fee.

Simon Pearce on the Brandywine is a combination art glass studio and restaurant (1333 Lenape Rd, West Chester; 610/793.0949; www.simonpearce.com), with diners offered an up-close-and-personal view of glass blowers at work, along with a menu of creative American cuisine and a view of the Brandywine River. The establishment is open daily, 10AM-9PM.

After the Battle of Brandywine, rowdy redcoats caused serious damage to the **Dilworthtown Inn** (Old Wilmington Pike and Brinton's Bridge Rd, West Chester; 610/399.1390; www.dilworthtown.com), constructed in 1758. Restored to its handsome original state, the inn serves a fine, fancy supper (reservations are recommended). Vegetables and herbs used in the cooking are grown locally; local pheasant, quail, and partridge are featured entrées. A consistent winner of the Wine Spectator Award for Excellence, the Dilworth-